LIFE

OF

PHILIP MELANCTHON,

COMPRISING

AN ACCOUNT

OF THE MOST IMPORTANT TRANSACTIONS OF

THE REFORMATION.

BY

F. A. COX, A. M.

OF HACKNEY.

—In Necessariis UNITAS—in Dubiis LIBERTAS—in Omnibus CARITAS

LONDON

PRINTED FOR GALE, CURTIS AND FENNER, PATERNOSTER
ROW; AND OLIPHANT, WAUGH AND INNES,
EDINBURGH.

Printed by Stower & Smallfield, Hackney.

Printing Statement:

Due to the very old age and scarcity of this book,
many of the pages may be hard to read due to the
blurring of the original text, possible missing pages,
missing text and other issues beyond our control.

Because this is such an important and rare work, we
believe it is best to reproduce this book regardless of
its original condition.

Thank you for your understanding.

S   D   Serenissime ac Inclyte Rex

Deniq; norit

sunt historiar quæ exempla satis multa continent

Quare miror in ~~Epistola citra~~ Edicto citari

Epistolam ~~ex~~ corinthys, cu hic longe aliud

tradar de coniugio, ac præcipiar coningiu

ys qui non sut idonei ad coplibam.

Ex Francofordia cal. Aprilis . 1 5 3 9

R   M .   T

addictissimus

Philippus Melanthon

To

OLINTHUS GREGORY, LL. D.

OF THE ROYAL MILITARY ACADEMY, WOOLWICH,

THIS

LIFE OF MELANCTHON

IS INSCRIBED

AS A

MEMORIAL

OF THAT

MUTUAL ESTEEM

AND

AFFECTIONATE FRIENDSHIP

WHICH HAVE LONG SUBSISTED

BETWEEN

ONE OF THE MOST USEFUL WRITERS OF THE AGE,

BOTH IN

SCIENTIFIC AND THEOLOGICAL DEPARTMENTS,

AND

HIS HIGHLY OBLIGED

AND

DEVOTED FRIEND,

FRANCIS AUGUSTUS COX.

PREFACE.

NOTHING is more gratifying than to invite others to participate our honourable pleasures, especially those of a mental and moral description. The lives of great and good men if related with impartiality cannot fail of being at once entertaining and instructive. Invited to watch their progress and observe their character, we may learn the most valuable lessons. We are allowed to detect, in order to shun, their errors; to trace, in order to imitate, their virtues;--- to follow them into their retirements;---to become their associates and friends. From the forum of public debate and of unremitted exertion, we accompany them to the fireside, and the closet. Divested of the insignia of office, the pomp of authority and the glory of popular applause, we see them in the undress of friendship and private life. We sit with them in the domestic circle, and hear them converse and see them act at home. Human nature is developed ;--we gain comprehensive views of men and things.

Such a scene must be improving to every well-ordered mind, and if the biographer fail of exciting interest, it can only be in consequence of having performed his task badly, from the defect of necessary documents, or from having chosen an insignificant character.

The *execution* of this work I submit to the judgment of the public, not doubting that I shall meet with a due degree of justice and candour.

The requisite *materials* I have found by no means scanty, and whenever they were important or difficult to obtain I have spared no pains to procure them. My object has been to render Melancthon more fully known, that his character may be more completely understood and more justly appreciated. For these purposes SECKENDORF, DUPIN, MOSHEIM, CAMERARIUS, MELCHIOR ADAM, BAYLE, BRUCKER, and a variety of other writers have been carefully consulted, so that whatever information is communicated respecting persons or things may be deemed authentic.

Every reader must be aware that it is not an *obscure* or *insignificant character* which claims his attention in the following pages. As the intimate friend and distinguished coadjutor of Martin Luther, his name is already familiar and must be dear to every enlightened Protestant; for who can be uninterested in the lives of those illustrious heroes who first led on to the great conflict, in which the liberties of mankind, the rights of conscience, the independence of nations were contested, and by whose struggles they were secured?

In detailing the life of the celebrated Melancthon, I am deeply conscious of one disadvantage. Thoroughly to understand a character and to render the narrative of his life complete, who does not perceive the importance of personal knowledge? It is true, indeed, the colouring may be a little too high and glowing, yet the picture is almost sure to be truer to nature when the artist has drawn from life. It is likely to possess a certain character and expression which a mere copy will seldom exhibit. The tout ensemble will be far better preserved. But in the present case, the picture cannot be taken from life; the great original *cannot* sit to the artist! Though necessitated however to be in some degree a copyist, this misfortune is in part remedied by the well-drawn portrait of a very intimate friend and a learned man. I refer to the Latin life of Melancthon, by Joachim Camerarius.

I have long cherished a reverence

mingled with affection for the interesting
subject of these Memoirs.   I have been
accustomed to trace his exertions as a
scholar and a Reformer with admiration.
In both respects it must be admitted he was
a light in a dark place; and though it is
the province of an impartial biographer in
furnishing a detailed view of his life and
labours in connexion with other eminent
men of his remarkable age, to notice errors
of judgment and imbecilities of mind which
are indeed incident to every human character,
the reader will be presented with the view of
as much excellence, associated with as little
defect is to be expected in the present
world.

No one surely can mistake the purpose
of this volume so much as to suppose that

the author pledges himself to believe the creed or to vindicate all the opinions of its illustrious subject; it is sufficient for him to have rescued from the concealment of a dead language the rich materials which he has incorporated into the following pages, and to raise from the long interment of three Centuries, the character and the glory of one of the brightest ornaments of religion and literature.

HACKNEY, *Feb.* 27, 1815.

CONTENTS.

CHAP. I.

A. D. 1497 to A. D. 1518.

CHAP. II.

A. D. 1518.

CHAP. III.

A. D. 1518 to A. D. 1520.

CHAP. IV.

A. D. 1520.

CHAP. V.

A. D. 1520, 1521.

CHAP. VI.

A. D. 1522. to A. D. 1525.

b

CHAP. VII.

A. D. 1526 to A. D. 1529.

CHAP. VIII.

A. D. 1530.

CHAP. IX.

A. D. 1531 to A. D. 1536.

CHAP. X.

A. D. 1537 to A. D. 1545.

A General Council proposed—Meeting at Smalcald—Melancthon writes on the Pope's Supremacy, and against the manner of appointing the Council—Communications with Francis I.—Passage from the Recess *of Smalcald—Melancthon is solicited to visit Augsburg respecting the institution of a Public Library—Letter of Cardinal Sadolet—A second Commission from Henry VIII.—Persons sent into England—Melancthon's letter to the king—Second Letter against the Anabaptists—Another Deputation from Frankfort—Melancthon's*

CHAP. XI.

A. D. 1546 to A. D. 1550.

CHAP. XII.

A. D. 1550, TO A. D. 1557.

CHAP. XIII.

A. D. 1557 to A. D. 1560.

LIFE

OF

PHILIP MELANCTHON,

&c.

CHAP. I.

*The Reformation—Luther—Birth of Melancthon—His
education—Early proficiency—Residence at Pforzheim,
Heidelberg and Tubingen—Takes his degree—Obtains
an early and remarkable celebrity—Honored by Erasmus and Bp. Latimer—Edits Nauclerus—Renders assistance to Capnio in his contention with the monks—
His public lectures and literary zeal—His removal
to a Greek Professorship in the University of Wittemberg—Commencement of his friendship with Luther.*

THE commencement of the sixteenth century may be justly regarded as one of the best
and brightest periods in the annals of time. It
was distinguished by the release of Christianity
from those fetters of darkness in which she had
been bound for ages, and her triumphant assertion of that glorious liberty in which she now
walks abroad through the earth.

This great event cannot be too highly appreciated, especially as we are daily participating

B

the blessings which result from it. But un-
fortunately, the admiration of mankind is more
commonly bestowed upon the splendid atchieve-
ments of the Military than the Christian hero.
We overlook the miseries he inflicts, and the
wide spreading desolation that marks his course.
But were it even possible to separate these
images of horror from the consideration of his
successes, surely it must be admitted that the
bloodless victories of truth are nobler in themselves, and, accomplished by the exertion of
mental and moral energies, incalculably more
important. On this principle the Reformation
from Popery merits particular attention. Whether
we consider, on the one hand, the violent and
deep-rooted prejudices which were at that
period universally prevalent, artfully cherished,
and powerfully defended, the great and immediate danger resulting from the slightest attempt
at religious innovation, and the deplorable errors
which reigned by long usurpation and prescrip-
tive authority over the minds of men ;—or, on
the other, the seemingly accidental causes from
which the Reformation originated, the inconsiderable source from which it flowed, the slow
but irresistible progress it made, and the beneficial revolution it effected in the sentiments of
mankind, it is impossible not to perceive reasons
for astonishment and joy. No one ought to be
accused of credulity for calling it a miracle; a

moral miracle it undoubtedly was. The miracles which accompanied the first propagation of Christianity and secured its establishment were, it is true, a more direct appeal to the senses, but the same mighty power that established religion in the earth, evidently interposed in this case to rescue it from perishing.

Amongst the instruments of this remarkable change the name of Martin Luther stands preeminent. He was not indeed the *first* or the *only* advocate of this righteous cause, but he was in many respects the *greatest*. Others had inveighed against Popery, exposed the errors of that pernicious system with ingenuity and boldness, and even bled for the sacred cause of God and truth. Waldus, Wickliffe, Huss and Jerome of Prague,(a) are imperishable names ; but in vain did they struggle against the torrent of corruption that deluged the earth. They could oppose, in their respective times and stations, but a momentary resistance, and were swept away. Their efforts indeed produced *some* effects, but they were evanescent, for " darkness covered the earth, and gross darkness the people."(b) But when Luther appeared a variety of circumstances co-operated to produce a result which human skill could neither foresee nor prevent. An attentive observer cannot fail to notice the

(a) Vid. Appendix I.
(b) Isa. lx. 2.

very gradual manner in which truth was discovered to his own mind, by which means he
became fitted to act the part he did, when it is
probable a more full and sudden manifestation
would have disqualified him for the early part of
his career as a reformer. For a long time his
imperfect knowledge of the great principles of
Christianity and the rights of conscience operated
as a check upon the impetuous ardor of his
spirit, which, though afterwards essentially beneficial to the cause, would probably have impeded, if not have wholly prevented the great
work of Reformation, had it been at first unrestrained by lingering prejudices and superstitions.
The schisms which had divided the church
about the end of the fourteenth and at the commencement of the fifteenth centuries materially
diminished the popular veneration for the papal
dignity. The proceedings of some of the councils in deposing and electing popes at their pleasure produced a similar effect. Above all the
scandalous profligacy and venality of the court
of Rome, the voluptuous lives of the ecclesiastics, their intolerable exactions and the facility
which the sale of indulgences afforded to the
vilest offenders to obtain a ready pardon, prepared the minds of the people in general for
those doctrines which the Reformers afterwards
promulgated.

Luther possessed a vigorous and fearless mind.

He was qualified to take the lead and to head opposition in a servile age. His mind was incessantly active; his ardor in the pursuit of knowledge and in the propagation of what he knew, was inextinguishable. He did not " fight as one that beateth the air"*(c)* in the holy war he undertook. Having buckled on the armour he was impatient for the conflict, and rushed forward to an anticipated victory. He was one of the greatest of Christian heroes, and his faults were those of a first rate character. Never scarcely did the hand of God form a fitter instrument to do a greater work !

It was, however, happy for Luther that he did not stand alone, but was provided with an associate in his principal labours adapted in a remarkable degree to supply his deficiencies, to correct his errors, and to regulate his impetuosity of character. Independently of the interest which must necessarily be felt in any one who was the intimate friend and coadjutor of Luther, who was with him in all his struggles and helped him through them, Melancthon claims a distinguished notice on his own account. In tracing the history of his life it will be obvious that although inferior in courage he equalled Luther in ardent piety, and excelled him both in personal virtues and in literary attainments

(c) 1 Cor. ix. 26.

PHILIP MELANCTHON was born in Saxony, at the small but pleasant town of BRETTEN, in the lower Palatinate of the Rhine, on the sixteenth day of February, in the year one thousand four hundred and ninety-seven. The following inscription in his father's house records the event:

DEI PIETATE NATUS EST IN
HAC DOMO DOCTISSIMUS DN.
PHILIPPUS MELANCTHON, D.
XVI. FEBR. A. M.CCCC. XCVII.

The house which belonged to his parents, containing this inscription and his picture, remained standing in the market place till modern times. During the thirty years war many of the literati and inhabitants of Heidelberg took refuge within the walls of Bretten, but in 1632 it was taken by the Imperialists. In the year 1784 it contained, exclusive of the public buildings, two hundred and sixty-two dwelling houses, and upwards of two thousand inhabitants; but in 1789 it was taken, plundered, and almost exterminated by the French; and what their desolating rapacity spared, was at length destroyed under the orders of the Imperial General Ogilvi, by which act of indiscretion, however, he lost the favour of his master.

The mother of Melancthon was the daughter of John Reuter, a very respectable man, and for

many years mayor of the town. Her name was
Barbara, and she is represented as a truly estimable woman. His father, George *Schwartzerd*,
(for this was the German family name,) was a
native of Heidelberg, but settled at Bretten in
consequence of his marriage. He filled the
office of Engineer or Commissary of the Artil-
lery, under the Palatinate princes Philip and
Rupert. Distinguished not only by integrity,
prudence, fidelity, and many other virtues, but
by his remarkable ingenuity in the invention of
all kinds of instruments, adapted either for the
purposes of war, or for the fashionable tourna-
ments of the age, he attracted the attention of
Maximilian, son of the Emperor Frederic, and
became well known to many of the most powerful princes.*(d)* He died in the year 1508, in
consequence of having swallowed some water
from a poisoned well about four years before,
when engaged in the service of his country.
He is described not only as a man of the strictest
morals and of undissembled piety, but so
grave in his manners, as scarcely to admit even
of a joke in the ordinary intercourse of life.
His wife continued in a state of widowhood
twelve years, when, upon the marriage of her
son Philip, which gave her some offence, she
again entered into the conjugal state, with a
respectable citizen of Bretten.*(e)*

(d) Vid. Appendix II.   *(e)* Cam. Vit. Mel.

The early studies of Melancthon were chiefly committed to the management of his maternal grandfather Reuter. This is to be attributed to the numerous and public nature of his father's engagements. The choice could not have been better made, for his grandfather was unquestionably well qualified for such an important superintendence, and, at the same time, affectionately solicitous about his youthful charge. It must be understood, that he acted in concert with his mother, and by her advice.

Melancthon was at first placed with his younger brother George, at a public school in his native town; but, in consequence of a loathsome disease, at that time prevalent in Germany, having found its way into the school, he was soon removed, and put under private tuition.

Although native genius may have frequently surmounted the greatest disadvantages, it has in too many instances, been injured by an improper or defective education. Like the body that has been cramped in its growth, but which, notwithstanding, evinces its original strength of constitution by the very deformities into which it shoots, so the vigorous mind, checked or misguided at an early period of life, is prone to neglect the useful and pursue the trifling, to cherish unseemly prejudices and to take an erroneous course. Melancthon remarked of Lu-

ther, that, " If he had been fortunate enough to
have met with suitable teachers, his great capacity would have enabled him to go through all
the sciences. Nor is it improbable that the
milder studies of a sound philosophy, and a careful habit of elaborate composition, might have
been useful in moderating the vehemence of his
natural temper."(f)

Considering the age in which he lived, and
the state of depression which literature in general
suffered, Melancthon seems to have fallen into
very good hands; and though his natural capacity was the basis of all his future eminence,
much is doubtless to be attributed to the guides
of his early studies. His preceptor in the Latin
language was John Hungarus; a man of great
merit, and, at a very advanced period of life, a
faithful preacher of the pure word of God at
Pforzheim.(g) He was charmed with the rapid
proficiency of his pupil, who, like other youths
of superior talent, was fond of shewing his dexterity by discussing with boys much older than
himself the rules of grammar, or the elements of
language which they had been taught. In these
little contests he was usually victorious; but
whilst he never failed to impress others with a

(f) M. Luth. Op. Præf. Tom. II.
(g) Cam. Vit. Mel.

sense of his superiority, his excellent spirit and temper compelled them to mingle esteem with their admiration.   At this time he had a stammering, or rather, perhaps, a hesitating mode of pronunciation, which, though never very unpleasant, and probably the effect of modest timidity, and not of any natural impediment in the organs of speech, was so effectually cured by time and care, that afterwards it became scarcely, if at all, perceptible. *(h)*

The Academy at Pforzheim, under the immediate superintendence of George Simlerus, was highly celebrated.   Simlerus was distinguished by his classical learning.   He afterwards became a lawyer of considerable eminence, and a lecturer on jurisprudence at Tubingen.   At Pforzheim, Melancthon was introduced to the study of the Greek language, which he prosecuted with great diligence and proportionate success. His brother George and his uncle John were his school-fellows, and they all lodged together at the house of a relation, who was sister to John Reuchlin.   This elegant scholar, known to the learned by the name of Capnio, was a native of Pforzheim, and successively a teacher of languages at Basil and at Orleans.   His mind, naturally vigorous and industriously cultivated, became a storehouse of various erudition.   He

(h) CAM. Vit. Mel.

was the restorer of letters in Germany, and the author of several treatises on philosophy.*(i)*

Reuchlin, or Capnio, took particular notice of the three lads who were inmates at his sister's and frequently questioned them about their pursuits at school. The genius of Philip could not remain long undetected by so diligent an inquirer and so zealous a friend to literature. His prompt and accurate replies, indicating the rare combination of a studious habit with an extraordinary talent, instantly won his affections,

(i) It scarcely deserves the name of philosophy; perhaps it should rather be called mysticism, compounded as it was of the Platonic, Pythagorean and Cabbalistic doctrines. He wrote treatises entitled, " De Verbo Mirifico," and " De Arte Cabbalistica." Some have supposed him to have been the principal author of " Epistolæ Obscurorum Virorum;" a work replete with the most pungent satire against the persecutors of Reuchlin, in the controversy about the restoration of Greek and Hebrew learning. Others have believed the ingenious Ulrich de Hutten, of Franconia, to have been the original writer, but that Reuchlin rendered him essential assistance in the work. In fact, it was the joint production of several literary men, of whom these two were the principal. Hutten was probably the principal writer.

Erasmus allows this performance to be witty, but severely condemns it as anonymous and defamatory, and Leo consigned it to the flames; " But after all," says Jortin, " these *Epistles of the Obscure* may be considered as a piece of harmless mirth, levelled against men who were not only egregious boobies, but, which was infinitely worse, shameless calumniators and blood-thirsty persecutors." JORTIN's *Life of Erasmus*, Vol. I. p. 93. 4to.

and led him, in some degree, to prognosticate his future proficiency. To testify his regard and to encourage him in the prosecution of his literary studies, Capnio presented Philip with several books; amongst the rest, an enlarged Greek Grammar and a Greek and Latin Lexicon. This was a powerful stimulus to his ardent mind, and, dissatisfied with the mere performance of his ordinary exercises, he began to indulge his genius in poetical composition. Although he possessed sufficient inclination, yet he could not command leisure at any subsequent period of his life to devote himself much to this fascinating art; but he wrote several epigrams, epitaphs, prologues, and, occasionally, poetical epistles to his friends; and some very excellent judges, to whom may be added even the fastidious Julius Cæsar Scaliger, have commended his verses. *(k)* Probably the

(k) " Ne Melancthon quidem abhorruit ab ea laude quæ ex poëticis artibus comparatur. Tametsi nonnulli ejus populares insanis quibusdam præceptionibus è Christiana republica poëtas exigendos exclamarunt; quorum barbarissimam amentiam non verbis, neque enim nugis aut clamoribus vinci queunt; sed contrariis affectionibus doctissimus quisque damnavit. Illius igitur ingenium magnum atque ad omnia comparatum intelligemus ex iis poematiis quibus solis lunæque defectiones cecinit. Nam et tempora variè describit eadem versibus luculentis; et eodem nitore præsagia statuit, cujus vestigia sequuti sunt non ignobili ingenio Germani aliquot Stigelius, Æmilius, Acontius, Volfius, Camerarius. Idem Philippus in epigrammate

efforts of his premature age to which we have adverted, resembled the frequent productions of the same period, by youths of ability at school. He wrote also at the early age of *thirteen*, a humourous piece in the form of a comedy, which he dedicated to Capnio, to testify the sense he entertained of his truly parental kind. ness, and engaged his school-fellows to perform it in his presence. It was upon this occasion his patron and friend gave him the name of *Melancthon*, a Greek term of similar significa- tion with the German word *Schwartzerd.(l)* This method of substituting sonorous Greek ap- pellations for their proper names, was at that period a very common practice amongst the learned. Thus *Reuchlin* from the German word Reuch, *smoak*, was changed by Hermolaus Barbarus into *Capnio*, a term of similar import.

Melancthon appears to have cherished a high regard for his early preceptors, and to have re- tained it through life. His amiable spirit never undervalued the merit of others, or forgot their

jucundus atque festivus. Nam aliorum ingenia Germanorum rarò quicquam scribunt, quin jocorum aliquid agant: quò fit ut risus è vulgo non admiratio à sapientibus sequatur. Quæ tamen verterunt Græca (iis enim gens illa dedita est imprimis) non invita Minerva faciunt." SCALIG. Poët. Lib. VI. p. 798.

(l) The word Melancthon is compounded of Μέλας, *black*, and χθων, *earth.* In German, *Schwartz seyn* signifies *to be black*, and *die erde, the earth.*

claims upon his gratitude. In one of his writings, referring either to Hungarus or Simlerus,
he says, " My preceptor was an excellent grammarian, who took pains to make me understand
the construction of every sentence, giving me
thirty or forty verses at a time to construe. He
would not allow me to slur any thing over, and as
often as I blundered, he would correct me, but
with a proper degree of moderation. Thus I
learnt the grammatical part of language. He
was one of the best of men. He loved me as a
son, and I him as a father; and we shall soon
meet, I trust, in eternal life! Yes—I was truly
attached to him, although he were somewhat
severe; yet *severity* I cannot call it, but rather
fatherly correction to stimulate me to diligence."*(m)*

After a residence of nearly two years at Pforzheim, Melancthon was sent by his mother and

(m) MELANCTH. Op. Tom. III.   On another occasion he
writes thus : "Audivi enim adolescens duos viros præclarè eru-
ditos, Georgium Simler et Cunradum Helvetium, alumnos Academiæ Coloniensis, quorum alter Latinos et Græcos poëtas mihi
primùm interpretatus est, deduxit etiam ad philosophiam puri-
orem, sæpè conferens Aristotelicam lectionem quæ tunc erat
in manibus ad Græcos fontes; alter Cunradus doctissimi et
honestissimi viri doctoris Cæsarii auditor primùm nobis Hey-
delburgæ elementa doctrinæ de motibus cælestibus tradidit:
quam ob causam et doctori Cæsario peculiarem gratiam et
venerationem tanquam præceptori, debere me profiteor."
MEL. Declam. Tom I. *Responsio ad Scrip. quorund. delect. à
Clero Secund. Colon. Agripp.*

the relation who superintended his education, to
the University of Heidelberg; formerly the metropolis, now the second town, of the lower
Palatinate, and the birth-place of his father.
He was matriculated on the thirteenth of October, in the year 1509, the twelfth of his age.(n)
The University was highly celebrated for its
various professors in the different branches of
learning, who were soon attracted not only by
the extraordinary progress and amiable disposition of their young pupil, but by his zealous
efforts to excite his fellow students to the more
diligent cultivation of polite literature. Conscious of his own mental superiority, he felt no
envious apprehension of their outstripping him;
or, if they had, his future character renders it
evident, that he would have been the first to
rejoice in their success. It was impossible that
the union of so much application with so much
talent should fail of producing great results.
He was accordingly soon looked up to as a first-
rate youth, and though but a lad was employed to compose most of the public harangues
and discourses of eloquence that were delivered
in the University, and wrote some things even
for the professors themselves.(o) He was also

(n) MEL. ADAM. vitæ Germ. Theologorum. CAM. vit. Mel.
(o) BAILLET, des Enfans deven. celeb. par leurs Etudes ou
par leurs Ecrits, Traité Historique, p. 130. MEL. ADAM. Vitæ
Philos. p. 186, "Scripsit jam adolescentulus *professoribus*
in eâ scholâ orationes, quæ publicè recitatæ sunt."

entrusted with the education of the two sons of
Count Leonstein.   His proficiency in the Greek
was so remarkable, that even at this early age
he composed *Rudiments* of the language which
were afterwards published.*(p)*

During his residence at Heidelberg, Melancthon, who was so eminently formed for friendship,
contracted an intimacy with several persons of merit. Among these were Wimphelingus, Sturmius,
Gautherus, and Sorbillus. He was an inmate of
the well-known Pallas, a man pre-eminently distinguished for his wisdom, virtue and benevolence, and for many years the brightest ornament
of the academy.

Heidelberg had not the honour of educating
Melancthon more than three years. He was
naturally of a feeble constitution, and the situation of the place did not appear to agree with
him. This circumstance, together with a severe
disappointment he suffered in being refused a
higher degree in the university than he had
hitherto obtained, *solely*, as it was alleged, *on
account of his youth*, determined him to remove
to Tubingen, a town on the Neckar, in the duchy
of Würtemberg. The university was daily increasing in reputation, and he entered it in the
month of September, 1512. It had been founded
by Prince Eberhard I. about five and thirty years
before, who had been careful to procure the most

(p) BRUCKERI Hist. Crit. Philosophiæ, Tom. IV. p. 270.

celebrated men of the time for professors in every branch of literature and theology (q).

At Tubingen our aspiring youth attended all the different professors of classical and polite learning, devoting himself especially to mathematics, jurisprudence, logic, medicine and theology. In medicine he studied Galen so thoroughly, that he could repeat the greatest part of his treatises; and although theology, as it was then taught, consisted in little else than scholastic subtleties, knotty questions, unintelligible jargon, and absurdities compounded of superstition and profaneness, (r) he began to be much devoted to the more sober and rational part of it. Here he first became acquainted with Oecolampadius, who was his senior by several years: and as he mentions in one of his letters, they used to read Hesiod together. But, of all the professors, Henry Bebelius, distinguished for his skill in history, John Brassicanus, John Stofflerus in the mathematical department, and Francis Stadianus, the public lecturer on Aristotle, appear to have attracted his highest esteem. He has mentioned the two latter in particular with ap-

(q) MELANCTH. Declam. Orat. de Eberh. Duc. Wirt.

(r) " In theologia D. Lempum qui tum praecipuus habebatur; de quo hoc saepe retulit, solitum cum auditoribus depingere in tabula monstrum illud, quod vocant transubstantiationis et insulsitatem hominis tum quoque se miratum." MEL. ADAM. Vit. Germ. Theologorum, p. 329.

C

plause and affection in his writings. Stofflerus
had for many years the sole care of calculating
and arranging the calendar, a task which Melancthon affirms he executed with great labour and
with equal skill. " Had it not been," says he,
" for his indefatigable application, we should have
known nothing of the distinction of times and
the changes of the months—nor of the seasons
for ploughing, sowing, planting and other agri-
cultural pursuits, nor of a variety of other useful
and ingenious arts."*(s)*. He addresses him in
the dedication or preface to his public oration
on the Liberal Arts, in these terms : " I am indebted to your kindness not only for what I
know, but for what I am desirous of knowing ;
and I am desirous of knowing whatever becomes
me. How can I sufficiently testify my regard
and admiration for one who, during the many
years in which he has diligently investigated
the abstruse parts of mathematical science, has
been constantly stimulating the studious in general, and myself in particular, by every mark of
kindness, to pursue an honourable renown."*(t)*
Francis Stadianus he describes in the strongest
terms : " He was a man of learning, and lived
in such a manner as to deserve the affection of
all the learned and the good !"*(u)*

(s) MELANCTH. Declam. Tom. I. *Encomium Suevorum.*
(t) MELANCTH. Declam. Tom. I. *Orat. de Art. Lib. præf.*
(u) MELANCTH. Declam. Tom. I. *De Stud. Corrig.*

Melancthon had not yet attained the age of seventeen when he was created Doctor in Philosophy, or *Master of Arts.* This took place on the twenty-fifth of January, in the year 1513, *(x)* when he immediately commenced a course of private tuition; but not long afterwards he became a public lecturer at Tubingen. General admiration was soon excited by the profound knowledge and elegant taste he discovered in the Latin classics. A considerable portion of time was occupied every day in delivering public lectures, which were not exclusively devoted to the learned languages, but embraced an extraordinary variety of subjects, as rhetoric, logic, ethics, mathematics and theology. At the same time he particularly directed the attention of his scholars to the classical compositions of Virgil, Terence, Cicero, Livy and the Greek writers. He may be justly regarded as the restorer of *Terence*, whose poetical compositions, through the ignorance of his transcribers and publishers, had hitherto appeared only in a prosaic dress. *(y)*

(x) MELCHIOR ADAM calls it the *seventeenth* year of his age; but, according to the above date, which he has given, Melancthon was not quite *sixteen.* M. BAILLET says he took his diploma in 1514; but I am not certain whether we are to conclude that Melchior Adam commits a mistake in the year of the world or in the year of his age.

(y) The British Museum contains a very curious old copy of Terence, as it was published previous to this period at Strasburg. The title-page is wanting. It is crowded with a variety

Melancthon, having reduced them to a proper arrangement, presented them to the public in their present form. In this labour he shewed his discrimination and taste; for Cicero eulogizes Terence both for the purity of his diction and the beauty of his compositions, representing them as the rule and standard of the language. *(z)*

This bright star in the literary hemisphere, the brighter for the profound darkness which surrounded it, could not fail of attracting the attention of the great men of the age. So early as the year 1515 the sagacious and learned Erasmus of Rotterdam, exclaimed in terms of rapturous admiration, "At Deum immortalem quam non spem de se præbet admodum etiam adolescens et pene puer, Philippus ille Melancthon, utraque literatura pene ex æquo suscipiendus! Quod inventionis acumen! Quæ sermonis puritas! Quanta reconditarum rerum memoria! Quam variæ lectio! Quam verecunda regiæque prorsus indolis festivitas!" *i. e.* "What hopes

of marginal notes, and has several manuscript references. It is also ornamented with curious wood cuts, and the last page concludes with the following notification of the time and place where it was published: "*Impressum in imperiali ac libera urbe Argentina per Joannem Grüninger. Ad illam formam ut intuenti jocundior atque intellectu facilior esset per Joannem Curtum ex Eberspach redactum. Anno à nativitate Domini, 1499, tertio idus Februarii.*"

(z) The learned reader may feel gratified to peruse some of his Prologues to Terence, in *Appendix* III.

may we not conceive of Philip Melancthon, though as yet very young, and almost a boy, but equally to be admired for his proficiency in both languages! What quickness of invention! What purity of diction! What vastness of memory! What variety of reading! What a modesty and gracefulness of behaviour! and what a princely mind!" (a) An eulogium so remarkable, and bestowed by such a man, on a stripling of only *eighteen*, was surely no inconsiderable testimony to his wonderful merit.

Nor was this the only occasion on which this accomplished scholar expressed his admiration. His works abound with similar encomiums: it will be sufficient to select two or three. Writing to Oecolampadius he says, " Of Melancthon I have already the highest opinion, and cherish the most magnificent hopes: so much so, that I am persuaded Christ designs this youth to excel us all: *he will totally eclipse Erasmus!*"—Mosellanus having interceded with him upon occasion of some injurious reports that had been circulated respecting the remarks of Melancthon upon his paraphrase on the New Testament, and implored him not to suffer himself to be unfavourably impressed by them— Erasmus replied, " Philip Melancthon is in no need of my patronage or defence." In a letter

(a) GRYNÆI Epist. Select. Lib. I. p. 302.

which Erasmus addressed to him, he concludes
thus, " Farewell, most learned Melancthon, use
all thine energies that the splendid hopes which
Germany conceives of thy genius and thy piety
may not only be equalled, but exceeded." On
another occasion, in a letter to Julius Pflug, the
celebrated counsellor of George, duke of Saxony,
he gives Melancthon this character: " He not
only excels in learning and eloquence, but by a
certain fatality is a *general favourite*. Honest
and candid men are fond of him, and *even his adversaries cannot hate him!*" " Happy," exclaims Dr. Jortin, " is the person whom this
description suits! It is not safe to attack him;
the public will revenge his wrongs and take his
part against you"! Seckendorf remarks, that
were the various eulogies which literary men,
and *even religious opponents* have pronounced
upon Melancthon to be collected together, they
would fill a very considerable volume.*(b)*

To a much earlier period, probably, may be
referred the oration mentioned in a very curious
passage of one of Hugh Latimer's sermons,
which evinces the astonishing celebrity of this
youthful scholar and reformer.*(c)* " Heere I have

(b) SECKENDORF Hist. Lutheranismi, Lib. I. Sect. 16.
Add. 1. ERASMI Lit. Lib. V. ep. 38. Lib. VI. ep. 1. JOR-
TIN's Life of Erasmus.

(c) One is inevitably tempted to suspect an error here in
the chronology of biographers. Hugh Latimer was born in the

occasion to tell you a story which happened at Cambridge. Master Bilney, (or rather Saint Bilney that suffered death for God's word sake,) the same Bilney was the instrument whereby God called me to knowledge, for I may thanke him, next to God, for that knowledge that I have in the word of God. For I was as obstinate a Papist as any was in England, insomuch that when I should be made Batchelor of Divinity, my whole oration went against Phillippe Melancthon and against his opinions. Bilney hearde mee at that time and perceived that I was zealous without knowledge: and hee came to me afterward in my study, and desired mee for God's sake to heare his confession: I did so—and to say the very truth, by his confession I learned more than before in many yeares. So from that time forward I begunne to smell the word of God, and forsooke the schoole doctors and such fooleries."(d)

year 1486, and is commonly said to have been converted from Popery to the reformed religion, in which he was extremely zealous, at about *thirty years* of age, that is, in the year 1510: consequently, the philippic against Melancthon, to which he refers in the above quotation, must have been pronounced antecedently to this change; from which we must infer, that Philip Melancthon, a boy *not more than thirteen years old*, was characterised and inveighed against as a *reformer, in a public oration delivered by a student in a foreign university upon taking his divinity diploma!*

(d) BP. LATIMER's Serm. ed. 1635. fol. 124.

The same Latimer afterwards said, in a sermon preached before Edward VI. who expected
him in England, " I hear say Mr. Melancthon,
that great clerk, should come hither. I would
wish him, and such as he is, two hundred
pounds a year. The king should never want
it in his coffers at the year's end."

Melancthon took upon himself the laborious task of revising the works published by
Thomas Anshelmus, a noted printer at Tubingen. The greatest part of his time, not immediately devoted to his professional duties or his
private studies, was bestowed in editing a pon-
derous folio work of Nauclerus, to which a preface was prefixed by Capnio. Originally, it
was, in fact, nothing but a confused heap of
fables, mingled with historical facts; and Melancthon bestowed a labour upon it very dis-
proportionate to its intrinsic merit, in arranging,
correcting, purifying, and almost re-writing it.
In this case we can only praise him for his industry.(e)

During his residence at Tubingen, he had
an opportunity of rendering essential service to
his early friend and patron Reuchlin, or Capnio,
who was involved in a disagreeable contention

(e) The book is entitled, " Memorabilium omnis ætatis
et omnium Gentium Chronici Commentarii à *Joanne Nauclero*
J. V. Doctore Tubing. Præposito et Universitatis Cancellario,
digesti in annum M. D."

with certain ecclesiastics.   It happened thus.
The divines and monks of Cologne, instigated
by a Jew of the name of Pfefferkorn, who had
professed Christianity, obtained an edict from
the emperor to authorise them to burn all the
Jewish writings as heretical, excepting the Bible.
The Jews instantly implored the emperor to suspend his order till these books had been examined by a competent committee of learned
men.   To this very reasonable petition he consented.   Capnio, who had prosecuted the study
of the Hebrew language under some learned
Jews, both at Vienna and at Rome, and who
had become conversant with the Cabbalistic
writings, was appointed by the Elector of Mentz
to be an arbitrator in the controversy.   Having
given it as his opinion, that no other books
should be destroyed but such as were found to
be written expressly against Jesus Christ, the
emperor approved the decision, and restored
the books to the Jews.   At this the monks
and inquisitors of Cologne were violently exasperated, and not only loaded him with invec-
tives, but used every means to induce the court
of Rome to pursue him with the thunder of
excommunication.   At this critical juncture,
Melancthon was of essential use to his friend,
and frequent conferences took place between
them, both at Tubingen and at Stutgard, the
place where Capnio resided.   Neither the ad-

vice nor the zealous efforts of a warm friendship
were wanting in his defence, which, co-operating with his high literary reputation, the result
was, the honourable acquittal of Capnio. This
celebrated character died very poor at the age
of sixty-seven. " On account of his virtue and
merit," says Melancthon, " his memory ought
to be cherished. He served his country with
great diligence and judgment, promoted assiduously the Hebrew language, so important to
the church, lived in a moderate manner, and
was bountiful to the necessitous, especially to
scholars. His candour was remarkable, and he
was devoid of envy and malevolence. For these
reasons he was much esteemed by learned
men."*(f)*

One of the earliest of Melancthon's productions, now extant, is an Oration on the Liberal
Arts, delivered at Tubingen in the year 1517,
at twenty years of age. It indicates the elegance
of his mind and the variety of his reading. After a suitable introduction, he relates the
classical story of the seven stringed lyre, and the
origin of the liberal arts. The oration proceeds
with a detail of these arts and a brief recital of
their origin and progress. It glows with anima-
tion as it approaches the close. " Let the ex-

(f) Comp. MELANCTH. Declam. vit. Reuchl. *passim.*
BRUCKER. Hist. Crit. Philosophiæ.

ample of those illustrious persons who surround me, inspire you. Be animated by the great and glorious expectations of your country, and apply the utmost vigour of your minds to what you know to be of pre-eminent importance, the attainment of sound learning and real virtue. Do not be seduced from this noble course by flattering pleasures or by evil examples. Let no dishonourable principle influence your minds: and *that* I call dishonourable which diverts you from the literary pursuits and from the sacred studies to which you are devoted."

Considering the very important part Melancthon was destined to act in the Reformation, it would be pleasing, were it possible, to trace the formation of his religious principles and modes of thinking with as much exactness as we are able to detail his literary career. The history of piety is even more interesting than the history of genius. To discriminate with accuracy the different states of the mind, to ascertain the changes of feeling at successive periods of early life, to witness at once the progressive establishment of moral character and the developement of intellectual capacity, is, and ever must be, highly instructive. Melancthon was endowed with a soul formed of the finest materials, cast in the gentlest mould, and ever ready to listen with attention to reason and argument; but in proportion as the original pre-

judices of education had entrenched themselves
in a mind delicate, discerning, and full of sensibility like his, the attempt to dispossess principles so dear to him, must have been difficult
and hazardous. It is long before one, so constituted, can renounce what has been held sacred ;
then, not without obvious and substantial reasons. Offence is easily taken at the first and most
distant appearances of what is deemed error, and,
under favouring circumstances, in an unenlighten-
ed age, an extraordinary degree of superstition is
the natural result. Melancthon expresses, on one
occasion, the pungent sorrow which the recollection of his former zeal in the idolatrous services of the Catholic church occasioned.(g) It
is easy to believe, therefore, that he must have
endured many secret conflicts, many heart-rend-
ing struggles, previously to his separation from
that communion. The only illustrative fact
that has been transmitted to us affords some good
evidence that his convictions originated in the
best manner, and that his early religious views
were derived from the only pure source of instruction. Capnio having presented him with
a small Bible which had been recently printed
at Basil by the well-known John Frobenius, or
Froben, Melancthon accustomed himself to write

(g) " Cohorresco quando cogito quomodo ipse accesserim
ad statuas in Papatu." *Explic. Evang.* P. II. p. 592.

down upon the margin such explanatory hints
and such useful illustrations of particular passages, as either occurred to his own reflections
or could be collected from the different ancient
writers with whose works he was conversant;
a practice which at least proves the diligent attention he began to pay to the sacred volume.
This Bible was his constant companion. Where-
ever he went he never failed to carry it with
him, and during the public service at church
he constantly held it in his hand, to direct and
enliven his devotions. This practice furnished
an occasion to his bigotted and no less malignant adversaries, who perceived he made use of
a volume of a different size from the prayer-book,
to represent him as engaged in reading even in the
public church, what was very improper both to the
occasion and the place! No efforts were omitted
to render him odious: but Envy and Persecution waged an unequal war and were defeated.*(h)*

The spirit manifested by these religious
barbarians on this occasion, perfectly harmonised
with the language of one of the monkish fraternity, whose preposterous ignorance and bigotry
have furnished a standing joke ever since the
Reformation. " A new language," says he, " has
been invented, which is called *Greek;* guard carefully against it, it is the mother of every species

(h) CAM. Vit. Mel.

of heresy. I observe, in the hands of a great many people, a book written in this language, which they call the *New Testament;* it is a book full of thorns and serpents. With respect to Hebrew, it is certain, my dear brethren, that all who learn it are instantly converted to Judaism."!! *(i)*

After a residence of about six years, Melancthon removed from Tubingen to THE UNIVERSITY OF WITTEMBERG, the metropolis of the Circle of Upper Saxony. In this situation he was immediately introduced into a scene of great labour and extensive usefulness. This university was founded so recently as the year 1502, under the auspices of the Elector Frederic, who spared no pains to advance it to respectability and distinction. The licence of the Emperor Maximilian, and the bull granted by the Pope, for its establishment, are still extant. *(k)* The celebrity of Melancthon, seconded by the powerful recommendation of Capnio, induced the Elector to determine upon giving him employment in the university. Several letters were interchanged on the subject, and the result was, the formal appointment of Melancthon to the Greek Professorship. Upon this occasion, Capnio applied to him with prophetic accuracy the

(i) CONRAD DE HERESBACH, cited by GERNLER.
(k) Vid. HIST. ACAD. WITTEBERGENSIS, Edit. GOTTFRIDO SUEVO.

remarkable language of Jehovah to Abraham : *(l)*
" Get thee out of thy country, and from thy
kindred, and from thy father's house, unto a land
that I will shew thee . . . . . and I will bless thee,
and make thy name great, and thou shalt be a
blessing :" adding, " this accords with the pre-
sentiment of my mind ; and thus I hope it will
be with thee hereafter, my Philip, my care and
my comfort !" He went to Wittemberg on the
twenty-fifth day of August, in the year 1518, at
the age of twenty-one. *(m)* His name is inserted
in the documents of the university with marked
distinction. *(n)*

(l) Gen. xii. 1, 2.

(m) Seckend. Hist. Luth. Lib. I. Sect. 16. Adam.
Vit. Germ. Theologorum.

(n) The following entrance is extracted from the Catalogue of Rectors in the *Hist. Acad. Witteb. à Gottfr. Suevo.*

RECTOR

Johannes Stöb aliàs Güngelyn de Wangen. Diac. Con-
stantiens artium ingenuar. Magister . . . . *d.* 1 *Maii,* 1518

Inscripti

Inter inscriptos reperiuntur

Illustris Princeps Dominus Dn. Barnimus Stetinens.
Pomeraniæ Cassubiæ Sclavorumque Dux Princeps Rugiæ,
Comes Gutzkoviæ.

Johannes Vonder Osther, Canonicus Caminens.

Philippus Melancthon, Artium Magister Dubingens.
de Pretten. Græcarum literarum Lector primus.

Ad latus hujus nominis quidam subsequentium Rectorum
uti ex comparatione literarum apparet Paulus Eberus hæc
verba adscripsit :—

Vivat omne in ævum decus unicum Academiæ hujus et

The general sensation excited at Tubingen on this occasion may be imagined from the language of Simlerus. " The whole city lamented his departure. No one can conceive or estimate how much the Academy lost of distinction and of emolument when he departed." His journey was performed on horseback, by way of Nuremberg and Leipsic ; and he availed himself of the opportunity of contracting a friendship with Picamerus, Mosellanus, Camicianus and other eminent characters.

Upon the fourth day after his arrival at Wittemberg he commenced his public duties as a Professor in the customary mode of delivering an oration, which attracted an unusual degree of applause. Luther is lavish in his commendations, and in a letter addressed to Spalatine he says that it was inconceivably learned and elegant, and excited such universal admiration, that every one forgot the comparative meanness of Melancthon's personal appearance. (o)   In consequence of his

Ecclesiæ ornamentum perpetuum. Sit in recordatione felici et sempiterna beata anima magni illius Melancthonis nostri : Amen.

(o) " Habuit Philippus orationem quarto die postquam venerat, planè eruditissimam et tersissimam, tantâ gratiâ et admiratione omnium ut jam non tibi id cogitandum sit : quâ ratione eum nobis commendes. Abstraximus citò opinionem et visionem staturæ et personæ et rem ipsam in eo gratulamur et miramur." LUTH. Ep. Tom. I. p. 81. b.

settlement at Wittemberg, immense numbers crowded to the university, and his audience sometimes amounted to fifteen hundred persons. *(p)* He had the honour of being Luther's instructor in the Greek language. *(q)*

It is amusing enough to hear the terms in which M. Baillet mentions the intimacy which from this moment commenced between Melancthon and Luther. " Being called to Wittemberg," says he, " in the twenty-second year of his age, *Melancthon fell into the hands of Luther, who abused his easy disposition, and availed himself of all those fine talents which ought to have been devoted to the service of the Catholic church !" (r)*

In truth, this was an event of the utmost importance, not only in reference to these eminent individuals themselves, but on account of the influence of their ardent friendship upon the Reformation in general. The profound learning and cultivated taste of the one, the vigorous zeal, independent spirit, and dauntless heroism of the

(p) TEISSIER Eloges des Hommes Savans, Art. *Melancthon*. It has even been asserted that his hearers sometimes amounted to *two thousand five hundred*—but I think without sufficient authority—" Son nom pénétra dans toute l'Allemagne, et il eut quelquefois jusqu'à deux mille cinq cents auditeurs." CHAUDON et DELANDINE Nouveau Dict. Hist. Art. *Melancthon*.

(q) LUTH. Com. in c. 5. ep. *ad Gal.*

(r) BAILLET Trait. Hist. des Enfans dev. Celebres, &c. p. 133.

other, alike conduced to dissipate the delusions of the age. Both adopted the same general views; and each was equally solicitous of removing that veil of Egyptian darkness that overspread the face of the world: yet they were constitutionally different. The one verged to the extreme of boldness, the other to that of caution; but, like Moses and Aaron among the ancient Israelites, their different talents were admirably suited to promote the general object. Truth would undoubtedly have suffered had the one been less energetic and daring, or the other less moderate, and cultivated.

It would not be difficult to speculate on the ill effects likely to have resulted to the interests of true religion, if these eminent men, instead of being united in strict friendship, had cherished hostile sentiments towards each other. This would probably have been the case, had Melancthon continued a Papist, or had he promoted the views of those who appeared to " halt between two opinions."(s) The impetuous temper and resolute firmness of Luther could neither endure opposition nor neutrality. By the collision of contending parties a third was in reality produced, whose leading maxim was to avoid extremes, and who were ready to make every sacrifice to obtain a delusive peace or to secure

(s) 1. Kings xviii. 21.

personal convenience. They would have abandoned what they even esteemed sacred, in order to terminate this religious war; and, it is to be feared, would have willingly entered into negociations with the advocates of error and superstition, upon the principle of relinquishing the conquests which Truth had already acquired, and which Conscience demanded of them never to cede. At the head of this party the learned, witty, vacillating, avaricious and artful Erasmus is unquestionably to be placed. Too anxious to obtain a Cardinal's hat to enlist himself under the banners of the Reformation, he aimed to please the partizans of Rome; and too penetrating to be ignorant of the abuses of the Catholic system or blind to its excessive absurdities, he was aware the Reformers had reason and truth on their side, and was solicitous, especially while the victory was doubtful, of conciliating their esteem without unwarily pledging himself to act a conspicuous part in what he termed the *Lutheran tragedy*. The consequence was, he dissatisfied both, and failed of acquiring the honours it was in the power of Popes to bestow, and the more valuable distinction which they could *not* give, but which the unbought affection of independent minds and holy reformers would have conferred. *(t)*

(t) JORTIN's Life of Erasmus, *passim*.

It is obvious, that the Papists and the coadjutors of Erasmus would have been equally
glad of Melancthon. His influence in the university of Wittemberg, and his literary fame,
now diffused to the extremities of the empire,
and swiftly circulating throughout the whole ci-
vilized world, would have invigorated the hostility of the one, or promoted the temporizing policy of the other. It would have proved a mighty
bulwark of defence, which, in case of the pre-
ponderance of either party, would have been
strength to the weak, and power even to the
strong. Melancthon was scarcely less detested
than Luther by the violent Catholics ; and
Erasmus, in the course of a long letter addressed
to him, alludes to his having exhorted him to
abandon the Reformers, though he declares he
had not very strenuously urged him to it, knowing it would be labour lost, but still he could
have wished he had applied himself entirely to
good literature. His purpose, he says, was to
promote the good of both parties and dissuade from
tumults, and he wished a reformation might be
made without strife or contention.

The removal of Melancthon, therefore, to
Wittemberg, by which he was introduced to the
immediate and intimate friendship of Luther,
ought to be regarded as a most memorable event.
Luther freely unbosomed all his feelings to this
new and invaluable associate, consulting him on

all occasions, and anxiously availing himself of
his superiority in literary acquirements. *(u)*

Whoever is accustomed to observe the movements and to admire the wisdom of a superintending Providence will mark this occurrence.
He will not be disposed to attribute it to a happy
casualty, but consider it as the result of a superior and wise arrangement. He will connect
it with all its circumstances, and trace it to all
its consequences. Accustomed to comprehensive
views of things, he will not resemble the ignorant
rustic that steps across the spring whence a
Nile, a Euphrates, a Ganges or a Ohio originates,
without any emotion, and without the capacity
to realize those images of grandeur and sublimity
that present themselves in a similar situation to
the enlightened philosopher ; but he will pause,
ponder, compare, and look around him. The
Almighty Ruler of the world proceeds in the
large system of his operations in a similar manner, in some respects, to every intelligent agent
acting on a smaller scale. Does the skilful archi-
tect prepare his materials for the building which
he is about to construct, and fit in each particular stone or ornament to its place with discriminating care ? And is there any improbability in
the belief that when the Universal Agent is about
to produce an extraordinary work, he prepares,

(u) CAM. Vit. Mel. p. 31.

by a process adapted to the purpose, whatever
materials are proper for its execution? Moral
operations require moral instruments, and in the
whole machinery of circumstances an intelligent
and pious mind will see much to admire.
Amidst the rubbish of error which had accumu-
lated century after century till the Reformation,
God determined to erect the temple of Truth,
and his providence cleared an ample space, chose
a variety of workmen, and reared the admirable
superstructure.   And as in the erection of a
building there must be different kinds of labourers, all co-operating together and all essential to complete the undertaking, so it was
requisite, in erecting this great edifice, to prepare and to employ persons very differently
constituted, but all capable of useful co-operation.   In this point of light it becomes us
to contemplate the preparatory course of Melancthon's education, the important station he
filled and the celebrity he obtained at Tubingen,
and particularly his removal thence to the scene
of his future labours.   He was selected by Providence for great purposes, and qualified by a
suitable process for the part he was destined to
act. His literary fame and his vast acquirements
were not only of essential service, but were particularly needed at that precise period when they
were ready for public use.   Short-sighted indeed or criminally blind must he be, who does

not perceive the same superintendance here as in the guidance of Joseph to Egypt, or David to the camp of Saul. If the Reformation claimed the steady efforts of true courage and inextinguishable zeal, be it remembered also, that it no less required a proportion of nice discernment, elegant taste and literary skill ;—if a superstition which invested a mortal with the prerogative of infallibility were to be attacked and levelled with the dust, the ignorance which, with its characteristic blindness, supported that superstition, was at the same time to be dethroned and demolished ; —if old abuses were to be removed, and a new order of things to be introduced and systematized, it was desirable to find not only a nervous arm, but a polished mind, at once to clear away the rubbish of error, and clothe unwelcome novelties with attractive beauty ;—in a word, if existing circumstances called for a MARTIN LUTHER, they also demanded a PHILIP MELANCTHON!

CHAP. II.

A. D. 1518.

General Observations—Sketch of the Life and Doctrines
of Aristotle—Progress of the Peripatetic Philosophy—
Its intermixture with the Scholastic Theology—Its
revival and purification by Melancthon—His early
labours at Wittemberg, and his increasing influence
throughout Germany—Extracts from his Oration
" de Corrigendis Adolescentiæ Studiis."

AFTER long ages of depression, and almost
of total extinction, philosophy, literature, and
theology at length revived. It was impossible
that either of them should prosper during a period in which the human mind was burdened by
innumerable superstitions, gigantic in magnitude
and ferocious in character. The mental faculties were unable to expand or even to stir beneath the oppressive weight ; and century after
century rolled on, scarcely presenting any
thing worthy of the historian to record or
the moralist to admire. But from the moment
that the circulation of thought commenced and

public opinion became comparatively free in its
movements, the superincumbent pressure was
in a measure removed, and the sixteenth century
marked a new era in the calendar of time. In proportion as it became possible to think with freedom,
to express sentiments and to announce discoveries
in science or religion, without instantly incurring
the charge of heresy and being inevitably consigned to perpetual imprisonment or death,
knowledge increased and truth lifted up her
drooping head.*(x)* It is true, the imperfections
which usually characterize first discoveries were
in this instance apparent, but the clouds of prejudice and the mists of ignorance gradually
melted away ; objects which were blended together became distinctly perceived, and this
" morning light" of scientific and religious dis-

(x) This consideration must be restricted to those countries or places where a degree of successful resistance had been
opposed to the papal domination, such as Germany and Switzerland ; for, as we shall afterwards see, light was very far from
being generally diffused ; and even at that period Copernicus,
an eminent astronomer, and native of Thorn, in Prussia, was
confined to a prison by Pope Urban VIII. for daring to maintain the solar system, and the annual and diurnal motions of
the earth. The celebrated Florentine Galileo, also, was twice
summoned before the Inquisition, and twice sent to grace the
cells of a prison for heretically maintaining the truth of the
Copernican system. Copernicus was born Jan. 10, 1472, and
expired in the seventieth year of his age, May 24, 1543.
Galileo was born in 1564, and died at Arcetti, near Florence,
in January, 1642.

covery " shone more and more unto the perfect day."*(y)*

To trace the almost infinitely diversified causes, remote and proximate, of this mighty change would be an interesting, though perhaps a very difficult undertaking. It would be necessary to shew, not only the effects produced by the various great events that have occurred in the moral world upon the general state and character of the particular nations whence they originated, and where they particularly influenced, or upon human character in general in the age in which they occurred ; but also the manner in which they resulted from the previous state of the world and affected succeeding times, as well as the intimate connection and reciprocal influence subsisting between them or resulting from their operation.

A writer of very considerable merit*(z)* remarks, that " A man who, without knowing the nature of the course of a river, should arrive on its banks, seeing it here gliding through an extensive plain, there confined within narrow vallies, in another place foaming beneath the precipice of a cataract ; this man would take the first turning where it might be concealed by a projection for the origin of the river ; ascending

(y) Prov. iv. 18.

(z) Villers on the Spirit and Influence of the Reformation by Luther, p. 7.

higher, a new turn, the cataract, will occasion
the same illusion ; at length he reaches its source,
he takes the mountain from which it issues for
the first cause of the river : but he will soon
think that the sides of the mountain would be
exhausted by so continual a torrent ; he will
see clouds collected, the rains, without which
the dried mountain could not supply a spring.
Then the clouds become the first cause ; but it
was the winds which brought these here, by
passing over vast seas ; but it was the sun who
attracted the clouds from the sea ; but whence
arises this power of the sun ?   Behold him then
soon entangled in the researches of speculative
physics, by seeking a cause, an absolute foundation, from which he may finally deduce the
explanation of so many phenomena.

"Thus the historian who inquires what was the
cause which led to the reduction of the authority of the popes, to the terrible thirty years'
war, to the humiliation of the house of Austria,
the establishment of a powerful opposition in
the heart of the empire, the foundation of Hol-
land as a free state, and so of other occurrences,
will at first see the origin of all these events in
the Reformation ; and will attribute them absolutely to its influence.   But urging his inquiries
further, he discovers that this Reformation itself
is evidently only a necessary result of other circumstances which precede it ; an event of the

sixteenth century, with which the fifteenth, to use the expression of Leibnitz was pregnant ; at most the cataract of the river."

But at present it will be necessary to wave these considerations, which, though attractive in themselves, do not strictly comport with the nature and design of this biographical memoir. In order, however, duly to appreciate the character of Melancthon, and as a general introduction to his literary labours, it will be proper, previous to our entering upon a circumstantial detail of his exertions in conjunction with Luther, to give a rapid sketch of preceding times, and of existing circumstances. The attentive reader will not deem this brief digression from the immediate course of the narrative uninteresting or uninstructive ; nor will he feel it difficult to trace its real connection with the principal subject of consideration. It is proposed to furnish a general outline of the Peripatetic philosophy, its progress in the scholastic form, its relation to theology, and its revival and purification by Philip Melancthon.

Aristotle was born in the first year of the ninety-ninth Olympiad, B. C. 384, at Stagyra, a town of Thrace ; on which account he is called the Stagyrite. At seventeen years of age he went to Athens and studied in the school of Plato, by whom he was denominated the *mind of the school.* In the year B. C. 345, the second of the hundred and ninth Olympiad, he took up his residence in the court of Philip, and became preceptor to his son Alexander.*(a)* Philip and Olympia both became attached to the philosopher, and he obtained considerable influence in the public councils. When Alexander formed the plan of his Asiatic expedition, his preceptor, who preferred literary to ambitious projects, retired to Athens, but carried on a friendly correspondence with the conqueror, although they were afterwards alienated. At Athens he founded a new sect of philosophy in opposition to the academy in which, after Plato, Xenocrates at that time presided. Having made choice of the Lyceum for his school—which was a grove hitherto devoted to military purposes only, he adopted the singular method of walking about as he taught his disciples, on which account they were called *Peripatetics*, and his doctrine the *Peripatetic Philosophy*. After continuing his school twelve years he retired, in consequence of the hatred of his numerous rivals and enemies, to Chalcis, where he died in the sixty-third year of his age.

(a) Philip had addressed to him the following extraordinary letter--- " *Philip to Aristotle wisheth health* : Be informed that I have a son, and that I am thankful to the gods, not so much for his birth, as that he was born in the same age with you : for if you will undertake the charge of his education, I assure myself that he will become worthy of his father, and of the kingdom which he will inherit."

Aristotle appears to have been the first amongst the ancients who attempted a regular inquiry into the process of general reasoning, and though he mistook the subject and wasted a fruitless ingenuity and research upon what is placed beyond the reach of investigation, yet his efforts mark a new era in the history of the human mind. As a writer he was voluminous, and profound, but too anxious to depreciate the labours of his predecessors. From a variety of causes he is extremely obscure. The subjects on which he treats are commonly abstruse and metaphysical : he affects a concise diction, abounds in sudden transitions, technical words, new invented terms, mathematical modes of discussion, and even contradictory statements. Sometimes he misrepresents the opinions of other philosophers, and always seems gratified to depreciate their merits. His writings too have unquestionably been mutilated. A considerable part of his books found their way into the Alexandrian library, and of course shared its fate ; and the rest were afterwards buried in a subterraneous cavern a hundred and thirty years, to prevent their being seized by the kings of Pergamus : after which they suffered a still greater injury by ignorant or officious transcribers and commentators. *(b)*

(b) BRUCKERI Hist. Crit. Philosophiæ.

The logic of Aristotle comprises analytics, or the investigation of truth by incontestible proof, and dialectics, or investigation by probable arguments. In each course truth is to be sought by syllogisms ;—syllogisms consist of propositions, and propositions of simple terms. Terms are of three kinds, homonymous, paronymous, and synonymous. The latter are divided into ten classes, called categories or predicaments--- comprising substance, quantity, relation, quality, action, when, denoting time, where, denoting place, situation and habit.

Every proposition consists of a subject, a predicate, and a copula, or the thing concerning which an assertion is made, the accident asserted of it, and the assertion itself. Syllogisms arise out of propositions. A complete syllogism consists of three propositions, of which the two former are the premises, and the latter the conclusion. They are called the major, minor, and middle terms. The predicate of the conclusion is called the major term, the subject the minor, and both together the extremes. For example--- the sentence, *God is omnipotent*, is a proposition, in which *God* is the subject, *omnipotent* the predicate, and *is* the copula. In the syllogism *Our Creator must be worshipped—God is our Creator—Therefore God must be worshipped ;* the two former propositions are the premises, the latter the conclusion. The three terms are worship—God—Creator. The first the major, the second the minor, the third the middle term, introduced to shew the connection between the two ideas of God and worship. This method of reducing every proposition to the syllogistic form is capable of being almost infinitely diversified, and bears the stamp of its master's originality.

Demonstration arises from principles true in themselves, which involve in them by consequence the truths to be demonstrated, and which are clearly perceived. There are two kinds of demonstration, the one τῶ ὅτι which proves the existence of the cause from its effects; the other τῶ διότι which reasons from the nature of causes. *Dialectics* deduce conclusions from probable premises, or which appear so to the intelligent part of mankind. *Refutation* contradicts a conclusion drawn by the opponent from assumed premises, and either uses legitimate syllogisms or sophisms. Of sophisms the principle are, by departing from the point, and proving something which does not really belong to the question—by taking for granted what is neither allowed nor proved—by reasoning in a circle—by assigning a false cause, or one which does not belong to the question—by representing an accident as essential to the subject—by deducing an universal assertion from what is true only in particular cases, and the reverse—by asserting any thing in a compound sense which is true only in a divided sense, and the reverse — by the use of ambiguous words.

In Physics he taught that matter and form are the constituent principles of things. Matter is neither produced nor destroyed. *First matter,* as he termed it, is a primary substance without quantity or quality, form or figure, and the eternal subject on which forms might be impressed. All things are formed from it and resolved into it. Nature subsists in material substances and consists of matter and form. *Causes* are of four kinds : material, of which things are made; formal, by which any thing is what it is ; efficient, by which things are produced ; and final, or the end for which they are produced. *Substances* are of three kinds ; the first, eternal, as the heavens ; the second, perishable, as animal bodies ; the third, the immutable nature. The heavens are perfect. The natural motion of the heavenly sphere is circular ; but there are other spheres moving in a different direction to produce terrestrial vicissitudes. The primum mobile, or first sphere and first mover, are eternal and immutable. The stars are supported by the sphere, and communicate light and heat by friction. The earth is spherical, and fixed as the centre of motion. The world is eternal, without beginning or end. Bodies are simple, as the elements ; and compound, produced by their combination. The First Mover, and the celestial sphere act perpetually on matter. In sensible bodies there are primary qualities, and mixed bodies are formed from a combination of the elements. In consequence of the agency referred to, bodies suffer a constant succession of dissolution and reproduction.

Aristotle divides Metaphysics into the doctrine of being, the Deity, and the soul. The first axiom concerning being is, that it is impossible for the same thing to be and not to be in the same subject, at the same time, and in the same respect. Being is either by itself or by accident; in power or in act, either notional or real—the former as it is conceived in the mind, the latter as it exists in nature. The essence of the First Mover is incorporeal, indivisible, immutable, eternal, and intelligent: the cause of all motion and the being of beings, or God. This pure intelligence operates upon inferior ones, and they move the heavenly spheres and orbs in imitation of the first power. These he supposed to be eternally connected with their respective spheres.

He taught that the soul has three faculties; the nutritive, by which life is produced and preserved—the sensitive, by which we perceive and feel—and the rational. The production of animal life arises from the union of the nutritive soul with animal heat: life is the continuance of this union, death its dissolution. His writings do not determine whether or not he conceived the soul to be immortal.

In Ethics he taught that felicity consists not in bodily pleasure or external glory, but in the virtuous exercise of the mind. A virtuous life is a source of delight. Virtue consists in the proper exercise of the understanding, and in the pursuit of what is right and good. As it respects ourselves, it consists in preserving a due medium, such as reason prescribes. Fortitude, Temperance, Liberality, Magnificence, or the medium between grandeur and meanness, Moderation, Gentleness, Affability, Urbanity, Modesty, Justice, Equity, and Friendship, are to be esteemed virtues. The purest pleasures are those which a good man derives from the practice of virtue. *Contemplative happiness* consists in the pursuit of wisdom, and is the noblest: *active happiness* arises from external possessions: *both* are necessary to perfect felicity.

Such is a very concise and cursory statement of the doctrines of Aristotle, whose name was reverenced almost to adoration for many centuries; and upon whose principles, partly understood and partly mistaken, disguised, or corrupted, was grafted the scholastic theology, the nature and history of which it will now be proper briefly to detail.

During the four first centuries of the Chris-

E 2

tian age the Platonic appears to have prevailed more than the Aristotelian philosophy; but in the fifth, in consequence of the Platonics themselves adopting the dialectics of Aristotle in their schools, and of the adaptation of his mode of philosophizing to the Arian, Pelagian, Nestorian and other intricate controversies of the age, the Stagyrite openly triumphed. The incursions, however, of the Goths, Vandals, Heruli, Huns and other barbarous nations into the Western Empire proved extremely prejudicial to the interests of learning, which in the sixth century was only preserved from absolute extinction by the monastic orders. Schools were attached to cathedrals under the immediate direction of the Bishops, who caused the youth to be instructed in the seven liberal arts : others were formed in the monasteries, in which the abbot or some of his ecclesiastics presided. Persons devoted to the monastic life were obliged to employ a portion of their time in studying the ancient doctors of the church. From this connection of schools with cathedrals and monasteries, the term schoolmen, or scholastics, was at length applied to those who *professedly* taught philosophy and the liberal arts, for the whole business was *really* and most wretchedly neglected.

The seventh century presents to our view nothing but the midnight of superstition and ignorance. Aristotle was in vogue because his

dialectics were of use in the ridiculous controversies between the Monophysites, Nestorians
and Monothelites. "About eight hundred years
ago," says Melancthon, "nearly the whole world
being in a state of disturbance through the irrup-
tion of the Goths, and Italy laid waste by the
Lombards, Roman literature declined with the
Roman empire. The fury of war destroyed the
libraries, and extinguished the Muses ; for war,
you know, neither conduces to the study of wisdom nor to the due cultivation of civil affairs. On
this principle Homer represents Mars contending
with the bitterest animosity against Pallas. At
that period, Gregory, whom I may call the great
reviver of expiring theology, and a man of most
eminent piety, presided over the Roman church,
and, by promoting study and letters in general,
ameliorated, as much as he could, the ruined
condition of that unhappy age. But he stood
alone."(a)

The whole history of the Church, from the
eighth to the twelfth century, proves that the
scholastics studied and taught philosophy for
no other purpose than to afford support to the
hierarchy by their quibbles and subtleties. Great efforts were indeed made, from
time to time, by distinguished individuals, but
to little or no purpose. Charlemagne, who be-

(a) MELANCTH. Declam. Tom. I. *De Corrigendis Adolescentiæ Studiis.*

came Emperor of the West in the year 800,
was not only a great conqueror and a wise legis-
lator, but a zealous patron of learning.

The Arabians, in the course of their Asiatic
conquests, became acquainted with some of the
ancient Greek authors ; and the Caliphs, procuring from the Eastern Emperors copies of the ancient manuscripts, had them translated into Ara-
bic, particularly those which treated of mathematics, physics, and metaphysics. Charlemagne
caused Latin translations to be made from the
Arabian, and founded the universities of Bono-
nia, Pavia, Osnaburg and Paris. " Long peace,"
says Malancthon, in speaking of this period, " was
the means of promoting letters in Scotland and
Ireland. Amongst others, the Venerable Bede
was pre-eminently illustrious for his uncommon
skill in Latin and Greek, in philosophy and mathematics. So profound was he in sacred learning, as to be comparable to the ancients. Italy
and France, in the mean time, were in the most
degraded state ; while Germany, always better
skilled in arms than in letters, was pursuing hostile and violent measures in Italy. Such was
the state of affairs when Charlemagne was born,
who, as soon as he had subdued the Roman
empire, devoted himself to the restoration of
literature ; and, in addition to his very extensive
knowledge of the doctrines of the schools, he
was an experimentalist and discoverer. It was

by his means Alcuin was induced to settle in France, where he became eminently useful."(d)

Lewis the Meek, Charles the Bald, his brother Lothaire, and the English Alfred, with many others, highly distinguished themselves. Johannes Scotus, an Irishman, the intimate friend of Charles, a man of superior genius and well acquainted with Greek and Roman litera- ture, was the first who blended together the mys- tic and scholastic theology. It was, however, the prevalent opinion that philosophy was to be pursued merely in subservience to theological disputation, and to furnish weapons for contro- versy. Nothing but abstruse and subtle ques- tions were proposed, which generated a war of words. It was characteristic of the scholastic philosophy to display all possible ingenuity in reasoning about nothing, or nothing better than the merest trifles. Dialectics were employed not to assist the understanding in the search for truth, which is their only legitimate application, but to perplex what was plain, to distinguish what did not differ, and to entangle the mind in a labyrinth of inexplicable absurdities. The topics of discussion were intention and remission, proportion and degree, infinity, formality, quid- dity, individuality, and others equally *intelligi- ble* and *edifying !* Aristotle was considered as

(d) MELANCTH. Declam. Tom. I. *De Corrigendis Adoles- centiæ Studiis.*

having reached the utmost limit of human knowledge ; a convenient opinion it must be admitted for those who were desirous of being spared the trouble of thinking or examining for themselves !—and so preposterous was their attachment to this heathen oracle that they blasphemed the great Teacher of the world by publicly. reading to the people in sacred assemblies the Ethics of Aristotle, instead of the Gospel of Christ !/e/

At the opening of the twelfth century the dialectic philosophy took the lead of every other description of knowledge, and was every where taught in the schools. It was imagined to be utterly impossible to understand the mysteries of sacred wisdom without it, and consequently those who excelled in it were regarded with the highest admiration. The theologians were the only philosophers : the scholastic philosophy, supported by the authority of Aristotle, became completely established by its alliance with theology, and opened the only avenue to ecclesiastical preferment. Those who excelled in this jargon—and assuredly it required no ordinary degree of penetration to comprehend it—were dignified with the most splendid titles, and obtained the most eminent situations. They were created professors, abbots, bishops, cardinals, and even popes, and were known by the epithets

/e/ MELANCTH. Apol. A. C. p. 62.

*most profound, angelical, wonderful, most sub-
tle, perspicuous, wise doctor,* or by some other
equally flattering appellation. And what could
be a more suitable finish to this colossal glory,
than the crown of posthumous canonization ?—
Who then will dispute the authority or the wisdom, for instance, of Pope John XXII. in
conferring this distinction upon the *angelical*
Thomas Aquinas, or of Pope Sixtus IV. in
sainting the *seraphic* Bonaventure ? Still if these
decrees had not proceeded from the chair of infallibility one would be tempted to submit an
inquiry, whether some kind of mistake were
not committed, and whether, after public opinion had made *angels* and *seraphs* of these renowned doctors, instead of acquiring additional
honour, which, no doubt, was the true intent
of the statute of canonization, they did not in
fact rather suffer in point of dignity, by being
changed into mere *saints?* But *tacere est
sæpe tutum !—*

About this period the Greek copies of the
writings of Aristotle, which were brought from
Constantinople into the West, were diligently
studied in Paris, and thence introduced in the
time of Abelard into Germany; but taking
alarm at the prevalence of logical diquisitions the
Synod of Paris, and the Council of the Lateran
under Pope Innocent III. prohibited the use
of the physical and metaphysical productions of

Aristotle in the public schools. These measures however, tended to increase rather than diminish his celebrity, and it was afterwards found necessary to admit of their use under certain restrictions, till they were eventually appointed by express statute in the Parisian University. In Italy and Germany the Emperor Frederic II. a patron of learning, encouraged the study of Aristotle and other ancient writers, by employing persons to translate their works into Latin; but this task was very imperfectly executed, owing to their general ignorance of the Greek language.

From the twelfth to the fourteenth century true philosophy made very little progress. The spirit of disputation originated a variety of sects and parties who were mutually enflamed with the most violent animosities. Ranging under different leaders they were denominated *Albertists*, *Thomists*, *Scotists*, and *Occamists*.

But of all these disputes none were more vehement, more lasting, or more nonsensical than that which existed between the *Nominalists* and *Realists*. The case was briefly this : Plato taught that ideas were intelligible natures, having a certain and substantial existence, whose origin and seat is the Divine Mind, and the immediate objects of contemplation to the human understanding. Universal essences of this kind Aristotle considered as mere fictions, but yet not denying the existence of essential forms or ideas, he affirmed they were eternally united to matter, and that from this union arises existing bodies. Zeno and the Stoics acknowleged primary principles, but ridiculed those who affirmed the substantial existence of ideas or universals. The Eclectic Philosophers endeavoured to reconcile. these differences of opinion ; and a fine field they afforded to them and to succeeding *wise men* for subtle distinctions and endless contests. The opinion of Aristotle that universals do not subsist *prior* to individual bodies, nor *after* them, but *within* them, and are forms eternally united to matter, prevailed till the eleventh century, when Rosceline adopted and propagated the Stoic opinion that universals have no real existence, but are mere names and terms by which the kinds of individuals are denoted. This was maintained by Abelard, and produced the sect of Nominalists. Their opponents were denominated Realists. *(f)*

In the thirteenth century, the state of literature and philosophy was somewhat ameliorated both by means of the Italian poets Dante, Allighieri, Petrarca, and Boccaccio, who fixed the standard of their own language ; and of the two Englishmen, Chaucer and Roger Bacon. Possessed of a discriminating judgment and a sublime

(f) BRUCKERI Hist. Crit. Philosophiæ.

genius, Bacon observed the defects of the scholastic philosophy, and recommended the pursuit
of Truth by experience and observation. He
made numerous discoveries in science, particularly in optics, astronomy, and mechanics. The
Italian poets promoted the study of philosophy
and letters. They were all warm admirers of the
ancients, and cultivated the Latin language with
considerable success.

A critic, however, quoted by Roscoe, says
that the Latin writings of Dante were like a picture that has lost its colour, and exhibit little
more than an outline. " Happy had it been
had this author been enabled to convey his sentiments in Latin as advantageously as he has
done in his native tongue. The numerous works
of Petrarca, the offspring of that solitude in which
he delighted, are lasting monuments of his industry and his talents. Yet his style is harsh,
and scarcely bears the character of Latinity.
His writings are indeed full of thought, but defective in expression, and display the marks of
labour without the polish of elegance; but as
we sometimes take a potion, not for the sake of
gratification but of health, so from these writings we must expect to derive utility rather
than amusement. Rude as they are, they possess however some secret charm which renders
them engaging. The distinguished talents of
Boccaccio sunk under the pressure of the general

malady. Licentious and inaccurate in his dic-
tion, he has no idea of selection. All his Latin
writings are hasty, crude and uninformed. He
labours with thought, and struggles to give it
utterance; but his sentiments find no adequate
vehicle, and the lustre of his native talents is
obscured by the depraved taste of the times."(g)

About this period many eminent Greeks
were induced to quit their native country in
consequence of the barbarizing effects of the
Turkish conquests in the East, and to settle in
the western parts of Europe. The precursor of
these eminent refugees was Emanuel Chrysoloras,
who, having been sent to solicit the protection
of the Christian princes against the Turks, visited
Venice, Florence, Rome and other cities, and
was at length prevailed upon by the Florentines
to fix his residence amongst them. Others, following his example, brought with them into
Italy a store of Grecian books and ancient literature. These were read with great avidity, and
translated. Learned men were welcomed at
Rome, where many translations, especially of
the works of Aristotle, were patronized by Pope
Nicholas V. (h)

(g) Cortesius, quoted in Roscoe's Life of Lorenzo de'
Medici, Vol. II. p. 53, 4to. Comp. Bruckeri Hist. Crit.
Philosophiæ, Tom. IV. Pars I. Lib. I. Cap. I. Sect. 8.

(h) It is not to be imagined, as most writers have represented, that the Greek language was absolutely unknown in

The Medicean family also highly distinguished themselves, by whose means several libraries were established in different parts of Italy.
Cosmo de'Medici founded the library of S. Mar-
co : his son Piero pursued the same laudable
course, and Lorenzo sent Lascaris into Greece
to purchase valuable manuscripts while his great
coadjutor Politiano, who had the care and arrangement of his collection, made several ex-
cursions into Italy to purchase the remains of
antiquity. If the ancestors of Lorenzo laid the
foundation, he raised the superstructure of the
Laurentian library. Corvino, the King of Hun-
gary, and Federigo, Duke of Urbino, who were
permitted to copy such of the manuscripts of
Lorenzo as they wished to possess, proved also
distinguished patrons of learning. *(i)*

The thirst after knowledge which such illustrious individuals manifested led to the discovery of many important remains of Greek and
Roman literature. Quintilian and several of

Italy previous to the European journey of Chrysoloras and the
learned Greeks. Leontius Pilatus of Thessalonica instructed
Boccaccio in that language about the year 1350, and gave public lectures on Homer at Florence. Guarini, also, a Veronese,
used his efforts for the restoration of Greek literature, and probably other solitary examples might be adduced; but after the
death of Boccaccio no progress was made; on the contrary,
Greek literature declined till the arrival of Chrysoloras and the
Constantinopolitan fugitives.

(i) Roscoe's Life of Lorenzo de' Medici, Vol. II. 4to.

Cicero's compositions were recovered. By means of the discovery of the art of printing in the fifteenth century the Latin Classics were easily multiplied, and several learned men published both the Greek and Roman writers with scholia and notes. Amongst the labourers in this vast field the name of Politiano stands pre-eminent. Besides the academy at Pisa, established by Lorenzo de'Medici, another and still more important institution was formed at Florence, where the Greek language was taught by learned Greeks and Italians, under his auspices, and by his liberality. Men of rank, and illustrious females also devoted themselves to study; of the former, Giovanni Pico, of Mirandula, who, at the age of twenty-one, had the reputation of being acquainted with twenty-two different languages; and of the latter, Cassandra Fidelis, were the most remarkable. But it must not be imagined that this taste was universally diffused; for though the fragrant flowers of poesy grew in a few places, and some fruit-bearing trees were planted here and there in classic ground; the general aspect which the world presented to the eye was that of a thorny wilderness or a barren desart.

The revival of letters, however, and the reformation of religion at the beginning of the sixteenth century reciprocally influenced and promoted each other. The reformers were con-

vinced that ignorance had been one of the principal causes of the corruption of doctrine, and
hence they were solicitous of seeing philosophy
restored to its purity, and truth to her throne.
The boldness with which they attacked religious
error and despotism contributed to the advancement of literature : the zeal with which some
of them cultivated literature by reflecting a beam
of light on biblical criticism, contributed to the
cause of religion. When the Romish church
reigned with unrivalled dominion in the West,
she resisted the study of the oriental and other
languages. She decreed the faith of others upon
the sole authority of her popes, her councils,
and her charters, and too tractable slaves submit‑
ted to the imposition. The attack of this system
demanded a knowledge of languages, of the principles of sound criticism, and of sacred and profane antiquities. The New Testament, and the
Septuagint Version of the Old, required an ac‑
curate and extensive acquaintance with Greek,
the study of which was particularly promoted
by MELANCTHON. The reforming spirit diffused
itself beyond the Reformers themselves, and
many even in the bosom of the Catholic
church, as Erasmus, Ludovicus Vives, Faber,
and Marius Nizolius, censured the scholastic
method of philosophizing, inveighed against the
corruptions of the age, and assiduously cultivated general literature. Besides, the zeal-

ous supporters of the Romish hierarchy finding
themselves attacked by literary weapons so ably
wielded were necessitated to have recourse to
measures of defence, which must of course consist in the cultivation of all possible familiarity
with letters, and with ecclesiastical antiquities.
But these studies were never pursued to the
same extent as amongst Protestants, who gave
the first impulse to improvement, and the finishing blow to the massive edifice of corruption.

In the beginning of the sixteenth century
though the scholastic philosophy thus began to
fall into contempt, Aristotle retained a considerable degree of authority. The Platonic system
having totally declined, the peripatetic philosophy became universally victorious. The Catholics zealously promoted it because of its adaptation to the defence of their system, and amongst
the Protestants many learned men were followers
of Aristotle, so far as their superior reverence to
evangelical truth would permit. On this point
Luther and Melancthon differed in opinion. The
former who had studied the schoolmen, at first
attached himself to the *Nominalists*, but afterwards rejected the whole system with contempt.
Melancthon is also to be classed amongst the
principal supporters of this party.

The controversy which had so long subsisted between these parties was marked by every
species of polemic, and sometimes even of pu-

F

gilistic violence.   Ludovicus Vives represents
himself as having been witness of disputes in
which after having vented upon each other
every species of abusive language the parties
proceeded to blows, and this not only with their
fists, but with clubs and swords, so that many
have been wounded and even killed ; and Camerarius states that similar disorders prevailed in
the academy at Tubingen, which Melancthon
could scarcely suppress.*(k)*   Erasmus in his
joking manner, alludes to these evils in one of
his epistles.   " We are making preparations (he
writes) for a war against the Turks (A. D. 1518).
With what view soever this be underaken we
ought to pray God that it may be profitable not
to a few, but to all of us in common.   Should
we conquer them it is to be supposed (for we
shall hardly put them all to the sword) that attempts will be made to bring them over to
Christianity.   Shall we then put into their hands

(k) " Atque non solum contentiones et jurgia inter dissentientes sed dimicationes etiam ac pugnæ commissæ fuerunt,
interdum concertationibus non tantum pertinacibus verborum
sed manuum quoque violentis.   Hæc dissidia et Tubingensem
Academiam invaserant, contubernio bonarum artium et philosophiæ studiis destinato, in duo quasi castella diviso, ex quibus de opinione sua factiones illæ acerrimè præliantes inimici-
tias graves exercebant.   Philippus qui certam docendi disse-
rendique rationem probaret, et Aristotelica in hoc genere primas
tenere intelligeret, magnificas et splendidas et amplas alteras
disputationes non amabat."   CAM. Vit. Mel. p. 22.

an Occam, a Durandus, a Scotus, a Gabriel, or an Alvarus ? What will they think of us (for after all they are rational creatures) when they hear of our intricate and perplexed subtleties concerning instants, formalities, quiddities and relations ? What, when they observe our quibbling professors so little of a mind, that they dispute together till they turn pale with fury, call names, spit in one another's faces, and even come to blows ? What, when they behold the Jacobins fighting for their Thomas, the Minorites for their most refined and seraphic doctors, and the Nominalists and Realists each defending their own jargon, and attacking that of their adversaries ?"(l)

When Louis XI. king of France, published an edict against the Nominalists, in the year 1474, ordering their books to be fastened up with iron chains in the libraries, that they might not be read, and requiring the youth of the academies to reject their doctrines, their principal leaders fled into England and Germany, and attached themselves to the Reformers.(m) Luther, however, perceiving the support which the scholastic philosophy afforded to the errors of the Catholic church, and conceiving that the logical and metaphysical sentiments of Aristotle incorporated with it, had occasioned all the

(l) ERASM. Epist. 329.
(m) BRUCKERI Hist. Crit. Philosophiæ.

celebrated disputes and divisions of previous ages, rejected both; but it is to be remarked that he rather opposed the false doctrines founded on Aristotle, through the ignorance and perversity of mankind, than the principles of philosophizing which he established. " I am persuaded," says he, " that neither Thomas, nor all the Thomists together, ever understood a single chapter of Aristotle."

At first Melancthon united with Luther in condemning Aristotle, from a conviction that his principles and modes of reasoning were injurious to genuine Christianity, but he very soon altered his opinion, and thought he might be employed as a valuable auxiliary in the propagation of truth. This circumstance has occasioned his being much misrepresented by certain writers, to whose statements, the system upon which, during his whole future life he conducted the education of youth, is an ample refutation.(n)

(n) " Pour ne rien dissimuler, il faut que je dise ici que Melancthon suivit au commencement le branle que Luther lui avoit donné: il parle mal d'Aristote ; mais il changea bientôt de langage et il persévéra dans la recommendation de la philosophie de ce fondateur du Lycée••••••On peut confirmer ceci par ces paroles d'Erasme, *Epist. ad Fratres Germaniæ inferioris,*" p. m. 2127. " Nonne Melancthon aliquando damnavit scholas publicas? Nunc hic dicit maneant scholæ quæ bonæ sunt, vitia corrigantur." BAYLE Dict. Hist. Art. *Melancthon.* Note (K). Comp. BRUCKERI Hist. Crit. Philosophiæ, Tom. IV.

Melancthon attempted the revival of the pure peripatetic philosophy, though he agreed with Luther on the subject of the scholastic system. In several passages of his writings he utterly condemns the latter as generating dissention rather than promoting truth; and though he took Aristotle for his guide, be it remembered, this was only in philosophical inquiries, and so far as his principles might be connected with utility. His devout and penetrating mind always paid a superior deference to the dictates of Revelation. In his oration on Aristotle, he thus expresses himself, " I will add something concerning philosophy, and the reasons for believing that of Aristotle to be the most useful for the Church. It is agreed, I think, by all, that logic is of prime importance, because it teaches method and order, it defines fitly, divides justly, connects aptly, judges and separates monstrous associations. Those who are ignorant of this art, tear and mangle the subjects of discourse as puppies do rags. I admire the simile of Plato, who highly extols it as resembling the fire which Prometheus brought from heaven, to kindle a light in the minds of men by which they might be able to form correct ideas. But he does not furnish us with the precepts of the art, so that we cannot dispense with the logic of Aristotle. That of the Stoics is not extant, and instead of being a simple method of reasoning fit for the explanation of profound subjects, it appears to have been a complete labyrinth of intricacies, and in fact a mere corruption of the art." *(o)*

Melancthon was considered in the German schools in the light of a COMMON PRECEPTOR.*(p)* Uniting the study of the Aristotelian philosophy with ancient learning in general, the plan which he adopted was to extract out of Aristotle all that was essentially good, to illustrate it by the aids of literature and genuine criticism, and to adapt it to the principles of true religion.*(q)* Nor did he follow Aristotle implicitly; whatever was valuable in the writings or doctrines of the Stoics and Platonics he adopted for his use, and, whatever his own genius suggested, incorporated into his system.

This plan was pursued in most of the German academies under the sanction both of the civil and ecclesiastical authorities, and from its first promoter was denominated the *Philippic* method. In all the Lutheran schools abridgements of the various branches of philosophy by Melancthon, composed in a familiar style, were

(o) MELANCTH. Declam. Tom. III. *Orat. de Aristotele.*

(p) BRUCKERI Hist. Crit. Philosophiæ.

(q) " Eruditam philosophiam requiro, non illas cavillationes, quibus nullæ res subsunt. Ideo dixi unum quoddam philosophiæ genus eligendum esse, quod quam minimum habeat sophistices, et justam methodum retineat; talis est Aristotelis doctrina." MELANCTH. Declam. *de utilit. Philos.* Tom. I.

constantly and for a long period taught; of this nature were his *Logic*, *Ethics*, *Physics*, and his *Treatise on the soul*. Nor did he confine his attention to a few subjects only, but with the most exemplary zeal and assiduity, reduced almost every art and science into a form and arrangement which inconceivably abbreviated the labour of the student.

Vitus Winshemius, a very competent judge, speaks of these publications in the highest terms of commendation, as shortening the Aristotelian road to knowledge.*(r)* He characterizes their author, with great propriety, as resembling the industrious bee flying through the fields of universal science in all directions, and collecting the choicest and sweetest portions from the prime productions of every writer. So sings the poet—

Floriferis ut apes in saltibus omnia libant
Omnia nos. Itidem depascimur aurea dicta,
Aurea perpetua semper dignissima vita.

As bees in flowers their honied treasure find,
So on thy precepts feeds the searching mind,
Thy golden precepts —yes, illustrious sage,
GOLDEN—and formed to bless the latest age.*(s)*

On various occasions Melancthon publicly delivered discourses on the method of studying

(r) WINSHEM. Oratio in Funere Melancthonis.
(s) BUSBY's Lucretius, B. 3.

philosophy, and his opinions were so universally reverenced, that he acquired the highest fame and the most useful influence. The precepts of art and science had been hitherto very imperfectly taught, and with a great intermixture of truth and error. These he systematized and reduced to order ; rejecting what was erroneous, explaining what was obscure, and arranging what was confused. *(t)*

Several learned men from Italy and Great Britain, who became tutors in the German schools, and assiduously promoted the peripatetic philosophy, materially assisted him in these laudable efforts. It is to be lamented indeed, that the learned of Italy, France, England, and Germany, did not totally discard Aristotle as a guide, and strike out a more independent plan ; but we must not despise the light though it be mingled with some darkness, nor undervalue the labours of distinguished men, because they did not undertake what we deem desirable, or accomplish what is now perceived to have been practicable.

In the genuine spirit of a literary Reformer, instead of merely pursuing the course which custom had prescribed or indolence would have dictated, Melancthon applied his active mind to the discovery of the best means of inspiring a

(t) ADAMI Vit. Germ. Theol. p. 331.

taste for literature, and of promoting the great ends of study. When he first arrived at Wittemberg nothing could exceed the miserable condition of philosophy and letters as well as of religion, so that he found an ample and unoccupied field of important labour. The liberal arts and sciences were sunk into the most wretched state, and were concealed in the profoundest darkness. So completely were all men plunged into abject barbarism, that though they dare not venture upon open hostility, being restrained by the authority of the prince, yet they secretly despised and disparaged learning, and slandered Melancthon ; the printing offices did not possess any copies of the Greek writings, and the students were necessitated to write out passages as they were explained to them for their own use.*(u)*

Melancthon, with a laudable impatience, instantly applied himself to the removal of these evils. The desart which spread its vast and cheerless extent before his eyes overgrown with weeds, he was anxious by assiduous cultivation to convert into a literary paradise. In the first year of his residence at Wittemberg he read lectures to crowded auditories upon Homer, and upon the Greek text of St. Paul's epistle to Titus. Luther speaks of him in various letters

(u) WINSHEM Vit. Mel. BRUCKERI Hist. Crit. Phil. Tom. IV.

to his friends in the highest terms of commendation, stating that his lectures were so extremely popular, that all the principal theologians attended him, and high and low became
inspired with the love of Greek.   Amongst other
epithets, he calls him the *most learned and most
truly Grecian Philip Melancthon. (v)*   " He is
a mere boy and a stripling if you consider his
age ; but our great man and master, if you reflect
on the variety of his knowledge, which extends
to almost every book.   He is distinguished not
only for his acquaintance, but for his critical
knowledge of both languages, nor is he unskilled
in Hebrew learning."

The excessive ardour of his mind produced
a considerable effect upon his constitution, and
the Elector Frederic addressed an affectionate
letter to him on the subject, wherein he admonishes him to be careful of his health, and not to
exert himself too much, offering him the best
wines his cellar could produce, and reminding
him of Paul's language to Timothy, to " use a
little wine for his stomach's sake and his often
infirmities."*(w)* " This," he stated, " was no less
obligatory than any other admonition."*(x)*

(v) " Philippum Græcissimum, eruditissimum, humanis-
simum, habe commendatissimum."   *Luth. ad Spalatinum.*
" Eruditissimus et Græcanicissimus Philippus Melancthon
apud nos Græca profitetur," &c.   *Ad Langum.*

(w) 1 TIM. v. 23.

(x) VAN DE CORPUT Leven ende Dood van Phil. Mel.

Melancthon was scarcely seated in his professor's chair, when he commenced an attack
upon prevailing prejudices, and announced a
plan of reform.   He determined that youth
should *study* as well as frequent the university,
and that they should be put in possession both
of motives and means for this purpose.   His
zeal appears never to have diminished through the
course of his long and laborious life.   It was the
least of all his distinctions to have acquired a
great name, for he rendered essential service both
to the cause of literature and religion.

A few weeks only had elapsed since his
arrival at Wittemberg, when he delivered in the
month of October an oration, to which some
references have already been made, on reforming
the studies of youth. *(y)*   He congratulates
them on being placed under the auspices of the
illustrious Frederic, and on their numerous advantages for the acquisition of learning ;   and
while attentive to the various other departments
of human knowledge, he particularly urges them
to the study of the Greek writers and philosophy ;
" but·let no one trifle in philosophizing lest he
should at length totally lose sight of common

p. 7. *Amstcrd.* 1662.   Winshem. Oratio in Funere Melancthonis.   Mel. Adam. Vit. Philosophorum, p. 188.

(y) Melancth. Declam. Tom. I.   It is entitled " *Sermo
habitus apud Juventutem Academiæ Wittebergensis de Corrigendis Adolescentiæ Studiis.*"

sense. Let him rather select the best things
from the best authors, for the purposes of improvement both in the knowledge of nature and
in morals.   The study of Greek literature is of
essential importance; it in fact comprehends
universal science, for their writers discuss morals
in a most copious and appropriate manner. The
treatise of Aristotle on this subject, the laws of
Plato, and the best of their poets, may be read
with the utmost advantage. Homer amongst
the Greeks may be called a fountain of knowledge ; Horace and Virgil hold a similar preeminence amongst the Romans."

He speaks in recommendation of history as
calculated to direct us in the skilful management of public and private affairs.

" But," he adds, " the manner in which
you apply to *sacred studies*, is of the greatest
importance. These, above all other pursuits,
require judgment, experience, and diligence; and
remember that the perfume of divine ointments,
so to speak, far surpasses the aromatics of human literature.   Under the guidance of God,
the cultivation of the liberal arts will be rendered
subservient to sacred objects, as Synesius intimates to Herculianus " the noblest employment of life, is to use philosophy as a guide to
divine knowledge." If this should not be quite
obvious to any one, let him consider that brass
was sent by the King of Tyre for the temple of

Solomon as well as superior metal : so it is in reference to theology which comprehends Hebrew and Greek literature, for the Latins drink from these streams and sources, and those foreign languages are requisite to be known, lest we should appear nothing better than ciphers amongst theologians. *(z)* But there the accuracies and beauties of language will be seen, and the genuine sense of terms and expressions discovered with noontide evidence. Having ascertained the literal meaning of words, we shall be able to pursue the course of argument notwithstanding any frigid glosses, discordant comments, or any other hindrances that may be interposed.

Whenever we approach the fountains of truth we shall begin to grow wise in Christ, his commandments will become obvious, and we shall be regaled by the blessed nectar of heavenly wisdom. When we have gathered the clusters amongst " the vineyards of Engedi," the bridegroom will come " leaping upon the mountains, skipping upon the hills," and with the " kisses of his mouth," and the " savour of his good ointments poured forth," will anoint those who are conducted into the palaces of Eden. United to him we shall live and thrive, contemplating Zion and Salem in the secret silence of adoration. *(a)*

(z) κωφὰ πρόσωπα literally *senseless masks.*

(a) The allusion is to the language of the *Song of Solomon,* Ch. i. 14. Ch. ii. 8. *et passim.*

Such is the fruit of celestial knowledge, which will always prove worthy of our supreme regard when pure and unimpaired by human subtleties.

The great importance then of giving a new impulse and direction to your studies, and the manner in which they are likely to become conducive to your mental and moral character is sufficiently obvious. Who can help deploring the state of our immediate predecessors, who, abandoning the light of learning, plunged into Tartarean darkness, and took up with the very dregs of knowledge? And who is not affected at the lamentable state of our own times deprived by negligence of our ancient authors, and of all the advantages which would have accrued from their writings had they been preserved? You should understand, therefore, the difficulties which attend the acquisition of the most valuable knowledge; nevertheless, industry will so overcome them, that I trust you will obtain that which is of real importance with far less expense of time and trouble than is generally devoted to what is absolutely useless.

Your tutors will undertake the labour of making proper selections for you, and separating the frivolous from the useful in conducting you to the stores of Roman and Grecian literature. Let some of your leisure hours be occupied especially with the latter, and I will use my utmost endeavours to afford you every facility. From the very first I shall be careful to alleviate the laboriousness attending the grammatical part of language, by reading portions of the best writers for illustration. I shall notice, in passing, what-ever may relate to the conduct of life, or the general knowledge of obscure subjects, so that by proper application we shall be able to accom - plish the circle of human learning, and it will devolve on me to stimulate your diligence. Homer is in our hands and the Greek of Paul's Epistle to Titus, and you must pay great atten- tion to ascertain by the strain of the discourse, the divine truths intended to be revealed.

Here it is proper to remark, how much grammatical accuracy in language conduces to the knowledge of sacred mysteries, and what a difference appears between commentators, some of whom are versed in the Greek language, others ignorant of it; and in various cases what mis-takes are the consequence. If we trifle on this subject, be assured we shall inevitably suffer for it.

Enter then, O ye youths, enter upon your course of wholesome instruction with this sen- timent in your constant recollection *whoever determinately sets about a business has half ac-complished it.* Do not be afraid of becoming wise : study the Roman authors, but especially attach yourselves to those of GREECE, without the know-ledge of whom the former cannot be properly

understood, and whose compositions will conduce to the knowledge of general literature, and
more than any others to the formation of the
mind to taste and elegance.   I cannot help looking forward to anticipate the effect of your example, and I fancy that I can see a few years hence
Germany in various parts reviving in literature,
the general state of morals ameliorated, and the
minds of men, at present barbarously wild and
barren as the desart, at length *tamed*, so to speak,
and cultivated !

Henceforth then you will devote yourselves
to study, not only for the sake of your own personal advantage and that of posterity, but for the
honour of our immortal Elector, who is by universal concurrence the best of princes, and has
nothing more at heart than the promotion of
literature. For myself I am resolved to try my
utmost, both to accomplish the desires of the
most pious of princes and the success of your
studies. And with this design I solemnly devote myself, O ye illustrious princes and su-
perintendents of this university, to your service:
consecrating my youth to solid learning and not
to useless or injurious pursuits, and confidently
depending upon your kindness and protection.

CHAP. III.

,,,,,,,,,,

A. D. 1518, to 1520.

,,,,,,,,,,

The State of Religion—Relics—Indulgences—Tetzel—
Progress of the Controversy with the Court of Rome—
Melancthon's Narrative of Luther—Public Disputation
at Leipsic—Its Effects—Paper war between Melanc-
thon and Eckius—Concise but satisfactory Pamphlet
and admirable Spirit of the former.

TURNING from the schools of literature to
the church of Christ, we find that, in reference to religion as well as science, Melancthon
was called to Wittemberg at a most critical juncture. That we may duly appreciate his labours
and form a correct idea of the posture of ecclesiastical affairs, it will be requisite to glance at a
a few preceding events.

The state of the Catholic church was at this
period quiet and reposing. Though many circumstances had occurred to prepare the public
mind for the introduction of a new order of
things—though some portentous gatherings of
the no distant tempest might have been discern-

G

ible to attentive observers, when not only private persons but distinguished princes upbraided the despotism, the fraud, the avarice, the extortion, the licentiousness of the Popish hierarchy, and even demanded a reform of abuses by means of a general council,—yet the right of private judgment was not asserted, the supreme authority and infallibility of the Pope in religious affairs was not disputed, and the Roman Pontiff felt the utmost self-consciousness of security. The commotions which had been excited in some former ages by the Waldenses, Albigenses and Beghards, and more recently by the Bohemians, seemed to be at an end : and as in nature, the storm is frequently preceded by a peculiar stillness diffused around, when the winds are hushed into peace— not a leaf of the forest stirs—not a wave ripples on the tranquillized surface of the lake—not a bird flutters through the air to dissolve the universal enchantment ;—so was the atmosphere of Rome at this time hushed into the deepest calm—not a breath of murmur stirred—not a tongue moved—not a voice was heard to excite alarm, and ecclesiastical authority lolled at perfect ease in the Papal chair. If the low mutterings of discontent began to roll, they were too distant to be heard or too contemptible to be feared. If any intimation were given of the existence of rebellious feelings, they were only treated with the smile of ridicule. What mortal

power could storm the citadel of St. Peter, and
overturn the turrets of superstition? Who dare
resist the well established power of Papal domination? Where was a son of Jesse to be found,
who could hope to slay the giant in his strength
and glory ?—

After the execrable pontificates of Alexander
VI. who expired in the year 1503, and of Julius
II. whose sanguinary course was arrested by the
arm of death in the year 1512, Leo X. assumed
the ecclesiastical sceptre. His character was in
many respects different from his predecessors.
He was of a disposition more gentle, and of
a taste far more refined. Historians have celebrated him as the patron of arts, sciences, and
literature. Learned men resorted to his court,
were honoured by his friendship, and were employed to assist in the plans for promoting knowledge which his elegant mind devised ; but he
was a lover of pleasure, an opponent of reform,
and a crafty politician. Every means which he
considered as conducive to the grandeur of the
Roman See he instantly adopted, though at the
same time he was dissipating its treasures by a
boundless luxury.

The state of religion was inconceivably deplorable, and its very foundations were sapped
by the substitution of public prayers to the
Virgin, and to saints, in the place of those devotional sacrifices of the heart which are due ex-

clusively to the eternal God. *(b)* The bishops
and canons devoted themselves to sensuality,
and even used the wealth intended for charitable
purposes to support their personal grandeur and
extravagance.   They were oppressive to their
inferiors, and servile, as might be expected, to
those from whom they had any reason to anticipate emolument or patronage.   All orders of the
clergy, imitating their ecclesiastical superiors,
who copied from the luxurious court of Leo, became utterly contemptible, and as a necessary
consequence of these disorders, dissoluteness
was associated with idleness, and every religious
office publicly bought and sold.   The discourses
of those who pretended to preach, consisted of
fabulous tales, reports of miracles and prodigies,
scholastic subtleties, or grave assertions of the
necessity of obedience to the decisions of the
holy mother church, the merits of saints, the
glory of the Virgin Mary, the virtue of relics, the
duty of endowing churches and monasteries, the

(b) The Popish churches resounded with such petitions
as the following:

" Maria, mater gratiæ
Tu nos ab hoste protege
In hora mortis suscipe,
et
Sancta Dorothea, *cor mundum in me crea* :
Sancta Catharina ab astu mundi transfer nos ad amæna
Paradisi : *aperi januas Paradisi.*"

Vid. MELANCTH. Declam. Tom. VI.

flame of purgatory, the utility of indulgences and other topics equally *edifying!* A monk of the Franciscan order at Basil, assured his audience from the pulpit, that *Scotus* had rendered greater services to the church than *St Paul! (c)*

Luther says of the monks, " Their fasting is more easy to them than our eating is to us. To one fasting day belonged three days of devouring. Every friar to his evening collation has two quarts of beer, a quart of wine, spice cakes or bread prepared with spice and salt, the better to relish their drink. Thus went these poor *fasting* brethren, they grew so pale and wan that they were like the *fiery angels."(d)*

There existed a particular order of friars in Italy, called *Fratres Ignorantiæ,* that is, *Brethren of Ignorance.* They were obliged to take solemn oaths that they would neither know, learn, nor understand any thing at all, but answer all questions with the word NESCIO. Truly, said Luther, all friars are well worthy of that title, for they only read and babble out words, but feel no concern to understand them. They say, although we understand not the words, yet the Holy Ghost understands them, and the devil flies away. This was the friars' highest argument who are enemies to all liberal arts and learning, for the Pope and the Cardinals conclude

(c) HOTTING. Hist. Eccles. Tom IV. p. 383.
(d) COLLOQ. MENSAL. p. 413.

thus: " Should these brethren study and be learned, they would master us, therefore *saccum per neccum*, i. e. *hang a bag or sack about their necks*, and send them begging through cities, towns, and countries." *(e)*

But something worse than ignorance attached to the monkish fraternity, of which two notable instances mentioned by Luther, will abundantly satisfy the reader. In the monastery at Isenach, says he, stands an image which I have seen. When a wealthy person came thither to pray to it, (it was Mary with her child), the child turned away his face from the sinner to the mother, as if it refused to give ear to his praying, and was therefore to seek mediation and help of Mary the mother. But if the sinner gave liberally to that monastery, then the child turned to him again ; and if he promised to give more, then the child shewed itself very friendly and loving, and stretched out its arms over him in the form of a cross. But this picture and image was made hollow within, and prepared with locks, lines, and screws ; and behind it stood a knave to move them, and so were the people mocked and deceived, who took it to be a miracle wrought by divine providence !

A Dutchman making his confession to a mass-priest at Rome, promised by an oath to

(c) COLLOQ. MENSAL. p. 415.

keep secret whatever the priest should impart to him till he came into Germany, upon which the priest gave him *a leg of the ass on which Christ rode into Jerusalem*, very neatly bound up in a silken cloth, and said, " This is the holy relic on which the Lord Christ did corporeally sit, and with his sacred legs touched this ass's leg !" The Dutchman was wonderfully pleased, and carried the holy relic with him into Germany, and when he came upon the borders, boasted of his holy possession in the presence of four others of his comrades, at the same time shewing it to them ; but each of the four having also received a leg from the priest and promised the same secresy, they inquired with astonishment " whether that ass had *five* legs ?"—By the way, they forgot that the latter would have been much less of a miracle than the former.

A Dutch schoolmaster in contempt of a shameless friar, who had expressed his dislike of the liberal arts and sciences, gave his school boys this Latin for an exercise, *monachus* a devil, *diabolus* a friar.*(f)*

The subject of *sacred relics* is inexhaustible, but we will only add a few words. Spalatine, the celebrated secretary of Frederic, Elector of Saxony, drew up a curious catalogue of sacred relics preserved in the principal church at Wit-

(f) COLLOQ. MENS. p. 315 & 326,

temberg.   It contained the enormous number of *nineteen thousand three hundred and seventy-four.* Previous to the more correct ideas of religion which he received from Luther, the Elector was a great collector of these rarities.   But the relics in the churches of Hall were still more curious. *(g)*   These precious specimens of superstition are of very high antiquity.   In the year 359, the Emperor Constantius caused the remains of St. Andrew and St. Luke to be removed to the temple of the Twelve Apostles at Constantinople, from which precedent the search for saints and martyrs, whose bodies were supposed to possess extraordinary virtues, became general.   The wonder seems to be how a sufficient number could be procured, to serve even by piecemeal for the purpose of so many ages and churches ; but this apparent difficulty is solved by father John Ferand, who asserts, that " God was pleased to multiply and re-produce them for the devotion of the faithful."   Instead of swelling the inventory to thousands, a specimen of a few may afford the reader some data by which to ascertain whether the probability is that they were multiplied by divine omnipotence, or by human credulity.

" *The rod of Moses with which he performed his miracles.*
" *A feather of the angel Gabriel.*

(g) Seckend. Hist. Luth. Lib. I.   p. 221-223. Lib. III. p. 372.

" *A finger of a cherub.*

" *The slippers of the antediluvian Enoch.*

" *The spoon and pap dish of the Holy Child.*

" *A lock of hair of Mary Magdalene.*

" *A tear our Lord shed over Lazarus, preserved by an angel who gave it in a phial to Mary Magdalene.*

" *One of the coals that broiled St. Lawrence.*

" *The face of a seraph with only part of the nose.*

" *The snout of a seraph, supposed to belong to the defective face.*

" *Some of the rays of the star that appeared to the magi.*"

The bishop of Mentz, says Luther, *(h)* boasted that he had A FLAME OF THE BUSH WHICH MOSES BEHELD BURNING !

The necessity of some reform of abuses, even the more enlightened Catholics themselves have always admitted, and the manner in which it was accomplished, is worthy the most attentive consideration. Man usually employs great means to accomplish insignificant purposes ; but God produces the greatest effects by the smallest apparent effort. Hence there is a characteristic difference between divine and human methods of operation, which perhaps was never more remarkably conspicuous than in the history of the Reformation. Never, consequently, did any work exhibit more visible traces of a divine interposal.

When Leo X. took the Papal chair, he found the revenues of the church exhausted by the vast projects and ambitious enterprizes of his immediate predecessors, and not only was he

(h) Colloq. Mensal. p. 314.

naturally disinclined to economize, and liberal in his encouragement of the arts and learned men, but extremely desirous of aggrandizing the Medicean family, of maintaining a splendid establishment, and of contributing to the exterior magnificence of the Catholic church. Julius II. had granted indulgences to all who contributed to the building of the church of St. Peter at Rome, and under the same pretext Leo adopted a similar plan of obtaining money. " Pope Leo X.," says Sleidan, " making use of that power which his predecessors had usurped over all Christian churches, sent abroad into all kingdoms his letters and bulls, with ample promises of the full pardon of sins, and of eternal salvation to such as would purchase the same with money !"

It is obvious that the multiplication of crimes in a superstitious and dissolute age, would be proportionate to the facility of obtaining pardon. It had been a practice in the different governments of Europe, to allow the payment of a fine to the magistrate, by way of compounding for the punishment due to an offence. The avaricious and unprincipled court of Rome adopted a similar plan in religious concerns, and intent only on the augmentation of revenue it even rejoiced in the degradation of the human mind and character. The officers of the Roman chancery published a book containing the exact sum to be paid for any particular sin. A deacon

guilty of murder was absolved for twenty crowns.
A bishop or abbot might assassinate for three
hundred livres. An ecclesiastic might violate
his vows of chastity even with the most aggra-
vating circumstances for the third part of that
sum. To these and similar items, it is added,
" Take notice particularly that such graces and
dispensations are not granted to the POOR, *for not
having wherewith to pay they cannot be comforted.*" (i)

The origin of indulgences is to be traced
to a time far antecedent to the period now
under review. They were resorted to in the
twelfth century for the purpose of private emolument, the bishops assuming to themselves
this dispensing power, whenever they wanted
money for their private pleasures, or for the
exigencies of the church. They soon became
a source of inexhaustible opulence, and the abbots
and monks who did not possess the same authority, but quite as much avarice and craft, invented the counterpart of this plan by carrying
about the relics of saints in solemn procession, and
permitting the infatuated multitude to touch and
kiss them for certain stipulated prices.

The Roman pontiffs soon interposed to

(i) TAXA CANCELLAR. ROMANÆ. This book was first
printed at Rome, in 1514, and at Cologne the following year.
Consult SCHELHORNII Amænit. Literar. *Francof.* 1725.
Vol. II. 369. BAYLE, Art. *Banck* and *Tuppius.*

share this profitable traffic of indulgences with
the bishops, and at length to *appropriate* it to
themselves.   And with strange temerity they
ventured not only to publish plenary remission
for all temporal penalties, but for all the punishments predicted for transgressors in a future state
of existence.   The first pretence to justify this
proceeding, was the holy war carried on by European princes against the infidels of Palestine,
but this benefit was very soon extended to less
important occasions.

The monstrous doctrine thus originated was
modified and embellished by *Saint* Thomas in
the following century, and contained these propositions, " that there existed an immense treasure of *merit*, composed of the pious deeds and
virtuous actions which the saints had performed
beyond what was necessary for their own salvation,
and which were therefore applicable to the benefit of others ; that the guardian and dispenser of
this precious treasure was the Roman pontiff,
and that of consequence he was empowered to
assign to such as he thought proper a *portion* of
this inexhaustible source of *merit*, suitable to
their respective guilt, and sufficient to deliver them from the punishment due to their
crimes." *(k)*

In the pontificate of Leo X. Albert, Elector
of Metz, and archbishop of Magdeburg, who was

(k) MOSHEIM. Eccles. Hist. Vol. III. p. 86, 8vo.

soon afterwards made a cardinal, *(l)* had the
commission for dispensing indulgences in Germany, and enjoyed a considerable share of the
profits.   His agent in Saxony was John Tetzel,
a Dominican friar, a profligate in his morals, but
a man of popular eloquence, and what was still
better for the purpose, of most consummate
effrontery.   He carried on a very extensive traffic in indulgences, in consequence of offering
them to the ignorant multitude at a very low
price.   He boasted that " he had saved more
souls from hell by his indulgences, than St. Peter
had converted to Christianity by his preaching."
He affirmed, if any man purchased them, his
soul may rest secure respecting its salvation—
that the souls purchased, as soon as the money
tinkles in the chest, escape and ascend to heaven—and that the cross erected by the preachers
of indulgences, was as efficacious as the cross of
Christ itself.—The usual form of absolution by
Tetzel, was as follows, " May our Lord Jesus
Christ have mercy upon thee, and absolve thee
by the merits of his most holy passion.   And I,
by his authority, that of his blessed apostles Peter
and Paul and of the most holy Pope, granted and
committed to me in these parts, do absolve thee,
first from all ecclesiastical censures, in whatever
manner they have been incurred, and then from
all thy sins, transgressions and excesses, how

(l) DUPIN's Eccles. Hist. B. II. Ch. I.

enormous soever they may be, even from such as
are reserved for the cognizance of the Holy See ;
and as far as the keys of the holy church extend,
I remit to you all punishment which you deserve in purgatory on their account, and I restore
you to the holy sacraments of the church, to the
unity of the faithful and to that innocence and
purity which you possessed at baptism ; so that
when you die the gates of punishment shall be
shut, and the gates of the paradise of delights
shall be opened, and if you shall not die at present, this grace shall remain in full force when
you are at the point of death. In the name of
the Father, and of the Son, and of the Holy
Ghost."

The audacious Tetzel was particularly successful in his impious traffic in the neighbourhood of Wittemberg, a circumstance which
roused the righteous spirit of Luther to a determined opposition. He declaimed both publicly
and privately against the vices of the monks who
published indulgences, and pointed out to the
people from the pulpit, the danger of relying on
any other means of salvation than those which
God himself had appointed in his word. Luther
was at that time about thirty-four years of age,
and a professor of theology and philosophy in the
University of Wittemberg. On the thirtieth of
September, 1517, he maintained publicly at
Wittemberg ninety-five propositions against in-

dulgences, by which he opened the long and glorious campaign which eventually secured the rights of conscience, and established the cause of protestantism.

These propositions which were affixed to the church adjoining the castle of Wittemberg, were much welcomed, and obtained a wide and rapid circulation in Germany. The Augustinians, particularly the prior and sub-prior of the monastery, endeavoured to dissuade Luther from thus exposing himself and his order to danger, but nothing could extinguish or abate his zeal. Tetzel soon afterwards published two theses against the Reformer at Frankfort, the former consisting of a hundred and six propositions, the latter of fifty, but all deduced from one general principle, as liberal and as enlightened as a Catholic commissioner of indulgences might be expected to assume, namely, the Pope's infallibility. As a further incontestible proof of victory over his opponent, he committed his writings to the flames. The students of the University at Wittemberg instantly resented the indignity, very much to the dissatisfaction of Luther and totally without the knowledge of the elector, senate, or rector, by treating Tetzel's propositions in a similar manner. The controversy, however, was for a long period entirely of a private nature, and Luther himself relinquished his prejudices in favour of the hierarchy slowly and reluctantly.

His letters to the Pope and the bishops were expressed in respectful, and even in submissive terms, for no one was less aware than himself of the great work he was employed by Providence to accomplish.

Some of his Augustinian brethren differed from Luther respecting several of his doctrines, which determined him to embrace the favourable opportunity of an annual meeting of the order at Heidelberg, in the summer of 1518, to publish and publicly defend his sentiments on justification, faith, good works, and other theological topics. The effect produced by this discussion was considerable, especially upon the minds of two persons afterwards distinguished in the annals of the Reformation, Martin Bucer and John Brentius.

In the course of the same year three powerful antagonists arose, Silvester Prierio, master of the Apostolic palace at Rome, James Hoogstraat, an inquisitor of Louvain, and John Eckius, professor of divinity, and vice-chancellor at Ingolstadt. In his controversies with these dignified ecclesiastics, he displayed the most intrepid firmness of character, and an increasing knowledge of the truth. In reply to Prierio's extravagant representations of the Pope's power and of his superiority to a general council, he exclaims, " If such are the sentiments entertained at Rome, happy are they who have se-

parated from the church and are gone out from
the midst of that Babylon ! Cursed are they who
hold communion with her ! If the Pope and cardinals do not check this mouth of Satan and
compel him to recant, I solemnly declare before
them that I dissent from the Roman church, and
renounce her with the Pope and cardinals as the
abomination of the holy place "

Leo X. reclining upon the lap of sensuality
and indolence, cheered by the beams of prosperity, and lulled by the echoes of parasitical adula-
tion into luxurious repose, took no notice of the
progress of opinion in Germany. He expected
the contentions which had arisen would cease
of themselves, and like a few bubbles on the
surface of a stream produced by some temporary
and slight agitation of the waters would gradually, and without any interference, disappear.
When Prierio referred to the heresies of Luther,
he replied with the utmost indifference, *Che fra
Martino aveva un bellissimo ingegno, et che coteste
erano invidie fratesche.* " Martin is a man of
talents, but these are only the squabbles of
monks." But from the moment the innumerable reports he heard of the fatal divisions of
Germany, and especially a letter from the Emperor Maximilian I. on the subject, convinced
him of his mistake, he became infuriated, and
acted with a precipitancy no less conducive
than his previous indifference to the advantage of

the reformed cause. He summoned Luther to
appear before him at Rome within sixty days,
to answer for his heresy in the presence of select
judges, of whom Prierio was nominated as one.

Frederic, justly surnamed the *wise*, adopting
the only measure that could have successfully
averted the impending danger represented to the
pontiff, that Luther's cause belonged exclusively
to the jurisdiction of a German tribunal, and
ought to be decided by the ecclesiastical laws of
the empire. This induced the Pope to refer the
case to Cardinal Cajetan, a Dominican, and his
legate at that time at the diet of Augsburg.   In
a letter dated the eleventh of October, addressed
to Melancthon from this place, which evinces at
once the ardour of his friendship and the peculiarity of his situation, he thus expresses himself: " There is nothing, my dear Philip, new
or remarkable here, unless it be that the whole
city is full of the rumour of my name, and every
one is desirous of seeing this new Erostratus, the
incendiary. Persevere manfully in what you are
doing for the right instruction of youth ; for my
part I am ready, if such be the will of God, to
suffer any thing for you and for them. I would
rather die, and lose for ever, what would indeed
be a most painful privation, your most delightful society, than recant any part of the truth I
have spoken, or furnish those with an occasion
of disparaging the most important studies, who

are both the silliest and the bitterest enemies of sound learning. Italy is plunged into the profoundest Egyptian darkness, all are ignorant of Christ and the things that are Christ's. Yet these are the lords and masters of our faith and morals! Thus the anger of God is evinced in the accomplishment of that prediction; ' I will give children to be their princes, and women shall rule over them.' Farewell, my dear Philip, and pray fervently that the divine displeasure may be averted." (m)

Luther held three different conferences with the cardinal, in the month of October, but to no purpose: after which, Charles Miltitz, a Saxon knight belonging to the court of Leo, and well qualified for such a commission by prudence and sagacity, was sent to supersede Cajetan. (n) At his first conference in the year 1519, at Altenburg, he succeeded so far as to persuade Luther to write a submissive letter to Rome, and after two other interviews great expectations were entertained of a speedy and complete reconcilia-

(m) Luth. Op. Tom. I. p. 163.

(n) For the double purpose of conciliating the Elector of Saxony, and avoiding the humiliating appearance of sending a messenger expressly to treat with Luther, the Pope sent the golden or consecrated Rose to Frederic, by Miltitz, which was an annual present to some distinguished favourite of the court of Rome. It was received, however, with coldness, and even contempt.

tion. Happily the inconsiderate violence of the Papal advocates defeated these hopes, and stimulated Luther and his followers to still greater diligence in the investigation of truth, and to increased activity in the propagation of it.

The origin and early progress of this extraordinary controversy, together with the motives which influenced the great *heresiarch* of the sixteenth century, are so admirably stated by Melancthon in his preface to the second volume of Luther's works, that the substance of it cannot with propriety be omitted in this narrative.

"THE REVEREND MARTIN LUTHER gave us reason to hope, that in the preface to this part of his writings, he would furnish a narrative of his own life, and of the occasions of those contests in which he was engaged : and he would have done it, if, before this volume was printed, he had not been called from this mortal life to the eternal society of God and the heavenly church. A clear exposition of his private life would have been peculiarly useful, for it abounded with profitable examples for the confirmation of the pious, and the admonition of posterity. It would also have refuted the calumnies of those who insinuate, that he was excited by princes or others to undermine the dignity of bishops, or that he was animated through the expectation of private gain to break the bonds of monastic servitude.

" The parents of Martin Luther originally lived in the town of Eisleben, where Martin was born, and afterwards removed to Mansfeldt, in which place his father became a magistrate and obtained the highest reputation for his integrity. His mother was remarkable for every virtue, and especially for the fear of God and a devotional spirit. They were peculiarly diligent in their daily instructions to educate their son in the knowledge and fear of God, and in a proper sense of every duty. Luther was placed under the tuition of a pious tutor at the school of Eisleben, and at the age of fourteen was removed to Magdeburg, along with John Reineck, who afterwards rose to considerable distinction, and with whom he formed a lasting friendship. In the course of a year he was sent to the school of Eisenach, where he applied to grammatical studies with the utmost diligence. He far surpassed his schoolfellows in talent, especially in eloquence and copiousness of language, in prosaic and poetical composition. Captivated with the love of literature he panted for academical instruction, and if he had met with suitable teachers, his capacity would have enabled him to go through all the sciences, nor is it improbable that the milder studies of a sound philosophy and a careful habit of elaborate composition, might have been useful in moderating the vehemence of his natural temper. But at Erfurt he was introduced to the thorny logic of the age, which his penetrating genius soon completely understood. Eager for knowledge he was not satisfied with this, but hastened to read Cicero, Virgil, Livy, and most of the Roman writers; whom he studied not as boys do for the sake of the words, but for instruction. He entered into the meaning and spirit of the authors, and as his memory was tenacious, almost every thing he read was ready for use. Thus, even in his early youth he excited the admiration of the whole university.

" Having taken the degree of master of arts at the age of twenty, his relations urged him to embrace the profession of the law, thinking that his genius and eloquence might be employed advantageously to the state, but he very soon disappointed their wishes by entering the Augustinian monastery at Erfurt. There he not only pursued ecclesiastical studies with the closest attention, but submitted to the severest discipline, and far surpassed others in the various exercises of reading, disputation, fasting, and prayer. As he was neither little in person nor feeble in constitution, I have been astonished at the small quantities of food he required, for I have known him when in perfect health, neither eat nor drink four days successively, and for a considerable length of time subsist on a slight allowance of bread and a herring day after day.

" The occasion of his commencing that course
of life, which he considered most suitable to
piety and sacred learning, was this, as he related
it himself, and as many know. When deeply
meditating on the wonderful instances of divine
wrath and judgment, he was frequently so
alarmed, that he was ready to die with terror. I
saw him once wrought up to such a pitch of feeling in the course of an argument on some doctrinal point, that he threw himself on a bed in a
neighbour's chamber, and amidst the most fervent
supplications, frequently exclaimed, ' he hath
concluded all under sin, that he might have
mercy upon all.'

" It was not poverty, therefore, but religion
which induced him to seek a monastic life, in
which though his proficiency in scholastic learning, and his skill in the inextricable labyrinths of
disputation were remarkable, yet as he was
rather in quest of solid improvement than of
fame, he regarded these pursuits as only ornamental and subordinate. He eagerly resorted to
the fountains of heavenly knowledge, that is, the
writings of the prophets and apostles ; that he
might ascertain the will of God and have his
faith established upon the firmest evidence. To
this he was the more disposed, in consequence
of those anxieties which preyed upon his mind.

" He used to relate that an elderly priest in
the monastry at Erfurt, to whom he explained

his feelings, consoled him by discoursing on the nature of faith, and directing his attention to the article in the creed, ' I believe in the remission of sins.' This he interpreted not merely as implying a general belief, for such a faith even devils possess, or a conviction that some persons of peculiar excellence as David or Peter are pardoned, but that it was the divine command that each individual should personally appropriate the doctrine. This interpretation he confirmed by a reference to St. Bernard, and to the language of St. Paul, ' We are justified by faith.' Luther was thus led to pay greater attention to the doctrine of justification by faith, so much inculcated by Paul, and by the study of the different passages on this subject in the writings of the prophets and apostles, accompanied by daily prayer, he acquired increasing light.

" At that period he began to read the works of Augustine, where, particularly in his commentary on the Psalms and his book concerning the Spirit and the Letter, he found many decisive passages which confirmed his idea of faith and afforded him much consolation. Nor did he altogether relinquish the Sententiarii. He was studious of Occam, Gerson, and others, and some of their writings he could almost repeat by heart, but Augustine was his favourite author.

" Staupitz, who was anxious to promote theological studies in the recent academical establishment at Wittemberg, recommended Luther to a professorship in 1508, in the twenty-sixth year of his age. His genius was soon noticed in the daily exercises, especially by Martin Mellerstadius, who plainly predicted the mighty change he was likely hereafter to accomplish in the current doctrine of the schools.

" Here he expounded the logic and physics of Aristotle, but continued to pursue his theological studies. Some time afterwards he went to Rome to settle a dispute with the monks, and upon his return the degree of Doctor of Divinity was conferred upon him at the expence of the Elector Frederic, who had heard him preach and admired the force of his genius, his nervous language, and the excellent matter of his discourses.

" Afterwards he expounded the Psalms and the epistle to the Romans, and in such a luminous manner, that truth seemed to arise with new splendour after a long and cloudy night. He pointed out the distinction between the law and the gospel, he refuted the Pharisaical error at that time inculcated both in the schools and the pulpit, that men may merit the remission of sin by their own works and become righteous before God. Thus he directed the minds of men to Jesus Christ, and like John the Baptist, pointed to the Lamb of God who taketh away the sins of the world.

" This revival of important truth procured

him a very extensive authority, especially as his
conduct corresponded with his instructions, and
these proceeded not merely from the lip, but
from the heart. This purity of life produced a
great effect upon the minds of his hearers, and
the old proverb was verified σχεδον, ὡϱ ειπεῖν, κυϱιω
τα την εχει πιϛιν τὸ ἠϑος. ' Piety makes the speech
persuasive.' Wherefore many worthy men influenced by the excellence of his doctrine and
the sanctity of his character, were afterwards induced to comply with some of the changes which
he introduced in certain established ceremonies.

   " Not that Luther at that time meditated an
innovation upon the customary observances, or
broached any alarming opinions, but he was
illustrating more and more the doctrines so essential to all, of repentance, the remission of sins,
faith, and salvation by the cross of Christ.
Every pious mind was charmed with these lovely
truths, and the learned were pleased to see Christ,
the prophets and apostles, brought as it were, out
of darkness, mourning and imprisonment, the
differences between the law and the gospel, and
between philosophy and evangelical doctrine
established, nothing of which was to be discerned
in Thomas Aquinas, Scotus, and other scholastics. Add to this, the study of the Greek and
Latin languages was promoted by the writings of
Erasmus, and many persons of cultivated minds
began to despise the barbarism of the schools.

Luther himself studied Greek and Hebrew, that he might enjoy access to the fountains of sacred wisdom.

" Such was the course which Luther was diligently pursuing at the moment when the impudent Dominican Tetzel published his prostitute indulgences in these parts ; who was so irritated by Tetzel's impious discourses, and so inflamed with the love of pure religion, that he issued those propositions concerning indulgences which are inserted in his works. These he posted up in Wittemberg on the day of the feast of All Saints, in the year 1517. Tetzel, hoping to ingratiate himself into the favour of the Roman pontiff, immediately convoked his monks to assist him in writing against Luther. But this did not satisfy him. He thundered against Luther as a heretic, and publicly committed his propositions to the flames, threatening a similar fate to their author. This conduct compelled Luther to discuss the subjects of difference at greater length, in support of the Truth.

" In this manner the great controversy commenced, when Luther did not in the least suspect or dream of the change about to be accomplished, nor indeed of even rooting out indulgences. It is therefore calumnious in those who say that he only made use of this affair as a plausible pretext to subvert the establishment, and to introduce himself and his friends into power. So far from this, the Elector Frederic in particular beheld these contentions with sorrow, and acted with extreme caution. Frederic was distinguished above all his contemporary princes as a lover of peace, neither stimulating nor even applauding Luther, and frequently expressing his apprehensions of future discords. But he was a wise man, by no means disposed to follow the advice of those who are for crushing every innovation in the bud, but rather regarding the admonitions of heaven, to listen to the gospel, and not resist the truth. He read the word of God for himself, and submitted to its authority. I know, too, that he often asked wise and good men to give their opinion; and particularly at Cologne, at the time of the coronation of Charles V., he affectionately urged Erasmus to speak freely on the subject of Luther and the existing controversies. To which Erasmus replied, ' Luther is right in his sentiments, but he wants more mildness.' Frederic took occasion afterwards to exhort him to moderate the asperity of his style.

" Luther promised Cardinal Cajetan to be silent, if silence were also imposed upon his adversaries; from which it is evident that he was at that time solicitous of peace, and not of contention : but he was provoked into disputation by illiterate writers, who obliged him to publish on the sacraments, on the distinction between divine and human laws, on vows, and other subjects. Eckius, for the purpose of rendering him hateful to the hierarchy, moved the question respecting the supremacy of the Roman see.

" Human policy detests changes and innovation ; and it must be confessed that, in the present unhappy state of mankind, there will always be a mixture of good and evil in the very best of causes : but in the church the command of God is paramount to all human authority. ' This,' says the eternal Father, ' is my beloved Son, HEAR YE HIM ;' and he denounces eternal vengeance against those who impiously endeavour to abolish any part of revealed truth. Luther, therefore, was engaged in a work both of piety and necessity, especially as a teacher in the church of God, when he opposed pernicious errors. If innovation be odious, if the prevalence of discord be unpleasant and we cannot witness it without grief, be it remembered, the blame attaches to the promulgators and abettors of error.

" I state this not merely for the sake of defending Luther and his adherents, but that pious people now, and in future ages, may perceive what is, and always will be, the ruling principle in the true church of God ; and how God, by the word of the gospel, selects his eternal church from the great and corrupt mass of sinners, amongst whom his word shines as a light in a dark place. Thus, in the time of the prevalence of Pharisaical impiety, Zacharias, Eliza-

beth, Mary, and many others, preserved the purity
of truth; and previous to that age there were many
who saw, with greater or less degrees of clear-
ness, the genuine gospel, and worshipped the
true God.   Such an one was that aged priest I
have mentioned who encouraged Luther amidst
his conscientious convictions and struggles, and
was in some respects his teacher in the faith.
Let us then join in the fervent supplication of
Isaiah for his hearers, ' Bind up the testimony,
seal the law among my disciples.' *(o)*   This
statement will tend to show that base superstitions cannot last for ever, and will explain the
causes of religious innovation.

    " No private ambition induced Luther to
undertake this cause at first; and though he was
naturally ardent and passionate, yet he was always
mindful of his peculiar department; and, discriminating wisely between the office of a magistrate
who wields the sword to govern the multitude,
and that of a Christian preacher who is to instruct
the church of God, he disclaimed the use of
arms or coercive measures.   Whenever Satan,
who perpetually aims to disgrace the cause and
subvert the church of God through the errors of
miserable men, excited several seditious characters to tumultuous irregularities, he condemned
them in the severest manner, and both adorned

(o) Isa. viii. 16.

by his example, and strengthened by his eloquence, the bonds of social order. But when I
reflect on this subject, and consider how many
great men in the church have committed sad
mistakes in this point, I do affirm that no human
care, but a divine principle alone, could have
sufficed to keep him so constantly within the
limits of duty.

" He constantly exhorted every one to ' render unto Cæsar the things which are Cæsar's,
and to God the things which are God's ;' that is,
to worship God in the exercise of genuine repentance, in an open avowal of the truth, in prayer
and in a conscientious discharge of duty ; and
in the fear of God to regard all the civil regulations of the community. Such was Luther.
He gave to God the things which are God's, he
taught the truth, and prayed aright, and possessed
all those virtues which are well-pleasing to God ;
and, as a citizen, he shunned every thing seditious. Virtues greater than these cannot, I think,
be desired in the present life.

" But though we extol the excellencies of the
man, and the use he made of the gifts of heaven,
yet we ought to feel peculiar gratitude to God,
who, by his means, restored the true light of
the gospel, which we should preserve and dif-
fuse.... It is this doctrine of which the Son of
God says, ' If any man love me he will keep my
words, and my Father will love him, and we

will come unto him and make our abode with him.'"

The celebrated disputation at Leipsic claims some notice, both on account of its early occurrence in this great polemical campaign, and of Melancthon's concern with it. It lasted from the twenty-seventh of June to the fifteenth of July. Carolostadius, or Carlostadt, archdeacon of the church of All Saints at Wittemberg, and a zealous reformer, and Eckius of Ingoldstadt, the papal advocate, after some preliminary pamphleteering, agreed upon settling the controversy, after the fashion of the age, by a public debate. George, Duke of Saxony, uncle of the Elector, offered the city of Leipsic for the purpose, expecting, no less than Eckius himself, a triumphant issue to the Catholic cause. Thither the combatants repaired on the twenty-seventh of June, Luther and Melancthon accompanying their friend. The assembly was splendid. The Duke of Saxony, the Members of his Council, the Magistrates of Leipsic, the Doctors and Bachelors of the University, with a number of persons of quality, were present; and scribes were appointed to take notes of the debate. It is a curious circumstance that John Agricola, of Eisleben, who was employed on the Lutheran side, was afterwards an opponent of the Reformation, and John Poliander, who was amanuensis to Eckius, attached himself to Luther at the close of the disputation, and afterwards became a preacher of the gospel in Prussia.*(p)*

The first six days' discussion between Eckius and Carlostadt, on the subject of free-will, was conducted with considerable skill by both parties ; but if it were detailed would appear pre-eminently uninteresting. It is sufficient to state that the principal question was, " Whether the human will had any operation in the performance of good works, or whether it was merely passive to the power of divine grace?" Eckius maintained that the will co-operated with the grace of God, and Carlostadt asserted its total inefficacy to perform any meritorious act. Melancthon, who was a hearer, says, it first gave him a practical demonstration of what the ancients understood by *sophistry*. Eckius undoubtedly acquired the greatest share of popularity, from the superior ease and fluency he discovered to his antagonist. Luther soon afterwards obtained the Duke's permission to take the place of Carlostadt in the debate, at the particular request of Eckius who was impatient to encounter the leading Reformer. Each was in truth equally ardent, conscious that a mighty cause was at stake, which demanded the whole force of their respective energies of mind. On the one side was Eckius, impelled by no small degree of con-

(p) SECKEND. Hist. Luth. Lib, I. p. 92.

I

fidence in himself from previous conflicts,
especially the recent one with Carlostadt, supported by the plaudits of the Catholic party,
which was the prevalent one in point of numbers and splendour, and having acquired a
very high degree of popularity; *(q)*—on the
other, Luther, persecuted and defamed, conscious
that if he betrayed the least feebleness in argument, or the smallest degree of forgetfulness or
hesitation, it would be taken advantage of by
his wily adversaries, and thus prove detrimental to
the important cause he advocated ; and that even
though he should be completely triumphant in
argument, it would rather tend to irritate than
convince or silence his opponents.   Never was a
more important crisis—never a greater cause—
never more determined, more equalized, or more
impetuous antagonists :

> . . . . . . As when two black clouds,
> With heav'n's artillery fraught, come rattling on
> Over the Caspian, then stand front to front,
> Hovering a space, till winds the signal blow
> To join their dark encounter in mid air—
> So FROWN'D THE MIGHTY COMBATANTS—*(r)*

Eckius selected thirteen propositions from
the works of Luther as the subjects of " long

(q) Eckius had already engaged in public disputations
in eight different Universities.
(r) MILTON's Parad. Lost, B. II.

debate ;" but the principal one that engaged their
attention was the foundation of the supremacy
claimed by the Roman Pontiffs. After ten days
of violent and incessant discussion, in which
Eckius was obliged to admit the eminent " attainments of his reverend opponent," and even
to apologize for himself, the victory was claimed
by both parties. Luther says he must acknowledge that he and his friends were overcome—
" *clamore et gestu*," by noise and gesture.*(s)*
Hoffman, the rector of the university of Leipsic,
refused to give a decision in favour of either ;
in consequence of which it was referred to the
universities of Paris and Erfurt, who neglected,
though they did not refuse to do it. The immediate effect of this dispute upon Eckius, was that
of increasing his animosity against the Reformer,
on whom he determined to revenge himself in
every possible way. Luther considers it as
some good evidence that the duke felt the force
of his arguments, because on one of these controversial days when they were dining together,
he laid his hands on the shoulders of the two
combatants and exclaimed, " Whether the Pope
exists by divine or by human right, he is, however, the Pope !"*(t)*

If we may judge by the letter of Eckius
himself to his friend Hoogstraat, it will not be

(s) SECK. Hist. Luth. Lib. I. p. 73.
(t) LUTH. Op. Tom. I. SECKEND. Hist. Luth. p. 74.

difficult to ascertain the victorious party.   He
complains that the Lutherans had great advantages over him, because they brought several
books to which they had recourse, they had their
disputation in writing and conferred together
about an answer, and they were many against
one single man. *(u)*   It is no inconsiderable circumstance also, that a large number of the young
students immediately quitted Leipsic and repaired to the University of Wittemberg. *(v)*

Though Melancthon had undoubtedly favoured the designs, and aided the efforts of Luther
previously to this conference, he was roused
by the present occasion to a more particular study
of the points of difference, and a more vigorous
co-operation with the great champion of religious
liberty.   He had an opportunity of hearing
whatever one of the most zealous, eloquent, and
able advocates of Popery could say in defence of
his system, of perceiving the influence of that
system upon the minds of men in general, and
of estimating more correctly perhaps than under
any other circumstances he could have done the
great importance of the controversy itself. " From
the period of this famous public disputation, he
applied himself more intensely to the interpretation of the Scriptures and the defence of pure

(u) LUTH. Op. Tom. I. p. 303.
(v) SECKEND. Hist. Luth. Lib. I. p. 92.

Christian doctrine, and he is justly esteemed by Protestants to have been under divine Providence, the most powerful coadjutor of the Saxon Reformer. His mild and peaceable temper, his aversion to schismatic contention, his reputation for piety and for knowledge, and above all, his happy art of exposing error and maintaining truth in the most perspicuous language, all these endowments concurred to render him eminently serviceable to the revival of the religion of Christ. Little did Eckius imagine that the public disputation in which he had foreseen nothing but victory and exultation, and the downfall of Lutheranism would give rise to another theological champion, who should contend for Christian truth and Christian liberty, with the primitive spirit of an apostle. At Wittemberg, Melancthon had probably been well acquainted with Luther's lectures on divinity; but it was in the citadel of Leipsic, that he heard the Romish tenets defended by all the arguments that ingenuity could devise; there his suspicions were strengthened respecting the evils of the existing hierarchy; and there his righteous spirit was roused to imitate, in the grand object of his future inquiries and exertions, the indefatigable endeavours of his zealous and adventurous friend." (w)

(w) MILNER's History of the Church of Christ, Vol. IV. p. 428.

Melancthon represents himself as only a spectator and hearer of this celebrated dispute, *(x)* but he took the most lively interest in every part of the proceedings, and several writers *(y)* have stated that he often went up to Carlostadt and whispered so many useful suggestions, that Eckius was provoked to exclaim : ' *Tace tu Philippe, ac tua studia cura, nec me perturba,*' i. e. ' Hold your tongue Philip, mind your own business, and do not interfere with me.' His opinion of the different disputants is given in a letter to a friend, and may be relied on for candour and accuracy. *(z)* " Eckius was much admired for his various and striking ingenuities. You know Carlostadt, he is certainly a man of worth and of extraordinary erudition. As to Luther, whom I have known most intimately, his lively genius, his learning and eloquence I admire, and it is impossible not to be in love with his truly sincere and pure Christian spirit." It is difficult to ascertain how Eckius procured a copy of this letter, which also contained a general account of the transactions at Leipsic, but he instantly

(x) " Neque enim quidquam mihi cùm Eccio rerum unquam fuit, et *Lipsicæ* pugnæ ociosus spectator in reliquo vulgo sedi." *Defensio P. Mel. contra Eccium.*

(y) SECKEND. Hist. Luth. Lib. I. ADAM. Vit. Philosophorum, p. 189. WINSHEM. Oratio in Funere Melancthonis.

(z) LUTH. Op. Tom. I. p. 304.

published a most acrimonious reply, calling
Melancthon a mere grammarian, *(a)* and with
preposterous self-sufficiency affirming, that " although he might have some knowledge of Greek
and Latin," yet " he was not a person with whom
a divine could with propriety condescend to
enter the lists." Nothing can be inferred from
this contemptuous language, excepting the violent malignity of his temper, and the secret consciousness he felt of the talents of his opponent.

Melancthon replied, in a tract consisting
of only five folio pages, but written with so much
mildness, elegance, and acuteness, that it proved
extremely serviceable to the Lutheran cause.
To railing he opposes argument, to arrogance
modesty, to dogmatism, sound sense and genuine
piety. He contends without virulence and triumphs without parade. Some of the sentiments
are so excellent, and the manner in which they
are expressed so truly characteristic, that they
ought not to be suppressed.

After remarking that " in the epistle which
had excited so much indignation, he had merely
intended a slight sketch rather than a full description of the Leipsic disputations ; for to have
done otherwise would have required more time
than his numerous occupations admitted, he

(a) In his rage he even coins an epithet of contempt.
" Hic inquam, *Grammatellus.*"

solemnly disavows ever having intentionally
given offence to any one, deeming it both un-
christian and inhuman to injure or detract from
another's merit. If he had done wrong, he wished
it to be imputed either to incaution or accident,
and begged to be forgiven, conscious as he was
of being totally devoid of any malignity, and
forced as he felt himself into this unwelcome
arena of contention. He was resolved to be
deaf to the calumnies of Eckius, appealing to
what he had himself written for his best justification, and he would now conduct his argument
without uttering any petulant or unjustifiable
reproach against his antagonist, because he was
more solicitous for the glory of Christ than respecting the effect which any frivolous calumnies might
produce.

" Eckius," says he, " is confident of being
victorious, by appealing to the authority of the
holy fathers of the church. But how does this
avail him ? I am, indeed, by no means disposed
to depreciate, on the contrary, I highly reverence
those illustrious luminaries of the church and de-
fenders of Christian doctrine. But I cannot deem
it rash, as the fathers differ in their sentiments
to receive the SCRIPTURE, and not the vary-
ing opinions of men as the ultimate appeal. As
there is always some one simple meaning to the language of scripture, (for divine truth is most intel-
ligibly simple), this sense is to be sought by a

comparison of passages, and by the general strain of the particular discourse. In this manner we are enjoined to investigate the sacred writings, as we examine the sentiments and decrees of men, by bringing them to the touchstone and trying their consistency. Then it is more satisfactory to consult their judgment on the meaning of scripture, from those places where they professedly explained it, rather than where they are only indulging their own feelings in rhetorical descriptions. We all experience this fact, that scripture is variously interpreted according to our various dispositions of mind and cast of opinion. This or that interpretation pleases, because it seizes our feelings and captivates our passions, and as the polypus imitates the colour of the rock to which it fixes, so we are prone to use our utmost endeavours to conform our sentiments to the prejudices of our own minds. It frequently happens that the mind may admit, and for a time be wonderfully charmed with the genuine force and propriety of a sentiment, but afterwards be incapable of reviving such an impression; and thus the fathers of the church, wrought up to a pitch of feeling, make use of scripture in a sense not in itself bad, but sometimes inapplicable and foreign to the purpose. And though I do not totally condemn this, yet I think it cannot be of much avail in controversy, for according to the Greek adage, καλῶς τρέχϟσιν, ἀλλα ἐκτὸς ἰδϟ ' They run well, but then they do not keep in the course.' I dare affirm, that sometimes the fathers have given interpretations of scripture, suggested perhaps to the mind in a state of high religious feeling, and which might not be erroneous, but which to us inferior men and in a less glowing state of mind, have not seemed to accord with the literal sense. There is a secret manna and food of the soul, to which Paul alludes, when he speaks of *spiritually discerning* it, which is more easily felt than described.

But who does not perceive how often the scriptures have been misapplied in the different controversies that have been agitated at various periods, of which innumerable examples might be adduced, so that it has frequently happened, especially of late, that their exposition has been at complete variance with the original text. As to the scholastic method of interpretation it is any thing but simple, a very Proteus, transforming the sense of scripture into allegories, tropes, figures, and diverting the truth from its literal, grammatical, or historical meaning, into I know not what wretched and polluted channels.

After touching upon the various points of difference, he concludes by saying, " Eckius himself shall be witness if I have not avoided

those invidious reflections, which had I been so
inclined, might have been indulged." In writing
to his friends, he uniformly breathes the same
admirable spirit. " If," says he, " you perceive
any thing of an antichristian nature in what I
send, let me beg you to perform the duty of a
genuine friend, admonish me instantly, reprove,
yea, lash me as you please. He is, believe me,
the dearest of all my friends, who is most honest
and downright in his remarks, for you know, as
it is not my disposition to dissemble, so I always
look upon *flattering friends* as they deserve. But
as genuine Christian affection neither flatters nor
admits of flattery, so you will acquire the character of a friend with me, by being a faithful
adviser. Eckius rages against us in the most
coarse and violent manner, either from a natural
impetuosity of disposition or because he considers
himself aggrieved, and my purpose is not to inflict, but to compensate for any supposed injury.
He is undoubtedly very severe; but I have replied only in a small publication, and with as
much moderation as possible, for God is my
witness, that I do not cherish the slightest animosity. I might have said more, perhaps, without transgressing the bounds of propriety, but I
chose to refrain in order to write not what my
adversary deserved, but what was worthy of our
own character and cause. After our departure

from Leipsic, Eckius certainly reviled Luther in the most outrageous manner." *(b)*

Such was the temper of this amiable controversialist, who so well understood the wide difference between opprobrious epithets and solid arguments, and who it is obvious on every occasion sought *truth* rather than *victory*. He abhorred the field of strife, and hated Discord as an unnatural and ferocious demon. He valued peace as it ought to be valued, above gold and silver—above honours and empires. He was more anxious to do good than to shine, to carry the olive branch than to wield the sword, to be regarded or—for such was the temper of the times—to be *despised* as an humble peace maker, than to be blazoned forth as a polemical hero !

Still let it be recollected, and in this sentiment Melancthon would have concurred, that we ought not so much to lament that controversies have arisen, as that they have been conducted in an anti-christian spirit. Nothing, it is readily admitted, can be more detrimental to the interests of genuine religion than intemperate and ill-humoured debatings, but on the other hand—open, fair, and candid discussion is calculated to promote good will, to pacify resentments, to smooth the wrinkled brow of bigotry, to dissipate doubts, to clear up

(b) MELANCTH. Ep. II. *ad Joan. Langium.*

difficulties, and to elucidate truth. Melancthon may be exhibited as a bright example to all controversial writers of the spirit in which their arguments should be conducted—or rather, let them be induced to imitate a greater than he, who, " WHEN HE WAS REVILED, REVILED NOT AGAIN !"

CHAP. IV.

Melancthon's marriage—His domestic character—His exemplary virtues—His boundless liberality—Account of his favourite servant John—Epitaph on his tomb-stone—Candour of Melancthon—His Meekness—Sym-pathy—Interesting Letter written to a Friend, who had sustained a painful family bereavement—His Piety — Sincerity—Wit — Memory —Temperance — Modesty—Humility—Parental conduct—His value for Time — Marriage and Settlement of his two Daughters—Character of his Sons-in-Law, George Sabinus and Caspar Peucer — Notice of Thurzo, Bishop of Breslaw.

As the traveller at " the sweet approach of ev'n," hastens from incessant toils and conflict-ing elements, to the shelter of some hospitable roof, where, amidst the cheerfulness and comfort of the social circle, he forgets past difficulties and is strengthened for future exertion: so we may now be permitted to retire for a season, from the thorny paths and stormy atmosphere of polemical discussion, to the bowers of domestic peace. .

Although from the peculiarity of circumstances which surrounded Melancthon, and the
important period in which he lived, we are naturally anxious to trace his public career, and
follow him through the principal scenes of an active life, yet in order to accomplish the legitimate
purposes of biography, it will be proper to turn
aside for a moment to visit him in the recesses of
privacy, by this means aiming to impart various
instruction, as well as to prepare amusement.

Few persons can claim to rank amongst distinguished scholars or professors, and fewer still
are destined by Providence to undergo the struggles, to encounter the resistance, and to pursue
the high and holy course of Reformers ; but every
one occupies a place and possesses an influence
in the FAMILY.   One or other of the endearing
names of father, husband, parent, child, brother,
sister, friend, belongs to every human being ; to
these different relations, peculiar and appropriate
duties are attached, and from the manner in which
they are discharged or neglected, we have an opportunity both of noticing the developement of
individual character, and of ascertaining the principle upon which the felicity or infelicity of life
in a very considerable degree depends.   Here we
have all the advantage of *example*, arising from
the interesting consideration that another is acting
in our own circumstances, and moving in a
similar sphere ; and if our personal improvement

be not promoted, whether the example be good or bad, we must be strangely deficient in moral taste and right feeling.

The chief actors in seasons of great political change or great moral revolution, are unfavourably situated for the cultivation of the milder graces; by the collision of opposing parties and contradictory opinions, the sparks of intemperate anger are too apt to be struck out, and dispositions even naturally mild, have sometimes been inflamed. But in cases where it has been deemed necessary or prudent for the sake of the cause, to suppress the rising emotions of resentment, and to check improper violence of language in public, the rage of the heart has burst forth in the circle of unrestrained friendship, and disturbed the hour of private intercourse. Here, however, the character of Melancthon is particularly worthy of admiration. A meek and quiet spirit never forsook him.—He always engaged reluctantly in disputation, and was never or seldom irritated by it, even in the smallest degree. He harboured no resentments. When he retired from the field of strife, he laid aside his weapons and most willingly renounced the glory of the controversialist, for the peace and comfort of the domestic man. He did not bring malevolent feelings or angry passions into his family, for in truth he had none to bring. But it would be doing him great injustice to represent

him as a tame or effeminate character.   Passions
he had, but they were unde the due regulation
of reason and piety.   Religion had completed
the work of nature ; he was kind and gentle
upon principle, as well as by constitution.   If
the emotions of anger at any time arose in his
mind, they were instantly suppressed as a weakness unworthy of a man, as a sin unbecoming a
Christian.

In the year 1520, he married a very respectable young lady belonging to one of the principal
families in Wittemberg.   Her name was Catharine Crappin, and her father was a burgomaster
of the town.   She is described by Camerarius,
whose intercourse with the family was such as to
afford him every means of correct information,
as a truly religious person, most assiduously attentive to her domestic concerns, extremely
liberal to all, and not only benevolent to the
poor, and even lavish of her own means of supplying them, but urgent with others whom she
could at any time influence to minister to their
necessities.   With eminent piety of spirit she
united great purity of manners, and avoided all
extravagance in dress and all luxury in food.
Nothing could be more congenial to the taste of
Melancthon, who was never captivated by the
blandishments of pleasure, nor seduced by the
charms of sensuality.   In a letter to Langius,
dated in November, he speaks of her in terms of

high regard, as possessed of a disposition and manners which entirely corresponded with his wishes: and he represents his marriage as the result of serious deliberation, and conformable to the advice of his friends. *(c)* Seldom have two individuals become more completely one in spirit and character, and seldom has the marriage contract been more firmly sealed by mutual attachment. Reason, religion, and love, presided over their happy union, and confirmed their solemn vows.

During this year he commenced a course of lectures on the epistle of Paul to the Romans, and so indefatigable was he in the regular discharge of this and all his academical duties, that the suspension of the usual course even for the single day of his marriage was so remarkable, as to be publicly intimated in the following curious notice :

> A studiis hodiè facit ocia grata Philippus
> Nec vobis Pauli dogmata sacra leget.

> Rest from your studies, Philip says you may,
> He'll read no lectures on St. Paul to day.

Liberality was a distinguishing feature in the mind of Melancthon and his excellent wife ;

(c) " Uxor enim datur mihi Catarina Crapti, non dico, quam non sperata aut quam frigenti, sed iis puella moribus, ea animi indole qualem à diis immortalibus optare debueram : δέξια ὁ Θεος τεκμαίροιτο dextra Deus significet, i. Deus omina fausta firmet. Equidem expendi argumenta, quæ in hanc rem

and this was apparent both in the common
acts of charity and in the more diffusive spirit of universal benevolence. Neither of them
were disposed by oppressive exactions or parsimonious care to enrich themselves. They deeply
sympathized with the feelings of the needy and
the wretched; never being deaf to their impor-
tunities, but readily and most liberally supplying
them with money and sustenance. The necessitous might have applied to them the language
of St. Paul to the Corinthian church, with the
utmost propriety. "To their power, yea, beyond
their power, I bear record, they were willing
of themselves, praying us with much intreaty,
that we would receive the gift." (d) The house
was crowded with a constant succession of
comers and goers of every age, sex and condition,
some pressing in to receive, and others departing
well stored from this ample repository of kindness and bounty. It formed a part of their

incidere possunt, nisi fallor, omnia, ut satis sciam quid pro-
bandum fuerit. Verum secutus sum amicorum consilium, qui
me ad rem uxoriam hortati sunt *propter periculum ex infirmitate
carnis et carnalis libertatis improbitatem.* Neque enim verè
Christiana libertas fuit, qua literas deamavimus plus æquo. Et
cavendum nobis fuit quod monet Paulus *ne libertatem occa-
sionem faciamus carni.* Ne tu improbes cœptum opto. Majus
voto fuerit, si probaveris. Cordum nostrum admone promissi
ἐπιβαλαμις." Ep. 5. *ad Langium.*

(d) 2 Cor. viii. 3, 4.

domestic regulations, never to refuse an appli-
cant! *(e)*

In addition to those who frequented the
house to beg, the celebrity of Melancthon proved
a severe tax upon his time, for multitudes resorted
to him to seek his advice, to obtain recommendatory letters, to request the correction of their
compositions, to lay before him various complaints, to solicit his aid in literary pursuits, or
perhaps merely for the purpose of seeing so distinguished a person ; all of whom enjoyed free
access. Sometimes persons whom he could not
altogether approve would solicit his valuable re-
commendations; these he has been known to dismiss with pecuniary presents, as the best method
which his benevolent spirit could devize, of being released from their unwelcome importunity.

It seems scarcely possible to conceive how
amidst such a profusion of benevolence Melancthon could support his own family, especially
when it is recollected, that while none were sent
empty away, he not only did not aim to grow
richer, but frequently refused those emoluments
which others usually grasp after with the utmost
eagerness. Instead of availing himself of the
influence of the great with whom he was connected to advance him to dignity and opulence,
he was known to refuse even the presents of
princes. With an admirable disinterestedness,

(e) " Nam ea domus disciplina erat, ut nihil cuiquam
negaretur." CAM. Vit. Mel.

he lectured on divinity and the Holy Scriptures, two whole years without any salary; and when a pension of two hundred florins was assigned him by the Elector of Saxony, he excused himself, by saying, " I am unable to devote myself to the duty with sufficient attention and assiduity to warrant an acceptance of it." The Elector, however, by Luther's advice, intimated that it would suffice to give one or two lectures in a week, as his health might permit. *(f)*

At the time which will be hereafter more particularly noticed, when the Elector Maurice was desirous of attaching Melancthon to his interests, he made inquiry into his circumstances, and whether he was not in need of some pecuniary aid. Upon his dissembling this, the prince told him, he wished he would at least ask some favour, assuring him that whatever it might be, it should readily be granted. He replied, that " he felt perfectly satisfied with his salary, and was not anxious for any augmentation of it, or indeed for any thing else." Maurice still continued to urge him, and at length he said, " Well, as your highness requires me to ask some favour, I ask *my dismission.*"—The prince found it necessary, however, to solicit his continuance in his professorship, adding to the gentlemen of his court, " That he had never seen or experienced any thing like Melancthon's conduct, who was not only too disinterested to ask

(f) SECKEND. Hist. Luth. Lib. II. p. 164.

for any thing, but would not even accept it when proffered."(g)

It is proper to mention, with marked respect, an invaluable servant, of the name of John, who lived with him many years. John was a man of tried honesty and fidelity, adorning the humble sphere in which he moved, and very much beloved by his master. To his management we must in part look for an explanation of the mystery to which we have alluded, namely, the possibility of being so lavishly benevolent with such restricted and apparently inadequate means. The whole duty of provisioning the family was entrusted to this domestic, whose care, assiduity and prudence, amply justified the unbounded confidence reposed in him. He made the concerns of the family his own, avoiding all useless expenditure and watching with a jealous eye over his master's property. He was also the first instructor of the children in the family during their infancy. This merits to be distinctly recorded, not only because such a servant is a kind of *rara avis in terris*, but because, as in the present instance, he may contribute essentially to the general good, by preventing the waste of those means which a benevolent spirit will ever feel anxious to consecrate to purposes of public utility. John grew old in his master's service, and in the year 1553, expired in his house, after

(g) VAN DE CORPUT. Leven ende Dood van Phil. Mel. p. 667.

the long residence of almost thirty-four years,
amidst the affectionate regrets of the whole
family. He invited the academicians to his funeral, delivered an oration over his grave, and composed the following epitaph for his tombstone :

Joannes patrii Nicri discessit ab undis
   Huc accersitus voce, Philippe, tua
Quem comes exilii juvit precibusque fideque
   Nam verè gnato credidit ille DEI.
Ipsius hic dominus sepelivit corpus inane
   Vivit, conspectu mens fruiturque DEI.

Imitated.

Here at a distance from his native land,
Came faithful John, at Philip's first command ;
Companion of his exile, doubly dear,
Who in a servant found a friend sincere—
And more than friend, a man of faith and prayer,
Assiduous soother of his master's care ;—
Here to the worms his lifeless body's given,
But his immortal soul sees God in heaven.

Perhaps no one ever attended more scrupulously than Melancthon to the injunction of
Jesus Christ, " When thou doest alms, let not
thy left hand know what thy right hand doeth ;
that thy alms may be in secret." *(h)* He was
unostentatious in every thing, but especially in
works of charity. Satisfied with the approbation
of conscience and of God, he manifested no
solicitude for the applauses of men, and was content to do good without being praised for it. It
will be easy to believe, that he abounded in acts

(h) MATT. viii. 3.

of kindness, which being known only to himself,
no book records excepting the registers of heaven ;
especially when it is stated from unquestionable
authority, that on several occasions when his
pecuniary resources have been completely exhausted, he would contrive to supply the necessitous by privately taking cups and other vessels
appropriated to domestic use, to a trader to sell,
even at a very low and disadvantageous rate. *(i)*

Melancthon received many presents of gold
and silver coin. These he would often give to
the very first person, who from avarice or curiosity might be induced to ask for them; not from
any undervaluation of these ancient specimens,
but simply from a disposition to oblige. Mere
self-gratification appears seldom to have entered
into his views, much less did such a feeling
acquire any degree of ascendancy over him. His
prevailing desire was to communicate pleasure
to others and he was satisfied with the feast, the
intellectual and moral feast which a refined benevolence can alone provide; in which respect,
it must be acknowledged, that in a very important sense " he fared sumptuously every day."*(k)*
On one remarkable occasion when he had accu-
mulated a large collection of coins and curiosi-
ties, he offered a certain stranger who seemed
peculiarly gratified with the sight, to take any
one which he might happen to feel a wish to
possess ; upon which, the stranger said, with

(i) CAM. Vit. Mel.　　　　*(k)* LUKE xvi. 19.

consummate effrontery, " I have a particular wish for them all." Melancthon, though he did not dissemble his displeasure, nevertheless granted his unwarrantable request. *(l)*

If the parsimonious or the prudent should be disposed to censure this excessive and prodigal benevolence, alledging that if it be culpable to " withhold more than is meet," *(m)* it is at least not very laudable to squander the gifts of Providence indiscriminately upon every class of importunate beggars; be it remembered, that there is an essential difference between an obvious crime and an apparent excess of virtue—between the conduct of the spendthrift and that of the person who is lavishly bountiful. In the one you perceive the very essence of selfishness, in the other the exuberance of kindness. The one lives only to seek his own gratification; *self* is the end he pursues, and the contemptible idol he worships; no sacrifices are considered too costly to be offered to this paltry god, and every thing is rendered subservient to this infamous idolatry; the other, considering himself in some degree the depository and trustee of the divine beneficence, and valuing the possessions of life only so far as they provide for his own immediate necessities, and may be made to contribute to the comfort of others, becomes at least serviceable to a number of his fellow creatures. He feels the claims of humanity, and fulfils the high

(l) CAM. Vit. Mel. (m) PROV. xi. 24.

duties of a neighbour. If such a person be a little more liberal in distributing than the narrow calculations of human policy or prudence seem to admit, he acts in conformity with the dictates of a pure and disinterested benevolence, reaps a rich harvest of satisfactions, and manifests the spirit while he fulfils the precepts of the Saviour of the world.

If it be alledged that it is no one's duty to impoverish himself or to injure his family, even though it be the result not of a selfish but of a benevolent expenditure, this is conceded—yet in the present case, the question does not respect the waste of property *already possessed*, but the neglect to *accumulate*. If an individual be satisfied for himself with that station of life which Providence has assigned him, and with those pecuniary resources, small or great, which he already possesses, and if he prefer using that supply which industry, manual, or mental, procures for him, in doing good to others, instead of aspiring after the greater honours or emoluments within his power—if he chose even to *refuse them when offered*, either from an apprehension of moral danger or from mere indifference, will any one represent this as culpable? Surely we ought rather to admire than to censure such conduct; it evinces a noble spirit of disinterestedness, and a glorious superiority mind to the attractions of earthly splendour, which is worthy of imitation.

In this statement of some of the excellent qualities of Melancthon, his extreme *Candour* and *Kindness* must not be overlooked. He was never known to asperse any one, either openly or by insinuation. Nothing was further from his intentions than to injure another's character or reputation, and if his were attacked, no one could manifest a more exemplary patience. He not only could not be moved to resentment by the misconduct of offenders, but did not relax in his benevolence or familiarity with them. No dark suspicions pervaded his mind, no malevolence or envy disturbed his placid spirit. The calm summer of his soul was never beclouded or distracted with tempestuous passions.

Sympathy with the sufferings of others was not among the least of his eminent qualities, of which, perhaps, it will be the best possible illustration to insert a translation of one of his letters to an afflicted friend, whose sorrow for the loss of a beloved child he hastened, the moment he heard it, to alleviate. His sentiments are to be regarded as those of the heart, and not as the mere effusions of a formal or complimentary friendship. An affectionate disposition may, and indeed will, by a generous participation, share another's woes, even though it has not yet tasted the bitterness of bereavement or personal affliction of any kind; but in order to afford effectual consolation to the mourner, it seems requisite that the person whose friendly spirit hastens to his relief, should have been himself a sufferer, that he may be duly qualified to select appropriate language, and that the distressed individual himself may be impressed with a consciousness that his words are not words of course. Experience is the best of all instructors, and affliction superinduces a sensibility, and teaches a language which cannot possibly be attained in any degree of perfection by any other process. And, " As in water face answereth to face, so the heart of man to man."(n) In this view Melancthon was likely to prove a judicious as well as a sympathizing friend, for during the whole of his life he drank deep and drank often, of the bitter cup. The following letter besides claims insertion for its excellence, and as it is without date may be introduced here with propriety.

" *To John Pfeffinger, with affectionate salutations.*

" God has implanted the principle of natural affection in mankind, for the double purpose of strengthening the bonds of human society, and teaching us to realize the ardour of his love to his own Son and to us. He therefore approves the affection we cherish for our offspring, and the piety of our grief for their loss. Natural affection is peculiarly forcible in minds of a superior order ; on which account, I doubt not, that the loss of your son—a son too not only possessed

(n) PROV. xxvii. 19.

of the most amiable dispositions, but of a mind
well stored with literature, not only inclined by
his very constitution to moral habits, but under
the constant influence of true religion, and
already engaged in a course of study in which
his capacity promised so much—the loss of such
a son, I say, must affect you with the deepest
grief. And be assured, I am not disposed to
accuse you of weakness, on the contrary, I acknowledge—I commend your piety—I truly
lament your personal bereavement and the public
loss ; for I am apprehensive that in these times
the churches will feel the want of teachers properly instructed. But you are well aware that
we are permitted to mourn, though not immo-
derately. It is certain that these events are under
divine superintendance ; it becomes us, therefore, to manifest a due submission of mind to
God, and quietly to resign ourselves to his disposal in every season of adversity.

"I will not now advert to the physical
causes of death, for though naturally exposed
to various diseases, let us rather regard the will
of God in this dispensation, and not so much
our own loss ; and let us realize the blessings
which in being removed from this afflictive life
and these calamitous times he is called to share.
If we truly loved him, we shall rejoice in his
happiness ; and if we rightly understand Christian truth, we shall be disposed to congratulate

him upon the society of the heavenly assembly, where he no longer drinks the streams of knowledge mingled and polluted as they are in the present world, but enjoys free access to the pure and infinite fountain of wisdom, holds intercourse with the Son of God himself, the prophets and apostles, and with inexpressible delight joins in praising God for so early an admission to that illustrious assembly; the thought of which may well enkindle within us a desire to escape from our earthly imprisonment.

" Perhaps it increases your sorrow to recollect his capacity, his erudition, his virtue; and you fondly wish for the charming company of such a son. But these very excellences themselves ought to diminish your regrets, because you know how they contributed to the good of many during the short period of his mortal life, so that he was not a useless incumbrance upon society. You witnessed the evidences of his thriving piety in this world of trial, which were but the beginnings of celestial life, and proved that his departure hence was only a removal to the happy intercourse of heaven. In fact, as often as you reflect upon these qualities of your dear son, you have reason to be thankful to God, who has shewn such kindness both to you and to him, as to confer upon him the greatest of all favours: for a grateful mind will record mercies as well as crosses.

" It is becoming, therefore, as you know, to be resigned to the will of God who requires us to moderate our griefs, and to believe that no real evil has befallen your son. Let these considerations afford you comfort and repress undue anxiety. The minds of men are naturally influenced by examples, for it seems proper that we should not refuse to endure the afflictions incident to others, and which must be sustained as the common law of our nature. How calamitous must the death of Abel have appeared to our first parents, by the murder of whom their future hopes in reference to the church seemed to be cut off in regard to their own family, and how much greater cause for sorrow attached to them, when the human race consisted of so small a number, than can belong to you, who possess a surviving family, in which distinct evidences of piety may be traced? They were doubly wounded by the death of one son, and still more by the wickedness of his impious brother.

" Innumerable instances might be adduced from the history of all ages. Recollect the old Bishop of Antioch, whose three sons were slain by the tyrant Decius, in the very presence of their parents, who not only witnessed his cruel conduct, but exhorted and encouraged their children to suffer: after which, their mother beheld the murder of her husband, and having embraced the cold remains of her children and her husband, solemnly committed them to the grave.

"You remember also, the history of the Emperor Mauritius, who stood a silent spectator while his son and daughter were slain, but when the murderer approached his wife, he exclaimed, amidst a flood of tears, "Righteous art thou O Lord, and upright are thy judgments."(o)

"Wise men have often inquired with astonishment, for what reason the feeble nature of man is oppressed with such a weight of afflictions; but we who can trace the causes to a divine origin, ought to be resigned to the appointments of God, and avail ourselves of those remedies for grief which divine goodness has revealed : and while these are your solace, reflect upon this bright example of domestic piety.

"If when you are absent for a season from your family, and placed at a distance amongst persons uncongenial to your taste, the hope of returning home alleviates your vexations; so now you may be stimulated to patience by the consideration that in a little time you will again embrace your son in the delightful assembly of the skies, adorned with a more splendid distinction than any station on earth can command, I mean, with THE GLORY OF GOD, and placed among prophets, apostles, and the shining hosts of heaven, there to live for ever, enjoying the vision of God, and the enrapturing intercourse of Christ

(o) Ps. cxix. 137.

himself, the holy apostles and prophets. Let us constantly look forward to this glorious eternity during the whole of our troublesome pilgrimage as to the goal of our course ; and let us bear with the greater fortitude our present afflictions because the race is short, and we are destined not to the fugitive enjoyments of this life, but to the possession of that blessed eternity in which we shall participate the wisdom and righteousness of God.

" But as you, my learned and pious friend, are well acquainted with these truths, I have written the more briefly ; and I pray God to invigorate both your body and mind. You remember it is said, ' In HIM we live and move and have our being.' (p)—Farewell."

The preceding letter renders it almost superfluous to state as a matter of fact, what must be at once obvious to every reader, and what every future transaction in Melancthon's life will render increasingly evident, that he was remarkable for *Piety;* humble, genuine, undissembled piety. The association of great intellectual capacities with bad moral habits is always to be deeply deplored, and no exterior embellishments of nature or art, no power of mind, no fascination of manners, can render an infidel in principle and a profligate in character otherwise than offensive

(p) ACTS xvii. 28.

L

and contemptible. Vice always degrades even the great, while religion inexpressibly ennobles even the little. In the present instance we have not to weep over talent perverted and abused by vicious associations, but to rejoice in seeing it devoted to the best of purposes, and forming an alliance with true piety, which was in fact the pillar of his confidence, the brightest ornament of his unblemished character, the consolation of his most desponding hours, the stimulating motive of all his public exertions, and the LAW of his family.

Among other interesting fragments of Melancthon's composition, a short but expressive GRACE, designed for the table, and probably used by himself, is extant. *(q)*

BENEDICTIO MENSÆ.

His Epulis donisque tuis benedicite Christe
Ut foveant jussu corpora fessa tuo,
Non alit in fragili panis modo corpore vitam
Sermo tuus vitæ tempora longa facit.

THE TABLE BLESSED.

To these provisions which enrich our board,
The gifts thy liberal Providence bestows,
Saviour, thy benediction now afford,
From which alone their power to nourish flows.
A few short years material food supplies
Corporeal waste, and cheers our fainting hearts:
But thy imperishable word imparts,
A principle of life that never dies.

(q) MELANCTH. Epigrammata. *Hagan.* 1528.

Or,

O Saviour !——
Bless what thy providential care
Has for our bodies given ;
But thy good word (superior fare !)
Sustains the soul for heaven.

Melancthon was characterized by *Sincerity,*
and totally devoid of every thing like deceit and
dissimulation.   There were no reserves about
him ; all was transparent, open, and honest,
while at the same time, his manners were remarkably captivating.   From this temper resulted a freeness in common conversation, which
led him sometimes to express himself with a
degree of inconsideration : and even when his
intimate friends have endeavoured to check his
frankness from an apprehension of what indeed
not unfrequently happened, that his words would
be invidiously misrepresented, such was his
consciousness of entire purity of motive, that
they could seldom or never succeed in rendering
him cautious.   He was not only communicative,
but his conversation was seasoned with *Wit.*
Disputing one day with a certain Italian on the
real presence in the Eucharist, " *how is it,*" said
he, " *that you Italians will have a God in the
sacramental bread—you, who do not believe there
is a God in heaven ?*"   When he first changed
his religious views, he conceived it impossible
for others to withstand the evidence of truth in

the public ministry of the gospel, but after forming a better acquaintance with human nature, and living to witness the futility of those fond but ill-founded expectations which a warm hearted piety is at first disposed to cherish, he remarked, that " *he found old Adam was too hard for young Melancthon.*"

He was possessed of an extraordinary *Memory*, and maintained that temperance in eating and drinking, that equanimity of mind, and those habits of reflection which essentially conduce to the perfection of this faculty. He was also inquisitive and read much, but with proper selection ; retaining not only the general strain of the discourse, but the very words of the writer. *(r)* Nor were these merely lodged in his memory, for he was remarkable for the facility with which he could call into use whatever he knew. The various kinds of information he gained were so arranged in the different compartments of his great mental repository, that he could at any time, and without difficulty find whatever he wanted : for he had the power of *recollecting* as well as of *retaining* knowledge. This qualification fitted him for controversy and made him peculiarly feared by his opponents.

(r) " Fuitque in eo valde bona memoria non rerum modo et sententiarum sed verborum quoque et orationis. Quæ igitur legendo comprehenderat, ea hærebant in animo ipsius." CAM. Vit. Mel. p. 60.

Such was his *Modesty* that he would never
deliver his opinion upon important subjects
without deliberation and serious thought. He
considered no time misspent and no pains ill
bestowed in the search of Truth, and he was
incessantly occupied in examining for himself.
Sophistry and every species of evasion in argument excited his just abhorrence ; seldom or
never could it escape his penetrating eye, and
whenever he detected it no considerations could
deter him from expressing the most marked disapprobation.   His own conceptions were clear,
his language perspicuous, and his intentions
upright.   There was such a transparency in the
whole stream of his argument in public discourses or disputations, that you could see to
the very bottom of his motives and principles.

He was kind to a fault ; and so exceedingly
Humble, that in the common concerns of life he
was not ashamed to stoop even to menial offices
if they were not base or dishonourable.   Frequently he would put to shame the ill-humoured
disinclination of the lowest servants to discharge
any part of their duty, by doing it himself.

The same happy combination of modesty
and humility characterized all his deportment,
and in a very conspicuous manner influenced
his private conduct, his public transactions,
and his various writings.   It is not every author
however conscious of the blemishes which may

have disfigured his first publications, that would
be willing to make concessions of this description, " Nothing is more foolish than to attempt
the defence of folly. An ingenuous mind will acknowledge its mistakes, especially in subjects of
a literary kind, and candidly confess its weakness
or negligence in order that youth may learn from
the example of others, to be more diligent in investigation and more careful in their mode of study. I will not scruple therefore to censure some
things in this (the first) edition of my own
writings, and will not only recapitulate the
course of my juvenile studies, but explain my
meaning in some public transactions, and state
why I issued certain theological publications."(s)

M. Baillet, with a zeal natural to one of his
faith, is anxious that the church of Rome should
be duly honoured as the mother of so illustrious
an offspring. " His parents," says he, " were
most excellent Catholics, irreproachable in their
manners, exemplary in their conduct, careful to
maintain in their family the fear of God and a
due observance of his commandments, walking
before God with a simplicity, a fidelity, and a
zeal like that of primitive Christians. I feel
myself constrained to state these particulars, that
you may remember to attribute to Melancthon's
excellent education all that you read or hear

(s) MELANCTH. Ep. Lib. I. 110. *Ep. de seipso et de
edit. prima suorum scriptorum.*

said of his sweetness of temper, courtesy, temperance, modesty, and others virtues, for which the Protestants have so much extolled him: and that you may consider these qualities *as produced or cherished in the bosom of the Catholic church."* *(t)* Varillas, one of the greatest enemies of the Reformation, has nevertheless spoken of him in the following manner: " He possessed a sweetness and mildness of temper, that rendered him incapable of returning injury for injury. In observing the exactest rules of morality, he only followed his inclination, and notwithstanding the meanness of his birth, *(u)* he practised the utmost generosity his means would allow. No German wrote the Latin language with greater ease or in a more intelligible manner, yet he was never so attached to his own productions, or so prejudiced in their favour as to refuse making any corrections suggested by his friends." *(v)*

(t) BAILLET Trait. Hist. des Enfans devenues celeb. par leurs Etudes ou par leurs Ecrits, p. 130.

(u) The Papists were extremely fond of representing their adversaries as low and baseborn persons, in order as they imagined, to render their cause contemptible.

(v) VARILLAS Hist. des Heres. l. 7. So far indeed was he from any over-valuation of his own productions, that he suffered his papers, and what was most unjustifiably negligent, even the letters of his most distinguished friends to lie about exposed to any one's inspection. The consequence was, that many of them were lost. " Quinetiam libros scriptaque sua

Neither Melancthon's attachment to literature, nor his multifarious engagements in public seduced him from the cultivation of *domestic
feelings,* and the discharge of *parental duties.* His
wife and children, ever dear to his heart, were
not forgotten amidst the deepest abstractions of
study, or the greatest perplexity of engagement.

The habits of studious men have sometimes
been represented as tending to disqualify them
for the familiar intercourse of domestic or social
life. It is often long before the clouds which
profound study gathers over the mind can be
entirely chased away, even by the cheering influence of innocent conviviality. At the same
time a great man never appears greater than in
descending from the high station where public
opinion or extraordinary genius has enthroned
him to an approachable familiarity. It is then
his friends will no longer censure his abstractions
nor his affectionate family deprecate his fame.
Melancthon may be appealed to as a pleasing
illustration of this remark. A Frenchman one
day, found him holding a book in one hand and
rocking his child's cradle with the other. Upon
his manifesting considerable surprize, Melancthon took occasion from the incident to converse

omnia et litteras quæ afferebantur quotidie plurimæ à diversis
et dissimilibus conditione, loco, fortuna, relinquere omnium
oculis et manibus expositas, ex quibus subtractum plurimum
esse constat." Cam. Vit. Mel. p. 57, 58.

with his visitor on the duties of parents, and on
the regard of heaven for little children in such a
pious and affectionate manner, that his astonishment was quickly transformed into admiration.
The fondness he cherished for his own family
extended to children in general.   He possessed,
in a very eminent degree, the rare art of making
himself a captivating and instructive companion
to them.   He descended with the most happy
ease to their level, promoted by his jocularity
their little pleasures, and engaged with all his
heart in their games and festivities. He would often exercise their ingenuity, by devising fictions
and puzzles, and took great delight in relating
useful scraps of history or memorable tales. *(w)*

He always estimated *Time* as a most precious
possession. It is said of him, that when he
made an appointment, he expected not only that
the day or the hour, but that the *minute* should be
fixed, in order that time might not be squandered
away in the vacuity or idleness of suspense.

In his youth he was remarkably troubled with
sleeplessness, which the regularity of his general
habits at length overcame.   He usually rose at
TWELVE O'CLOCK, but when he retired to rest
we cannot tell, no doubt at an early hour.
When letters or papers arrived in the evening he
always referred them to the next morning for

(w) CAM. Vit. Mel.

inspection, lest the hours devoted to sleep which he found indispensible to the due preservation of health, should be disturbed.

His matrimonial connection was not only a happy, but a very lasting one. Formed for each other, this favoured pair were not destined to suffer the pangs of early separation ; but lived, so far as can be ascertained, in undisturbed harmony for thirty-seven years. They had four children, two sons and two daughters. Of the former little or nothing is known. It seems probable they died in early life, for in a letter written to Camerarius, his most intimate friend in April 1524, he intimates their delicacy of constitution which seemed to require some change of air, on which account he meditated their removal for a little time to Leipsic. *(x)*

Anne his eldest daughter appears to have been the favourite child, for she was not only handsome and accomplished, but of a very literary turn. Luther in one of his letters, calls her " the elegant daughter of Philip." *(y)* On the sixth of November 1536, she was married to

(x) " Pueros meos cogito Lipsiam ad Lottherum aliquantisper mittere, nam aër noster nescio quid minatur." MELANCTH. Ep. Lib. IV. 14. *ad Joach. Camerar.* He afterwards speaks of one of his sons accompanying him in his visit to Nuremberg in 1526, an account of which will be mentioned in the proper place. Ep. Lib. IV. 29.

(y) EP. II. 92.

George Sabinus. *(z)* This young man, a native of Brandenburg, being sent to Melancthon with the powerful recommendation of Erasmus to be educated, became an inmate of his family. His thirst after knowledge was so unbounded, that no labour however great, which was deemed requisite to attain it, damped his inextinguishable zeal. By day and by night he devoted himself to study, and overlooked or despised every obstacle in the path of knowledge. But his taste even surpassed his zeal, particularly in poetic compositions. Camerarius relates that he had seen him weep abundantly when reading an exquisite piece of poetry, and that though he would deeply deplore his own infelicity in composition, no one in reality excelled him. *(a)* His poem entitled, " *Res gestæ Cæsarum Germanorum,*" procured him not only a very extensive reputation in Germany, but the notice and patronage of the most enlightened princes of the age, and he became successively professor of the Belles Lettres at Frankfort on the Oder, rector of the New

(z) MEL. ADAM. Vit. Philosophorum, p. 227.

(a) " Vidi ego hunc Georgium, qui postea Sabini nomine celebris fuit valde tenera adhuc ætate, lacrimas profundentem ad lectionem boni et elegantis carminis. Audivi tristes querelas ejus deplorantis suam infelicitatem in scribendo, cum non solum per ætatem nihil quod perfectum esset ipse elaborare, sed ne intelligere quidem rationem perficiendi elaborandique adhuc valeret." CAM. Vit. Mel. p. 206.

Academy of Königsberg, and counsellor to the
Elector of Brandenburg.   It will not appear surprising that such a youth, and in such favourable circumstances should have ingratiated himself into Melancthon's esteem, and attracted the
affections of his accomplished daughter.

It is related of Sabinus, that on a certain
occasion when he was dining in company with
Stigelius and Melancthon, the latter engaged
them in an extempore poetical contest. Sabinus
being the elder of the two was required to begin,
which he did in these words :—

> " Carmina conscribant alii dictante Lyæo
> Multa sit in versu cura laborque meo;"
>
> Some silly scribblers soon their pages fill---
> Let care and labour regulate *my* quill !

to which Stigelius replied,

> Carmina componant alii sudante cerebro
> Nulla sit in versu cura laborque meo.
>
> Some toil and sweat to elaborate a rhyme---
> Let *no* such care nor labour waste *my* time.

The two poetical gladiators had the satisfaction
of being equally extolled by Melancthon, the
one for his attack, and the other for his defence. *(b)*

Stigelius obtained a considerable poetical
notoriety, and Melancthon has expressed a very

(b) TEISSIER Eloges des Hommes Savans---Art. *George
Sabin.* MEL. ADAM. Vit. Philosophorum, p. 231.

high opinion of his merit. *(c)* He wrote a variety of epitaphs, epigrams, and epithalamia, a metrical translation of many of the Psalms of David, with other little compositions, of which the following monumental inscription for himself is not the least curious :—

> Hic ego Stigelius jaceo ; quis curat ? ut omnis
> Negligat hoc mundus ; scit tamen ipse Deus.

> Here lies Stigelius ;---but who marks the spot?
> Well---let the world neglect me ! GOD will not.

But this apparently happy and suitable connection was destined to become a sourse of considerable affliction. Sabinus was very different in character from his father-in-law Melancthon. The elegant pleasures of literature did not satisfy him ; for he was naturally ambitious, and the fame he acquired by his poetic publications, fed the secret flame till it could no longer be suppressed. Melancthon was attached to the more humble life of a man of letters and a man of piety, nor could he be induced by the most pressing intreaties to pursue any

(c) " Etsi enim Italia una videtur suavia et venusta ingenia gignere, tamen ferè adfirmari potest, nondum post *Ovidii* ætatem cujusquam in Italiâ venam fuisse dulciorem et elegantiorem Stigeliana. Et in Germaniâ arbitror Micyllum et alios qui carmen felicissimè scribunt, libenter Stigelio proximum ab Eobano locum tribuere." MELANCTH. Ep. Lib. I. 49, *ad Georg. Princip. Anhalt.*

measures for the promotion of his children to
posts of civil distinction and emolument. He
employed all his skill to cure the raging fever of
Sabinus, but in vain ; for the poet worshipped
fame and wealth. They became therefore dis-
contented with each other, and found it best to
separate. The lovely spirit of Melancthon however prevented any serious dissention, and they
eventually parted with mutual good will and
kindness. Sabinus took his wife into Prussia,
where to her father's inexpressible grief she died
after a residence of four years at Königsberg.

The youngest daughter of Melancthon was
married in the year 1550, to Casper Peucer,
whose name is one of the most celebrated in
German literature, as well as in the annals of
the Reformation. He was a Physician, and
through the favour of the Elector of Saxony,
made professor of Medicine in the University of
Wittemberg. He was always sent for to Court
when any important deliberations of a medical
kind were held, and had the most free access to
the Elector. His writings are numerous in medicine, mathematics, and theology. Above all,
he is to be ranked amongst the illustrious sufferers
for the cause of Truth.

After the death of Melancthon, Peucer, in
conjunction with the divines of Wittemberg and
Leipsic, and of several ecclesiastics and persons
of distinction in the Court of Saxony, aimed to

introduce the Calvinistic sentiments respecting the Eucharist, denying most strenuously the Lutheran doctrine of the corporeal presence of Christ. Great commotions being excited, the Elector Augustus, in the year 1571, called a solemn assembly of the Saxon Divines, and of all persons concerned in the administration of ecclesiastical affairs, at Dresden. Augustus commanded them to adopt his opinion respecting the Eucharist, which at that time agreed with that of Peucer and the moderate Lutherans; but he was soon seduced by the insinuations of their adversaries, who represented the church as in danger, to change sides, and in consequence of finding that the Saxon Divines who were the disciples of Melancthon, propagated their sentiments with the utmost assiduity, he called a new convention at Torgaw in the year 1574, where he assumed the Dictator's chair and wielded the Persecutor's sword. Of those who denied the corporeal presence, some were imprisoned, others banished, and others compelled to renounce their sentiments. Peucer had the honour of suffering amongst the former. He endured the severities of a cruel imprisonment for ten years, and was only released at last through the intercession of the Prince of Anhalt. *(d)*

(d) ADAM. Vit. Medicor. Germ. MOSH. Eccles. Hist. Cent. 16.

Among the rare instances of eminent persons attached to the reformed cause in the early period of its progress which is now under review, comprising .the year 1520, the name of John Thurzo, Bishop of Breslaw, in Silesia, claims a distinguished notice.   It is true little, too little is known of him; but as the early traveller watches the commencement and the gradual progress of the dawning day, by the first beams that strike successively upon surrounding objects, so the observant reader will unite with the vigilant bioprapher, in hailing each indication of increasing light in a world enveloped in mysterious darkness.   The Bishop of Breslaw, therefore, ought to be mentioned for the pleasing singularity of his character, as the decided friend of the infant Reformation.   He died in peace in the month of August, meriting this noble eulogium. *(e)*

    " Who is there," says Melancthon, " that does not love the man, who, so far as I know is the only man in Germany, that by his authority, learning, and piety, has furnished an example of what a bishop ought to be?   If the

----

(e) This was expressed in a letter addressed to the good bishop, which he did not live long enough to receive.   Luther wrote to him in language indicative of an equal esteem, and at the same time.   SCULTET. Annal. Evang. p. 61.   VON DER HARDT. Hist. Lit. Reform. P. 5. p. 33.

Christian world could but produce ten persons
of a similar *stamp and cast of thinking* (συμφράδμονες),
as Homer says, I should not doubt of seeing
the kingdom of Christ in some measure restored."

M

CHAP. V.

The Pope's Bull against Luther—His retaliation—Diet of Worms—Luther's seizure and imprisonment at the Castle of Wartenberg—Feelings of Melancthon—Condemnation of Luther by the Sorbonne—Melancthon's Satirical Rejoinder—His publication under the feigned name of Thomas Placentinus or Rhadin—His Declamation on the Study of Paul—Extracts from his Loci Communes, or Theological Common Places—Transactions relative to the Abolition of Private Masses.

RETURNING from the disputations at Leipsic, Eckius resolved if possible to ruin Luther, and pursued his purpose with inveterate malignity and unremitting zeal. He flew to Rome, implored Leo X. to excommunicate this heretic and obtained the vigorous co-operation of the Dominicans then in high favour at court, who were willing to revenge the quarrel of their brother Tetzel.

At length on the fifteenth of June 1520, the Pope issued a Bull against Luther, in which after calling upon Christ, St. Peter, St. Paul, and all the saints to interpose in behalf of the church *(f)* forty-one propositions are extracted from his writings, and condemned as pestilential, scandalous and offensive to pious minds; all persons are interdicted from reading them upon pain of excommunication, and unless the heretic should present himself at Rome within sixty days in order to take his trial before the supreme Pontiff,

(f) " Leo Episcopus, Servus servorum Dei. Ad perpetuam rei memoriam. Exsurge Domine et judica causam tuam: memor esto improperiorum tuorum eorum quæ ab insipientibus fiunt tota die...... Exsurge Petre et pro pastorali cura præfata, ut præfertur, tibi divinitus demandata, intende in causam sanctæ Rom. Ecclesiæ matris omnium Ecclesiarum ac fidei magistræ, quam tu, jubente Deo, tuo sanguine, consecrâsti...... Exsurge tu quoque, quæsumus, Paule, qui eam tua doctrina ac pari martyrio illuminâsti atque illustrâsti. Jam enim surgit *novus Porphyrius*....... Exsurgat, denique, omni sanctorum ac reliqua universalis ecclesia, cujus vera sacrarum literarum interpretatione posthabita, quidam quorum mentem pater mendacii excæcavit, ex veteri hæreticorum instituto, ud semetipsos sapientes, scripturas easdem aliter quam Spiritus Sanctus flagitet, proprio duntaxat sensu, ambitionis, auræque popularis causa (teste Apostolo) interpretantur, imo vero torquent et adulterant, ita ut juxta Hieronymum, jam non sit Evangelium Christi, sed hominis, aut quod pejus est, diaboli. Exsurgat, inquam, præfata sancta ecclesia Dei, et unà cum beatissimis apostolis præfatis apud Deum omnipotentem intercedat, ut purgatis ovium suarum erroribus, eliminatisque a fidelium finibus hæresibus universis ecclesiæ suæ sanctæ pacem et unitatem conservare dignetur." Bulla Leonis X.

M 2

he is fully EXCOMMUNICATED. But these menaces were ineffectual; in many places the decree
was delayed or evaded—even at Leipsic it was
violently opposed and at Erfurt it was forcibly wrested from Eckius, torn in pieces and
thrown into the river by a body of academicians.
Many of the Roman Catholic writers condemn
the imprudence of Leo in this and other hasty
proceedings against the Saxon Reformer, but it
is more than probable had the effect been different, they would have spared the Tiara.

Immediately previous to the publication of
this celebrated anathema, Luther had been offered
an asylum from his persecutors by Sylvester
Schaumberg, a Franconian knight, whose son
was under the tuition of Melancthon. " I offer
you," said he, " my own protection, and that of
one hundred noblemen in Franconia, with whom
you can live in safety until your doctrine has
undergone a deliberate investigation."   The state
of his mind at this critical juncture may be ascertained from his own language to his friend
Spalatine the Elector's secretary, upon transmitting to him the generous letter of Schaumberg. " As for me the die is cast. I equally
despise the favour and fury of Rome, I have no
longer any wish to be connected with or reconciled
to them. Let them condemn me and burn my
books, and if I do not in return publicly condemn
and burn the whole pontifical code, it will only

be from want of fire." In fact, on the tenth of December 1520, in the presence of an immense concourse of people of all ranks, he committed the Bull of Leo, the decretals of the Pontiffs and other similar documents to the flames, in testimony of his everlasting separation from the Romish Communion. Nor did he neglect to use the *pen* as well as the *torch*, by which he appealed from the Pope to a general council, and exposed the pretensions and corruption of the church of Rome in several tracts. A second Bull was issued against him in the month of January 1521, in which the Pope styles himself " the divinely appointed dispenser of spiritual and temporal punishments," and which consisted of a recapitulation of the former Bull, and a formal excommunication of Luther.

During these transactions the Elector Frederic acted with a prudence and discretion which proved eminently serviceable to the Reformation. Had he been *less* the friend of Luther and of truth, he would have delivered him up to his enraged adversaries ; had he been *more* zealous it would have been equally fatal by exposing himself to the papal anathemas, and the infant cause he secretly and therefore effectually patronized, to almost inevitable destruction. His conduct and character cannot be more accurately depicted than in the words of Melancthon. " This most excellent prince was much concerned to foresee the contests and disorders which would ensue, though the first attacks made by Luther were upon very plausible grounds By his own judgment and sagacity, and by long experience in the art of government, he well knew the danger of revolutions. But being a truly religious man and one who feared God, he consulted not the dictates of mere worldly and political wisdom, which might have inclined him to stifle at once all symptoms of innovation. He determined to prefer the glory of God to all other considerations, and to listen to the divine command which enjoins obedience to the gospel. He knew that it was a horrible profaneness to resist the truth when plainly seen and known. He had studiously examined Luther's works, and accurately weighed his proofs and testimonies ; and he would not suffer doctrines to be oppressed and smothered which he judged to be the word of God. The Holy Spirit confirmed and supported him in these excellent resolutions, so that though the Emperors Maximilian and Charles, and the Roman Pontiffs urged this prince, and not without menaces, to hinder Luther from writing and preaching in his dominions, he was not in the least degree shaken or intimidated. Yet he presumed not to rely entirely on his own judgment in a matter of such great importance, but took the advice of other persons who were venerable for their rank, learning, and experience."

After the death of Maximilian I. the unanimous vote of the electoral College placed Charles V. upon the Imperial Throne, who was publicly crowned at Aix-la-Chapelle, on the twenty-third of October 1520, the year after his election. *(g)* Leo immediately applied to him to inflict an exemplary punishment on Luther for disobedience to papal authority, while Frederic exerted his influence, an influence derived from the personal obligations of Charles who had been created Emperor chiefly through his exertions, to obtain a public and fair investigation of his cause in Germany previous to the publication of any condemnatory edict. The result was that the Emperor appointed a diet at Worms in January 1521, to which under the protection of a safe conduct Luther repaired in April.

His friends recollecting the fate of John Huss were extremely apprehensive, and would have dissuaded him from venturing amongst his enemies. Their fears increased as he approached the city. Every argument was used to prevent his perseverance and when at Oppenheim he was met by Bucer, *(h)* who had been sent to

(g) ROBERTSON'S Hist. of Charles V.

(h) Martin Bucer was born at Shelestadt in Alsace. He spent several days with Luther at Worms and embraced his opinions. He afterwards preached the doctrines of the Reformation at Strasburg and was extremely active in endeavouring to reconcile the Lutherans and Zuinglians. In the year 1549

entreat him to take refuge in a neighbouring castle; upon which occasion he uttered that heroic and most characteristic declaration which both Protestant and Papist historians have recorded. " I am lawfully called to appear in the city of Worms, and thither will I go in the name of the Lord though as many devils, as there are tiles on the houses, were there combined against me."

At this crisis Melancthon thus expresses himself in a letter to one of his friends. " Martin still lives and prospers notwithstanding the indignation and fury of Leo, to whom all things have hitherto been supposed possible. Nobody approves the Bull which Eckius is enforcing, unless it be those who are more concerned for their own ease and indulgence than for the success of the gospel. We are certainly in no danger from it at present though the hierarchy raves and thunders. O that you knew with what trembling hesitation this pontifical mandate is executed, for its abettors are in a complete strait between the general opinion on the one hand and the anger of the Roman Pontiff on the other, while there are many who would rather be openly accused of any crime than appear to be deficient in religious zeal for the Pope. You are doubt-

Archbishop Cranmer invited him to England, and he became a lecturer in Divinity in the University of Cambridge, where he died in 1551, at the age of sixty-one.

less acquainted with the proceedings at **Worms**, though I may say a word or two on that subject. Charles is constantly urged to proscribe Luther by an imperial edict, and there are great deliberations and debatings about it. If the Papists could prevail in their rage they would destroy us, and they are vexed at the inefficiency of the pontifical decrees. They are in hopes that those which they are using every means, but I trust in vain, to extort from the emperor, will prove availing. Nothing can terrify Martin Luther, who would willingly purchase the advancement and glory of the gospel AT THE PRICE OF HIS BLOOD."(i)

Private conferences and public examinations, violent threats and gentle entreaties, were alternately employed to cajole or to force him into a recantation of his heretical opinions and a submission to the Roman Pontiff. It was all in vain. He was neither to be compelled nor seduced into compliance. He COULD suffer death, but he COULD NOT violate the dictates of conscience! The wonder is, that when his enemies were so inveterate and himself so intrepid and resolute, he should have been allowed to depart from Worms in peace; but the members of the Diet refused to expose themselves to the reproach of a violation of faith, and the Emperor was unwilling to contend with them

(i) Ep. 5. ad Hessum.

from political motives. He was allowed twenty one days to return home, and required not to preach to the people in the course of his journey. A few days after he had withdrawn, an edict was issued by the authority of the Diet in the Emperor's name, declaring him a member cut off from the church, a schismatic, a notorious and obstinate heretic; and forbidding all persons, under penalty of high treason, loss of goods, and being put under the BAN of the Empire, to receive, defend, maintain or protect him, either in word or writing; and all his adherents, followers, and favourers to suffer the confiscation of their property, unless they had left his party, and had received *absolution by apostolic authority! (j)*

The formidable edict of Worms however was in a great measure superseded by two circumstances, namely, the multiplicity of the Emperor's engagements arising out of commotions in Spain, and the wars of Italy and the Low Countries; and a curious, but well concerted and well timed contrivance of his wary friend the Elector of Saxony. Foreseeing the meditated attack upon Luther, Frederic employed several trusty persons in masks to seize upon him as he was passing a forest in Thuringia, near Altenstein, and convey him to the castle of Wartenberg which was situated on a high moun-

(j) DUPIN's Eccles. Hist. B. 2. Ch. 10.

tain in the vicinity of Eisenach. *(k)* The consequence of this sudden disappearance was unfavourable to his adversaries who were suspected of having plotted his destruction, the Imperial Edict missed its aim, and his opinions—or rather, " The word of the Lord grew, and was multiplied." *(l)*

Luther's confinement in the castle of Wartenberg, placed Melancthon at the head of the reformed cause, who was well aware of the responsibility of his situation. After a considerable lapse of time he writes to his friend Hess; " I feel the need I have of good advice. Our Elijah is still confined at a distance from us, though we are expecting and anticipating his return. What shall I say more? His absence absolutely torments me." *(m)* Though there was indeed an alloy of constitutional timidity, which cannot but be considered as some depreciation of his sterling value in the peculiar situation of ecclesiastical affairs, no one was so well qualified to maintain the respectability and promote the success of the Lutheran cause. The

(k) SECKEND. Hist. Luth. Lib. I Sect. 44. p. 152. In his retreat he passed for a country gentleman, under the assumed name of Yonker George.

(l) ACTS xii. 24.

(m) The expression is very strong, and shews the agitated state of his mind. " Me desiderium ejus excruciat miserè." Ep. 7. ad Hessum.

great Reformer well knew his extraordinary merit, and requested him to assist in the discharge
of some of those clerical duties for which he was
incapacitated by absence.   In one of his letters he
addresses him thus: " For the glory of the word
of God and the mutual consolation of myself
and others, I would rather be consumed in a
blazing fire, than remain here half alive and
utterly useless.   If I perish, the gospel of Christ
will not perish, and you, I hope, like another Elisha, will succeed Elijah."   Again he
writes, " The accounts which I receive of your
abundant success in religion and learning during
my absence, rejoice my heart exceedingly and
very much diminish the miseries of separation.
The circumstance of your going on so prosper-
ously while I am absent, is peculiarly delightful
to me, because it may serve to convince the
wicked one, that however he may rage and foam,
their desires shall perish and Christ will finish
the work which he has begun." (n)

Melancthon was constitutionally hypochondriacal; and as even trifling circumstances frequently disturb the peace of such persons, it
was to be expected that the state of things at
this momentous crisis would produce a poweful
effect upon his mind.   His heart was interested
in the cause of pure Christianity, his happiness

(n) LUTH. Ep. 235, and 243.

was deeply involved in it, his sensibilities were perpetually wrought upon by surrounding occurrences, and his spirits ebbed and flowed according to the success or decline of that cause which was to him the dearest upon earth. In fact the situation of Melancthon and the friends of the Reformation was peculiarly afflictive. The transactions at Worms and the subsequent concealment of Luther, had inspired Frederic with an unusual degree of caution, amounting to timidity, in his proceedings. The writings of Luther were not allowed to be published and the academicians were interdicted the discussion of questions likely to offend persons of distinction, who were attached to Popery. That Luther deeply sympathized with his friend and participated in his sentiments, is obvious from his own words. " I sit here in my Patmos, reflecting all the day on the wretched condition of the church. I bemoan the hardness of my heart, that I am not dissolved in tears on this account. May God have mercy upon us." It would however be flagrantly unjust to impute the strong sensation of either of these exalted characters to pusillanimity. Though much distressed, they fully coincided in the principles recognized in another of Luther's epistles. " The peace and approbation of God is ever to be preferred to the peace and approbation of the world. . . . . . In all circumstances we ought to adhere strictly to the simple word of God and not merely when that word happens to thrive and be respected among men. Let those who please take against us. But why are we to be always looking on the dark side of things ? why not indulge hopes of better times ?"

At length these bosom friends contrived a mode of alleviating the anxiety that was so intolerable and of obtaining each other's mutual assistance in the present crisis. This was a secret visit of Luther to Wittemberg, which was hastened by the prevalence of various evils, especially the conduct of Carlostadt. which will be noticed in a subsequent page. He states the circumstance to Spalatine : " I came to Wittemberg and amongst the delightful intercourse enjoyed with my friends, I found this bitter, that my little pamphlets and letters had neither been heard of nor seen, for which you shall judge, whether I was not justly displeased. However, on the whole, what I have seen and heard has afforded me the greatest satisfaction. May the Lord comfort those who are interested in the cause : but on my way I was vexed with the various rumours I heard of the imprudences of some of our friends and I propose to publish some suitable exhortation as soon as I return to my asylum. Commend me to our illustrious prince, from whom I wish to conceal my journey to Wittemberg, for a reason of which you are aware. Farewell. I am in Ams-

dorff's house with my beloved friend Philip Melancthon." *(o)*

In England Henry the Eighth published a
book against Luther and in defence of the seven
sacraments of the Roman Church, for which
he received the title never yet relinquished by
his successors, of *Defender of the Faith.* In
France, the Divines of the Sorbonne *(p)* published a formal condemnation of the Reformer's
writings (dated the 15th of April, 1521), in which
they show the danger to which Christians are
exposed from his *poisonous* errors, and charge
him with rashness in preferring his own judgment to that of the Universities and Holy Fathers of the Church, *as though God had given
him the knowledge of many truths necessary for
salvation, which the Church had been ignorant of
during past ages, being left by Jesus Christ her
spouse in the darkness of error. (q)*

Melancthon immediately took up his pen
and gave them a very suitable flagellation in a
small piece, entitled " Adversus furiosum Pari-

(o) LUTH. Ep. 253.

(p) The term applied to the faculty of Theology at Paris.
The College of the University in which they assembled was
called the house of the Sorbonne, which was first erected and
endowed in the year 1250, by a wealthy favourite of St. Lewis,
whose name was Robert de Sorbonne. This Theological Society was, at that period, in the highest repute.

(q) DUPIN's Eccles. Hist. B. 2. ch. 11.

siensium Theologastrorum decretum pro Luthero apologia ;" or, " *An Apology for Luther, in opposition to the furious decree of the Parisian Theologasters.*" *(r)* This, we may be certain, was gratifying to his friend *Yonker George,* in confinement at Wartenberg. " I have seen," says he, " the Decree of the *Parisian Sophists,* together with the Apology of Philip, and from my very heart I rejoice : for Christ would not have given them up to such blindness had not he determined to promote his own cause, and to put a stop to the despotism of its adversaries." *(s)*

In this satirical pamphlet he begins by remarking, that, " during the past year, the Sophists of Cologne and Louvain condemned the Gospel, in a set of naked propositions, unsupported by either Reason or Scripture, and that now the Parisian Divines had acted in the same irrational manner. By the spirit which pervades the Decree it may be determined whether it is from God, who is not the author of malice, or *from another quarter !* It appeared almost incredible that *such* a work should have proceeded from

(r) A term of ridicule as we speak of a *poetaster, witling,* &c.

(s) LUTH. Ep. 236, *ad Spalat.* Lib. 1. Luther is not quite so delicate in his epithets when he is writing familiarly to Melancthon on the subject ; for he does not scruple, in conformity to the *fashionable* language of the age on controversial occasions, to call these Parisian doctors, *asses* and *madmen.*

such a University, distinguished as it had been by remarkable men, and especially by the great and pious Gerson. *(t)*   A letter was prefixed to the Decree which he supposed must have been written by some hired declaimer, because it displayed such womanish violence, that it was too silly for a divine to be sure!   What does it contain? 'Oh ! Luther is a Manichæan! a Montanist! he despises us forsooth!—he is mad!—he must be brought to his senses by fire and flames!' What feminine, what *monkish* weakness !

  " Luther is accused of heresy, not because he differs from SCRIPTURE, but from the *Holy Fathers*, *Councils*, and *Universities*, whose opinions are received as the first principles of religion ! ! But are Holy Fathers, and Councils, and Universities to decree the articles of Christian faith?— And how can this be the case, when they are so liable to err, Occam himself being judge, if you will not credit me ?   Is our faith to depend upon the opinions of men ?—So did not Paul determine when he affirmed, that ' other foundation can no man lay than that is laid, which is Jesus Christ.' *(u)*

(t) John Gerson was Chancellor of the University of Paris in the Fifteenth Century, and the most distinguished person of his age.   The Council of Constance regarded him as its oracle, and his publications were eminently calculated to promote the cause of religious liberty and reform.

(u) 1 COR. iii. 2.

N

" Luther then does not dissent from SCRIP-
TURE, but from YOUR judgment, and from the
sense which the *Fathers, Councils,* and *Schools*
have adopted ; and this I see is the great cause of
the controversy, and the great sin he has committed ! But what after all is decreed by the
Councils, when some things are false and some
true, some conformable to Scripture, and some
contrary to it; so that Scripture must be the
final appeal, and if any passages be obscure, they
are to be compared with others, and thus Scripture will explain itself. ' If an Angel from
Heaven,' says the Apostle, ' preach any other
gospel than what I preach let him be accursed.' *(v)* Surely then Luther may oppose
the obvious sentiment of Scripture to Councils,
Fathers, and Universities ! What can these
Sophists reply ? What sort of logic and what
kind of glosses can they use to avoid the inference
from these statements ? Either deny that there
is any certain sense in Scripture, or acknowledge
that Luther is justifiable in placing its dictates in
opposition to human opinion.

" After all he is not inclined to concede that
Luther and the ancient Fathers and Councils
disagree. On various points he is completely
supported by the sentiments of Augustine, Cyprian, Hilary, and Chrysostom; though it is

(v) GAL. i.x.

true many things are to be found in the writings
of Luther on the Sacraments, vows and other
subjects, which cannot be discovered in them.
No wonder, for that age knew nothing of the ty-
rannical laws of Roman Pontiffs, nothing of our
Parisian Masters and their articles of faith.   That
period may, perhaps, be considered as the noon-
day of evangelical truth ; ours as the declining
evening in which darkness covers the minds of
sinners as a punishment for their guilt; and that
is darkness indeed in which the Sorbonne divinity
prevails, a divinity which extols *human opinion*
as paramount to *Scriptural Truth!*   Does not the
spirit of God, by his prophets, threaten such a
punishment, and does not Paul speak of those
who should teach for doctrines the commandments of men ? and to whom can he refer but—to
the *Sorbonne Divines,* or *such as they ?*

"Nay more, whatever criminality may be supposed to attach to any persons for opposing the
fathers, is to be charged upon these very Parisian
disputants themselves, who diametrically contradict them.   The very best of the Fathers denounce whatever is not from the spirit of Christ,
as sinful ; but these not only do not allow of
their guilt, but absolutely affirm many of them to
be meritorious.   The Fathers deny that mere
human strength is adequate to fulfil the divine
law, these Parisians state the very reverse.

N 2

" It is written, if an offender refuses to hear the church let him be as a heathen man and a publican. I pray now what do you call the church? No doubt, the *French*, or *Sorbonne Church*. But how can that be the church of Christ which has not the word of Christ, who testifies that his sheep hear his voice? We denominate *that* his true church which is built upon THE WORD OF GOD, and which is nourished, fed and governed by it; in a word, which derives every thing and judges of every thing, by THE GOSPEL OF CHRIST, for " he that is of God heareth the words of God."

Again, " You, the Sorbonne Church, without appealing to Reason or Scripture, condemn Luther and exclude him from the communion of the pious. But it did not become you to *condemn*, but to *accuse*. You do not accuse or convince by argument, but contrary both to divine and human laws, at once *condemn*, and for no other reason than because you are the Sorbonne divines and lords of our faith to be sure! For shame! for shame!!! But stay,—I must not treat the *Sorbonne* so irreverently!—for these lords over our faith say they imitate the example of the Apostles, when they issue decisions without Scripture authority. I wish, however, they would verify this statement by some reference. Christ himself quotes the authority of Scripture, Paul does the same; and what are all the apostolic discourses but the testimonies derived from the records of the Old Testament concerning Christ. The *Sorbonne only* is to be believed *without* SCRIPTURE!

" He imagines this fraternity must be of Egyptian origin, and the descendants of Jannes and Jambres who resisted Moses. The truth of the Lutheran doctrines, however, he is satisfied will remain immoveable and unshaken, not only by their opposition, but in spite of the rulers of darkness."

Soon after the publication of this performance a mock answer appeared in the name of the Parisian Divines, written in a ludicrous style and intended to make them appear ridiculous. Dupin imputes it to Luther, and Seckendorf expresses a doubt whether it were written by him or some other friend.

Another controversial piece of the present year, under the feigned name of Didymus Faventinus, against Thomas Placentinus, and on behalf of Luther, is to be attributed to Melancthon. *(w)* It consists of forty-four folio pages. In this performance he details the history of the Lutheran controversy, and refutes the various calumnies of

(w) It is published by his son-in-law in the second volume of his works. *Placentinus,* or *Rhadin,* as he likewise called himself was an assumed name, the real writer being Emser. Comp. MELANCTH. Ep. 5, 6. *ad Hessum.*

the enemies of truth and the reformation. " Luther," says he, " is most iniquitously condemned for having delivered his country from the papal impositions, for daring to root out the errors of so many centuries, and restoring to the light pure Christianity which had been nearly extinguished by the impious decrees of the Popes, and the vain sophistries of the schoolmen. I am not alone in ascribing this merit to Luther ; the learned universally do the same : and I state this lest you should imagine that he is the sole author of the present commotions, which ought rather to be imputed to those who have done nothing else during the past three years than plotting the destruction of Luther. Do not suppose their object is the peace of the Christian community— no—it is solely that they might be able to tyranize completely over it."

Emser, in his declamatory publication, banters Luther, telling him that he ought to feel himself very much obliged to his friend Philip Melancthon, for taking the pains to *polish up his writings and enable him to cut a better figure than he would in his own barbarous style*: and censures him for discountenancing liberal studies. " Luther," replies Melancthon, is no enemy to Mathematics and Natural Philosophy. He thinks the study of coins, plants, and the habits of animals, conducive to the knowledge of the sacred writings, and ought to be encouraged in the Academy.

He approves authors of this class which we use, as Pliny, Athenæus, and, if you please, Aristotle, Theophrastus, Dioscorides, not to mention the poets."

After exposing the errors of the scholastic divinity, both in metaphysics and in morals, " with prodigious force of argument and fluency of language," (x) and discussing a variety of other topics, he proceeds to the subject of grace. " Philosophers imagine that men may obtain the highest pitch of virtue by exercise and habit; on the contrary the sacred writings teach that all human performances are polluted by sin, and can only be cleansed by the Spirit which Christ procured for men. Philosophers attribute every thing to human power; but the sacred writings represent all moral power as lost by the fall. The Scholastics, in imitation of the Philosophers who ascribed the merit and the goodness to human power, affirmed, that the Spirit was delighted to dwell with us after this self-created excellence, but not to transform or purify the soul by his agency. Who does not perceive how the truth of Christ is obscured and lost by this statement; this utter rejection of the scriptural representations of the Spirit as the author of sanctification and of every thing good in man ; and

(x) " Magno pondere argumentorum & verborum flumine." SECKENDORF.

this shameless, this arrogant assumption of human merit? Hence have originated those endless disputes respecting offerings, rewards, and cardinal virtues, in which every thing is attributed to human nature, and nothing to Christ.

" The terms grace, faith, hope and charity, are so abused, that they have quite a different meaning in the sacred writings from that which is given them in the controversies of scholastic divines, so that we have not only lost the doctrine, but the very language of Christianity. Grace, denotes the favour of God through Christ —but where does it ever signify, as they assert, *a form of soul?* Whence originated the terms *faith infused* or *acquired, formed,* and *unformed?* What is their authority for teaching that Christian minds must hope for salvation from human merits? Whence indeed is this profane, impious and arrogant word, *merit?*

" The church, ye Princes, appeals to your faith and piety, that, enslaved as she has hitherto been by vain philosophy and human traditions, you would at length emancipate her from her wretched state, her Babylonian servitude."

He complains bitterly of the state of the Universities, and entreats the different Princes to use their utmost exertions to procure that reform which was so essentially requisite. " The youth, the most tender and susceptible part of the community, are perishing in luxury, gluttony and excess. And what are they likely to do with such masters? And if they should have a diligent tutor, what will it avail if he cannot instruct them, or only in the most sparing manner, in sacred wisdom? For it is in vain you attempt to govern the youthful mind unless you arm it, by evangelical truth and holy example, against the lusts of the flesh, the influence of the world and the machinations of Satan.

" Every one of the ancient Republics paid the greatest possible attention to the instruction of their youth; we, we only, who are denominated Christians, totally disregard and despise this, which is of all others the most important object. O ye Princes, if no other consideration affect your minds, at least compassionate the situation of our youth, who are ruined by the wickedness of others. I have seen some of them by no means ill disposed, who would however rather continue in ignorance of letters, than purchase knowledge at so dear a rate ; and who carried away nothing from the Universities but a wounded conscience."

It is needless to quote any of those passages which are merely controversial, though they are in themselves witty, and were at the time extremely necessary. Poor Emser published a reply in the following year full of *feeling* and furnishing ample proof that Melancthon had trod upon a rattlesnake.

Amongst the " Select Declamations," we find one of the present year on a subject which he was peculiarly qualified to discuss. It is entitled, " Adhortatio ad Christianæ Doctrinæ, per Paulum Proditæ, Studium ;" or, An Exhortation to the Study of Chistian Truth, as stated by the apostle Paul. After shewing the superiority of Paul's doctrine, and the institutions of Christianity to human laws, and of Paul's eloquence to that of the most celebrated orators of antiquity, he concludes with the following solemn appeal : " If, O ye youths, you have any concern for your own best interests, devote your minds to the study of Paul. Inform yourselves from him of the genuine principles of the Christian life, the true means of religious consolation, and the estimate to be formed of all divine and human things. It concerns youth especially to embrace a doctrine of preeminent importance, as conducive to the felicity of man in his passage through the present life, and in prospect of departure from it. Paul instructs you how to live holily and to die happily, by warning the unwary of the snares which their formidable adversaries the flesh and the devil, have prepared for their ruin. You may without moral danger neglect other arts and studies, but it is impossible to despise the truth of the gospel, without sacrificing the hope of salvation. It becomes bishops to use their utmost endeavours, not only

to see that those particularly devoted to sacred
studies are well instructed, but to promote this
knowledge throughout the whole Christian community; and it is incumbent on the Academies
to inculcate it with the greatest zeal, and substi-
tute it for that barbarism and disputation falsely
called Philosophy, which our ancestors unhappily sanctioned.   If it please God the brass shall
become gold.

"It is with the deepest affliction of mind I
observe that our public seminaries are nothing
but the temples of Tophet, and the gloomy
valley of the children of Hinnom.   Christianity
is banished.   Athens had its Areopagus, and
Sparta its School, where youth were trained up
after the very best models, and were better instructed by these heathens than they are in our
Universities at this day.   But do you yourselves,
ye studious youth, seriously undertake the diligent study of St. Paul's writings, where Christ
Jesus is evidently set forth, and his Spirit will
unquestionably prosper your endeavours.   No
service is more acceptable to God, and no conduct can be more pious and praiseworthy than
to aim at truth, and to acquire its transforming
influence; and being once attempted, the labour
will become so delightful that it will never be
relinquished.   The knowledge of any truth is
pleasant, but the knowledge of Christian truth is

singularly beneficial, and you will find the writings of Paul both agreeable and useful.

" It is said that the Egyptians, a people unexampled for superstition, kept an annual festival in honour of Mercury, the reputed author of their laws and literature, on which occasion the multitude were accustomed to offer sacrifices of honey and figs.   This rite proves the antiquity of the festival; for in the golden age, as it is called, almost all public entertainments and feasts were of a sacrificial nature, and honey and figs the most usual offerings to the gods, of which there is ample evidence.   In the midst of these public solemnities the voice of melody was heard in a hymn to Mercury, neither rudely composed nor badly recited.   It expressed the grateful sense they cherished of his having given them laws and formed a variety of institutions, and celebrated the praise of truth in general.   May I not indulge the hope that the discovery of truth by the study of Paul, will excite similar sensations and strains of festive joy; for what can be more just and proper than that after being instructed in the best and most important knowledge, the burden of our song should be as their's constantly was, γλυκὺ ἡ ἀληϑεια, " O lovely truth."

The " LOCI COMMUNES THEOLOGICI," or " Theological Common Places," which was first Published at this time, demands, on account of its magnitude and subsequent celebrity, a particular notice. None of the works of Melancthon, and scarcely any amongst the numerous productions of his illustrious contemporaries, ex-cited greater attention, or circulated to a wider extent. It was very popular both in France and Italy. At Venice, it was published under the name of *Messer Philippo de Terra Nera*, which is the Italian translation of the word Melanc-thon, and was extensively read. Not a syl-lable of disapprobation was expressed, till one Cordelier, who had read the work as it was first published, with the author's real name affixed, gave information to the inquisitors, who, though they approved, or at least did not censure it, as the writing of *Philippo de Terra Nera*, instantly suppressed it as the production of *Philip Me-lancthon! (y)*

" He that intends to be a good divine," says Luther, " hath a great advantage; for, first, he hath the Bible, which I have so plainly translated out of the Hebrew into the High German lan-guage, that every one may read it without diffi-culty. Afterwards he may read the Loci Com-munes of Philip Melancthon ; and let him read with diligence, so that he may have it perfectly in his memory. When he has these two pieces,

(y) HERMANNI VAN DER HARDT Hist. Literar. Re-formationis. P. IV. p. 30. DUPIN Eccles. Hist. Cent. 17, T. I. p. 220.

then he is a divine, against whom neither the devil, nor any heretic can be able to take advantage, for the whole of divinity lies open to him, so that he may read what and when he will for his edification." Again, "we find no book where the sum of religion or divinity is more finely compacted together than in Melancthon's Loci Communes; all the Fathers and Sententiarii are not to be compared to it. It is the best book next to the holy Scriptures." *(z)*

To an edition published in French, at Geneva, in the year 1551, the illustrious John Calvin has prefixed an advertisement, in which he eulogizes the author in the strongest terms : and of the Common Places in particular he very justly remarks, " it is a summary of those truths which are essential to the christian's guidance in the way of salvation." A very cursory analysis of the sentiments contained in this celebrated performance is all the reader can expect or would deem admissible. *(a)*

Of God.

"The human mind, originally formed in the image of God, and capable of knowing him, is, however, in consequence of sin, enveloped in darkness, and can scarcely of itself determine whether there be a God or a Providence. Al-

(z) Colloq. Mensal, p. 298.
(a) Vid. Appendix IV.

though nature is every where marked with traces of the divinity, and with evidences of his interference in human affairs, such is the weakness of man, that he is full of doubt and hesitation on the subject. It is, therefore, a proof of divine goodness to enlighten and instruct us by his word.

" God is a spiritual essence, possessing eternity and the attributes of power, wisdom, goodness, justice and mercy, in an infinite degree, which are not separable from himself, or incompatible in their operations. The unity of God is stated in the following passages : ' Hear, O Israel, the Lord our God is one Lord.'—' I am the first, and I am the last, and besides me there is no God.'—' I am the Lord and there is none else, there is no God beside me.'—' We know that an idol is nothing in the world, and there is none other God but one.'—' One God and Father of all.' (b)

" The scriptures teach us, however, that the essence of God consists in three persons, infinite and co-eternal, the Father, the Son, and the Holy Spirit.

" The Son is denominated by John the LOGOS or WORD. In the epistle to the Hebrews he is called ' the brightness of the Father's glory, and the express image of his person;' and ' all things' are said to have been ' made by him.' In the

(b) Deut. vi. 4. Is. xliv. 6. Is. xlv. 5. 1 Cor. viii. 4. Eph. iv. 6.

Colossians he is termed ' the image of the invisible God.' *(c)*

"The third person, or HOLY SPIRIT, is represented by John as proceeding from the Father
and the Son.   The Son, at the predestined period of time, assumed human nature and was
born of the Virgin Mary.   He was THE CHRIST,
one person consisting in two natures, the divine
and the human.   Neither the Father nor the
Spirit assumed human nature, but the Son.

" The doctrine of the Trinity is supported by
Scripture.   In the last chapter of Matthew mention is made of ' baptizing in the name of the
Father, of the Son, and of the Holy Spirit.'
Three persons are here distinctly named, and
each is assigned an equal power and honour. The
appeal or invocation is equally made to each, and
so as to imply an equal authority.

"Christ must have been possessed of a divine
nature, or it would not be proper to adore and invoke him.   And the adoration, as stated in various passages, was not merely external, as we
bow before kings and potentates, because omnipotence is attributed to him, and John affirms,
' in the beginning was the word, and the word
was with God, and the word WAS GOD.' *(d)*

A copious variety of passages is here quoted
from the Old and New Testaments, in proof of

(c) HEB. i. 3.   JOHN i. 3.   COL. i. 15.
(d) JOHN i. 1.

prayer and other acts of worship being presented to Christ, and the opinions of the Arians and So- cinians are opposed by arguments and quotations from the fathers.

In speaking of the HOLY SPIRIT, Melancthon remarks, that " the general signification of the term *spirit* is motion, either natural, or by means of external impulse ; but it is used in a variety of senses by the prophets and apostles, which must not be absurdly confounded together. Often it means the wind, the life of man, and the various movements of passion good or bad. In the phrase ' God is a spirit,' it signifies a spiritual es- sence, or a pure incorporeal intelligence. It is applied to the Father, but not to him only, and it is requisite to distinguish those places where it refers to the Holy Spirit, whose office is to sanc- tify and animate the soul."

The divinity and personality of the Holy Spirit is then maintained in a series of explanatory remarks on his appearance, at the Baptism of Christ, in the form of a dove, and on the day of Pentecost; and on a variety of passages common- ly recited in the Trinitarian controversy.

The Creation.

" All creatures are the workmanship of God ; angels, men, and every other existence and sub- stance. They were created from nothing, for

' by the word of the Lord were the heavens
made, and all the host of them by the breath of
his mouth.' *(e)*

" If all things were made by the *word of the
Lord*, they were not formed, as the stoics
imagined, from matter antecedently existing.
And as God created, so he perpetually sustains
all things and all beings. The fertility of the
earth year after year, and the perpetuation of
human life is to be attributed to what is called
his general operations. ' In him we live and
move and have our being.' ' Who upholds all
things by the word of his power.' ' He giveth
life to all flesh.' ' Are not two sparrows sold
for a farthing, and not one of them shall fall to the
ground without your father. Even the very
hairs of your head are all numbered.' ' All
wait on thee that thou mayest give them their
meat in due season.' ' He covereth the heavens with clouds, he prepareth rain for the earth,
he maketh grass to grow upon the mountains.' *(f)*

" A variety of special promises have been
given to the church, relating to the care of a superintending providence, and are to be found in
every part of the scriptures. The prayer which
our Saviour directs us to present, ' give us this

(e) Ps. xxxiii. 6.
(f) Acts xvii. 28. Heb. i. 3. Mat. x. 29. Ps. civ. 27.
Ps. cxlvii. 8.

day our daily bread,' intimates our constant dependance, so that second causes cannot operate or avail us unless God give them efficiency.

" Other proofs of this subject might be adduced; as, *first*, the order of nature, that is to say, a series of effects, shewing an agent and cause. The regularity of these operations, as the course of the heavenly bodies, the succession of animals, and of the various productions of the earth, and the course of rivers, demonstrate they are not accidental coincidences, but resulting from an intelligent agent. *Secondly*, the nature of the human mind : what is devoid of intelligence cannot produce it, but the human mind possesses intelligence, and since each derives his being from another, the original being must be an intelligent one. *Thirdly*, the distinction between virtue and vice, and the varieties of knowledge. It is not possible these should exist in the human soul without an adequate cause and by mere accident. *Fourthly*, the uniform impression of the truth that there is a God—all acknowledge it. *Fifthly*, natural conscience: persons guilty of notorious crimes, suffer great alarms of mind, and yet do not apprehend that any punishment will be inflicted by man. They have a certain internal conviction of right and of wrong. *Sixthly*, the constitution of civil society, which could not be organized and maintained in its various relations, but for the wisdom imparted and the regulations maintained by an eternal Providence. *Seventhly,* the knowledge which is obtained and can be obtained only by the continuance of efficient causes. These are not infinite, we must therefore recur to a first cause. *Eighthly,* the existence of final causes.—All things are destined to some use, but this appointment of a suitable end and purpose could not have been fortuitous nor can it continue by chance. It implies a superintending intelligence. *Ninthly,* prophetic signs and intimations of futurity. These are not only such signs as are notorious to the heathen world, but especially particular predictions to the church—often involving the fate of empires, as the predictions of Balaam, Isaiah, Jeremiah and Daniel. A foreseeing mind is necessarily pre-supposed. These considerations demonstrate both the being and the presiding providence of God.

THE CAUSE AND CONSEQUENCE OF SIN.

" This has been a fruitful subject of disputation, and many great men on both sides have involved themselves in inextricable difficulties and absurdities. Let youth be admonished to lay aside contention, and seek only that simple truth which is conducive to genuine religion and sound morality. All wise men agree in one point, that God is not the author of sin, that he neither desires it nor impels the will to commit sin, but abhors it; but it is to be attributed to the influence of the devil and to the will of man. God when he had created the universe pronounced all very good, and Christ imputes evil to Satan, when he represents him as ' a liar and the father of lies.' The New Testament every where states the same sentiment. ' Whosoever committeth sin is of the devil—for the devil sinneth from the beginning,' that is, the devil was the original author of sin. *(g)*

" Such expressions as ' I will harden Pharoah's heart' do not contradict this representation, because they are mere Hebrew idioms, signifying the permission and not the effectual operation and impulse of the divine mind.

" The nature of original sin is hence apparent. It is not the original nature which the Deity implanted in man, but the corruption arising from disobedience. God then is not the author of sin, but properly speaking, it arose from the temptation of Satan and the will of man which was created free.

ON THE FREEDOM OF THE HUMAN WILL.

" By the term free will, is to be understood a faculty and power in the human will, to choose or reject whatever is presented to it; which power was far greater before nature was corrupted, but is now impeded by various means to be

(g) 1 JOHN iii. 8.

hereafter stated.   The apostles speak of the *heart* and the *mind*, that is, the will and the understanding.

   " Many disputes have been agitated upon this subject, and the grand question is, in what manner can the will be free, or how can it obey the law of God?   This question can only be resolved by considering the magnitude of that sin, or inherent infirmity which is contracted by our very birth, and the requirements of the law of God as extending not only to external obedience, but to that of the whole nature, perpetual and perfect.   If the nature of man were not corrupted by sin, its knowledge of God would be more clear and certain ; it would be affected with no doubts, but possessing a genuine fear and confidence would render a perfect obedience, that is to say, all the feelings of the soul would harmonize with the divine law like those of holy angels.   In consequence of original sin, however, the nature of man is now full of doubts, darkness and error,   destitute of true fear and confidence in God, and polluted with vile affections.   Hence the question arises, what kind of power does the human will possess ?   I reply, that since the understanding of man is corrupted, and the choice of those things which are subjected to reason or to sense is perverted, so also is his external and civil obedience.

   " The gospel teaches us that such is the

dreadful depravity of nature, that it is totally repugnant to the law of God, so that we cannot
obey; and the human will cannot, by any exertion
of its own, eradicate this depravity. Such is the
blindness of human nature, that we do not even
discern this moral infirmity and corruption, for
if we did, the reason of our incapacity to satisfy
the divine law would be at once apparent. The
law requires perfect obedience, but our corrupt
nature cannot render it; and it is of this corruption we speak, not in reference to external acts
but internal affections and conformity to God,
when discoursing on the freedom of the human
will.

" To this let it be added, that without the
Holy Spirit we cannot exercise spiritual affections
as love to God, faith in his mercy, obedience and
endurance in afflictions, delight in him and others
of a similar nature. Many passages of Scripture
confirm this statement, ' As many as are led by
the Spirit of God they are the sons of God.'
' If any man have not the Spirit of Christ he is
none of his.' (h) These two are sufficiently obvious, for they distinctly intimate that we can
only obey by the grace of the Holy Spirit. To
these may be added a multitude of others, as
' the natural man receiveth not the things of
the Spirit of God, for they are foolishness unto
him, neither can he know them because they are

(h) Rom. viii. 14. Rom. viii. 9.

spiritually discerned.'—' Except a man be born of water and of the Spirit, he cannot enter into the kingdom of God.'—' No man can come to me except the Father which hath sent me draw him.'—' Without me ye can do nothing.' *(i)*

" The question then being proposed respecting spiritual actions, this seems to be the truth which it becomes us to maintain, that without the aid of the Holy Spirit the human will can perform none of those spiritual actions which God requires, namely, the genuine fear of God, faith in his mercy, perfect love, patience in affliction, persevering constancy even to death, of which holy Stephen, Lawrence and Agnes, with innumerable others are illustrious examples.

On the Gospel.

" This term is used in the most ancient of the Greek writers. In Homer it signifies the reward which is bestowed on the messenger of good tidings, and in Aristophanes and Isocrates, it denotes the sacrifice which is offered when any good news is announced. In other authors it is used for the *message itself, the news communicated,* in which sense the apostles have adopted it. Plutarch in the life of Artaxerxes, plainly speaks of the reward of *the gospel* or *good news,* for to

(i) 1 Cor. ii. 14. John iii. 5. John vi. 44. John xv. 5.

this the reference is obvious. In the life of Pompey, he says, ' the messengers arrived at Pontus bringing *the gospel*,' that is, *the good and joyful intelligence.* Cicero uses it in a similar sense in an epistle to Atticus.

" Let Christians then learn in the use of this term the delightful nature of this new doctrine, and consider the distinction between the Law and the Gospel. This is very clearly expressed by John, ' the law was given by Moses, but grace and truth came by Jesus Christ:' *(k)* the the distinction is between the commandments and the remission of sins, between gratuitous promises and those of a different description. The law requires perfect obedience to God, by which sins are not gratuitously pardoned, for we are not justified before God, or received into his favour according to its requirements unless we have entirely satisfied its demands. On the contrary, the gospel speaks of repentance and good works, and contains what is indeed its grand and characteristic doctrine, the promise of salvation through Jesus Christ.

" In Scripture therefore there are two kinds of promises ; the one attaches to the law and includes the condition of the law. For example ; the law proclaims the goodness and mercy of God, but it is to those who are sinless, and human reason inculcates a similar principle. Let every

(k) JOHN i. 17.

one reflect within himself and he will find that naturally he judges of God in the same manner, namely, that he is merciful, but only to the worthy and virtuous, that is, to those who are without sin ; and cannot be persuaded that they can please God when they are unholy and unworthy. So that as the law and its promises are conditional they leave the Conscience in a state of doubtful anxiety.

" The other description of promise is peculiar to the gospel not deriving its condition from the law, that is to say, not given upon the condition of fulfilling the law, but is gratuitously bestowed for the sake of Christ and includes the forgiveness of sin, reconciliation and justification before God. These blessings are certain, and not dependant on the condition of fulfilling the law ; for were we to suppose it necessary, in order to obtain the remission of sins to fulfil the law, we should justly despair. Hence these blessings are freely bestowed, and not as a reward for our worthiness or merit ; not however without a meritorious sacrifice on our behalf, for Christ gave himself for us as a propitiation for our sins, that for his sake we might be accepted of God.

Good Works.

" Five questions are proposed :—

1. What good works ought we to do ?—The reply is, summarily, not only external acts of

morality, but whatever is commanded by God and comprised within the decalogue.

2. How can we do them?—By the effectual aid of the Holy Spirit, who can enable us to render an internal and spiritual obedience—a service of *the heart* to God.

3. In what manner are our good works *acceptable* to God?—Christians are exceedingly desirous of this, but are at the same time deeply conscious of their imperfections, infirmities, and corruptions, as Paul says, ' the evil that I would not that I do.' *(l)* After admitting all this in the fullest extent, the reply is, that notwithstanding all the imperfection and infirmity of the Christian in the present state, and his incapacity to perform that perfect obedience which the divine law requires, he is nevertheless acceptable to God, for the sake of Christ the Mediator, who presents our prayers to the Father as our intercessor, and remits the infirmity and unworthiness of our services. Peter maintains this sentiment, ' offering spiritual sacrifices *acceptable to God by Jesus Christ.' (m)*

4. For what reasons ought we to perform good works? Many present themselves, arising *first*, out of the necessity of duty and the command of heaven, that we do not grieve the Holy Spirit and injure our own consciences or incur punishment; *secondly*, from a consideration of

(l) Rom. vii. 19.   *(m)* 1 Pet. ii. 5.

dignity ; not the dignity or merit of our works, but of our character and persons as servants of God ; the dignity of our vocation of which the apostle speaks, as the magistrate or minister ought to magnify his office, and to be loyal and diligent in the discharge of it ; *thirdly,* as an evidence and assurance of our reconciliation with God and the enjoyment of a gratuitous pardon through the love of his Son. Such as obey God have the promise of eternal life ; ' Godliness hath the promise of the life that now is and of that which is to come.' *(n)* The Scripture abounds with promises to believers, inclusive of temporal, spiritual, and eternal blessings.

5. What difference exists between the nature of different sins, since it is confessed there are remains of depravity in the most holy of Christians ?—Some kinds of sins are sins of infirmity only, sins which the regenerate person resists and abhors ; but others are sins *against conscience,* grace is forfeited, the Holy Spirit grieved, faith lost, that is, the confidence we ought to cherish in the mercy of God. The Apostle Paul says, ' If ye live after the flesh ye shall die, but if ye through the spirit do mortify the deeds of the body ye shall live,' that is, if ye obey wicked affections ye shall be exposed to the divine displeasure and to eternal death.

(n) 1 Tim. iv. 8.

It is said in the same chapter, ' As many as are
led by the Spirit of God they are the sons of
God;' but such as commit sin against their consciences, grieve and drive away the Spirit of
God, for they are no longer the children of God.
' Be not deceived, neither fornicators, nor ido-
laters, nor adulterers, nor effeminate . . . . . shall
inherit the kingdom of God.' John says, ' He
that committeth sin is of the devil.' (o)

THE KINGDOM OF CHRIST.

" The gospel plainly teaches us that the
kingdom of Christ is spiritual, that is to say,
Christ being seated at the right hand of the Father intercedes for us, pardons the sins of his
church, and bestows the Holy Spirit on those
who believe in him and approach God in his
name ; whom he sanctifies and will raise again
at the last day to everlasting life. And that we
may obtain these blessings, the ministry of the
gospel is appointed by which mankind are called
to the knowledge of Jesus Christ. But the true
church will always suffer persecution from the
wicked to the end of time, and in the church
itself the good and the evil will continue blended
together. It is necessary therefore to reject the
old Jewish error revived by the Anabaptists of
this age, that in the last times the church will
become a worldly empire in which Christians

(o) ROM. viii. 13, 14. 1 COR. vi. 9. 1 JOHN iii. 8.

will reign, destroying the wicked by force of arms, and seizing upon all the kingdoms and sovereignties of the earth.

PRAYER.

" There is an essential difference between genuine prayer as offered to God by his real church and the prayers of Pagans, Mahometans and Jews. This difference arises from two sources, the one respects the Essence of God of which they formed no just conceptions, and the other the means of acceptance with him, namely, by Jesus Christ the Mediator.

" This subject may be divided into five parts :—

1. In approaching God by prayer, it is requisite to consider WHO and WHAT HE IS to whom we address ourselves. Let us reflect there is no other God, and that from the very commencement of time he has manifested himself to his church by the word of his truth and the Son of his love, Christ our Mediator.

2. Let us remember that prayer is A COMMANDED DUTY. We are not to imagine that murder, theft, adultery, are the only sins ; it is one of the greatest of sins, not to render to God that service he demands, not to supplicate his throne, not to depend upon his aid in our necessities, and not to express our gratitude for the blessings we receive.

3. It is proper for a Christian to recur to THE PROMISES, that he may know that God hears and *why* he hears us, though we are unworthy and merit of ourselves the severest punishments.‡ The promises in their proper order include the remission of sins and reconciliation with God, the communication of all spiritual and all temporal blessings. Inexpressible kindness! Boundless mercy to the church! He commands us to ask mercies, and then adds an ample promise to encourage us to pray! But how surprising is the folly and weakness of the human heart, to draw back instead of approaching God! Nevertheless the innumerable examples and promises of Scripture excite us to dismiss our doubts, to approach God through his beloved Son, and not to imagine that his promises are as the Epicureans suppose, mere idle words. Surely the Divine Being has not given so many indubitable manifestations of himself for no purpose; he has not declared his will in vain; but would have our ignorance and our doubts removed by his word. Taulerus very justly remarks, ' that the mind of man is never so eagerly disposed to pray, but God is still more ready to give.'

4. It is necessary that FAITH should accompany supplication; for it is for the purpose of encreasing our faith that the promises are given. In reference to *spiritual blessings* which

God has expressly promised, as the remission
of sins, deliverance from the dominion of sin,
and from eternal death, the gift of the Holy
Spirit and eternal life, no condition is subjoined :
those who repent of their sins and believe in
Christ may rest assured of divine favour.   Faith
must also mingle with our request for *temporal
blessings;* and we must recollect three things—
first, that God is truly the source and dispenser of
these favours, that we do not possess them by
chance, that we cannot certainly secure them
by any personal exertion or diligence, they are
absolutely the gifts of God and of him we must
solicit life, protection, peace, tranquillity, prosperity in our different callings and bodily health.
Secondly, although it is the will of God that his
church and people should be subject to afflictions,
yet he will certainly bestow temporal good so far
as is requisite for their support and preservation.
Thirdly, it is the will of God that when we
request temporal blessings, our faith in the
great reconciliation should be exercised and
encreased.

    5. Let us RENEW AND REPEAT OUR RE-
QUESTS; for it is honourable to the character of
God to trust in him continually amidst our diversified afflictions, and to rely upon his hearing
those who supplicate his throne."

The transactions relating to the abolition of private Masses, constitute a very important part of the proceedings of this extraordinary year. It afforded the highest satisfaction to Luther in his retirement to find that the Augustinian Friars at Wittemberg had ventured upon an attempt to abolish the popish mode of celebrating private Masses; but the Elector felt some alarm, and deputed Pontanus, one of his counsellors, to remonstrate with the church and university upon their proceedings. Melancthon was chosen, with five others, Justus Jonas, John Doltz, Andrew Carlostadt, (p) Jerome Schurff, and Nicholas Amsdorff, to investigate the business; and in their report, they not only expressed their approbation of this zeal, but urged the Elector " to put an end to the popish Masses throughout

(p) He had three names, *Andrew Bodenstein Carlostadt*; and in allusion to his initials A, B, C, Melancthon frequently designated him by the term *Alphabet.* "Hic nihil est novi quæ de alphabeto scribis, nonnihil commoverunt. Vereor enim ne vir ille privatam contumeliam, quam putat ulturus novo scandalo causam evangelicam oneret." *Ep. ad Cam.* " Tuas literas longiores περὶ τᾶ ά, β, accepi." *Ep. p.* 2. It was no uncommon practice with Melancthon to amuse himself by punning upon names in his familiar letters : e. g. " Dux Georgius dicitur affuturus intra triduum adducens secum *Cochlæum*, qui paucis literis mutatis fiet avis κόλοιος, de quo genere nobis scripsisti quàm suaviter in tuâ viciniâ rhetoricentur. Et ut intelligas neutiquam vanum esse *Eckius* qui geminatus reddit vocem monedularum *Ekekekel* magnum acervum conclusionum congessit." *Ep. ad Luth. Lib. I. 3.*

P

his whole territory, and not to be deterred by the reproaches of those who would brand him with the name of *Heretic*, or *Hussite*: this Christ required of the Elector, whose mind he had enlightened with the knowledge of the Truth above all other Princes." The Elector directed Professor Bayer to return an answer, importing, that he was desirous of acting like a Christian Prince, for the glory of God and the establishment of his gospel, but that he thought nothing ought to be done with precipitation; that the truth would be discovered by others, and he might then undertake the change; and that as many churches and monasteries had been founded for the purpose of saying Masses, it should be considered whether upon their abolition their revenues might not be withheld—but that he was only a layman, he desired them to consult with the rulers of the church and university, that every thing might be peaceably settled."

To this they replied in a manner worthy of themselves and of the noble cause in which they were engaged, stating that " they adhered to their former opinion given against private Masses, that they could be abolished as they believed without tumult or scandal ; but if not they were instructed by Christ to *let them alone, for they are blind leaders of the blind;* and by the apostles to *obey God rather than men.* From the beginning of the world it had always been found that a small proportion of mankind acknowledged the truth, and according to the testimony of Christ himself, the gospel was to be preached to the weak, the few, the despised, and the unlearned; so that it was not surprising that Priests and the wise of this world apprehensive of losing their power, dignity, and other advantages, should not admit the preaching of the truth, or consent to wise and pious changes, unless they were likely to become sources of emolument to themselves. The ancient colleges and monasteries were founded not for the purpose of saying Masses, but for the instruction of youth and the support of the poor: and that even to the time of Augustine and Bernard. These institutions were only appropriated to Masses within these three or four hundred years, and for the Dead scarcely two hundred. Still they ought to be abolished as errors, even though they could boast of great antiquity. Besides, the very principle on which Masses are celebrated is sinful, namely, that they are good works, or sacrifices, or satisfactions for sin. It appeared that even to the time of Cyprian it was the custom of receiving the Sacrament in *both kinds*, and that this practice prevails even to the present day in Greece and the Eastern churches. It was not therefore their fault if tumult should arise ; but *they* were to be censured, who, to keep up their dignity, their income, and their luxury, continue to obstruct the light of truth, and cruelly wage war against the altars of God.   Christ predicted and his apostles experienced that the gospel was a *stone of stumbling, and a rock of offence.*   The Christian rule was neither to regard the madness of the enemy, nor the greatness of the danger.   Christ was not silent, though he foresaw the preaching of the gospel would be attended with discord, seditions, and the revolution of kingdoms; nor were his apostles less strenuous in instructing the people, because the wise men of the world detested the very name of the gospel, looking upon it as the firebrand of those disturbances, schisms, and tumults, which raged amongst the Jews at Jerusalem."   The result of these communications was, that though the timid Elector refused to give them a public sanction, he connived at these innovations. *(q)*

The life of Leo **X.** terminated with the closing year.

(q) Seckend. Hist. Luth. Lib. I. p. 216.

CHAP. VI.

....

....

The Anabaptists—Disturbances of Carlostadt—Luther's return to Wittemberg—Account of his German version of the Scriptures, with the assistance of Melancthon and others—Luther's conference with Stubner—His letter of Apology for stealing Melancthon's MS. Copy of his Commentary on the Romans—Extracts from that Commentary—Progress of the Reformation— Rise of the Sacramental Controversy — Death of Muncer—Melancthon's excursion in Germany—Death of Mosellanus—His Epitaph—Melancthon's introduction to the Landgrave of Hesse—Death of Nesenus—His Epitaph—Death of Frederic the Wise— Translated extracts from Melancthon's Funeral Oration—His Epitaph—Luther's Marriage—Controversy with Erasmus—Melancthon's visits to Nuremberg to found an Academy—Translated extracts of his Oration at the opening of the Institution—Publications.

FANATICISM soon made her unwelcome appearance in this season of religious commotion. In the spring of 1522, Nicholas Storck, Martin Cellarius, and Mark Stubner, who had been for some time engaged with the notorious Muncer in propagating the wildest sentiments at Zwickau, in Misnia, came to Wittemberg. The former was a baker, and a zealous leader of this enthusiastic band. They had harangued the populace in the church of St. Catharine, and pretending to enjoy visions and inspirations from heaven, acquired a very considerable ascendancy over the minds of an ignorant populace. Storck imagined he had seen an angel in a vision, who amongst other things, said he would be elevated to Gabriel's seat, from which Storck supposed that he was to become the head of a new empire. *(r)*

These persons have been usually designated by the term ANABAPTISTS, on account of their denying the validity of infant baptism; a name sufficiently vague and inappropriate, as this sentiment, even if it were acknowledged to be erroneous, cannot with any candour be classed amongst their *fanatical* opinions. This epithet is deduced from their representing the office of magistracy as subversive of their spiritual liberty, affirming that civil distinctions, such as rank birth and opulence confer, ought to be abolished, that Christians may enjoy all things in common ; and maintaining that they were favoured with visions and revelations from heaven. They

(r) MELANC. Ep. Lib. IV. 17. *ad Joach. Camerar,* VAN DE CORPUT Leven ende Dood Phil. Mel. p. 15.

branched out into various subdivisions, and some of them approached very nearly to the sentiments of modern Sandemanians. *(s)*

Although it was one of their principles to explode human science, Mark Stubner was a man of some learning, having been a student at the University of Wittemberg. *(t)*   Melancthon, with his characteristic goodness, received and treated him with the utmost hospitality, patiently investigated his pretensions, and scrupulously avoided any precipitancy in his decisions.   The state of his mind is obvious from a letter which at this critical juncture he addressed to the Elector.   " Your Highness is aware of the great and dangerous dissentions about religion which have distracted your city of Zwickau.   Some have been imprisoned for their innovations, and three of the leaders have fled hither, two of them ignorant weavers, the third a man of learning.   I have heard their statements; and it is astonishing what they relate of themselves as commissioned from heaven to teach; as having a familiar intercourse with God, and able to foresee future events; in a word, as having the authority of prophets and

(s) Comp. HOORNBEECK Summa Controversiarum Religionis Art.   *De Anabaptismo.*

(t) CAM. Vit. Mel.   Dr. Robertson follows Dupin in asserting that some of these pretenders had been disciples of Luther, but of this there is no evidence.

apostles.   How much I am struck with this
language it is not easy for me to say; but certainly I see great reason not to despise them, for
they have many arguments to adduce, and something of an extraordinary spirit about them, but
no one can judge so well upon the subject as
Martin Luther.   For the peace and glory of the
church, therefore, he should have an opportunity of examining these men, especially as
they appeal to him."

The Elector immediately had recourse to
his most confidential counsellors, who, being
unable to come to a decision, Melancthon continued to urge the necessity of obtaining Luther's sentiments, stating that Storck and his
associates had raised disputes concerning the
baptism of infants, and had appealed to divine
revelations ; and that for his own part he could
not positively pronounce upon the merit of the
case.   The Elector alleged, that were he to
recal Luther it would endanger his life, and advised Melancthon to avoid disputes with those
fanatics; but in the mean time if he knew what
justice required, he was ready to discharge his
duty.   Spalatine, who was present in the council, has recorded these memorable words which
the Elector pronounced in a manner that produced the deepest impression upon the whole
assembly of ministers and counsellors, and
which, he remarks, were expressive of his views

to the very last day of his life.—" This is a most
weighty and difficult affair, which I as a layman
do not profess to understand. God has given to
me and my brother considerable wealth; but if
I could obtain a right understanding of the matter, I declare I would rather take my staff in my
hand and quit every thing I possess, than know-
ingly resist the will of God." Luther, in a
letter to Melancthon, expresses himself in a
very judicious manner. It was written on the
seventeenth of January. " In regard to these
prophets I cannot approve of your timidity,
though you are my superior both in capacity
and erudition. In the first place, when they
bear record of themselves they ought not to be
implicitly believed, but their spirits should be
tried, as John admonishes. You know Ga-
maliel's advice, but I have heard of nothing said
or done by them which Satan himself could not
imitate. I would have you examine whether
they can produce a proof of their commission,
for God never sent any one, not even his own
Son, who was not either properly called to the
office, or authorized by miracles. The ancient
prophets were legally appointed; and their mere
assertion of being called by a divine revelation is
not a sufficient warrant for receiving them, since
God did not even speak to Samuel but with the
authority of Eli. So much for their public character. You should also examine their private

spirit, whether they have experienced spiritual distresses and conflicts with death and hell, and the power of regeneration.   If you hear smooth, tranquil, and what they call *devout and religious raptures*, though they speak of being caught up into the third heavens, do not regard them, while the sign of the Son of Man is wanting, THE CROSS, the only touchstone of Christians, and the sure discerner of spirits."

In addition to the affair of Storck and his associates, Melancthon was exceedingly afflicted by another untoward circumstance.   At the very moment when union amongst themselves, and a vigilant discretion in all their proceedings was of the greatest importance, Carlostadt was guilty of excesses, which were not only disapproved by the other Reformers, but highly prejudicial to their cause.   He was heard to say, that " he wished to be as great a man and as much thought of as Luther;" for which he was properly reproved by Melancthon, who reminded him, " that such language could only proceed from a spirit of emulation, envy and pride." *(u)*   So long as he steadily pursued the great object of reforming the church from Popery by sound argument, and firm but Christian conduct, the other Reformers united to assist his efforts; but when motives of vanity, concurring

(u) SECKEND. Hist. Luth. Lib. I. p. 199.

with violence of temper, occasioned his zeal to degenerate into wild-fire and extravagance, they were compelled to discountenance him. But instead of being induced to correct his errors, he instantly aspired to become the leader of a turbulent mobility, whose minds he enflamed by popular harangues, and whom he encouraged to enter the great church of All Saints at Wittemberg, to break the crucifixes and images in pieces, and throw down the altars. Misled by a strange spirit of infatuation, he began to despise human learning, and to encourage the youths of the University to quit their studies. Yet with all this perversion of mind and impetuosity of conduct, which no remonstrances could check, it must be admitted that he held some important truths, particularly the real doctrine of the Sacrament, which the Lutherans misunderstood, and which afterwards occasioned violent controversies. And yet, even in maintaining acknowledged truth, his *manner* of doing it was equally disapproved by the gentle Melancthon and the impetuous Luther. The former, who was never addicted to exaggeration, represents him in a most unamiable light, as " a man of savage disposition of no genius and learning, or even common sense; as having plotted against the reputation of Luther out of revenge for his opposing his fanatical practises; but at the same time as possessing a very insinuating and plausible exterior, though unable to disguise his violent ambition, passion, and envy, for any long period." *(x)*

The state of Luther's mind during these transactions can be more easily imagined than expressed. Every day increased his anxieties, every occurrence excited fresh alarm. The foundations of that noble structure he had been so actively engaged in erecting seemed to be endangered. What could be done ?—Was he to remain at a distance from the scene of action at a period when his skill and heroism appeared peculiarly requisite; or, could he venture upon incurring the Elector's displeasure by a clandestine and unauthorized return ?—Restless with increasing impatience he determined to hazard every thing, and at length on the third of March 1522, hastened to Wittemberg. An apology for this proceeding was written to the Elector, pleading the urgent necessity of the case arising out of the existing irregularities; but in two other communications, the one a letter addressed to Melancthon and the other to Amsdorff, he assigns an additional reason for his return, namely, the assistance he wished to obtain from them and others in the translation of the Scriptures into the German language. *(y)*

For the purpose of engaging in this import-

(x) Ep. ad Fred. Mycon. in HOSPIN.
(y) ADAM. Vit. Germ. Theologorum, p. 123.

ant labour, Luther had devoted the previous summer to the study of Greek and Hebrew. His skill in German is universally admitted. Versions of a very inferior kind had been published at Nuremberg in the years 1477, 1483, 1490 and at Augsburg in 1518, which were not only ill calculated to attract public notice, but interdicted from being read. The gospels of Matthew and Mark were first published by Luther, then the Epistle to the Romans and the other books in succession, till the whole New Testament was circulated by the month of September. In a letter which Melancthon addressed to the celebrated physician George Sturciad, dated the fifth of May 1522, he speaks of the whole version being in the hands of the printers. The essential assistance he rendered in completing the work is likewise apparent, for he states that he had paid particular attention to the different kinds of money mentioned in the New Testament, and had consulted with many learned men that the version might express them with the utmost accuracy. He begs his correspondent to give his opinion, and to consult Mutianus as being profoundly skilled in the knowledge of Roman antiquities. He entreats him to attend to his application from a regard to the general good, and to do it immediately because the work was in the press and printing with great expedition. " I wait your

reply," he adds, " with the utmost anxiety, and
I beseech 'you for faith, love and kindness' sake,
and every other urgent consideration not to disap-
point us." *(z)*

The difficulties of the undertaking particularly pressed upon Luther when he proceeded to
the translation of the Old Testament, but he
persevered with indefatigable zeal. It appears
that Melancthon was deeply engaged in revising
this important work for his friend two months
previous to his return. *(a)*

The utmost pains were taken to ensure the
accuracy of the translation, for a select party of
learned men at Wittemberg assembled every day
with Luther to revise every sentence ; and they
have been known to return *fourteen successive
days, to the reconsideration of a single line or
even a word.*   Each had an appropriate part assigned him according to his peculiar qualification.   Luther collated the ancient Latin versions'
and the Hebrew, Melancthon the Greek original,
Cruciger the Chaldee, and other professors the
Rabbinical writings.   At the request of Luther,
Spalatine afforded them every assistance, by
sending them specimens from the Elector's col-

(z) MELANCTH. Ep. I. *ad Geo. Sturciadem Erphordiæ.*
(a) " Vetus Testamentum cuditur, in quo recognoscendo
modò nonnihil negotii nobis fit." MELANCTH. Ep. Lib. IV.
1. *ad Joach. Camerar.*

lection of gems. *(b)* The Pentateuch went to press in December, and a second edition of the New Testament appeared at the same time. A Version of the Prophets was published in the year 1527, and the other books in succession till the whole laborious task was completed in 1530. He states how much he was indebted to his particular friend in writing to Spalatinus. " I translated not only the gospel of John, but the whole New Testament in my Patmos, but Melancthon and I have begun to revise the whole, and by the blessing of God it will prove a noble labour, but your assistance is sometimes requisite to suggest apt words and turns of expression. We wish it to be distinguished for simplicity of style." The whole was republished in a new edition in 1534, which was followed by others in 1541 and 1545. The names of Luther's principal coadjutors in this great undertaking ought to be had in everlasting remembrance—PHILIP MELANCTHON, CASPAR CRUCIGER, JUSTUS JONAS, JOHN BUGENHAGIUS or POMERANUS, and MATTHEW AUROGALLUS: the corrector of the press was GEORGE RORARIUS. *(c)*

After completing this translation of the

(b) SECKEND. Hist. Luth. Lib. I. p. 204. ADAM. Vit. Germ. Theologorum, p. 160. " Sæpè ut ipsemet fassus cum *Philippo, Aurogallo, aliis* totos quatuordecim dies in interpretatione unius voculæ aut lineolæ hæsit."

(c) SECKEND. Hist. Luth. Lib. I. p. 204.

Scriptures into the German language, Bugenhagius annually kept the return of the day on
which it was finished, by inviting a select party
of friends to his house in order to celebrate so
important an achievement. This social meeting
was usually designated THE FESTIVAL OF THE
TRANSLATION OF THE SCRIPTURES. *(d)*

To the fastidious we must leave it to censure the desire which may probably glow, at
least for a moment, in many a bosom, to have
been contemporary with these benevolent spirits,
to have shared their noble labour, and to have
annually participated in their pious conviviali-
ties. Never was a festive board more nobly
surrounded or more religiously devoted—never
did a more splendid occasion of holy triumph
present itself. Germany had already hailed her
Reformers, heard their discourses and witnessed
their progress with mingled emotions of fear and
satisfaction ;—already was she deeply indebted
to them for a series of disinterested efforts to
deliver her from the abject slavery in which superstition and tyranny had combined to chain her
down during past ages ; but a new obligation of
far greater extent was incurred by their furnishing to every man the means of the most direct
acquaintance with divine communications
through his vernacular language. Nor was

(d) ADAM. Vit. Germ. Theologorum, p. 318. *in Vit.
Joan. Bugenhagii.*

the mere accomplishment of this difficult undertaking the only subject of generous exultation
to these eminent men, every year and almost
every day exhibited great and good effects resulting from their labour.   " The different parts
of this translation," observes a learned historian,
" being successively and gradually spread abroad
among the people, produced sudden and almost
incredible effects, and extirpated root and
branch, the erroneous principles and superstitious doctrines of the church of Rome, from
the minds of a prodigious number of persons." (e)

Let us pause for a moment to reflect on
the wonderful concatenation of a few past
events by the invisible but efficacious agency
of a superintending Providence.   Leo X. had
issued a Bull against Luther which totally
failed of its object; the Pope exasperated at
witnessing his own impotency, appealed to
Charles V. newly promoted to the empire upon
the death of Maximilian I. to inflict exemplary vengeance upon his heretical subject;
Charles being under personal obligations to
Frederic Elector of Saxony, who had materially
assisted his advancement in opposition to his
rival Francis I. King of France, was disposed
to concede to his wishes by refraining from the

(e) MOSHEIM's Eccles. Hist. Vol. IV. p. 60, 8vo.

Q

publication of a condemnatory edict, but, not to
offend the Pope, he resolved to summon Luther
to the diet of Worms as a previous and pru-
dential measure : at Worms he appeared, where
he breathed the spirit of an apostle and exhibited the heroism of a martyr; but he was
declared an enemy to the holy Roman empire
and became instantly exposed to its vengeance.
At this crisis Frederic screened him from the
storm, by a friendly seizure and imprisonment
at the Castle of Wartenberg, *by which means*,
while his sudden disappearance operated to the
benefit of the reformed cause, by exasperating
the minds of men against the Roman See for a
supposed violation of its promise of security,
his confinement furnished him with leisure
which even had his life been spared, he could
not otherwise have enjoyed at such a turbulent
moment, for prosecuting the study of original
languages, and preparing for the translation of
the holy Scriptures into the vernacular language
of Germany. While his enemies and country-
men thought him dead and his particular
friends lamented his absence, trembled for his
safety, and mourned over the calamitous circumstances in which they became involved,
the Providence of God had unexpectedly
and at the fittest moment set him about a work
in the forests of Thuringia, which was hereafter

to gladden the hearts of Germany and more than any other circumstance to promote the Reformation. Amidst a universal pause of wonder and apprehension, God was mysteriously and secretly operating his own great purposes!

It was to be expected that the Catholics should endeavour to disparage the version of Luther, and yet Maimbourg confesses it was elegant and very generally read, although Jerome Emser one of the counsellors of Duke George of persecuting notoriety, and Cochlæus, attacked it in terms of bitter reproach. The former under the patronage of his master, published what he called a correct translation of the New Testament in opposition to it, and which as it consisted of little else than a republication of Luther's very version almost verbatim, but with a *Preface of his own,* was in reality the highest compliment he could have paid to his antagonist and the most effectual condemnation of himself. The result however of this animosity was most gratifying to every pious mind, Luther's version was read even in the pages of his adversary; and he expresses himself upon the occasion in language which strikingly illustrates his character, " There is a just judge who will see to this. The best revenge which I can wish for is that though *Luther's* NAME is suppressed, and that of his adversary put in its place, yet

Luther's BOOK is read, and thus the design of his labours is promoted by his very enemies."*(f)*

This German translation of the Scriptures was proscribed by an Edict of Ferdinand, Archduke of Austria, the Emperor's brother, forbidding the subjects of his Imperial Majesty to have any copy of it in their possession. The same interdiction extended to all his writings. Several princes issued similar prohibitions, among whom we can feel no surprize at discovering Duke George, but with what kind of *effect*—such as are acquainted with the history of persecution may easily conjecture. *(g)*

(f) The learned reader may find a complete vindication of Luther's Version, against the cavilling criticisms of Cochlæus and Emser in SECKEND. Hist. Luth. Lib. I. Sect. 127 and *add*. 1.

(g) The particularity of detail into which it has been deemed proper to digress upon this subject, will be more than justified by the reader from a consideration of the interesting nature of these facts in themselves, the great importance of the work achieved and the extensive exertions of Christian benevolence in a similar way at this moment by the British nation. The circulation of the Holy Scriptures is justly deemed an object worthy the utmost efforts of the most expansive philanthropy and the most assiduous zeal, and while competent men are stationed in different parts of the world to translate the inspired volume into the respective dialects of various tribes and nations whose very name was scarcely heard of before, princes and peasants, rich and poor, young and aged are concurring to

Soon after his return from the Castle of Wartenberg, Luther consented to hold a conference in the presence of Melancthon with some of the chief fanatical pretenders to prophetic inspiration before mentioned.   Mark Stubner, Cellarius and another, met the Reformer and his friend on this occasion.   Stubner related his visions and inspirations to very patient hearers, and when he had finished Luther coolly replied, " that nothing he had said was supported by the authority of Scripture, but seemed to result from a deluded imagination, or the suggestions of some evil spirit."   This enraged Cellarius, who with the voice and gesticulations of a madman, stamping the ground and beating the table, exclaimed against the audacity of Luther for insinuating such things against so *divine* a person ! Stubner, however, was more composed, possibly fancying himself in a *tranquil and devout rap-*

support by their voluntary liberalities the necessary expenditure.

I cannot dismiss this subject without informing the reader that, besides a valuable collection of other literary and classical remains, *James Edwards, Esq. of Manor House, Harrow-on-the-Hill,* has in his possession Luther's OWN COPY of his own German Version of the Scriptures.   To this gentleman I beg to express my public acknowledgements not only for pointing out this invaluable curiosity, but allowing me to transcribe some of the original writing of *Luther, Bugenhagius,* and *Melancthon,* by whose autographs in the blank pages it is fully authenticated.   One page is also occupied by *George Major.* Vide Appendix V.

ture. (h) " Luther," says he, " I will give you a proof that I am influenced by the Spirit of God, by revealing your own thoughts. *You are at this moment inclining to believe in the truth of my doctrine.*" The prophet however was mistaken, for Luther afterwards affirmed he was thinking of that sentence, " the Lord rebuke thee, Satan ;" and he very soon dismissed them with these words, " The God whom I love and serve will confound your impotent pretensions." They retired full of self-sufficiency, pouring out execrations upon Luther and promising what mighty things they would do to demonstrate the reality of their commission. They left Wittemberg the same day. *(i)*

A genuine FANATIC is one of the most pitiable objects in creation; a compound of ignorance and enthusaism. Enflamed with self-importance he mistakes the conceits of his own disordered imagination for the dictates of inspiration, and fancies his intercourse with the Deity to be of a sublimer nature than that of his inferior fellow mortals. He believes himself gifted above others, destined to move in a higher sphere, to walk in the precincts of heaven, to hold an immediate connexion with the Divine Spirit, which elevates him above the laws and ordinances, the instructions and the guidance of

(h) Vide p. 118.   *(i)* CAM. Vit. Mel. p. 51, 52.

Scripture. But surely nothing can be more degrading to reason than such absurdities, nothing
more disparaging to religion. The mischief such
a person is calculated to do results from this circumstance, that he denominates passion by the
sacred name of religion ; a passion which, heat-
ed to intemperance and kindling into the ardours
of rapture, spurns at reason, and substitutes a
man's own fancy and good opinion of himself
for the true foundation of piety. When such
sentiments as these prevail, it is impossible to
calculate or to conjecture the monstrous excesses into which they may precipitate the ignorant classes of mankind, who are soon attracted by plausible however ridiculous novelties.
But genuine religion and wild fanaticism are
perfect antipodes ; and intelligent persons, of an
observing cast of mind, will always look upon
the latter as a beacon to warn them away from
the dangers attending *any* deviation from the
plain course of scriptural instruction.

Should any be disposed to censure the conduct of Melancthon for that extreme leniency
which he manifested to Storck and his associates from Zwickau, be it recollected, that
though Luther's zeal charged him with undue
timidity, a word which both he and historians after him have applied with great incaution, several extenuating circumstances must
not be overlooked. Stubner being a man of

learning, and probably of some address, **and** knowing the importance of obtaining if possible the influence of Melancthon, probably resorted to every insinuating method to gain his support, disclosing his sentiments only in a very gradual manner.   The real goodness and amiable temper for which Melancthon was so remarkable, predisposed him to judge favourably of others, especially if they were professedly in pursuit of Truth.   He was himself a diligent and patient inquirer.   It was a period of religious discovery, and he daily felt he had much to learn.   The very extravagancies of these prophets were not more abhorrent to the present views of the Reformers, than the tenets of Lutheranism were to the mind of Luther himself at a former and not very remote period of his life.   Every impartial person must perceive what many transactions hereafter to be recorded will fully prove, that the hesitation of Melancthon in deciding upon new subjects or in difficult cases, which seemed to require a promptitude of action, resulted not so much from *timidity*, as from *conscientious scruples of mind*.   It was not that he feared temporal, but moral consequences ; and though Luther may be excused in a period when the mind was habitually kept warm and irascible by controversy, for using such an epithet; those who are solicitous of forming a correct idea of him will rather deem it

slanderous than descriptive to call him the *timid*
Melancthon.   If, after all, his first treatment of
Storck and his associates be considered as an
unwarrantable excess of candour, his language
became more decided as his convictions of their
delusion and misconduct increased: *(k)* and if
this be a shade in his character, it is otherwise
so bright that the admitted imperfection will
not materially obscure it; and the biographer can
feel no very powerful temptation where such a
splendour of excellence is discernible, to become
the labored apologist. *(l)*

Luther, besides many useful tracts of his
own, having secretly taken from Melancthon a
manuscript Commentary on *the Epistle of Paul
to the Romans*, printed it without his knowledge.   It was afterwards published in the year
1540, with a dedication to Philip, landgrave of
Hesse.   Luther's apology for this proceeding
is curious and characteristic.   It is prefixed to
the Commentary of his friend.

" Martin Luther to Philip Melancthon,
grace and peace in Christ.

" ' Be angry and sin not: commune with
your own heart upon your bed and be still.'—I

(k) Vid. MELANCTH. Epistolæ, *passim.*

(l) Whoever wishes for further information respecting
the enthusiasts above referred to, may consult HOORNBELCK
Summa Controversiarum Religionis.—SPANHEMII Orig. Prog.
Sect. & Nom. Anabaptistarum.—BAYLE Dict. Hist. & Crit.
Art. *Anabaptistes*—Notes (C) and (K), in which most of the
principal works written on the subject are mentioned.

am the person who dares to publish your Annotations, and I send you your own work. *(m)* If you are not pleased with it, it may be all very well, it is sufficient that you please us. If I have done wrong, *you* are to blame; why did not you publish it yourself? why did you suffer me so often to ask, to insist, to importune you to publish it, and all in vain?—So much for my apology *against* you; for you see I am willing to turn thief, and am not afraid of your future accusations or complaints. As to those whom you suspect of being disposed to sneer, I have this to say to them—' *Do better !'*—What the impious Thomists *falsely* arrogate to their leader, namely, that no one has written better upon St. Paul, I *truly* affirm of you. Satan himself influences them to boast in this manner concerning their Thomas Aquinas, and to spread his doctrines and his poison far and wide. `I know in what sort of spirit and with what correctness of judgment I pronounce this of you. If these famous and mighty men should choose to sneer at my opinion, the consequence belongs to me, not you. But I wish to vex these scorners more and more; and I say that the Commentaries of Jerome and Origen are mere trifles and follies compared to your Annotations. But what, you will say, is the purpose of aim-

(m) The Latin expresses it in a stronger manner, and with more of *pun* than our idiom will quite allow: " teipsum ad te mitto."

ing to provoke these great men against me?
Well—you may be humble if you please, but
let me boast for you.   Who has ever prohibited
persons of great capacity from publishing something better *if they can*—and thus demonstrating
the rashness of my judgment For my part, I
wish we could find out those who could and
would publish something better.   I threaten
you, further, to steal and publish your remarks
upon Genesis and the Gospels of Matthew and
John, unless you supersede me by bringing them
forward.   You say, Scripture ought to be read
alone and without a commentary; this is right
enough if you speak in reference to Jerome,
Origen, Thomas Aquinas, and others of the
same class, for their commentaries are the mere
vehicles of their own notions, rather than the
sentiments of Paul, and the doctrine of Christianity ; but no one can properly call yours
a commentary ; it is rather an introduction to
the study of scripture in general, and a guide to
the knowledge of Christ : in which it surpasses
all the Commentaries hitherto published.   As
to what you plead, that your Annotations are
not in all respects satisfactory to yourself, it is
difficult enough to believe you.   But behold I do
believe—you are not fully satisfied with yourself,
nor is this asked or desired of you : we would
have Paul maintain his preeminence, lest any
one should insinuate that Philip is superior or

equal to Paul. It is sufficient you are only second to Paul; but we shall not dislike any body for coming still nearer to this great original. We know very well that you are nothing; and we know also that Christ is all and in all, who if he pleases can speak as he did to Balaam by an ass; why then should he not speak by a man? Art thou not a man? Art thou not a servant of Christ? Has not he endowed thee with capacity? If thou shouldest choose to improve and enlarge this volume by elegant and learned additions, it will be a grateful service; but in the mean time we are determined to be gratified in spite of you, by possessing ourselves of the sentiments of Paul by your means. If I have offended you by this proceeding, I do not ask pardon; but lay aside your displeasure, by which you will rather give offence to *us*, and *you* will have to ask forgiveness. God preserve and prosper you for evermore. *Wittemberg*, July 29, 1522."

If Luther did not ask pardon for publishing Melancthon's Annotations on the Epistle of Paul to the Romans without his consent, the reader will not demand an apology for inserting some extracts from this valuable performance.

"CHAP. I. *v.* 1.—' *Paul......separated unto the gospel of God.*' Here the apostle states the business he was commanded to execute, namely, to preach the gospel. The reader

should remember that there is a material difference between the law and the gospel, to which
we have already adverted, and of which more
will be said in remarking upon the third chapter. The description which he gives of the
gospel is, that it is a divine promise communicated in the sacred writings, concerning Jesus
Christ the Son of God, of the seed of David according to the flesh, declared to be the Son of
God with power, through sanctification of the
Spirit, and resurrection from the dead : that he
is the Messiah or King, by whom deliverance
from sin and eternal life are dispensed.

" This description will be more obvious
by noticing the contradistinction between law
and gospel. The LAW represents what we are,
and what we are required to do. It demands
perfect obedience, without providing for the
forgiveness of sin, or liberating us from the power
of sin and death ; but rather arming sin against
us, by accusing transgressors, and alarming them
with the terrors of death. But the GOSPEL
freely promises the remission of sin and deliverance from death, by Jesus the Son of God, who
was descended from David according to the prophetic declarations. Paul states this at the
outset of his discourse, that we might know his
meaning, and distinguish properly between the
law and the gospel ; as though he had said,

' Paul divinely called to teach the gospel of
Christ; not to teach the law or to teach philosophy.'

"*V.* 3, 4.—' *Concerning his Son Jesus Christ
our Lord, &c.*" In this phrase he opposes the
vulgar notions of the Jews, who expected a
Messiah that would be—not *the Son of God by
his own nature,* but only *a man like the other
prophets,* though surpassing them in wisdom,
virtue, and capacity to obtain and govern the
whole world.   But the patriarchs and prophets
knew their Messiah to be the *Son of God,* who
was at that period their governor and their guide.
Jacob said, ' The Angel who delivered me out
of all evil bless the lads,' speaking of the deli-
verer whom he knew to be promised, and whose
proper office is to deliver out of all evil.   Jacob,
Moses, Daniel saw him by faith, and John
testifies that the Messiah was the Son of
God, and constantly present with the patriarchs.
' In the beginning,' says he, ' was the Word,
. . . . all things were made by him,'—referring to
those illustrious victories over the devil which
this glorious leader and captain enabled Noah,
Abraham, Joseph, Moses, Samuel, David, Isaiah, and Jeremiah to obtain.

"The term ὁρισϑέντος, which the Greeks explain
by another, ἀποδειχθέντος, is singularly emphatical,
and it refers to the manifestation of the Son of

God, as having risen from the dead, and as possessed of inconceiveable power, evinced by numerous miracles.

" The verb ὁρίζεσθαι, signifies to be certainly
proclaimed ; in opposition to the opinions of the
Jews, who expected a Messiah to be an extraordinary man indeed, but only a man, distinguished by heroic achievements, and who should
bestow riches, but not a *new nature and eternal
life.* But Paul says this Messiah would be powerful, and would give that holy Spirit by which
new light, justification and eternal life would be
dispensed, and the devil vanquished. This he
calls a real deliverance, which our forefathers
both understood and experienced in the various
trials of their faith, their dangers, and their conflicts with Satan and with death. And how
much greater is this deliverance than that which
some anticipate in the appearance of a Messiah,
who like Alexander is to divide kingdoms and
provinces amongst his soldiers.

" *V. 7.*—' *Grace to you and peace from God
our Father, and the Lord Jesus Christ.*' He
unites God the Father and the Lord Jesus Christ,
for three reasons ; namely, to intimate, that grace
and other divine blessings are dispensed by God
through his Son the Mediator—that if we enjoy
these mercies, it must be by praying for them
through the Son—and that Christ is by his nature God, equal in power with the Father, and ca-

pable of affording us every requisite assistance
by his own divine energy.

" *V.* 17.—' *The just shall live by faith*'. You
will observe that two important benefits are
attributed to faith—that we are *justified*, and
that we *live* by it. God sent his own Son into
the world to be our propitiation, lest we should
perish, as he says with an oath, ' As I live
saith the Lord, I have no pleasure in the death
of a sinner, but rather that he should be converted and live.' To the terrified conscience he
proclaims the forgiveness of sin by faith, that its
fears may be removed, and genuine consolation
imparted, which is the very commencement of
eternal life ; for ' this,' said Christ, ' is eternal
life, to know thee the only true God, and Jesus
Christ whom thou hast sent.' We know therefore that the gift of the Holy Spirit is joined with
the remission of sins, and reconciliation with
God ; we know that the dominion of Christ in
the church is not indolent, but his presence is
constantly with us to destroy the works of the
devil, to fight our battles, and to assist our progress ; these ideas are included when the prophet promises *life*, that is, joy, victory, and everlasting salvation to all believers.

" Chap. V. *v.* 2.—' *We rejoice in hope of the
glory of God*.' It may be asked, what is the
value of this justification and deliverance from
sin and death, when sin still adheres to us, and

we continue obnoxious to death, and all the
various afflictions incident to human life? In
what respects are Christians happier than others?
for Christians are often derided for speaking
about deliverance from sin and death, when they
are equally with other men exposed to calamities. Saints themselves are often ready to
acknowledge their infirmities, and are agitated
with doubts whether if God really delighted in
them, they should be the subjects of such infirmity; and this is no trifling temptation, because when faith realizes, according to the Scriptures, that God is propitious through Jesus
Christ, our weakness expects to see this kindness in some manner visibly displayed. So the
Anabaptists despise the doctrine of faith, and
affirm that we are to seek for celestial visions;
and there are others who dream they have already perfectly obeyed, and are acceptable to
God, as having satisfied the claims of his law,
and being without sin.

     " Paul therefore opposes each of these. He
administers consolation to those who acknowledge their infirmities, and commands them to
rejoice, but with hope; and to consider that
they shall enjoy the glory of eternal life, which
though not at present revealed, shall certainly be
bestowed. On which account it became them
to acquiesce, and not to doubt or despair, though
they were at present exposed to infirmities.

R

He directs them to rejoice *in hope*, that is, they are not to suppose that this perfection of nature and enjoyment is now to be attained, nor are they to expect any new manifestations from heaven, but to stand fast in the truth of Scripture, and aim to please God by faith in Christ, considering that a present perfection in this sinful state is not to be expected.

" The sentiment therefore is, that although the world, and even our own reason, may determine that we do not yet possess glory, or complete emancipation from sin and death, yet we rejoice, that is, we indulge the hope of that glory with which God will eventually distinguish us. We cleave to this hope, for it is not falacious.

" *V. 3.*—' *And not only so, but we glory in tribulation also,*' &c. He as it were corrects the former statement. We have not only a glory in expectation, but in present possession ; and what is it? *Affliction.* He is opposing the opinions and reasonings of the world.

" In the view of the world we are afflicted: we seem abandoned and rejected by God; and this reproach upon the gospel deters the generality of mankind from embracing it. This mode of reasoning indeed seems legitimate enough— afflictions are curses, that is, evils: and therefore signs of God's displeasure. But Paul on the contrary assures us that they are not curses, but are proper occasions of glorying; for they are not signs of the divine displeasure, but intimations of the love of God.

" We have then a double glory—the one which is the greatest is in expectation, consisting in the renovation of our nature, and the enjoyment of eternal life; but this glory we possess in hope : the other glory is in present possession, and it consists in affliction : for although the world judges that affliction is an evidence of divine anger, yet we know it to be an indication of his love; and obedience to his afflictive dispensations to be a new and acceptable kind of worship.

" Four things, therefore, ought to be well impressed upon our minds respecting afflictions:

" 1. They are appointed. We do not suffer affliction by chance, but by the determinate counsel and permission of God.

" 2. By means of affliction God punishes his people, not that he may destroy them, but to recal them to repentance, and the exercise of faith: for afflictions are not indications of displeasure, but of kindness—' He willeth not the death of a sinner.'

" 3. God requires our submission to his afflictive dispensations, and that we should expend our indignation and impatience upon our own sins; and as God determines to afflict his church in the present state, submission tends to glorify his name.

" 4. Resignation however is not all; he requires faith and prayer, that we may both seek and expect divine assistance. Thus he admonishes us, ' Call upon me in the day of trouble, I will answer thee, and thou shalt glorify me.'

" These four precepts are applicable to all our afflictions, and are calculated if properly regarded to produce that truly Christian patience which essentially differs from mere philosophical endurance.

" CHAP. VIII. *v.* 3.—' *God sending his own Son in the likeness of sinful flesh for sin condemned sin in the flesh.*' It is elsewhere stated, he was ' *Made sin for us.*' These words are peculiarly emphatical—Christ is represented as being *made sin* or a *sacrifice for sin :* it is a Hebrew form of expression, corresponding with the Latin term *piaculum* and the Greek κάθαρμα. A similar idea is conveyed in the use of the word *curse* or *anathema* and which signifies any thing devoted to punishment in order to propitiate the offended Deity. In this manner Isaiah speaks of Christ, ' thou didst make his soul a *sin,*' that is, an offering or sacrifice for sin : and Paul frequently inculcates the same sentiment in his second epistle and fifth chapter of the Corinthians, ' He who knew no sin was made *sin* for us,' that is,

an offering or *victim* who sustained the punishment of sin and satisfied the demands of justice
for us. In writing to the Galatians he suggests
a similar sentiment, ' Christ was made *a curse*,'
that is, *piaculum, a sacrifice*, sustaining the curse
and displeasure of God against sin.

" *V. 22.*—' *We know that the whole Creation
groaneth and travaileth in pain together until
now.*' This is an argument from the example of
the Creation. All things are subject to corruption and to the abuse of the wicked till the period
of deliverance, which therefore we expect.

" In this place Paul contemplates with
great emotion of mind the dreadful confusion
and corruption of human affairs, war, bloodshed, devastation and other evils prevalent in the
world. He contemplates the mighty power of
sin and the tyranny of Satan, and how degrading
it is that universal nature should be subjected to
the devil and to death in consequence of human
transgression.

" Here then in the first place is to be considered the feelings of Christians amidst their
afflictions. Delay is tormenting to the mind
and we are incapable of foreseeing the method of
deliverance. Troubles are daily increasing and
the truly pious are deeply afflicted to witness the
great dangers which surround the church of
Christ, and while its distresses multiply, its deliverance appears to be delayed.

" Whatever therefore may be the source of our grief, whether public or private, the apostle endeavours to impart consolation by referring us to the heavens and the earth, to the creation at large as subjected to the abuse of the wicked. Tyrants possess the dominion of empires—the impious enjoy the riches of the world, but the church of Christ for which all things were created, suffers martyrdom and is deprived of life, light and every other advantage. But these things were formed that they might be in subserviency to the saints for the glory of God, and as they are at present subjected to abuse and the power of corruption through the transgression of Adam, the creatures themselves wait for the promised deliverance."———

The Popish writers agree in lamenting the increase of Lutheranism during the years 1522 and 1523; its opponents, however, amongst whom George Duke of Saxony, Henry Duke of Brunswick, and Ferdinand Archduke of Austria may be considered the principal ones, were by no means asleep. The former, the most violent bigot of the day and the most inveterate enemy of Luther and the Reformation, used every means to influence Frederic and his brother John to adopt hostile measures : but their prudence frustrated his views in Saxony. The light spread rapidly in Europe, and Caspar Hedio,

Martin Bucer, and John Oecolampadius were diffusing it in Alsace and Switzerland.

Frederic however felt himself in a most critical situation. The Pope, Adrian VI. who had succeeded Leo X. had sent his legate Francis Cheregato to the Imperial Diet of Nuremberg, to demand the immediate execution of the sentence pronounced against Luther at the Diet of Worms. The Emperor concurred in his views and the Popish princes were evidently concerting measures to crush the Reformation. In this situation the Elector applied to Luther, Melancthon and Bugenhagius for their opinion on this question, " Is it lawful for your prince if his subjects should be attacked on account of religion by the Emperor, or any other ruler to protect them by arms?" To this they replied, " *it was not lawful*, chiefly because the princes were not yet convinced in their consciences of the truth of the reformed doctrine, neither had their subjects implored protection against violence, nor had the states of the provinces deliberated on the subject of war: above all, those who took up arms for their defence ought to be well satisfied of the justice of their cause." *(m)*

Clement VII. being elevated to the Papal Chair upon the decease of Adrian, selected Cardinal Campeggio a skilful negociator for his

(m) HORTLED. Hist. T. 1. Lib. II.

legate to the Imperial Diet at Nuremberg, where he arrived in the early part of the year 1524. He was commissioned to insist upon the princes uniting to execute the decree of Worms against Luther; and the Emperor gave similar instructions to his minister. After some debate it was resolved by the Diet that the Pope, with the consent of the Emperor, should at an early period summon a free council in Germany to deliberate upon the Lutheran affairs, and that in the meantime a Diet should be held at Spires to deliberate on the mode of proceeding. This of course did not satisfy Campeggio, and retiring to Ratisbon he held a private assembly with some of the princes and bishops of the empire, whom he engaged to resolve upon executing the decree of Worms. This unwarrantable procedure induced those who differed from Campeggio to pursue a measure of self-defence, by holding a similar Convention at Spires to confirm the decrees of Nuremberg.

At this period what has been called the *Sacramental controversy* originated. Carlostadt resolutely denied what Luther no less resolutely maintained the doctrine of *Consubstantiation*, or that the real body and blood of Christ were received together with the bread and the wine though they were not absolutely transubstantiated. This controversy divided the early friends of the Reformation, and long threatened the most serious consequences. The Reformers of Switzerland and many in Germany dissented from Luther and Melancthon, maintaining that the Lord's Supper was to be observed only as a commemoration of the death of Christ. It must be owned that *Consubstantiation* and *Transubstantiation* are as similar in nature as in name, and it would require good spectacles to discern any very essential difference between these two species of nonsense.

Carlostadt found it necessary to retire to Orlamund, and became the Pastor of the village in defiance of the right of appointment vested in the Elector and the University, where he not only railed against Luther's view of the Eucharist, but appears to have been hurried on by his violence of temper to very enthusiastical pretensions. He was at length expelled by the prince and his brother from their dominions, but afterwards recalled by the Elector John.

Carlostadt by raising mobs, pulling down images and railing against learning gave the final impulse to the fanaticism of Muncer, Storck and their associates. " It may be true," says Luther, " and candour may require me to believe that Carlostadt does not *intend* to promote sedition and murder, yet so long as he persists in raising headstrong mobs and exciting them to demolish statues with unauthorized violence, he possesses the same seditious sanguinary spirit that has

shewn itself at Alsted. How often has Melancthon in vain admonished him not to raise tumults
respecting ceremonies, and yet he has continued
to defend the breakers of the peace to the
last." (n)

These irregularities like a large tributary
stream, swelled the torrent of insurrection that
was at this moment rushing through the provinces of Germany. What has been termed *the
Rustic war* or *war of the Peasants* arose indeed
from the dissatisfaction of the lower classes with
the civil restraints and oppressions of their chiefs
which they *affirmed* to be no longer tolerable,
but it received an accession of strength and a character of fanaticism from the union of the Anabaptists, who hastened to wage war against their
lawful governors and the rights of civil society.
Muncer placed himself at their head, and was at
last taken and put to death after being defeated
by the confederate princes of Germany in a
pitched battle at Mulhausen in Thuringia. This
terminated the rebellion.

From public it is necessary to turn to more
private transactions. By the advice of his friends
who perceived it necessary to recruit his health
and spirits, Melancthon devoted part of the year
1524, to a journey on horseback to different
places in Germany. He was accompanied by
Nesenus and Camerarius, two intimate associates, the former distinguished for prudence,

(n) LUTH. cont. Proph.

knowledge and amiableness of disposition, the
latter who was afterwards his biographer for very
eminent literary attainments. Two youths, Burcardus and Silberbornerus, both of whom afterwards acquired a considerable reputation, attended them.

The travellers arrived at Leipsic the first
place of notoriety in their route, on the very day
when Peter Mosellanus, the Greek professor,
breathed his last. Melancthon and Camerarius
had just time to visit him, and mingle their tears
over his dying bed ; the former deplored a friend
and the latter a tutor. Mosellanus was a man of
erudition. He is praised by Erasmus as a wit
and a scholar ; and at his decease, which took
place at the early age of *thirty-one*, Melancthon
composed the following tribute to his memory.

Κεῖται τῷδε τάφῳ πέζος ποτάμοιο μοσελλα
   Τοὔνομ' ἔχων, ῥήτωρ ὃς ποτε ηδὶς ἔην
Τῷ μακρόν τε βίον γῆρας τε φθόνησε ποθεινὸν
   Αντὶ δὲ ἄσβεςον μοῖρ' απεδωκε κλέος
Πᾶς δὲ μινυθάδιος καὶ τειρεσία πέλετ' αιὼν
   Κρείτονος οὖν δώρε γῆρας ἄμειψε θεός.

Beneath this tomb that meets the stranger's eye
The dear remains of Mosellanus lie ;
In vain might friends protracted life implore,
The lovely rhetorician speaks no more ;
But in the records of eternal fame
Ages to come shall find inscrib'd his name,
While from this transient life of tears and sighs
God has removed him to yon fairer skies.

Melancthon and his friends proceeded from Leipsic across Upper Saxony to Fulda, where they heard of the death of the celebrated Ulric Hutten, an ingenious and learned man, but of a most waspish temper which was abundantly displayed in a book against Erasmus. Melancthon and Luther both disapproved his ferocious hostility. Though descended from a noble family of which he was sufficiently vain, he died in extreme poverty at Zurich.

After visiting Frankfort they remained some time with Melancthon's mother, who had married a second husband at Bretten. Parting at length most reluctantly from endeared relatives they reached Heidelberg, where the University received their former student with every mark of distinction and regard.

Upon their return not far from Frankfort they unexpectedly met Philip, the Langrave of Hesse on his way to Heidelberg. The Landgrave rode up to him intimating that he understood his name was Philip Melancthon; to which he replied in the affirmative, and alighting from his horse in token of respect to the illustrious stranger, he was requested to remount and turn back to spend the night with him. The prince assured him his intentions were not hostile, but simply to converse upon some particular topics. Melancthon replied in a suitable

manner and signified he entertained no apprehensions from the Landgrave. " But," said he,
smiling, " if I should deliver you into the hands
of Campeggio, I fancy he would think me doing
him a very grateful piece of service." On their
way, for Melancthon had turned back in com-
plaisance, the prince put a number of questions of a casual nature, which he answered briefly
and without entering into much explanation,
both on account of the unfitness of the time and
place and because the prince appeared to have
his thoughts occupied with other concerns. At
length he requested the prince's permission to
return and prosecute his journey which he
granted, stipulating that upon his arrival at
Wittemberg he should send him in writing his
deliberate opinion upon the subjects he had
referred to in his conversation. He also gave
him a safe conduct through his dominions.
This inquisitive disposition of the Landgrave
terminated in the happiest consequences, for he
soon became the decided supporter of the Reformation. His allusion to Campeggio was
sufficiently significant, for previous to this interview that subtle legate had sent to sound Melancthon upon the subject of coming over to the
Papal party, but was dismissed with the following spirited reply—that, " what he maintained
to be true and *knew* to be so, he did not embrace

or avow to gain the respect and favour of any living mortal, or from the hope of emolument or from any ambitious motives, nor would he cease to esteem and aid those who promoted it. In those exertions he had hitherto made for the knowledge and advancement of truth, he was determined in a spirit of meekness to persevere. Let all who are truly desirous of the general peace and safety of the community confer and co-operate to heal the wounds which cannot possibly be any longer concealed, and to restrain the fury of those who will not desist from tearing and fretting with their malicious nails the existing sores. If this be not done and the violent bigots still pursue their course, they may expect to be the first to suffer."

Soon after returning to Wittemberg Melancthon was plunged into the deepest affliction in consequence of the tragical death of Nesenus. He was lying at his ease in a fishing boat which he had hired as he frequently did for the purpose of recreation on the river Elbe, and which he had fastened to the trunk of a tree. The boat suddenly heaved about and whirled him into the water where he perished. The great men of the day were deeply affected by this fatal accident. Luther exclaimed in the transports of grief, " O that I had power to raise the dead !"—Micyllus by no means, says Seckendorf, a contemptible

poet of the day, honoured his memory with an
elegant epitaph. We insert a similar tribute
from the pen of Melancthon.

Ὡς τὸ βροτῶν γένος ἐς᾽ ἀν᾽εμώλιον ἠδ᾽ ἀμενηνὸν
Ω νέοι ὡς αἰὼν πᾶσιν ἄπιςος ἔνι.
Απροϊδὴς Θάναφς Νεσσηνὸν ἔμαρψε νέον περ
Αξενον ὃν ςυγερῦ ἀλϚιος οἴδμ᾽ ὄλεσε·

How vain and fleeting is the race of man ;—
And how uncertain when we yield our breath !
So sunk Nesenus 'neath the wave of death,
Nor knew the treacherous stream so near him ran.

It is known that Melancthon placed considerable confidence in dreams, and that both he
and Luther were addicted to astrology. In the
course of his late journey he expressed a presen-
timent of the death of one of the three fellow
travellers Camerarius, Nesenus, or himself, from
the occurrence of what he considered an ominous circumstance; and on the very day when
Nesenus was drowned, he often related to
those who were inclined to be jocose upon superstitious notions, that in his afterooon's nap
he saw in a dream every circumstance of his
friend's deplorable end. (o)

Another event of the present year was still
more afflictive. Henry von Zutphen, to whom
Melancthon and the whole University at Wittemberg was much attached on account of his

(o) CAM. Vit. Mel. p. 97.

wisdom, modesty and piety, had gone to preach
the reformed doctrines in Ditmars, a county of
Holstein in Denmark, the neighbouring priests
like tygers watching for their prey, instantly
sprung upon the victim and put him to death
by the most exquisite tortures. *(p)*

On the fifth of May 1525, FREDERIC,
ELECTOR OF SAXONY, surnamed the WISE,
departed this life. His death was peaceful and
pious, and as he was the early friend as well as
the constant protector of the reformed cause, it
was an event which could not fail of producing
a strong impression on the minds of Luther and
Melancthon. To them was entrusted the management of his funeral, which was conducted
in an unostentatious manner, omitting the superstitious practices which the Papists had been
accustomed to observe on similar occasions.
Luther delivered a short discourse in German
and Melancthon pronounced an oration in the
Latin language. From the latter the reader is
presented with the following extracts. *(q)*

" Amidst this public, universal and most
acute sorrow, in which the removal of one of the

(p) CAM. Vit. Mel.

(q) Seckendorf has detailed a variety of particulars respecting the will and last moments of the Elector, which it
would not comport with the plan of this work to insert, but
which will be interesting to peruse. Vide SECKEND. Hist.
Luth. Lib. II. Sect vi. p. 34.

wisest of princes, a loss so calamitous to this
state, is deplored, I feel myself scarcely possessed of sufficient presence of mind to attempt
by a formal oration to alleviate the affliction of
the nobles and the populace, with a voice too
so faultering with grief. Though the extraordinary virtues of this prince peculiarly deserve
the funeral honours which well constituted nations have always bestowed on their distinguished men ; I am deeply conscious that our
tears cannot express his superlative merits.
Deeply affected as I am with the loss of the
state which in a season of public commotion,
and amidst the universal darkness of the age required the light of his wisdom, private feelings
mingle with the general lamentation. I could
not but honour him while living and mourn him
when dead, not only for his signal virtues, but
for the innumerable favours of which I have been
the recipient. Incapacity of mind, however,
and excess of grief forbid a minute encomium
upon all his merits ; let these flowing tears and
this tremulous voice suffice to express the sin-
cerest feelings of a grateful heart.

" That this assembled multitude may form
a correct idea of how much they are indebted to
this prince, I propose slightly to allude to some
things worthy of praise and present as it were a
distant view of them ; and though I would by
no means assume so much as to hope that I shall

be able to cure the grief of those who are aware
of the magnitude of that calamity which the
state has sustained, yet I may at least assuage
their sorrow by reminding them of his virtues.

" This nation is highly indebted to the
higher orders for the advancement of sacred literature, and under Providence for the existence
of a prince, who as he was formed by nature
pacific, humane and merciful, so nothing was
more dear to him than the best interests of his
people. The Saxon princes are notorious for
their noble lineage, but Frederic was still more
illustrious for his knowledge of the science
of government and for genuine greatness of
mind. I am mistaken if any one was so mighty
in arms, and yet so anxious to render the employment of power subservient to the establishment of peace. He was just, gentle, firm, careful of the public welfare, diligent in ascertaining
the rights of others, and pacifying the contentions of fellow-citizens, patient toward the faults
of the people, aiming mildly to restore those
who were capable of amelioration, but severe in
punishing the wicked and incorrigible.

" The multitude I am aware are smit with
an admiration of heroic achievements and esteem
the soldier above the quiet citizen. The virtues
of domestic life are overlooked, and they who
cultivate peace and the arts acquire but a slender
praise. But I confess myself of a far different

opinion, for if you consider utility, if you remark the design of man's creation, peace is preferable to war. I cannot prefer the great but
warlike Anthony, to the peaceful Augustus,
nor admit that Alcibiades was of more service
to Greece than Solon, of whom the former ruined
his country by promoting eternal war, the latter
not only preserved but constituted it a great
state by furnishing it with ample laws. Frederic was formed to excel in the more useful and
therefore the superior virtues. It was for him
to preserve his people in peace amidst the most
turbulent times. Who will venture to compare
a victory with the more splendid achievement of
securing tranquillity during many years (more
than thirty) of commotion, while many envied
and many endeavoured to excite war. Believe
me the wisdom and the real fortitude of Frederic
were of no common cast, co-operating to overcome the impetuosity of anger, to spare the lives
of his subjects and to allay the violence of armed
hostility by reason, by counsel and even by purchase. When the friends of Pericles were enu-
merating his trophies and congratulating him
upon his victories, he replied, the praise did not
belong to *him* so much as to his *soldiers* or to
fortune, but he would claim this as his just distinction, *that no citizen through his means ever
put on mourning*—intimating that he had never
been guilty of any treacherous violence to ad-

vance his own dignity ; but our illustrious prince not only never revenged private injuries, but he made even war itself yield to reason and become subservient to spare the blood of his citizens.

" He possessed the greatest *private* virtues and a peculiar devotedness to the study of the *Christian religion.* He always treated sacred things with the utmost seriousness, and amidst the contrariety of opinions prevalent in the present age he diligently aimed to discover the best and most indubitable. Before the present period of reform, when human rites were appointed in the churches by pontifical authority, he ever preferred what was most conducive to morals ; and, because he felt persuaded that the common people were allured by these means to pay attention to religion he erected churches, devised ceremonies and exerted himself to procure teachers of sacred doctrine. Often would he confer with learned men on the nature and power of religion. These I consider proofs of a well disposed mind.

" When Christianity began to rise again as it were from the dead and to be purified from her corruptions he entirely devoted his mind to it, neither approving nor condemning any thing with precipitation. Wherever he saw the evidence of religious truth he embraced it with all his soul, and it became the means of establishing and nourishing his piety. He shunned insignificant disputes which did not conduce to edification; and when he observed certain impious men, upon pretence of enjoying evangelical liberty, debasing themselves and religion by a ferociousness of conduct and a contempt of public decency, he cautiously avoided giving them or others occasion of introducing rash changes through his example, perceiving the dangerous tendency of such innovations.

" I omit the detail of a variety of excellencies for which he was distinguished. I say nothing of his character as a peacemaker, or his fidelity in friendship—of his care to avert dangers, or his firmness in sustaining them—of the suavity of his manners, his gentleness, or his remarkable acuteness of intellect—of his management of his financial resources, by which of late they were so much recruited—these things are all known to you, and while you cherish gratitude to God for having bestowed such a Prince, ought never to be obliterated from your memories. Our country, alas! has lost not only a useful and gracious Prince, and one who has for a long period preserved public peace, but also a Father endowed with every various excellence. They merit the highest honour in every place who assiduously cultivate the country; he did indeed cultivate it, devoting the years of peace which he procured to its improvement, to the education of youth, and to the promotion of

commerce. Our Academy has lost a Mecænas;
no Prince possessed more capability, more devoted attachment, or knew better how to promote its interests. All Germany has lost—a
Prince and a Counsellor in every important
affair; for so great was his wisdom in German
affairs, and his general influence, that he was
deemed a proper person for the Imperial dignity,
and was consulted as an oracle—lost too at a
moment when Germany is ripe for civil war, and
as the poet says,

> Vicinæ ruptis inter se legibus urbes
> Arma ferunt, sævit toto Mars impius orbe—

lost—when his authority, discretion, and superiority of mind were peculiarly requisite for
the restoration of peace, the regulation of the
laws, and the reformation of religion.

" And shall we not mourn thy death, O
Frederic ? May we not lament our bereavement at so inauspicious a moment, not only of
a *Ruler*, but of a *Father ?* All eyes are turned to
thy illustrious brother, and the country feels that
in him it may safely repose the utmost confidence;
but he is himself most painfully sensible that by
thy removal he is deprived of another self, of
another mind capacitated to aid amidst surrounding difficulties. This weeping senate too,
the director of public affairs, seems almost ex-
animate with excess of sorrow, engaged as in a

dubious strife, and accustomed to follow thy signals and thy well-known voice!".

Such was the language of unaffected grief, and not exaggerated praise. On the Elector's monument the following Epitaph, written also by Melancthon, was inscribed.

Ante petet cursu Bojemica rura supino
   Unde in Saxonicos defluit Albis agros;
Inclyta quam possit meritorum fama tuorum
   Occidere in populis, Dux Frederice, tuis.
Aurea viderunt hæ gentes secula, regni
   Dum tibi Saxonici sceptra tenere datum est.
Pace frui placida campique urbesque solebant
   Horrenda extimuit classica nulla nurus
Bella alii ferro, sed tu ratione gerebas
   Et sine vi victi sæpe dedere manus.
Ingenio claros meruisti sæpe triumphos
   Militeque haud ullo fixa tropæa tibi:
Et pacis studiis florere ac artibus urbes
   Contigit auspicio, Dux Frederice, tuo.
Fovisti spretas hâc tempestate Camænas
   Unicus et studiis præmia digna dabas
Namque tuo sumptu flavum schola condita ad Albim est
   Ut vitæ verum traderet illa modum.
Hic Evangelii primum doctrina renata
   Deterso cæpit pura nitere situ.
Induit hic veros vultus, iterumque colorem
   Accepit taudem religio ipsa suum.
Et cùm Germani sumpsissent arma tyranni
   Contra Evangelium sanctaque jussa Dei;
Doctores tibi cura pios defendere soli,
   Et Christi latè spargere dogma fuit.
His tibi pro meritis gratâ præconiâ voce
   Posteritas omnis, virque puerque, canent.

Nulla tuas unquam virtutes nesciet ætas
Non jus in laudes mors habet atra tuas.

....

Beyond the utmost of Bohemia's bounds,
  Where Albis *(r)* pours along his lazy stream;
From every tongue our FREDERIC's name resounds,
  And all thy people hail the glorious theme.

Whilst thou the sceptre of these regions held,
  No rude alarms of war disturb'd our rest;
Another golden age our eyes beheld,
  While quietness our fields and cities blest.

Thy rule was reason, and thy trophy peace,
  Thou hast deserv'd the triumphs of the field,
But 'twas thy glory to bid discord cease,
  And though *victorious*, the first to *yield*.

Learning and Science by thy fostering care
  Adorn'd our cities, and proclaim'd thee WISE;
But not to thee were Muses only dear,
  Restor'd religion now delights our eyes.

Again we see her own celestial hue,
  Stripp'd of the meretricious modes of art;
And when to arms against her, tyrants flew,
  Thine was the care to shield the poison'd dart.

The truth of Christ, the doctrines brought from heaven,
  By thee were well discern'd and spread around;
To thee by present times applause is given,
  And future ages shall thy name resound.

    Yes—distant times thy virtues shall proclaim,
    Nor death extinguish thy immortal fame !

(r) The river *Elbe*, which rises in the mountain of the
Giants, on the confines of Bohemia and Silesia, and flows to the
German Ocean

In the midst of these public calamities, Saxony recently afflicted with the loss of Frederic, and Germany bleeding from the deep wounds of a civil war, occasioned by the rebellious conduct of the peasants, Luther, quite unexpectedly to most of his friends, married Catharine de Bora. Long in relinquishing his prejudices against the marriage of monks, he had once written thus to Melancthon; " It should seem that because I supplied you with a wife, you wish to be revenged upon me; but depend upon it I will take effectual care not to be caught in your snares"—but affection charmed away his resolution. The *time* of this union was considered by some of his best friends as rather ill-chosen, amongst whom was Melancthon, who thought it would give occasion, as it assuredly did, to the numerous adversaries of Luther to make uncandid animadversions. *(s)* These occasioned him some temporary depression of spirits; but a consciousness of acting right, and an ardent attachment to his new companion, notwithstanding the dissatisfaction of some intimate friends with the *time*, dissipated his gloom. Melancthon addressed an apologetic letter to Camerarius on the subject. It was written in Greek, *(t)* and is as follows: " As some un-

(s) CAM. Vit. Mel.
(t) " Elle est écrite," says the Bishop of Meaux, " toute

founded reports will probably reach you respecting the marriage of Luther, I think it proper to write to you the true state of the case, and to give my own opinion. On the thirteenth of June, Luther, to our great surprize, and without saying a word to his friends, married Catharine de Bora, and only invited Pomeranus, Lucca the painter, and Apellus the lawyer to supper in the evening, celebrating the espousals in the customary manner. Some perhaps may be astonished that he should have married at this unfavourable juncture of public affairs, so deeply afflictive to every good man, and thus appear to be unaffected and careless about the distressing events which have occurred amongst us; even though his own reputation suffers at a moment when Germany most requires his talents and influence. This however is my view of the subject. Luther is a man who has nothing of the unsocial misanthropist about him; but you know his habits, and I need say no more on this head. Surely it is no wonderful and unaccountable thing that his great and benevolent soul should be influenced by the gentle affections, especially as there is nothing reprehensible or criminal in it. The falsehood and calumny of the general report of his having been guilty of some mis-

en Grec; & *c' est ainsi qu' ils traitoient entre eux les choses secretes!*" BOSSUET Hist. Des Variations Tom. I. p. 65.

conduct is evident. He is in fact by nature fitted for the married state, and it is pronounced honourable in the sacred Scriptures. The allegation that it was unseasonable and unadvised, which our adversaries are so fond of producing, is not to be regarded, much less the derisions and reproaches of the vicious and profligate. I saw that his change of situation produced some degree of perturbation and gloom of mind, and I have done my utmost to cheer him: for I cannot condemn him as having committed a fault, or fallen into sin, though I grant God has recorded many sins which some of his ancient saints committed, in order that we might be stimulated to repose our confidence, not in men however dignified and distinguished, but in his word alone. It would be impious to condemn a doctrine because of the errors of its professors, but in the present instance I verily believe our friend has done nothing which is not fully defensible, or for which he ought to be accused. I have in possession the most decisive evidences of his piety and love to God, so that the malicious reproaches heaped upon Luther are nothing else than the inventions of scurrilous sycophants, who want employment for a slanderous tongue. In my opinion, however, this discouraging misrepresentation may be of some use, because it is dangerous, not only to persons who sustain ecclesiastical functions, but to every class of men, to enjoy too high a reputation. For, as a certain orator remarks, wise men as well as fools may be betrayed into an undue self-estimation and vanity of mind, through being gifted with some happy art or talent. But as the proverb says, " another kind of life, another kind of living."

" I have said so much on this subject lest this unexpected occurrence should have occasioned you an unnecessary degree of uneasiness, for I know you are concerned for the reputation of our friend Luther." *(u)*

It would be scarcely worth while in this place to introduce to notice the controversy between Erasmus and Luther, were it not for the illustration it affords of the character of Melancthon, who both on account of his connexion with the parties, and his general celebrity, was almost necessarily implicated in any public transaction that affected the reformed cause. No reflecting person will be surprized that they should become avowed antagonists. The character of each must naturally be disagreeable to the other. Erasmus could not approve the undaunted and untractable heroism of Luther, nor could Luther endure the trimming artifice and sycophancy of Erasmus.

The immediate occasion of this controversy

(*u*) MELANCTH. Ep. Lib. IV. 24.

was an essay called Diatribe, on the freedom of the human will, which Erasmus ventured to publish in the autumn of 1524 and for which as he expresses it, he "expected to be pelted." Upwards of a year elapsed before Luther produced his reply in a treatise de Servo Arbitrio, "on the Bondage of the Will." His antagonist re-appeared in the field of strife, in a book in two parts entitled Hyperaspistes. "Did you ever read," says Melancthon, "a more bitter publication than this of Erasmus? He calls it Hyperaspistes, but it is absolutely *aspis*, that is, a wasp." *(v)*

During this contention Erasmus wrote some long and artful letters to Melancthon. He assures him that he felt impelled by the peculiarity of his circumstances and situation to write against Luther—that if Wittemberg had not been so distant, he should gladly have sought an interview and should have been happy in a visit from Melancthon—that he had read his "Loci Communes" and admired more than ever his candid and happy genius—that he had given the most moderate counsel to popes and princes, but that the Reformers used him very ill in giving him the nick-name of Balaam who was hired to curse Israel—that Cardinal Campeggio had sent one of his agents to discuss with him

(v) MELANCTH. Ep. Lib. IV. 28. *ad Camerar.*

the propriety of removing Melancthon from his present situation. " My answer," says he, " was that I sincerely wished such a genius as yours to be perfectly free from all these contentions, but that I despaired of your recantation. *I open this secret to you in the entire confidence that you will be candid enough not to divulge it among the wicked ones!*" In a subsequent letter written with much irritation of mind, obviously because Melancthon was not to be taken in the snare he had laid for his religious integrity, he professes that he did not bestow much pains to persuade him to forsake the Reformers as he foresaw it would be useless, but he wished he had devoted his genius solely to literature, for there were plenty of actors in the religious tragedy!

Who does not perceive the insinuating purpose of Erasmus? Vexed at heart that the Lutheran cause should be strengthened by the literary authority, unquestionable moderation and superior talents of Melancthon, he employed every means to separate him from it. Yet with his characteristic duplicity he disclaims the real motives which all his letters betray. He fully believed that the Reformation could not ultimately prevail and he wished to avail himself of every means that might facilitate his progress to the possession of a Cardinal's cap. Let us hear the noble language of Melancthon. " For my

part I cannot with a safe conscience condemn
the sentiments of Luther, however I may be
charged with folly or superstition—*that* does not
weigh with me.   But I would *oppose them*
strenuously if THE SCRIPTURES *were on the other*
side; most certainly *I shall never change my sen-*
timents from a regard to HUMAN AUTHORITY *or*
from the DREAD OF DISGRACE." These are
the words of the *wavering* and the *timid* Melancthon !

In the autumn of the year 1525, by the
Elector's permission and at the express solicita-
tion of the Senate of Nuremberg, *(w)* he repaired
thither to assist in forming a plan for the establishment of a public seminary.   When he first
received the application, he writes thus to his
particular friend the senior Senator. " It afforded
me great pleasure to be informed from you that
your citizens were so anxiously disposed to erect
a public literary institution ; for nothing can be
a nobler ornament or a surer defence to a city
than such an establishment properly formed.
And I consider you, my friend, as meriting no
small praise, for stimulating your fellow citizens
to the maintenance and cultivation of letters.
I promise you most readily all the assistance in
my power, although I am not so ignorant of
myself as not to perceive that I am incapable of

(w) ADAM. Vit. Germ. Theol.   CAM. Vit. Mel.

fulfilling your wishes and your too partial opi_
nion of me." *(x)* This journey in which he
was accompanied by Camerarius was of a preparatory nature; in the ensuing year he visited
Nuremberg for the purpose of establishing the
academical institution and of giving his advice
in the management of ecclesiastical affairs. So
indefatigable was Melancthon in his attention to
the interests of religion and literature! He
was appointed to deliver an oration at the public
opening of this academy, which is preserved in
the volumes containing his select declamations.

The following passages are extracted from
it :—

" Consider the manners and general course
of life for which those nations are distinguished,
which are totally unacquainted with letters, as
the Scythians. Having no cities under the regulation of wholesome laws and no courts of
justice, those who prevail by force or faction
dictate the law; commercial intercourse with
neighbouring states is precluded; there can be
no interchange of property; public robbery is the
only means of escaping from the miseries of fa-
mine; every supply must depend upon the flesh
or fowl accidentally procured, and not only is
there no discipline at home, but even those domestic affections which are implanted in the

(x) MELANCTH. Ep. p. 51. *ad D. Hieronym. Baumgartn.* 7.

human bosom, conjugal fidelity, parental tenderness, the attachments of consanguinity and
friendship, become utterly extinguished by excessive barbarism. The science of education the
foundation of future excellence is unknown, virtue is disregarded, no sense of propriety prevails,
none of the assiduities of friendship, none of the
charities of life ; nor, finally, the least correctness
of sentiment respecting the will of God to man
and religion in general. Such is the cyclopic
nature of savage life only with somewhat different shades and degrees of barbarism ; and to
this state these nations must always tend unless
by imparting knowledge to them they become
excited and formed to virtue, humanity and
piety. You therefore have acted wisely and
nobly by introducing learning into your city and
studying to give it a permanent establishment
from a conviction it will be your best defence.
In this tempestuous age, your zeal merits peculiar applause, because amidst the general storm
that agitates the empire literature seems in danger of being wrecked."

After this he proceeds to complain bitterly
of the priesthood for their negligence of learning,
and declares that their fraternity have shewn
themselves the greatest enemies of the liberal
arts, so that the institution at Nuremberg is peculiarly well-timed. " And," says he, " do not be
loth to add this to the other ornaments of your city

T

which is already so distinguished for its wealth, its edifices and the ingenuity of its artificers, as to bear a comparison with the most celebrated cities of antiquity.   There is not a place in Germany more remarkable for well informed citizens who having added the establishment of the liberal sciences to their excellent civil polity, will be long regarded as pre-eminent in rank above all the cities of the empire ; for it is impossible to express what an accession of honour to that already acquired, will result from the erection of this institution of useful learning.

" If you proceed to cultivate these studies you will not only be illustrious in your own country but renowned abroad.   You will be regarded as the authors of your country's best defence, for ' no walls or bulwarks can prove more durable memorials of cities than the learning, wisdom and virtues of its citizens.'   A Spartan said, that their walls ought to be constructed of iron and not of stone, but I am of opinion that wisdom, moderation and piety, form a better protection than arms or walls."

The orator then endeavours to inspirit and excite the citizens of Nuremberg to a noble emulation of Florence, which had been so distinguished for the encouragement of the exiled literati and the cultivation of Greek and Roman lore : at a time too when the Roman Pontiff refused the great Theodore Gaza the least remu-

neration for his laborious services. He traces
the revival of letters in Europe to the example
of Florence, respresenting it as " the harbour
into which shipwrecked literature was received
and secured."

He adds, " It is not only a sin against heaven, but betrays a brutal mind whenever any
one refuses to exert himself for the proper instruction of his children. One great distinction
between the human race and the brute creation
is this, that nature teaches the animal to desist
from all further care of its offspring as soon as it
grows up, but enjoins it upon man not only to
nourish his children during the first and infan-
tine period of life, but as they rise into maturer
age to cultivate their moral powers with increased
assiduity and diligence.

" In the proper constitution of a state, therefore, schools of learning are primarily requisite
where the rising generation, which is the foundation of a future empire should be instructed,
for it is a most fallacious idea to suppose that solid
excellence is likely to be acquired without due
regard to instruction ; nor can persons be suitably qualified to govern the state without the
knowledge of those principles of right government which learning only can bestow.

" Having devoted yourselves then to this
object, do not be thwarted by the efforts of malice or by any other difficulties thrown in the

way to prevent the studies of your citizens.
Respecting your professors, this we may venture to promise, that they are equal to the task
they have undertaken and you may rely on the
diligent discharge of their important office.

" May the Lord Jesus Christ bestow his
blessing upon these transactions, and abundantly
prosper your counsels and the studies of your
youth !"

It appears from a long letter addressed to the
principal Senator of Nuremberg already mentioned, and with whom he maintained an uninterrupted correspondence of nearly thirty-seven years,
that he was invited to occupy a professorship in
the new institution, but he declines it in the
most modest yet firm manner, assuring his friend
that he felt the imperious nature of his obligations to his prince, and would rather perish with
hunger than abandon the duties of his station at
Wittemberg. *(y)*

During these almost innumerable public

(y) " Dum, meâ operâ uti volet Princeps Fredericus
non possum hinc honestè discedere. Nam cum is de me libe-
ralissimè meritus sit præstandum est vicissim mihi, ne quid in
ingratum putent collocatum esse. Itaque mihi curæ est per-
solvere, non modò quantum debeo sed etiam quantum ille sibi
de me pollicetur. Malim equidem fame mori, quam ab officio
discedere, præsertim cùm meo peccato literas ipsas non medio-
cri invidia gravarem τότε δὲ μοι χάνοι εὐρεῖα χθὼν tunc verò
mihi dehiscat lata terra, cum parum reveritus videbor digni-
tatem literarum." *Ep. ad Hieron. Baumgartnerum.*

and private engagements which Melancthon represents as both oppressive to his mind and injurious to his health, *(z)* he contrived to compose
and publish from time to time a variety of useful pieces ; amongst which were several intro-
ductions to different books of Scripture, a Latin
Version of the Proverbs of Solomon and an Epitome of the doctrines believed and taught in the
reformed churches. The latter is inserted in the
second volume of his works.

(z) " Nemo unquam servus in pistrino occupatior fuit,
atque ego sum, tametsi nihil agere videar. Et valetudo est,
ut scis, impar his laboribus, et malè me cruciant multa alia,
quæ tua unius consuetudine mitigari omnia poterant." ME-
LANCTH. Ep. Lib. IV. 32. *ad Joach. Camerar.*

CHAP. VII.

*John succeeds his brother Fredcric in the Electorate—
Changes—Diet of Spires—Melancthon's Memorial—
The Landgrave of Hesse promotes the Reformation in
his dominions — Melancthon's " Libellus Visitatorius" — Commissioners appointed to inspect the Reformed Churches—Second Diet of Spires—Anecdote
of the Landgrave of Hesse—Remarkable Story of
Grynæus—Melancthon's visit to his Mother—Continuance of the Sacramental Controversy—Conference at Marpurg—Melancthon's Commentary on the
Epistle to the Colossians.*

No circumstance could be more favourable
to the Reformation in Saxony, than the succession of John, brother of the deceased Frederic
to the Electoral dominions. Had he been influenced by the sentiments of the infatuated
Papist Duke George, unhappy consequences
might have been apprehended ; for though we
feel assured it was the cause of truth and righteousness, and possessed as such a principle of
imperishable vitality, had these princes " taken
counsel together against the Lord " it would doubt-

less have checked its growing prosperity and deferred its final triumphs. The wisdom of a superintending Providence was most apparent in all these transactions. The policy and prudence of Frederic resulting from conscientious scruples blended with some apprehensions of the over-awing domination of Rome, was admirably adapted to parry the repeated thrusts of ecclesiastical tyranny and to furnish opportunity for the Reformers to disseminate their principles; but when these had taken root it required a more decided protection and a firmer authority to favour the maturing harvest. John was of a bolder cast of mind than his deceased brother and avoided his temporizing caution, though it ought to be recorded to the honour of the latter, that a little previous to his death he had intended to give a more determined support to the reformed religion. The new Elector was warmly seconded by his son John Frederic. Philip, the Landgrave of Hesse also, might now be esteemed his zealous friend and coadjutor, for at a conference between the three princes at Creutzberg, he had most fully avowed the similarity of his views and determinations.

The Elector soon introduced important changes into the University and Collegiate church of Wittemberg. A new order of worship was provided, the Sacrament was administered in the German instead of the Latin language, and

Luther transmitted to him the new ecclesiastical rites practised by the Reformers, and drawn up with the advice of Melancthon and Pomeranus. A general visitation of the Saxon churches was also promised.

In the mean time Charles V. in letters to his brother Ferdinand, had commanded a Diet to be held at Augsburg, which though he wrote from Toledo in May 1525, was not assembled till the following November and was then so thinly attended as to be prorogued to the third of May 1526, when the place was directed to be exchanged for Spires. The Elector availed himself of this opportunity to form an association between the principal cities and princes of the empire who were moderately disposed, for the purpose of representing to Ferdinand the danger of attempting to execute the decree of Worms. At length Ferdinand confessed the necessity of adopting pacific measures and allowed the princes to send such divines to the Diet as they judged most capable of giving advice. The Elector of Saxony directed a brief memorial to be prepared, containing a reply to the principal objections of the Papists. It was written in German by Melancthon; the following is a specimen. (a)

(a) The original manuscript is extant amongst the Acts of the Diet. Reg. E. fol. 37. Vide SECKEND. Hist. Luth. Lib. II. p. 43.

" The first question to be considered is,
whether in preaching certain doctrines and omitting certain usages in opposition to the authority of the bishops and prelates we are guilty of
schism ; for though they cannot deny our doctrine they seek a pretext to condemn us from the
alleged defect of authority from the ecclesiastics.   They argue, 1. That the bishops possess
authority in the church and no one else—2. The
masses, monastic vows and other practices have
prevailed for so many ages—but the church is
infallible, therefore they cannot be abrogated.—
3. To obey is better than sacrifice, we ought
therefore to be obsequious.—4. Charity requires
the toleration of human infirmity.—5. Civil
commotion, to which disobedience to superiors
would expose us, ought by every means to be
avoided."

" To this it is replied:

" The ministers of the gospel are bound by
the precept of Jesus Christ, in Matthew x. 32.
to preach the primary article of the Christian
system, *justification by faith in Christ* and on no
pretence to omit or conceal it.   This doctrine
has been greatly misapprehended and to the dispa-
ragement of Christ, mankind have placed an unwarrantable dependance on masses, invocation
of saints and other works of their own : and these
things though they are manifest blasphemies it
is notorious have been taught in the Romish

church and substituted for the merits of Christ.
The Pope and the bishops neglect their duties,
usurp authority over emperors and princes, and
misapply the revenues of the church to tyran-
nical purposes; all this in the sacred name of
Christ himself.   Surely these are positive viola-
tions of the second commandment and require
the interference of our assemblies to rectify and
remove.

" On these grounds it is incumbent on the
pastors of churches from the very nature of their
calling to preach the truth, especially when the
bishops allowing their authority, neglect to do
it.   In vain do our ministers both by their voice
and their pen remonstrate; the only consequence
is they subject themselves to persecution—but
when placed in circumstances similar to Christ
and his Apostles before Anna and Caiphas, they
can adopt the declaration of the primitive disciples, ' We ought to obey God rather than
men.'

" We deny that the Pope and the clergy constitute the true church, though it is granted there
exist some among them who are real members of
that church and who renounce the prevailing errors; for the true church consists of those and those
only who have the word of God and are ' sanctified and cleansed.'—(Eph. v. 26.)   The Holy
Spirit expressly warns us against mistaking the
Pope and his Clergy for THE CHURCH, for

he has predicted by Paul that Antichrist
would come as God sitting in the temple of God,
that is, in the church. We are not departing
from the church, therefore in contending against
the errors of Antichrist which they themselves
who adhere to the Papal establishment acknowledge. Nor is it to the purpose to contend
about the alteration in external ordinances, for
the unity of the church does not consist in these
things and whoever affirms it does, ought to be
opposed.

"With respect to disobedience and the late
insurrections our conduct has not occasioned
them, but THE POPE AND THE BISHOPS THEM-
SELVES ARE THE CAUSE by their persecutions
and excommunications; and by demanding AN
OBEDIENCE WHICH AMOUNTS TO NOTHING
SHORT OF A RENUNCIATION OF THE WORD
OF GOD.

"The pretence of charity to the weak and
erring is altogether inapplicable, for our papistical adversaries who refuse all instruction and
act only as persecutors and tyrants, are not to be
classed amongst the persons of that description
to whom Paul refers."

He confirms his statements by an appeal at
large to the precepts of Christ and to examples
in the history of the Jewish and Christian
churches, and concludes by affirming that the
doctrine of justification by faith without works

ought to be maintained, though it expose us to persecution and every species of distress.

" The second question," says Melancthon, " is this, whether the princes have done right in authorizing the reformation of abuses in their colleges and monasteries ?" The reply is, " it has been shewn already that the princes have done right in receiving the doctrines of the gospel, it follows therefore that it is no less right to remove abuses which corrupt it. The question is whether the reformed doctrines are true or not ; if true they ought to protect them. The princes are no more under an obligation to obey the persecuting edicts of emperors and rulers, than Jonathan was to kill David or Obadiah the prophets. Nor ought they to be stigmatized with the name of *Schismatics*, because they do not separate from the church of Rome out of mere hostility and petulence of disposition, but because they are compelled to it by the express command of Scripture."

The Diet of Spires assembled in June. Several of the Lutheran divines were heard in explanation of their doctrines, and the deputies presented their memorial on the abolition of abuses. The result was favourable to the Reformation, a decree being obtained after much debate recognizing the necessity of a general council, appealing to the emperor for that purpose, and claiming

on behalf of the German Princes in the mean
time the liberty of acting independently in religion till such an appointment. *(b)*

The Landgrave of Hesse, upon his return
from the Diet, devoted himself with his characteristic ardour to the great and good work of promoting the Reformation in his own dominions.
He wrote letters to Melancthon soliciting his
advice; who in reply urged the Landgrave to
proceed in a gradual and cautious manner, con-
niving for a time at certain non-essentials, the
sudden abolition of which might be prejudicial to the cause he was desirous of promoting.   He laments the contentions which
subsisted amongst the Reformers themselves,
frequently about trifles, which should by every
means be avoided.   The preachers of the
gospel ought, he said, to inculcate not only the
doctrines of faith, but the practices of piety, the
fear of God, love to man, and obedience to
magistrates.   He besought his Highness to abstain from every attempt to extend the Reformation by military force; for the late occurrences
of the rustic war would evince that they who
delight in war should certainly be scattered. *(c)*

(b) Sleidan 149, 150.

(c) The impetuosity of this enterprising Prince could
scarcely be restrained within proper limits.   He was for the use
of arms, but was checked by Melancthon, and by the Elector
John, who acted with the advice of Luther.   The latter de-

" The Romish Ecclesiastics instigate to war, why do not the rest exhort men to gain a knowledge of the subject, and to preserve peace? Your Highness I am convinced might do a great deal with the Princes, if you would exhort them to take pains to understand the points in dispute, and endeavour to terminate these contentions." (c)

During the two years of peace to the reformed churches which succeeded the Diet of Spires, the Elector of Saxony employed himself in the very important work of regulating ecclesiastical affairs. Preparatory to a general visitation by persons suitably authorized and accomplished for the undertaking, Melancthon composed a directory for the use of the churches, which was published under the immediate sanction of the Elector. It is divided into eighteen sections, comprehending the doctrine of Forgiveness and Justification by faith in Christ—the Law—Prayer— the Endurance of Tribulation—Baptism—the Lord's Supper—Repentance—Confession—the Atonement—Public Worship —Marriage—Freedom of the Will—Christian Liberty—the Turkish War—the mode of Preach-

clared, " If the Landgrave were determined to have recourse to arms, it would be better for the Elector to dissolve alliance with him : but if force were to be first used by their adversaries, they then had a right to repel it."

(c) MELANCTH. Ep. Lib. III. 16.

ing—Excommunication—the Office of Superintendants or Bishops—Public Schools of Literature. The arrangement of these divisions
might perhaps be criticised, but the whole appears to have been written with the author's
characteristic skill and perspicuity. A preface
at the Elector's request was prefixed by Luther.

This publication, called *Libellus Visitatorius,* involved some unpleasant consequences to
Melancthon. The Papists professed to discover
in it a defection from many of the sentiments of
Luther, and hailed the imaginary difference with
a prodigious but premature exultation. It
cannot be doubted that such a circumstance
was eagerly desired, and it must be confessed
would have been worthy their mutual congratulations. Luther despised the charge—" Let our
adversaries," says he, " glory in their lies, as
they always do, for they take no pleasure in
truth." And again, " Their glorying is a miserable one, and will be of no long continuance;
but let them solace themselves with their vain
hopes and joys, as they often do, and let them
swell and bluster, I am very well pleased." *(d)*
At the same time Melancthon discloses a secret
in a letter to his confidential friend Camerarius.
" I am applied to from Bohemia to desert the
Reformed Cause, and promised any remuneration

(d) Luth. Ep. Lib. II. ad Spal. p. 345, 351.

from king Ferdinand. Indeed my defection is publicly reported as a fact, because in the little book written for the reformed churches I have shewn an increased degree of moderation, and yet you perceive I have really inserted nothing different from what Luther constantly maintains. But because I have employed no asperity of language, these very acute men judge that I necessarily differ from Luther." *(e)* Cochlæus does not scruple to charge Melancthon with a *crafty moderation*, and Luther with a *change of sentiment; (f)* but as Seckendorf observes, " Nothing better than such malignant insinuations was to be expected from him."

But the tauntings and misrepresentations of avowed adversaries were far less vexatious than the conduct of a friend and fellow-labourer. In the first article of the Libellus Visitatorius, the pastors of churches were admonished to instruct the people in the nature of true repentance, and to be careful not to separate repentance from the doctrine of faith, the former of which was stated to originate in the fear of divine judgments, and a just impression of the terrors of the Law, lest the vulgar should imagine that the remission of sins was attainable without the exercise of a penitent and contrite spirit. They were to press

(e) MELANCTH. Ep. Lib. III. 72. ad Cam.
(f) COCH. fol. 80.

the consciences of men on this subject, and urge to repentance, to prevent their placing dependance on any personal merit, for salvation. John Agricola, Chaplain to Count Mansfield, and his attendant at the Diet of Spires, loudly exclaimed against this advice, affirming that it was improper to make these statements and appeals to the common people, and that instead of attempting to work upon their fears, and terrify their consciences, they should be exhorted to faith in God as the commencement and essence of real religion. Instead of candidly representing his objections to Melancthon himself, he vociferated his complaints to the Papists, and it seems highly probable, from his whole conduct, that his intentions were to purchase a great name by obtruding himself forward as the head of a new party. In this he succeeded, for he became founder of the sect of the Antinomians, and afterwards a preacher at the court of Berlin.

Melancthon fully expresses his sentiments on the subject in his letters, one of which addressed to Justus Jonas, and not to be found amongst the published volumes of his correspondence, deserves to be noticed. *(g)* He begins by expressing his wish that Agricola had shewn a more friendly spirit, and that instead of circulating his censures throughout Germany,

(g) It is preserved in *Biblioth. Paulin. Lipsiensi.*

U

even in Leipsic, and in the very court of
Duke George, he had first informed him privately of any thing which he conceived objectionable in his writings.   He then alludes
to certain transactions relative to this document and the visitation, in the presence of the
Elector, Luther, Pomeranus and others.   Agricola referred to Luther as having stated that repentance originated in the love of righteousness;
quoted the story of the heathen mariners in Job,
and said that Christ commanded repentance to
be preached in his name, and not in the name of
Moses.   To this Melancthon replies, that terrors
of conscience must exist previous to justification, and these terrors seem to originate more in
the fear of punishment than the love of righteousness.   Agricola answers, that contrition
arises from faith in the divine threatenings—but
what, says Melancthon, is faith in the divine
threatenings but the fear of them?   Nothing,
he says, offends his opponent more than that in
the second article it is ordered that the ten commandments be taught; because we are free from
the law, and ought to study rather the writings
of Paul; to which it is answered, that Paul en-
forces the law, and Christ himself taught it and
explained its obligatory nature.   Agricola laugh-
ably enough, objects that Christ only spoke to
the Jews.   This war of words was sufficiently
disagreeable to the amiable Melancthon, and he

informs Jonas, that he had thrice solicited Agricola to bury what had passed in oblivion, and to renew their former friendship; but that he treated his overture with contemptuous silence. This disagreement however assumed so serious an aspect in the opinion of the Elector, that he immediately interposed; and summoning Melancthon, Agricola, and Luther to Torgau, stopped the further progress of the dispute for the present by an amicable adjustment. *(h)*

The commissioners appointed for the great purpose of inspecting the state of the reformed churches, were twenty eight in number, consisting of laymen and ecclesiastics. They were distributed into parties according to the different provinces. Melancthon, with five others, namely, John a Planitz, a knight, Jerome Schurff, Erasmus, (not of Rotterdam) Frederic Myconius, and Justus Menius, a clergyman of Eisenach, inspected Thuringia; Luther, Justus Jonas, Pomeranus, Spalatine, and other persons of eminence, were appointed in the general commission. All of them diligently laboured to fix suitable pastors in the respective parishes, to abolish ancient superstitions, to regulate the public seminaries ; in a word, to promote general good order and religious improvement.

The second Diet of Spires was convened in

(h) SECKEND. Hist. Luth. Lib. II. Sect. 12. p. 90.

the year 1529. A pleasant anecdote is related of the Landgrave of Hesse on this occasion. Faber, Bishop of Vienna, intending to ridicule the reformers, seeing the letters V. D. M. I. Æ. upon the sleeves of some of the courtiers of the Landgrave, chose to interpret them " Verbum Dei Manet Im Ermel;" i. e. The word of God remains in the sleeves: to which the Landgrave immediately replied, " No, this is not the meaning, but Verbum Diaboli Manet In Episcopis;" i. e. The word of the devil remains in the Bishops. The real signification of the letters however was, Verbum Dei Manet In Æternam; i. e. The word of God remains for ever. *(i)*

A curious circumstance occurred at this convocation, which Melancthon relates in his Commentary on the angelic appearance mentioned in the tenth chapter of Daniel, and which he affirms was but one out of many of a similar nature, which he could fully authenticate. The case was briefly this. Simon Grynæus, a very intimate friend of his, and at this period Greek Professor in the University of Heidelberg, who combined profound erudition with zealous piety, came over unexpectedly to see him at Spires. He ventured to encounter Faber, and to urge him closely on some of the topics in discussion be-

(i) Van de Corput, Leven ende Dood P. Mel. p. 155.

tween the Catholics and the Reformers. The
Bishop, who was plausible, but shallow, fearful
of engaging in argument, but cruelly ready to use
the sword, pretended that private business with
the king required his attention at that moment,
but that he felt extremely desirous of the friendship of Grynæus, and of another opportunity
of discussing the controverted points. No dis-
sembler himself, Grynæus returned to his friends
without the least suspicion of the wily courtier's
intentions; nor could any of them have known
it, but for what Melancthon deemed a supernatural interference. They were just sitting
down to supper, and Grynæus had related part
of the conversation between himself and the
Bishop, when Melancthon was suddenly called
out of the room to an old man whom he had
never seen or heard of, or could hereafter discover, characterized by a most observable peculiarity of manner and dress, and who said, that
persons by the king's authority would soon
arrive to seize Grynæus, and put him in prison,
Faber having influenced him to this persecuting
measure. He enjoined that instant means
should be adopted to secure the departure of
Grynæus to a place of safety, and urged that
there should not be a moment's delay. Upon
communicating this information he immediately
withdrew. Melancthon and his friends instantly
bestirred themselves, and saw him safe across the

Rhine. It afterwards appeared that the king's messengers were in the house almost as soon as they had left it, but Grynæus was out of the reach of danger; a danger, as Melancthon remarks, easily imagined by those who were acquainted with Faber's cruelty. He says they were all of opinion that this was a divine interposition, so singular was the appearance of the old man, and so rapid the movements of the instrument of vengeance, from whose power Grynæus scarcely escaped. *(k)*

Such is the narrative which the reader is put in possession of without note or comment. Some will think it supernatural, others will exclaim, *Credat Judæus Apella*, and many perhaps will consider it, though remarkable, capable of explanation without allowing it to have been miraculous. The use Melancthon makes of the statement must be admitted to be worthy of his exalted piety; " Let us," says he, " be grateful to God who sends his angels to be our protectors, and let us with increased tranquillity of mind fulfil the duties assigned us."

At this Diet the former decree, which allowed every Prince to manage his own ecclesiastical affairs as he thought proper till the appointment of a general council was revoked;

(k) MELANCTH. Op. Tom. 2. *in Comment ad Cap.* X. *Danielis.* CAM. Vit. Mel. MEL. ADAM. Vit. Germ. Philosophorum *in vit.* Sim. *Gryn.*

all farther innovation in religion was interdicted, the celebration of mass was no where to be disallowed, and the Anabaptists were made subject to capital punishment. *(l)* The resolutions of the first Diet had been carried *unanimously*, they were revoked, merely by a *majority* of Catholic votes procured by imperial influence. The arguments and remonstrances of the Reformers were useless, and the only measure left them to adopt was to enter a solemn *protest* against this decree which they did on the *nineteeth of April;* whence they acquired the name of PROTESTANTS. The first who thus obtained this glorious distinction were JOHN, ELECTOR OF SAXONY, GEORGE, ELECTOR OF BRANDENBURG, ERNEST AND FRANCIS, DUKES OF LUNENBURG, PHILIP, LANDGRAVE OF HESSE, and WOLFGANG, PRINCE OF ANHALT. They were seconded by thirteen or fourteen imperial cities.

The ambassadors commissioned by these noble Dissenters to communicate their proceedings to the Emperor in Spain, were immediately arrested upon their arrival. This unwarrantable violence only tended to strengthen their union and they held various meetings at Roth, Nuremberg and Smalcald, to concert measures for mutual defence. The Elector of Saxony however instructed by Luther and Melancthon, shewed

(l) SLEID. 171. Goldast III. 495.

a disinclination to form a military association and nothing decisive resulted at present from these deliberations.

The anxiety of Melancthon, who had accompanied the Elector to the Diet was extreme. During all these transactions he and Luther with whom a perpetual communication was maintained, were constantly consulted. In every struggle and difficulty they largely participated, for on them it depended in a great measure to pilot the new-launched vessel through the tempestuous seas. Melancthon was sometimes entreated by his friends who witnessed his extreme agitation, to suppress these anxieties and dismiss trouble from his mind. To which he would piously reply, " if I had no anxieties I should lose a powerful incentive to prayer ; but when the cares of life impel to devotion, the best means of consolation, a religious mind cannot do without them. Thus trouble compels me to pray, and prayer drives away trouble." (m)

Availing himself of a favourable opportunity, he went from Spires to pay a short visit to his mother. In the course of conversation she mentioned to her son the manner in which she was accustomed to attend to her devotions, and the form she generally used which was free from the prevailing superstitions. " But what," said

(m) CAM. Vit. Mel.

she, " am I to believe amidst so many different opinions of the present day?"—" Go on," replied Melancthon, " believe and pray as you do and have done before—and do not disturb yourself about the disputes and controversies of the times." *(n)*

The Sacramental controversy between the divines of Saxony and Switzerland continued to rage with unabated violence, neither party being disposed to retract in the smallest degree. Oecolampadius strongly solicited Melancthon to declare in favour of Zuinglius and the Sacramentarians, to which he ingenuously replied, " that after due examination he could not approve of their opinion, not finding sufficient reason in the literal sense of the words—that if he were to act in a politic manner he should speak otherwise, knowing there were many learned men among the Sacramentarians whose friendship would be advantageous to him, so that if he could have concurred in their opinion about the Lord's Supper he would have spoken freely. The Zuinglians supposed, he said, the body of Christ to be absent and only *represented* in the Sacrament, as persons are represented in a theatre, but he considered that Jesus Christ had promised to be with us even to the end of the world—that it is not necessary to separate the

(n) ADAM. Vit. Germ. Theologorum, p. 333.

divinity from the humanity—he was persuaded
therefore the Sacrament was a pledge of the real
presence and that the body of Christ was truly
received in the Lord's Supper—that the proper
import of the words ' this is my body,' was
not contrary to any article of faith, but agreed
with other passages in Scripture where the presence of Christ was mentioned—and that it was
unbecoming a Christian to believe that Jesus
Christ is as it were imprisoned in heaven—that
Oecolampadius had only alluded to some absurdities and the opinion of some of the fathers
against it, neither of which ought to influence
those who know that the mysteries of religion
are to be judged by the word of God and not by
mathematical principles, and that the writings
of the ancients abound in contradictions ; but, he
said the greatest number of the expressions in
the most eminent writers, proves the doctrine of
the real presence to be the general sense of the
church.   He desires Oecolampadius to consider
the importance of the question in dispute and
the ill consequences of maintaining his opinion
with so much warmth of temper, and adds, it
would be very proper for some good men to
confer together on the subject." To the latter
proposition Oecolampadius in his reply most
cordially assents. (o)

(o) MEL. Declam. T. II. OECOLAMP. Ep. p. 602.

Some years previous to this period Melancthon had thus expressed himself in a letter to
Camerarius; " I commit the affair to Christ
that his divine wisdom may best consult his own
glory. I have hitherto always entertained the
hope that he would by some means make it
plain what is the true doctrine of the Sacrament." It is deplorable that such men as
Luther and Melancthon should have wandered
so long in darkness; yet be it remembered,
though they erred. it was from a most anxious
solicitude of mind to adhere rigidly to scriptural
statements. They urged the *very words of Christ*
as their authority, but unhappily misinterpreted
them.

The excellent Landgrave of Hesse, with a
view to the adjustment of the differences which
had so long subsisted amongst the principal
reformers respecting the sacrament, procured a
friendly conference at Marpurg a city in his dominions. It took place in October. The leaders on both sides first held a private conference,
Luther with Oecolampadius and Melancthon
with Zuinglius. The prince, his courtiers and
chief counsellors were present at the public disputation, which was conducted on the one side
by Zuinglius, Oecolampadius, Bucer, Hedio,
Jacob Sturm, a senator of Strasburg, Ulrich
Funch, a senator of Zurich, and Rudolphus Frey
of Basil; on the other by Luther, Melancthon,

Eberhard, Thane of Eisenach, Justus Jonas,
Casper Cruciger, and others.   Jonas describes
Zuinglius as rude and forward, Oecolampadius
as remarkably mild, Hedio no less liberal and
good, and Bucer keen and cunning as a fox.

It appears that the Swiss and Saxon reformers discussed a variety of other topics, in
which they either did or supposed themselves to
differ, and though both parties afterwards claimed
the victory there is every reason to rely on the
statement of Melancthon.   " Zuinglius," he
says, " readily gave up several things which
he had advanced in his writings, particularly
his notion of original sin and came over to the
Wittemberg divines in all points, the single article of the Lord's Supper excepted." (p)

No doubt can be entertained that each of
the Protestant parties retired from this conference with too much self-satisfaction, and the
Papists ridiculed the Landgrave for his pious
zeal. (q)   If however the great purpose of perfect agreement were not obtained, it is much to

---

(p) MEL. in Scult. 198. in Hosp. 80--82.   Lit. Jonæ ad
Gulielm. Reiffenstein ap. SECK. Lib. II. p. 139.

(q) " De conventu hoc Marpurgensi ab omnium partium
scriptoribus agitur: *Pontificiis*, qui, ut noster hic, conatum
Landgravii inutilem irrident; *Zuinglio* cum suis, qui argu-
mentandi acumine potiores sibi fuisse visi sunt: *Nostris* qui
Luthero constantiæ et firmitatis laudem asserunt."   SECK.
Hist. Luth. Lib. II. Sect. xvii. p. 137.

their honour that all parties signed the following statement in reference to the excepted article in Melancthon's report. " We all agree in believing that the Lord's Supper is to be administered in both kinds conformably to its original institution, but that the mass ought not to be practised to procure mercy for the quick or the dead—that the Sacrament is truly a Sacrament of the body and blood of Jesus Christ, and that to eat of his body and blood in a spiritual sense is absolutely necessary for every Christian. We agree also respecting the utility of the Sacrament that like his holy word it is administered, and appointed by God to promote the faith and joy of his feeble and dependant people through the agency of the Holy Spirit. BUT THOUGH WE ARE NOT YET AGREED WHETHER THE BODY AND BLOOD OF CHRIST IS CORPOREALLY PRESENT IN THE BREAD AND WINE, YET AS FAR AS CONSCIENCE PERMITS, EACH PARTY SHALL MANIFEST A CHRISTIAN AFFECTION TO EACH OTHER, AND BOTH SHALL EARNESTLY IMPLORE ALMIGHTY GOD THAT HE WOULD BY HIS SPIRIT LEAD AND ESTABLISH US IN WHATEVER IS THE TRUTH !"

In the present year Luther wrote a preface to the second edition of Melancthon's Commentary on the Epistle to the Colossians. He speaks of it as a book small in size, but great in point of matter and useful tendency, and affirms with extraordinary frankness that he preferred the writings of Melancthon to his own, and was much more desirous that they should be published and read. " I," says he, " am born to be for ever fighting with opponents and with the devil himself, which gives a controversial and warlike cast to all my works. I clear the ground of stumps and trees, root up thorns and briars, fill up ditches, raise causeways and smooth the roads through the wood : but to Philip Melancthon it belongs by the grace of God to perform a milder and more grateful labour—to build, to plant, to sow, to water, to please by elegance and taste. O happy circumstance and shame to their ingratitude who are not sensible of it ! Had such a publication as this appeared twenty years ago what an invaluable treasure would it have been esteemed ! But now, we resemble the Israelites who loathed the manna and sighed for the garlic and the onions of Egypt. A time will come when the loss of such advantages will be deplored in vain."

So strong and so inviolable was the mutual friendship of these noble-minded Reformers. No root of bitterness grew in either bosom—no jealousy or envy divided them. Their only ambition seemed to be to promote each others reputation and strengthen by their zealous co-operation the common cause.

CHAP. VIII.

A. D. 1530.

*Brief notice of General Affairs—Appointment of the
Diet of Augsburg—Translation of the* AUGSBURG
CONFESSION—*Popish Confutation—Subsequent pro-
ceedings—Melancthon's Apology—Decree of the Diet
—Deliberation of the Reformers—Striking Anecdote
of Melancthon.*

SCRUPULOUSLY avoiding the minute and
intricate transactions of general history, excepting so far as they may be requisite to connect
the parts of this narrative together, it will not
be expected that the progress of the Turkish
war, or the contentions of the Emperor, the
Pope, and the king of France, should be detailed.
Suffice it simply to allude to these circumstances, that the wonderful movements of providence at this period may be duly remarked. The
Pope and the Emperor were both sufficiently
disposed to exert their respective authority as
the heads of civil and ecclesiastical affairs, to
extinguish the still increasing light of the Reformation. They were anxious to enforce the

intolerant edict of Worms, and to concert measures for the more effectual annihilation by force
of the Lutheran heresy. But at the very time
when it is probable their efforts would have been
most alarming, and when urged by the papal
party to exert their formidable power, they were
prevented from executing their purpose by personal contentions, as well as by the hostility of
a foreign enemy.

During some years France, Spain and Italy
had been in a state of commotion, and after the
battle of Pavia, in which Francis was defeated,
the Roman Pontiff becoming uneasy at the
growing power of the Emperor, entered into a
league against him, which so exasperated Charles,
that in the year 1527 he rushed into Italy, laid
siege to Rome, and blockaded Clement in the
castle of St. Angelo. Their differences however being at length adjusted, they were mutually pledged to the extirpation of Protestantism.

The appointment of a Diet at Augsburg to
deliberate on the Turkish war, and on the existing disputes in religion, forms a new era in the
history of the Reformation. Charles V. was
personally present. He arrived on the *thirteenth*,
and the first session was held on the *twentieth*
of June. *(r)* The Elector of Saxony selected

(r) DUPIN's Eccles. Hist. B. II. Ch. 22. p. 115.

his most eminent divines to accompany him. Luther, who could not with safety or propriety have appeared at Augsburg after being proscribed by the edict of Worms, was left at Coburg in Franconia, at a convenient distance for consultation, so that the principal labour and responsibility devolved upon Melancthon.

It had been deemed adviseable to prepare a statement of all the principal articles of the Protestant faith, in order to put the Emperor in full possession of the subject of dispute pending between the Papal and Reformed parties, and to facilitate the dispatch of ecclesiastical affairs. Luther and his friends had already sent a concise paper to the Elector of Saxony at his own request while at Torgau, on his road to the Diet. It consisted of seventeen articles, which had been already discussed in the conferences at Sultzbach and Smalcald. (s)

The Princes however solicited the pen of Melancthon to draw up a more extended and accurate statement. It was an important undertaking, and a critical moment. He naturally felt anxious for his own reputation, and while it was his desire to avoid unnecessary offence, he felt as a man of piety the paramount duty he owed to God and to his conscience. Often did he weep over the page—often did he complain

(s) Comm. de Luth. XLII. 4. &XLVIII. & Add.

X

with sentiments of genuine humility of his own incompetency. *(t)*

At length the celebrated *Confession of Augsburg* was completed. Luther's advice had been constantly sought, and there is no reason to doubt, while the mildness of the language scarcely comported with the vehemence of his temper, the skill displayed, and the sentiments stated met his entire approbation. *(u)* It was translated into almost all the languages of Europe, and read in the courts of kings and princes. *(v)*

Melancthon was desirous that it should be signed by the Theologians only of the reformed party, alleging as a reason, that the Princes would then be more at liberty to use their influence in promoting their mutual wishes, but he could not succeed. *(w)*

After the dispatch of other business the Protestant princes requested the Emperor to allow their confession to be publicly read. This

---

(t) Cam. Vit. Mel.

(u) Dupin says, that after revising and correcting it several times, he could hardly please Luther at last. Maimbourg on the contrary represents it as being highly gratifying to him. Seckendorf favours the statement of Maimbourg, by saying Luther was glad of this occasion to let the world see what he and his friends believed.

(v) Seck.

(v) Cam. Vit. Mel.

he would not permit in a full Diet, but commanding them to intrust it to him promised it should be read the next day in his palace; they however petitioned to reserve it. The next day in a special assembly of princes and other members of the empire, it was presented to his Imperial Majesty in Latin and German, with the offer to explain any thing which might appear obscure and an assurance they would refer the points of difference in religion to a general council. *(x)*

The reader shall now have an opportunity of inspecting this far-famed performance. *(y)* It will be found to contain many sentiments which to most Christians will appear strange and which we should be very far from defending, but

(x) DUPIN's Eccles. Hist. B. II. p. 116.

(y) Cœlestine in his history of the Diet of Augsburg, has inserted a summary of the Protestant faith in seventeen articles said to have been previously sent to Charles V. and which he imputes to Melancthon. He represents it as written at the request of Alphonsus Valdesius, Spanish Secretary to the Emperor, who said his Imperial Majesty had intimated his wish for such a statement. But Seckendorf assigns several satisfactory reasons for not believing it to be the production of Melancthon. It is written with considerable acrimony; and would have exposed him to great personal danger; it is not probable he would have done it without consulting Luther; such a proceeding would have been inconsistent with his natural timidity of disposition, and his learned biographer Camerarius mentions nothing of such a composition. CŒLESTIN. Hist. Comit. August. Tom. I. SECKEND. Hist. Luth. Lib. II. p. 165--167.

we have nevertheless thought it our duty faithfully to rspresent them.   Let the reader bear in
mind that the Reformers are to be honoured
chiefly for the grand principles of Christian liberty which they so strenuously asserted and
maintained in the face of the most powerful
opponents ; the detail of doctrine and practice
will always occasion difference of opinion.   That
they were too tenacious of their particular creed
and in many cases inconsistent with themselves
cannot be denied—but this period was only the
dawn of religious discovery, and it is not to be
wondered at that many objects appeared to them
at first in a very indistinct manner.   Many alterations were made in future editions of this very
document.   They ·were perpetually, with the
zeal of reformers and the genuine humility of
Christians, correcting their own errors.

THE AUGSBURG CONFESSION
As presented to Charles V. June 25, 1530.

ART. I.

   " Our churches are perfectly agreed that the
Nicene decree respecting the unity of the divine
essence and the three persons of the godhead is
true and worthy of the fullest belief ; namely,
that there is one divine essence which is called
and which is God, eternal, incorporeal, indivisible, infinite in power, wisdom and goodness, the

Creator and preserver of all things visible and invisible; and yet there are three persons co-equal in power and essence, and co-eternal, the Father, the Son and the Holy Spirit. The term person is used in the same sense as ecclesiastical writers have employed it, to denote a proper subsistence in distinction from a part or quality. Hence our churches condemn every heresy upon this subject that has arisen, as that of the Mani-chæans who assert two principles, the good and the evil, the Valentinians, Arians, Eunomians, Mahometans and all others of a similar descrip-tion.   They condemn also the Samosatenes both ancient and modern, who contend that there is only one person and speak of the word and the Holy Spirit in a very wily and wicked manner, affirming that there are no distinct persons, but that the Word signifies a mere voice, and the Spirit an influence or motion created in things.

Art. II.

" They teach also that since the fall of Adam all men are naturally born in sin, destitute of the fear of God and faith in him, and full of concupiscence ; and this disease or original de-pravity is sinful, even now condemning and ex-posing to eternal death all who are not born again by baptism and the Holy Spirit.

" They condemn the Pelagians and others who deny the sinful nature of this original depravity, disparaging the benefits which Christ dispenses to the exaltation of human merit, and contending that a man is justified before God by his own powers of reason.

ART. III.

" They also teach that the word, or Son of God assumed human nature in the Virgin's womb, in such a manner that the two natures the divine and the human were inseparably united in the one person of Christ, truly God and truly man born of the Virgin Mary, who really suffered, was crucified, dead and buried, that he might reconcile the Father to us, by his expiatory sacrifice for both original and actual sin. He descended to the dead (ad inferos), and really rising again on the third day ascended into heaven to sit at the Father's right hand, to reign for ever over all creation and to sanctify all who believe in him, by sending his Spirit into their hearts to rule, console and quicken them, that they may be able to resist the devil and the power of sin. Also Christ will return to judge the quick and the dead, &c. according to the Apostles' Creed.

ART. IV.

" They teach also that men cannot be justified before God by their own efforts, merits or works, but are justified freely through Christ by faith, and are received into favour and enjoy the remission of sins through Christ, who by his death gave a satisfaction for sin.

" God imputes this faith for justification before him.   Rom. iii. and iv.

Art. V.

" The ministry of the gospel and the administration of Sacraments was instituted that we might obtain this faith, for the word and the Sacraments are used as instruments by the Holy Spirit for the communication of faith, and where and wherever it is seen in those who hear the gospel ; that is, God justifies not for our merits but for Christ's sake.

" They condemn the Anabaptists and others, who suppose that the Holy Spirit comes to men through their own works and preparations without the external word.

Art. VI.

" They teach also that faith ought to be visible in its fruits, and that though good works are to be done as commanded and conformable to the will of God, we are not to confide in them as meritorious for justification before God. For remission of sin and justification is apprehended by faith, as Christ testifies : ' Having done all these things say we are unprofitable servants.' The ancient writers of the church teach the

same doctrine.   Ambrose says, ' This is the appointment of God, that whosoever believes in
Christ shall be saved without works, by faith
only receiving the remission of sins.'

Art. VII.

" They teach also that the one holy church
will continue for ever; but that this church
consists of a congregation of holy persons in
which the gospel is rightly taught and the Sacraments rightly administered ; and as to true
unity in the church, it is sufficient to agree concerning the doctrine of the gospel and the administration of Sacraments.   Nor is it universally
necessary that human traditions, rites, or ceremonies instituted by men be the same in all
places; so Paul says, ' One Lord, one faith, one
baptism, one God and Father of all, &c.'

Art. VIII.

" Although the church is properly a congregation of holy persons and genuine believers,
yet as there is a great mixture of characters in
this world, hypocrites and wicked persons, it is
lawful to use the Sacraments although administered by the wicked according to the language
of Christ ; ' The Scribes and Pharisees sit in
Moses's seat,' &c. so that the Sacraments and
he word of God become efficacious through the

appointment and command of Christ, even though dispensed by wicked persons.

" They condemn the Donatists and such persons who deny the lawfulness of making use of the ministry of the wicked in the church, considering such a ministry useless and inefficacious.

Art. IX.

" They teach concerning baptism that it is necessary to Salvation, because by baptism the grace of God is offered. ` Infants are to be baptized, who being brought to God by baptism are received into his favour. They condemn the Anabaptists who disallow the baptism of infants and affirm that they may be saved without it.

Art. X.

" They teach respecting the Lord's Supper that the body and blood of Christ are truly present, and are distributed to the recipients, and disapprove of those who teach otherwise.

Art. XI.

" Concerning confession they teach that private absolution may be retained in the churches, although in making confession it is not necessary that every particular delinquency be enumerated. This indeed is impossible according to the language of the Psalmist, ' Who can understand his errors ?'

Art. XII.

" Concerning penitence they teach that the remission of sins may be obtained by such as fall after baptism whenever they repent ; and that the church bestow absolution upon such returning penitents. But repentance may be divided into two parts, the one is contrition or the terrors which agitate the conscience under a sense of guilt; the other is, the faith derived from the gospel, or from absolution and which believes that sin is pardoned for the sake of Christ, the conscience pacified and released from its alarms.   Upon this good works ought to follow as the fruit of repentance.

" They condemn the Anabaptists who deny that once being justified it is possible to lose the Holy Spirit, as well as those who contend that a sinless perfection is attainable in the present life.   They condemn also the Novatians who refuse to absolve such as have fallen after baptism even upon their return to repentance ; and they are rejected who assert that the remission of sins is not connected with faith, but is obtained by our charity and good works.   They also are rejected who teach that Canonical satisfactions are necessary to make amends for eternal punishment or the pains of purgatory.

Art. XIII.

" Concerning the use of Sacraments, they teach that the Sacraments are instituted not only as the signs to men of our religious profession, but rather as the signs and evidences of the will of God to us to quicken and confirm the faith of those who observe them. The Sacraments are to be used therefore, that faith may be increased through believing the promises particularly exhibited and impressed by Sacraments. They condemn therefore those who teach that the Sacraments can justify as works of merit, denying that faith is requisite in the reception of them.

Art. XIV.

" Concerning church order, they teach that no one ought to teach publicly or to administer the Sacraments unless he be lawfully called.

Art. XV.

" Concerning rites in the church, they teach that those rites are to be observed which can be observed without sin and which conduce to the peace and good order of the church ; such as certain holidays and feasts. But in reference to these things men are to be admonished lest their consciences should be burdened with the idea that such worship is essential to Salvation. They must also be admonished that human traditions

instituted with a view of pleasing God, pur-
chasing his favour and atoning for sin are contrary to the gospel and the doctrine of faith.
Hence vows, traditions respecting meats and
drinks, &c. instituted to purchase divine favour
and satisfy for sins are useless and contrary to the
gospel.

Art. XVI.

" Concerning civil matters they teach that
lawful civil appointments are good in the sight of
God and that Christians may exercise the office
of a magistrate, may judge according to imperial
and other existing laws, inflict legal punishments, declare war, take up the military profession, make lawful contracts, hold property,
take an oath upon the requisition of a magistrate,
marry and trade.

" They condemn the Anabaptists who forbid the exercise of these civil offices by Christians, and they condemn those who do not place
evangelical perfection in the fear of God and in
faith, but in abandoning civil offices because the
gospel recommends the righteousness of the
heart ; but it does not abrogate political institutions, but requires the preservation of them as
ordinances of God and in such ordinances to exercise charity. It becomes Christians therefore
to obey their own magistrates and laws, excepting when they command them to do evil, in

which case we must obey God rather than men.
Acts v.

Act. XVII.

" They teach that Christ will appear in
judgment at the end of the world, that he will
raise the dead and bestow eternal life and everlasting felicity on his holy and elect people ; but
he will condemn wicked men and devils to endless torment. They condemn the Anabaptists
who imagine there will be a termination to the
punishment of wicked men and devils ; and also
others who are dispersing the Jewish notions that
previous to the resurrection of the dead the
righteous will occupy a worldly kingdom and
oppress the wicked.

Art. XVIII.

" Concerning free will they teach that the
human will is in a certain sense and in reference
to civil concerns and the exercise of reason free ;
but it has no efficiency in spiritual concerns
without the Holy Spirit, because the natural
man does not perceive the things of the Spirit ;
they are impressed upon the heart by means of
the word through the agency of the Holy Spirit.
Augustine delivers the same doctrine in his Hy-
pognosticon, Lib. III.—We admit that the will
is free in all men who can judge according to
reason, not indeed in divine things to begin or

go forward independantly of God, but only in
what pertains to the present life both good and
evil.   I say *good* referring to those things which
arise out of our natural welfare, as the cultivation of the soil, eating and drinking, friendship,
clothing, preparing a residence, marrying, tending cattle, acquiring the knowledge of various
arts and whatever pertains to the welfare of the
present life; all which things subsisting alone are
conducted without a *divine* direction.   By the
term *evil* I referred to the worship of idols, murder, &c.

" They condemn the Pelagians and others
who teach that we are able to please God su-
premely without the Holy Spirit and by the
power of nature alone ; and substantially to obey
his precepts.   For though nature can in some
respects perform external works, as abstaining
from theft and murder, it cannot command internal affections as the fear of God, faith in him,
purity, patience, &c.

Art. XIX.

" Concerning the cause of sin they teach
that though God is the Creator and preserver of
our nature, Sin originates entirely in the will
of evil beings, namely, devils and wicked men,
which apart from divine influence turns them
aside from God ; Christ says of the devil, ' When
he speaketh a lie he speaketh of his own.'   John
viii.

Art. XX.

" Our churches are falsely accused of prohibiting good works, for their writings now extant concerning the Ten Commandments and
others testify that they have given salutary instructions respecting every duty of life; what
kind of life and what works in every different
situation please God. Formerly public instructors
taught little of these things, but urged the practice of puerile and needless observances as certain feasts, fasts, fraternizations, peregrina-
tions, worship of saints, rosaries, (z) and the
like. Our adversaries have now learned to
do without these useless things and not to preach
them up so much as formerly. They moreover
begin to speak of faith respecting which they
were before wonderfully silent, although they
still obscure the real doctrine of faith by disre-
garding trembling consciences and commanding
the observance of good works in order to *merit*
the forgiveness of sin.

" As therefore the doctrine of faith which
ought to be regarded as of prime importance in
the church, was so long spoken of in an ignorant
manner however it was admitted to be necessary
by all, the most profound silence reigning in
public discourses respecting justification by

(z) A rosary is a mass with the prayers to the Virgin
Mary.

faith though the doctrine of works was continually canvassed, it was deemed proper to admonish the churches on the subject of faith.

" In the first place our works cannot reconcile us to God or merit the remission of sins, the
favour of God, grace and justification, for this
can only follow from faith, believing that we are
reccived into favour through Christ the only
Mediator and atoning sacrifice by whom the
Father is reconciled. Consequently whoever
trusts in his own works as meritorious despises
the merit and the grace of Christ, and seeks a
way to God without Christ, by human strength,
although Christ avers, ' I am the way, the truth
and the life.' Paul every where teaches this
doctrine concerning faith.—Thus, Eph. ii. ' By
grace ye are saved through faith and that not of
yourselves, it is the gift of God, not of works,' &c.
And lest a caviller should arise, saying that we
have devised a new interpretation for the language of Paul, we appeal to the testimony of the
Fathers. Augustine in many of his writings
defends grace and the righteousness of faith in
opposition to the merit of works. Ambrose
does the same in his call of the Gentiles and elsewhere ; for thus he speaks, ' The redemption of
Christ would be of little value and the mercy of
God must yield to the merit of human performances if justification were due to antecedent
merits, so as to be the reward of works and not
of free bounty.'

" Although the ignorant despise this doctrine, pious and trembling consciences derive from it much consolation because works cannot restore peace to the mind but faith only, by which they become assured of pleasing God through Christ. So speaks Paul, Rom. v. ' Being justified by faith we have peace with God.' The whole of his statement refers to the internal warfare of an alarmed conscience and cannot be understood unless this warfare is experienced. Ignorant and profane persons therefore judge most erroneously upon this subject, who dream that there is no such thing as Christian justification but only a philosophical and civil one.

" The consciences of men in former times who did not listen to the gospel were much tormented respecting the doctrine of works, some were driven into deserts and monasteries, hoping to merit grace by a monastic life ; others devised other works to purchase favour and make satisfaction for sin. The greatest necessity therefore existed to give a clear statement of the doctrine of faith in Christ, that the trembling conscience should not seek consolation in vain and should be instructed how by faith in Christ, favour, pardon and justification were to be obtained.

" Men are instructed that this term faith does not signify merely historical knowledge such as wicked men and devils possess, but it

Y

includes not only a credit of the historical fact
but of the effect resulting, namely, the remission of sins, that is, that through Christ we
enjoy mercy, justification and forgiveness.
Whoever knows that through Christ he has a
merciful Father truly knows God, knows that
he is under his care, loves him and calls upon
his name ; not living without God like the heathen.   Devils and wicked men cannot believe in
the doctrine of remission, consequently they
hate God as an enemy, neither calling upon him
nor expecting any good at his hands.   Augustine delivers the same doctrine respecting faith,
stating that this term is used in Scripture not
for such knowledge as the wicked possess, but
for that confidence which consoles and inspirits
trembling minds.

"Our churches moreover teach that good
works are necessary ; not as meritorious in procuring divine mercy, but such is the will of God,
for remission of sins and peace of conscience can
only be obtained by faith ; and the Holy Spirit is
received by faith and the heart being renewed new
affections are imparted that good works may be
produced.   Independently of the Holy spirit,
human nature is full of vile affections and totally
incapable of doing any thing good in the divine
sight, but, under diabolical influence men are
impelled to various sins, impious sentiments and
open immorality.   Thus we see philosophers

aiming to live in a moral manner, but they were unable to do so, and fell into open vice. Such is human imbecility when under the guidance of his own power, without faith and destitute of the Holy Spirit.

" Hence it is apparent that our doctrine cannot be accused of prohibiting good works, but is worthy of commendation as shewing in what manner they can be performed. For without faith human nature cannot fulfil the first or second precepts of the law ; without faith it cannot call upon God, or expect any thing from him, it cannot bear the cross, but seeks human support and confides in them. When faith and confidence in God are wanting vain desires and carnal principles reign in the heart. Hence Christ says, ' Without me ye can do nothing,' John xv. And the church says, ' Without thy Spirit there is nothing in man, nothing good.'

Art. XXI.

" Concerning the worship of saints they teach that their memory may be exhibited, that we may imitate their faith and good works, in the same manner as the Emperor could imitate the example of David in waging war to expel the Turks from the empire, both being kings ; but Scripture never instructs us to invoke saints or to implore assistance from them, because it presents Christ to us as the only Mediator, Sacrifice, Priest and Intercessor. To him we are to apply who promises to hear our supplications and who approves our worship, that is, that we resort to his aid in all our afflictions. 1 John ii. ' If any man sin we have an advocate with the Father Jesus Christ the righteous.'

" Such is nearly a summary of our doctrine which it may be seen does not disagree with Scripture nor with the universal church, nor with the Romish church so far as may be ascertained from its writers, so that we are injuriously treated by those who denounce us as heretics. But the dissension between us refers to certain abuses which have in an unauthorized manner crept into the churches, in respect to which difference it becomes the bishops to exercise lenity and to tolerate us on account of this our confession, because the canons themselves are not so severe as to require the same rites in all places, nor were the same rites ever exactly the same in all the churches. However, for the most part, the ancient rites are observed amongst us. It is therefore calumnious to represent all ceremonies and all the ancient institutions as abolished in our churches. But it has been the public complaint that abuses have adhered to the practice of the usual rites, and these, since pious sincere consciences could not approve them are in some measure corrected."

ARTICLES

In which the particular abuses that have been changed are recited.

" Since we do not differ from the Catholic church in articles of faith, but only omit some few abuses which are both novel and are received contrary to the canons through the corruption of the times, we implore your Imperial Majesty to give us a gracious hearing respecting these changes and the reasons for them, that the people may not be compelled against their consciences to observe such abuses.   Let not your Imperial Majesty listen to those who stir up hatred and distribute monstrous calumnies against us ; by which means the minds of good men being irritated against us, an occasion of disagreement and disord is furnished.   For your Imperial Majesty will doubtless perceive that our system both of doctrine and ceremonies is superior to what it is represented by the wicked and malevolent.   Besides the truth is not to be collected from the report of the multitude or the railings of adversaries, and it is easy to perceive that nothing conduces so much to preserve the true dignity of worship and the piety of the people, as the proper administration of the public services of the church. *(a)*

(a) In giving the remaining part of the Confession it has not been deemed requisite to adhere so closely to the words of

THE SACRAMENT IN BOTH KINDS.

" The Sacrament is administered to the laity in both kinds and not to the ministers only, because it is commanded by Jesus Christ— ' Drink ye *all* of this.' Whence it is apparent that *all* were to partake of the cup ; and lest there should be any dispute whether this injunction were applicable to the people, Paul testifies in the Epistle to the Corinthians that the *whole church* commonly received the Supper in both kinds. This was a long continued practice and it is uncertain who first introduced a different custom. Cyprian and Jerome relate that this was the usual practice and the decrees of several popes command it. We do not admit the division of the Sacrament, as such a practice would not comport with the original institution.

THE MARRIAGE OF PRIESTS.

" Upon occasion of a public complaint that some of the priests had violated their vow of celibacy, Pope Pius is reported to have said that

the writer, but rather to furnish a correct abstract of the statement, because the *doctrinal* is the most important part and furnishes a view of the sentiments of the Reformers, which Protestants will naturally feel anxious exactly to know; and because it would be tedious and useless to detail all that at the time of the Diet of Augsburg, it was thought necessary to state respecting those abuses of which but one opinion now prevails amongst Protestants.

there were several reasons why the priesthood should be forbid to marry, but many more and weightier why they should return to the practice of it. Our priests wishing to avoid all occasion of scandal, marry and plead its legality, *first*, from the language of Paul, ' Let every one of you have his own wife,' and ' it is better to marry than to burn.' *Secondly*, from the words of Christ, ' All cannot receive this saying, for some are eunuchs.'

" It is in vain to fight against the laws of nature and the appointment of God. Paul also expressly requires of a bishop that he be married. In Germany about four hundred years ago priests were compelled to marry, for they were so opposed to it that the Archbishop of Mentz, who was going to publish a decree of the Roman Pontiff on the subject, was borne down by a tumult raised by the incensed priests, so that not only was marriage forbidden in future but contrary to all divine and human laws, those which had been contracted were dissolved.

" God himself has pronounced marriage to be honourable and even in every well constituted heathen state it was equally sanctioned by the laws, and yet now the priests are to suffer capital punishments for it ! Paul expressly asserts that forbidding to marry is a doctrine of devils.—1 Tim. iv. And be it remembered, that as no human *law* so no human *vow* can annul the command of God.

The Mass.

" Our churches explode the general opinion of the merit and application of the mass, as false and impious ; the state of the controversy may be ascertained from the following abridgment of our arguments.

1. " The remission of sins as before stated, (Art. iv.) is enjoyed through faith in Christ, consequently it is impossible to obtain this remission through any other means or without the exercise of faith.

2. " The sufferings of Christ were expiatory ; and designed as an oblation not only for original guilt but for all kinds of transgression. ' We are sanctified,' says the apostle, ' by the sacrifice of Christ once for all.'—' By the one offering of himself he hath for ever perfected them that are sanctified.' The whole epistle to the Hebrews is occupied in establishing this doctrine, that the sacrifice of Christ is the only and exclusive means of pardon and reconciliation with God.

3. " In the institution of the Lord's Supper Christ does not command the priests to offer any sacrifice either for the living or the dead. By what authority therefore is this service appointed

as an offering for sin? The mass is absurdly applied to the release of souls from purgatory, whereas it was instituted for the purpose of *remembering* Christ, and thus confirming the faith and comforting the minds of his people. This misapplication therefore contrary to the authority of Scripture is censurable as a novel and impious service.

4. " A ceremony without faith is of no avail either to those who perform it or to others, for Christ affirms they are the true worshippers who worship the Father in spirit and in truth; and the apostle states that by *faith* Abel offered a more acceptable sacrifice than Cain, and ' without *faith* it is impossible to please God.'

5. " The proper application of the blessings procured by Jesus Christ is through faith, as Paul testifies in the third chapter of the Romans. ' Whom God hath set forth a propitiation through faith in his blood.' Consequently this application cannot be through or by the merit of any other work.

6. " The institution of the Sacrament is diametrically opposed to this abuse of it, for while there is no command respecting any offering for the sins of the living or the dead, we are enjoined to partake of the body and blood of Christ and for the express purpose of remembering him. The great design of the institution is to exercise and excite our faith in receiving this

pledge of love. Besides the communion of saints was intended, that the ministers of the church might impart the body and blood of Christ to others. That this was the primitive purpose of the institution we learn from Paul, ' the wine, is it not the *communion* of the blood of Christ, and the bread is it not the *communion* of the body of Christ?'

CONFESSION.

" This practice is not abolished amongst us, but the people are instructed, that a particular enumeration of all their delinquencies is not necessary, for in fact it is impossible. ' Who,' says David, ' can understand his errors?' ' The heart of man,' says Jeremiah, ' is deceitful and desperately wicked.' But if no sins could be remitted unless they were distinctly mentioned, a tender conscience could never be at rest, because the greatest number of our sins are perhaps neither observed nor can they be remembered. The fathers also sanction this omission. We do not therefore burden the conscience, but this we teach, that men must bring forth the fruits of genuine repentance, obedience, the fear of God, faith, holy joy, purity and a universal ' newness of mind.' We retain and enforce contrition, faith, remission and forgiveness of sin, reformation of life and mitigation of present punishments.

The distinction of Meats and other Traditions.

" It has been commonly believed by ecclesiastics as well as the vulgar, that a regard to the distinction of meats and drinks and other human traditions may conduce to the remission of sins. Hence an innumerable multitude of ceremonies, fasts and observances have been appointed. Many evils have resulted from this idea of traditions : as

1. " Such an opinion obscures the doctrine of grace and justification by faith, which is an essential part of the gospel and ought to be clearly stated in all the public assemblies of the church. The merit of Christ alone, as the cause of justification, is stated by Paul, but this reliance on human traditions annuls it.

2. " It operates further to abrogate the divine precepts, because tradition is more consulted than the authority of God and the whole of christianity is represented as consisting in the observance of certain days, rites, fasts and clothing. These observances are dignified by the name of a spiritual and perfect way, but the commands of God to attend to our duties, the education of our children, and to obey our rulers are deemed worldly and imperfect, and far inferior to these other splendid services.

3. " Tender consciences have been exceedingly disturbed by this doctrine of human tradi-

tions, from the conviction that they could not keep them all, though they have been represented as necessary to acceptable worship. Gerson mentions many who have fallen into absolute despair and some who have even committed suicide, because they found it utterly impossible to observe the traditions, and could not be consoled by the doctrine of grace and justification by faith.

" We teach that none can obtain the forgiveness of sin or merit justification by keeping the traditions of men, consequently they cannot be essential to the proper worship of God. The evidence of this is to be deduced from the Scriptures. Christ excuses the apostles from regarding the customary traditions, ' Do not ye understand that whatsoever entereth in at the mouth,' &c. (Mat. xv. 17—20.) ' The kingdom of God is not meat and drink,' &c. (Rom. xiv. 17.) ' Let no man judge you in meat or in drink, or in respect of a holy day,' &c. (Col. ii. 16.) Again, ' if ye be dead with Christ from the rudiments of the world, why, as though living in the world are ye subject to ordinances,' &c. (Col. ii. 20.) ' Why,' says Peter, ' tempt ye God to put a yoke on the neck of the disciples which neither our fathers nor we were able to bear ?' (Acts xv. 10.) ' The spirit speaketh expressly that in the latter times some shall depart from the faith, giving heed to seducing spirits and doctrines of devils......

commanding to abstain from meats,' &c. (1 Tim. iv. 1—3.)

" To this our adversaries object that we prohibit discipline and the mortification of the flesh, but this is incorrect, for we always teach that Christians ought to bear afflictions; and to be exercised with various afflictions and to be crucified with Christ is true and not pretended mortification.

" At the same time we do observe some traditions, but the people are admonished against trusting in them for justification before God, or supposing they commit sin by an omission of them.

Monastic Vows.

" Our opinions on this subject will be best understood by considering that such was formerly the state of the monasteries, that every day many things were done in violation of canonical authority. In the time of Augustine, their colleges were free colleges, and after discipline became lax vows were every where made that it should be restored, and with these vows for the restoration of good order were connected many new observances, which were imposed contrary to the canon upon many at an improper age. Multitudes of both sexes were allured into these establishments and subjected to the severest discipline.

" To these evils others were added, especially such a persuasion of the efficacy of vows
that they were even represented as meriting the
remission of sins and justification before God,
and a monastic life was not only extolled above
every secular duty and every religious office,
but made to supersede the precepts of the gospel
itself.

" Formerly there were schools attached to
the monasteries for the purpose of communicating
instruction in sacred and secular literature ; very
important they were and serviceable in supplying the church with pastors and bishops. How
different the case is now it is needless to state.
Instead of being appropriated to learning, now a
monastic life is pretended to be a life of perfection, conducive to justification and far preferable
to any other vocation, to which even God himself has appointed men by his providence.

" These are not exaggerated statements for
the purpose of rendering the monks odious, but
simple facts adduced to illustrate the nature of
our doctrines. First, in reference to matrimony ;
we admit all to marry who are not disposed to
celibacy, because vows cannot annul the divine
appointment and command. ' Let every one
have his own wife.' It was declared at the
creation of the human race, ' it is not good for
man to be alone.' What can be said in reply to
this ? Let the obligation of a vow be asserted as

firmly as you please, it cannot be maintained
that it discharges a man from his duty to obey
God. The canons expressly teach that in every
vow the command of a superior is to be obeyed,
how much more then is the authority of God to
be regarded! If no reasons can exist for changing the obligation of vows, the Roman Pontiff
himself cannot supersede them, for surely it is
not lawful for a man to rescind an obligation
which is purely divine. But the popes very
wisely judge, that the claims of equity are to be
observed in enforcing this obligation, and consequently we often read of their exercising a dispensing power in reference to vows. Many of
the canons rescind vows which have been made
previous to the age of fifteen and one of them
states eighteen, because it is presumed that at so
early a period a youth is incapable of forming a proper judgment on a subject which is to influence
the whole of his future life: hence a great number
are furnished with an excuse to desert the monasteries, because they made their vow previous
to the required age. After all, were it conceded
that the violation of a vow is represensible, it
does not follow that marriage ought to be dissolved, which as Augustine observes, is a serious
obligation whatever some may after contracting
it suppose.

" We plead also another reason to prove
that vows are not obligatory, namely, that all

religious services which are merely of human
appointment, having no authority from God
and represented as essential to forgiveness and
justification are impious, because ' in vain,'
says Christ, ' do they worship me, teaching for
doctrines the commandments of men :' and Paul
plainly states that remission and justification are
obtained by the propitiatory sacrifice of Christ
and through faith in his name. The monks
teach that these blessings are procurable by
those observances which are of human invention, and what is this but detracting from the
honour of Christ, obscuring his glory and denying the Scripture doctrine of justification by
faith. Vows are therefore both impious and
vain ; opposed to the gospel and a shameful substitution of a man's own works for the propitiation of Christ. ' Whoever of you,' says Paul,
' are justified by works are fallen from grace.'

" Moreover the monks represent their mode
of life as the state of perfection, because they obey
both the precepts of the gospel and the appointments of councils. This is a most awful error ;
for they boast of the meritorious works of supererogation and conceive they not only obey the
precepts themselves, but possess a superabundant
righteousness to satisfy for the sins of others.

" When the people are assured that the
monkish is the only perfect life, the precepts
and the whole service of God is undervalued,

because Christian perfection is to live in the habitual fear of God, to confide in his favour through faith in Christ, to seek and to depend on his help in all the various duties which devolve upon us in our respective situations ; to be holy in our conduct and to be devoted to our proper callings. Christian perfection consists not in celibacy, nor in mendicity and mean attire.

" The examples are sufficiently numerous of persons who deserting their families and offices in civil life have withdrawn into monasteries ; and this they call flying from the world and pursuing a kind of life more acceptable to God ; but surely to keep his commandments and not the traditions of men, is alone deserving the name of a good and perfect kind of life.

ECCLESIASTICAL POWER.

" This subject has proved a fertile source of the most violent contentions, while the ecclesiastical and civil power has been united in the same ruler. The Roman Pontiffs relying on their influence and authority, have not only oppressed the consciences of men with violent excommunications and appointed new modes of worship, but have even aimed to seize and appropriate imperial sceptres and gain the dominion of the world. This conduct has been long and often condemned by learned and pious men

z

in our churches, and we have endeavoured to console afflicted consciences by pointing out the distinction between the power of the church and the power of the sword, and shewing how each ought to be revered as appointed by God for the welfare of mankind.

" The power of bishops we apprehend to be a power or authority from God to preach the gospel, to remit and retain sins, and to administer the ordinances. The commission of Christ to his disciples is thus expressed, ' As the Father hath sent me even so send I you.—Receive the Holy Ghost—whosesoever sins ye remit they shall be remitted, and whosesoever sins ye retain they shall be retained.'—' Go and preach my gospel to every creature,' &c.

" This power is to be exercised only in teaching and preaching the gospel, and in administering the ordinances or services of their proper calling, because they are not entrusted with the temporal but spiritual concerns of men and whatever relates to an eternal life. These things belong to the ministry, and the gospel is ' the *power* of *God* unto salvation to every one that believeth.' Ecclesiastical power therefore is to be exercised in the preaching of the gospel and in reference to eternal things, but not to impede or controul the political administration of empires. Nor is it the business of the magistrate to legislate for the conscience, but for the tem-

poral interests of men to protect them from injuries, to coerce them by the sword, to inflict cor-
poral punishments, to administer civil justice
and to maintain social order and peace. The
ecclesiastical must not therefore be confounded
with the civil power. The former is to teach
and to administer the ordinances but ought not
to interfere with another office, to aim at secular
dominion, to abrogate the law of the civil magistrate, to prevent due subordination, or to obstruct
the course of ordinary justice. ' My kingdom,'
exclaimed the Saviour, ' is not of this world.'
Again, ' who constituted me a judge or a divider
amongst you ?' And the apostle intimates, that
' the weapons of our warfare are *not carnal*, but
mighty through God to the pulling down of
strong holds and casting down every *imagination*
that exalteth itself against the knowledge of
God.'

" If bishops possess the power of the
sword, it is given them not by the authority of
Scripture, but by the command of kings and
princes.

" Considerable disputes have been agitated,
whether bishops or pastors possess an authority
to institute ceremonies in the church and to pre-
scribe feasts, fasts and other observances. They
who assign this right to bishops, allege this
sentence, ' I have many things to say to you
but ye cannot bear it now, but when he the

z 2

Spirit of truth shall come he will lead you into all truth :' and they plead the example of apostolic injunctions which prohibited the use of blood and things strangled—which changed the day of the Sabbath contrary as it appears to the original appointment of the law.   But we reply, that the bishops have no authority to introduce another gospel.   Besides, to establish traditions is contrary to the Scripture, and the glory of Christ is tarnished when we expect by such observances to merit remission of sins and justification before God.   This vain hope has occasioned an almost infinite number of traditions to creep into the church.

    " If the bishops are endowed with authority to load the churches with endless traditions and thus to ensnare tender consciences, why does Scripture so frequently prohibit the multiplication of traditionary service ? Why does it denominate them doctrines of devils ?

    " It may be inquired, what then is to become of our dominical days and similar institutions ?   The reply is, that bishops or pastors may make appointments for the ordinary regulation of the churches, but not represent these services as necessary to the remission of sins, or in any degree so obligatory on the consciences of men as that they are to imagine themselves guilty of any crime in omitting them.   Such appointments conduce to the preservation of love and peace, that all things may be done decently and in order, but are not to be oppressive to the conscience or represented as essential to salvation.

" Such are the principal articles of our faith. We have omitted to notice many other abuses and subjects of violent contention in order to avoid prolixity. We are firmly persuaded that these our sentiments are conformable to the prophetic and apostolic writings, and the general opinion of the true universal church of Christ. We are ready to furnish any additional information or explanation whenever it shall be deemed necessary ; in the mean time we beseech the Father of our Lord Jesus Christ, that he would preserve, purify and increase his own church which is redeemed by the blood of his Son.

" Your Imperial Majesty's,

" Faithful and submissive Servants:

" JOHN, DUKE ELECTOR OF SAXONY.
GEORGE, MARQUIS OF BRANDENBURG.
ERNEST, DUKE OF LUNENBURG.
PHILIP, LANDGRAVE OF HESSE.
JOHN FREDERIC, DUKE OF SAXONY.
FRANCIS, DUKE OF LUNENBURG.
WOLFGANG, PRINCE OF ANHALT.
SENATE AND MAGISTRATES OF NUREMBERG.
SENATE OF REUTLINGEN."

The preceding confession was read in the German language by Christian Beyer, Chancellor of Saxony. A copy was also presented at the same time in *Latin*, by Pontanus. Cœlestine relates that when he gave it to one of the Emperor's secretaries, he had the boldness to exclaim, " By the grace and through the help of God, this confession will prevail against the gates of hell." This however was more probably said at some other less public moment. *(b)*

It is reported of William, Duke of Bavaria, who vehemently opposed the doctrine of the gospel, that as soon as the confession was read, he asked Eckius whether they might overthrow this doctrine out of the Holy Scriptures ; " No," replied Eckius, " by the Holy Scripture we cannot overthrow it, but we may by the fathers." Upon which Cardinal Albert, Archbishop of Mentz, said to the Duke of Bavaria, " Behold how finely our divines support us ! The Protestants prove what they say out of the Holy Scriptures, but we have our doctrine without Scripture." *(c)*

The Emperor immediately dismissed the assembly, and entered into a serious consultation with the Popish fraternity respecting the proper line of conduct to be adopted. Some were for enforcing the edict of Worms and compelling the consciences of their opponents to submit to imperial and ecclesiastical authority, others were

(b) SECKENDORF.   *(c)* COLLOQ. MENSAL. p. 152.

desirous of selecting a certain number of learned
men to consult and advise the Emperor. But
the prevailing opinion which Melancthon had
anticipated, *(d)* was to procure a confutation of
the Protestant articles from the Popish divines,
which should be read in a full Diet. Faber,
Eckius, Conrad de Wimpina, Conrad Collinus,
John Cochlæus and other select associates undertook and speedily completed the work. It
was reviewed by the Emperor and the Catholic
princes, who advised the omission of all expressions calculated to promote irritation. On the
third of August the Diet was convened to hear
it ; and on the sixth Melancthon thus expresses
his opinion in a letter to Luther. " At length
we have heard the confutation and at the same
time the Emperor's sentiments which were sufficiently bitter. Before this document was
read, he declared that he was resolved to abide
by the opinions he had caused to be there stated,
and desired that our princes would adopt the
same ; but if they refused, he as the defender of
the church would no longer tolerate the German
Schism. This was the sum of his oration,
which infamous as it was, the Catholics welcomed with prodigious applause. The same
may be said of their *puerile* confutation, for absolutely it is more foolish than any thing which

(d) MELANCTH. Ep. Lib. I. 12. *ad Luth.*

even Faber has published." *(e)* In another letter
to Luther two days afterwards, he intimates
" that their adversaries had used threatening language to terrify the princes from their adherence
to the doctrines of the Reformation," and it
appears that they had distinctly assured the
Elector John, that " unless he would abjure the
Lutheran doctrines which he had embraced, the
Emperor would raise an armed force to oblige him
and that he should be deprived of his dignities,
his possessions and even his life with all who professed the same faith, their wives and children."
It was some time before the Elector could re-
cover from the agitation which such a violent
philippic had produced, but the effect was temporary. *(f)*

Though many articles of the confession were
approved ; others, especially the fourth, fifth,
sixth, seventh, twentieth and twenty-first were
totally rejected.   The second respecting original
sin they admitted, excepting the definition which
appeared to them more descriptive of actual than
original sin ; the eleventh was only objected to
in reference to what was said of confession ; and
the several anti-catholic intimations in the twelfth
and fifteenth were of course the subjects of
animadversion.   They affirm in contradiction to
the second part of the Augsburg Confession, that

(e) MELANCTH. Ep. Lib. I. ep. 12.
(f) CŒLESTIN. Hist. Tom. III. 26.

Communion in one kind, the Celibacy of Priests, the Mass, Monastic Vows and the other subjects of objection introduced by the Protestants are not abuses, but religious and holy usages commanded by Scripture and confirmed by tradition. At the same time they admit that some degree of Reformation in the practice of them was requisite, to which the Emperor would pay due attention. They finished by expressing a hope that the Protestants would return to the communion of the church.

To the concluding intimation, the Elector of Saxony who spoke in the name of the Protestants replied, that they were ready to do any thing which conscience would allow for the sake of promoting union in religion, that if the Catholics could prove from Scripture that they had advanced any error, it should be recanted and were ready to furnish any explanation that might be demanded, and they wished to have a copy of the refutation of their articles. This request the Emperor refused, but two days afterwards offered it upon condition of its not being published. This was not agreed to, but seventeen persons were nominated by the Catholics to discuss religious differences, whose conferences were however of no avail. The Elector of Brandenburg pressed the necessity of satisfying the Emperor, by uniting in matters of faith with the princes and members of the empire, otherwise they might incur the reproach of involving Germany in war and tumult. After due deliberation, they communicated their answer by their deputy George Brucke to this purpose, " that they took it ill to be threatened, the Emperor would not give them a sufficient hearing, and that they were not allowed but upon a severe condition, a copy of the refutation of their articles. It was expected they should assent to it without examination, which their consciences disallowed, and notwithstanding the promise of a general council in the last Diet at Spires, it had not been convened." To this the Roman deputies replied in a defensive and explanatory paper, and finally it was agreed at the suggestion of the Protestants, that a smaller number should be appointed for the determination of the present controversy. Two princes, two lawyers and three divines were selected on each side conformably with this resolution. The Catholics were the Bishop of Augsburg, Henry, Duke of Brunswick, the Chancellor of the Archbishop of Cologne, and the Chancellor of the Marquis of Baden, John Eckius, Conrad Wimpina and John Cochlæus: the Protestants were, John Frederic, son of the Elector of Saxony, George, Marquis of Brandenburg; the lawyers, Gregory Pontanus and Heller; and the divines, Melancthon, Brentius and Schnepfius.

After conferring together they managed a

mode of expression, in which fifteen articles of the Augsburg Confession were mutually subscribed and only six remained; of these three were only in part disputed and the rest remitted to the second division of the confession, upon which they still continued and were likely to remain disunited.

The state of the question being reported to the Diet, it was resolved that a smaller committee consisting of three only on each side, two lawyers and one divine would be more available. Melancthon was nominated for the Protestants, and Eckius for the Catholics. The principal points of debate were the Mass, Vows and the Celibacy of Priests. The Catholics agreed that the Priests who were married might live with their wives, but they would make no concessions respecting the Mass and Vows.

The Emperor was extremely anxious to reconcile contending parties, and endeavoured to win over the Protestant princes by the most attentive behaviour and the most alluring promises. In particular he urged the Elector of Saxony and the Landgrave of Hesse; but to their immortal honour be it recorded, they were neither to be allured nor alarmed into a dereliction of the noble but too often persecuted cause of Christian liberty. *(g)*

(g) SLEID. 132. SCULTET. Annal. 158.

All hopes of an accommodation were now at an end and the worst was anticipated. " We expect," says Melancthon, " violent measures, for no moderation can satisfy the Popish faction. They, in fact, seek our destruction. Pray that God may preserve us." *(h)*

" An APOLOGY for the Augsburg Confession," drawn up by Melancthon, was on the twenty-second of September presented by the Protestant princes to the Emperor, who declined receiving it. Though not published till the following year, the insertion of a few short extracts in this place seems appropriate and will be acceptable.

" To represent justification as by faith *only* has been considered objectionable, though Paul concludes that a ' man is justified by faith without the deeds of the law ;' *(i)* that we are ' justified freely by his grace,' *(k)* and that ' it is the gift of God not of works lest any man should boast.' *(l)* If the use of the exclusive term *only* is deemed inadmissible, let them expunge from the writings of the apostle the exclusive phrases *by grace, not of works, the gift of God* and others of similar import. We exclude all notions of human merit, but not as our adversaries calumniously insinuate the use of Sacra-

(h) Ep. 12. ad Hess.   *(i)* ROM. iii. 28.
(k) ROM. iii. 24.   *(l)* EPH. ii. 8, 9.

ments and means. It has been already stated
that faith cometh by hearing, and we most highly
estimate the ministry of the word. Love and
obedience must be connected with faith, so that
they are only excluded as the meritorious source
of justification.

" We state that love is essentially connected with faith," for according to Paul, ' In
Christ Jesus neither circumcision availeth any
thing, nor uncircumcision, but faith which
worketh by love.' But we do not admit that
the remission of sins and reconciliation with
God, are obtained for the sake of love as a me-
ritous act, or for any other kind of work, but by
faith only or faith properly so called, because
the promise of forgiveness respects the exercise
of faith. It is faith which assents to the promise and is every where referred to in Scripture.

" In our churches the members are instructed into the true design of the Sacrament
as a sign and testimony of the free forgiveness of
sin, a doctrine highly consolatory to trembling
spirits and in which they ought to be admonished
to place their confidence. The preaching of the
gospel and the legitimate use of the Sacraments
is with us a perpetual sacrifice, and the resort
to our services is far more numerous than to those
of our adversaries, because they are more useful
and intelligible. But their doctrines neither the

learned nor the ignorant can comprehend. Truth,
holy doctrine, the proper use of Sacraments,
affectionate discourses, constitute the proper ornaments of churches, but wax tapers, golden
vases and other things of a similar nature though
ornamental in themselves do not constitute the
glory of the Christian church: and if our adversaries mistake these for worship, instead of
the preaching of the gospel and the exercises of
faith, they must be numbered amongst those
whom Daniel describes, as ' honouring their own
God with gold and silver, and with precious
stones and pleasant things.' *(m)*

   " We are not fond of invidious comparisons,
but as our adversaries are perpetually urging them
we cannot omit mentioning some of their evil
practices.   What mischief is done by the profa-
nation of the Mass !   What evils result from
their law of celibacy !   What a manifest piece
of idolatry is the worship of saints !   Then will
it be affirmed there is nothing reprehensible in
the ambition of their Pontiffs, who for upwards
of four hundred years have waged an incessant
war with our Emperors in Italy, and sometimes
even in Germany itself, arming sons and fathers,
relatives and citizens against each other ?   And
if the records of history be searched to ascertain
the true causes of such hostilities, I use the

(m) DAN. xi. 38.

most moderate terms when I say no cause, worthy of the station and character of these dignitaries can be found. What mischief ensues from the delegation of unfit persons to the sacerdotal office and from trafficking in benefices! And is there no fault in the dangerous disputes that are prevalent, which indeed might be pardoned if the purity of doctrine were preserved in the churches? But, what impious opinions and traditions are introduced and practised, let the writings of canonists and divines testify which abound in discussions some useless and some opposed to the gospel of Christ. Then, in interpreting Scripture they trifle and take the most unwarrantable liberties."

On the subject of ecclesiastical jurisdiction and the power of bishops, Melancthon had conceded in his conferences with the Papist committee more than many of his own party thoroughly approved, and yet Luther himself in his admonition to the princes of the empire, allowed that the bishops might retain their authority both civil and ecclesiastical, if they would employ it to the glory of God and not support the Pope's supremacy. The fact was, that Melancthon entertained hopes of an essential reformation in the spirit and conduct of the bishops, while Luther despaired of the possibility of effecting it, and was therefore extremely cautious of any concession to their authority. *(o)* In all doctrinal points Melancthon proved himself a firm, enlightened, inflexible Protestant. The testimony of a good conscience supported him amidst the perpetual calumnies which his zealous, disinterested and pious labours incurred; and if as many suspected, the Catholics selected him and Eckius finally to adjust the points of difference from an expectation that his characteristic gentleness and dislike of contention would induce him to sacrifice truth to peace, they were completely disappointed. It is agreed he went as far as possible, and further probably than his stern friend Luther could have been induced to do; but it would be difficult to prove that impetuosity and violence are conducive to conviction, or in any respect auxiliary to truth. Inflexibility is a virtue, but not the more estimable for assuming a military dress or a menacing air.

A celebrated ecclesiastical historian *(p)* has judiciously remarked, " it was in these conferences (at Augsburg) that the spirit and character of Melancthon appeared in their true and genuine colours; and it was here that the votaries of Rome exhausted their efforts to gain over to their party this pillar of the Reformation, whose abi-

(o) SECKEND. Hist. Luth. Lib. II. p. 159.
(p) MOSH. Eccles. Hist. Vol. IV. p. 96.

lities and virtues added such a lustre to the Protestant cause. This humane and gentle spirit
was apt to sink into a kind of yielding softness,
under the influence of mild and generous treatment. And accordingly while his adversaries
soothed him with fair words and flattering promises, he seemed to melt as they spoke and in
some measure to comply with their demands ;
but when they so far forgot themselves as to
make use of imperious language and menacing
terms, then did Melancthon appear in a very
different point of light; then a spirit of in-
trepidity, ardour and independance animated all
his words and actions, and he looked down with
contempt on the threats of power, the frowns of
fortune and the fear of death. The truth is, that
in this great and good man, a soft and yielding
temper was joined with the most inviolable fidelity and the most invincible attachment to the
truth."

In the midst of these multifarious transactions a correspondence was maintained between
Melancthon and many distinguished characters.
Scarcely a day passed in which there was not
some kind of communication with Luther, who
suggested various consolatory sentiments to his
friend and not unfrequently rallied him with
some severity respecting his apprehensive state of
mind. The following illustrative anecdote however ought by no means to be omitted, because

it evinces the sterling integrity of his principle, notwithstanding the imputations of historians, amidst his constitutional infirmities. After the Protestant confession had been presented to the council, Cardinal Campegius and his party inquired of Melancthon if he still persisted in his opinion. Upon which he replied, that " neither he nor his associates could abandon the known truth, and he besought him not to denounce their sentiments, but to allow them to avow what they never could deny with a good conscience." Campegius answered, " I cannot allow it, for the successor of Peter is infallible." " Well then," rejoined Melancthon, " we commend ourselves and our concerns to God. If HE be for us who can be against us ?—We shall await with patience whatever may happen to us. In our provinces we have upwards of forty thousand persons including poor ministers, their families and parishioners whose spiritual interest we cannot abandon, but will do whatever we are able for them praying for the help of Jesus Christ whose cause we espouse; and in our calling we are prepared to labour with patience and endure all difficulties. If it be necessary we would, if such be the will of God, rather fight and die than betray so many souls." (q)

The decree of the Diet was at length pub-

(q) VAN DE CORPUT Leven ende Dood van Phil. Mel. p. 179.

lished on the nineteenth of November. It assumed a tone of high authority, asserting the Catholic doctrines and condemning the tenets of Protestantism. The people were exhorted to hear mass, to pray to the Virgin and to saints, to observe holy days ; images and statues were ordered to be replaced where they had been removed, and all alterations or innovations in religion were strictly prohibited. This decree was to be put in execution whatever opposition or appeals might be made against it, and all who refused to obey it subjected themselves to be put under the ban of the empire, and were declared incapable of being admitted to the Imperial Chamber. The princes, states and cities which had rejected the Papal authority, were required under pain of exemplary punishment to return to their allegiance to Rome. The only consolatory circumstance amidst this imperial thunder, was a faint whisper that an application should be made to the Pope respecting the appointment of a general council within six months to decide religious controversies. (r)

The Protestants in general and the anxious mind of Melancthon in particular could not but feel deeply affected with this termination of the conferences at Augsburg. The disposition of

(r) SLEID. Hist. 139.

2 A 2

their adversaries was sufficiently obvious, for in addition to this persecuting decree the Emperor had pledged himself to unite with the confederated forces of the Popish princes, to compel the execution of it and maintain the established religion. *(s)*

The Protestant princes retired from the Diet with the strongest feelings of dissatisfaction and disappointment. Instead of despairing however, they re-assembled at Smalcald, and the result of this conference was, the adoption of *defensive* measures for the preservation of their religious liberties. *(t)*

Soon after these transactions Melancthon with Luther and other divines, met together for the purpose of consulting respecting the proper measures to be adopted in the present exigency, and after having spent some time in prayer to heaven, whence only they could expect adequate assistance, Melancthon was suddenly called out of the room from which he retired under great depression of spirits. He saw during his absence some of the elders of the reformed churches with their parishioners and families. Several children were also brought hanging at the breast, while others a little older were engaged in prayer. This reminded him of the pro-

(s) SLEID. 140.   *(t)* SLEID. Hist. 142.

prophetic language, " out of the mouth of babes and sucklings hast thou ordained strength because of thine enemies, that thou mightest still the enemy and the avenger." *(v)*   Animated by this interesting scene he returned to his friends with a disencumbered mind and a cheerful countenance. Luther astonished at this sudden change said, " What now! what has happened to you, Philip, that you are become so cheerful ?"   " O sirs," replied Melancthon, " let us not be discouraged, for I have seen our noble protectors, and such as I will venture to say will prove invincible against every foe !"—" And pray," returned Luther, thrilling with surprize and pleasure, " Who and where are these powerful heroes ?"— " Oh !" said Melancthon, " *they are the wives of our parishioners and their little children whose prayers I have just witnessed—prayers which I am satisfied our God will hear :* for as our heavenly Father and the Father of our Lord Jesus Christ has never despised or rejected our supplications, we have reason to trust that he will not in the present alarming crisis." *(u)*

It is said that during the Imperial Diet at Augsburg, Albert, Archbishop of Mentz, had by some means obtained a bible and read it attentively for four hours, when one of his

(v) Ps. viii. 2.

(u) Van de Corput Leven ende Dood van Phil. Mel. p. 224, 225.

council suddenly entering his chamber, asked with much astonishment what his Highness was doing with that book ? To which he replied, " *I know not what this book is, but sure I am, all that is written therein is quite against* us." *(w)*

(w) COLLOQ. MENSAL. p. 11.

CHAP. IX.

Smalcald—Unfavourable circumstances announced—The Emperor retracts at Ratisbon and agrees to the suspension of all legal processes against the Protestants—Death of the Elector JOHN—*Melancthon's Funeral Oration—His Epitaph—Succeeded by John Frederic—The Emperor urges on the Pope a general Council—Continuance of the Sacramental Controversy—Melancthon and Bucer confer with the Landgrave—A vain attempt at Leipsic to restore union between contending parties—*FRANCIS I. URGES MELANCTHON TO REPAIR TO FRANCE—*Their Correspondence—Entreaties of the Langœan family to the same purpose—Bellay goes into Germany and invites Melancthon into France--The Elector interposes to prevent the Journey--*HENRY VIII. INVITES MELANCTHON INTO ENGLAND—*Their Correspondence—The King of England's eagerness in dispatching Messengers to France to prevent Melancthon's continuance there if he were arrived, or otherwise to dissuade him from going—Curious original documents on the subject—A larger Commission sent into Germany—Melancthon's Communication with Archbishop Cranmer—State of his health—Takes a Journey—Injurious reports circulated—Writes against the Anabaptists—Conferences with Bucer and Capito.*

Two unfavourable events were announced to the Protestant princes, when they were as-

sembled a second time in the early part of the
year 1531, at Smalcald ; the one the Election of
Ferdinand to be king of the Romans, which was
considered as an artful proceeding of his brother
the Emperor for the purpose of rendering the
imperial crown hereditary in his family, and
consequently subversive of the liberties of the
empire—the other the commencement of prosecutions against some of their number on account
of their religious principles. It was deemed
immediately necessary to renew their defensive
league, and by means of their ambassadors to
implore the protection and support of the Kings
of England, France and Denmark.

Providence again interposed to rescue the
oppressed. It was not long before the Emperor
perceived that it was essential to his political
interests, rather to retrace his hasty steps than
by pressing on in his persecuting career to involve
Germany in a civil war. He found that his
peace with France and his friendship with the
Pope were both precarious, and that the Turkish
army was advancing upon Austria with recruited
forces. The malcontent princes were therefore
to be conciliated and not coerced, and it was
stipulated at Nuremberg and finally agreed upon
at the Diet of Ratisbon in August 1532, that
upon condition of their rendering the requisite
assistance in the war with the Turks, the Emperor would suspend all legal processes against

the Protestants on account of religion, use his utmost endeavours to procure the appointment of a general council within six months, to meet within twelve ; and that no person should at present be molested for his religion.

At this juncture the Elector JOHN was removed from his useful labours and exalted station by an apoplexy. The event occurred on the sixteenth of August 1532, and though Melancthon and Luther were immediately sent for they only arrived in time to see him expire. (x) The former delivered a Latin oration at his funeral, in which he thus admirably pourtrays the character of his prince.

" I shall not speak of his noble birth for which indeed the Dukes of Saxony are sufficiently distinguished, nor of his youthful pursuits though he might be highly eulogized for modesty and temperance, but confine myself principally to the delineation of his character during the period of his public life since the decease of his illustrious brother Frederic. Amidst a thousand difficulties, the genuine piety of the Elector John, his firmness, moderation, peaceful intentions and every other virtue which can constitute a good prince were conspicuous. It is a glorious trophy characteristic of his reign and demands our gratitude, that in a most turbulent period, these realms by the interposing

(x) SPALAT. Hist. MS. ap. Seck.

mercy of Providence have been preserved in
tranquillity though many endeavoured to stir up
war. The preservation of peace was doubtless
also a duty incumbent on a prince so favoured
of heaven, and his authority, moderation and
zeal eminently conduced to it by frequently and
forcibly disappointing the designs of ambitious
men. It is easy to judge of the extent of the
benefit derived from these exertions, when it is
recollected that the cause in which he was engaged did not respect a single province or state
only but the whole of Germany. If war had been
once kindled it would have raged throughout the
empire, so that by preserving domestic peace he
was instrumental in securing the tranquillity of
many other states.   Nor were his enemies alone
restrained by his authority and moderate counsels, but his violent confederates were checked
by perpetual efforts on his part which it would
not be proper on this occasion to particularize.
We have seen them taking up arms and in a situation to command victory, yet induced by the
prince's justice though contrary to their inclinations to adjust their respective claims without
bloodshed, in which he displayed an extraordinary heroism.   When he could have gained the
most decisive advantages over his most inveterate enemies who were at the very moment
plotting his ruin, he spared them.   How often
has he shewn a mind impregnable to sentiments

of private cupidity, for after composing strife he never cherished the spirit of revenge, but was satisfied with maintaining public tranquillity. This, this is truly worthy of a great and wise man, to conquer anger and to prefer the welfare of his country to the gratification of his private feelings. It must indeed be acknowledged that war is sometimes necessary, the enemy must be opposed and states must be roused to hostile preparations, but it is no less so that the turbulent emotions of the mind should be repressed and restored to reason, and that contention should be prevented by mild and judicious counsels.

"What, shall I say of his domestic administration which was replete with clemency and humanity? Homer represents Ulysses as ruling the Thracians like a good father, and Xenophon who proposes Cyrus as a perfect pattern for a prince, says that a good prince resembles a good father: and who ever had it in his power to say any thing worse of our departed prince who was incapable of acting with cruelty or pride? To me he appeared to cherish the most paternal feelings for all his subjects, and I have often noticed the most striking indications of it both in private discourse and in public transactions.

"His private life was most unostentatious, free from all disgraceful excess and dissipation, and all the leisure hours he could command at intervals of business were devoted to sacred literature and especially to the study of the Christian religion. To this he gave his principal attention in the latter period of his life, and as I know from indubitable authority he abounded in the exercises of devotion. No one is ignorant of the dangers he incurred through his attachment to evangelical truth ; and God eminently honoured his exalted virtue, by protecting him through so many years, and liberating him from so many dangers, as he did Hezekiah when blockaded by the Assyrian army in Jerusalem. Now in a period of public tranquillity he is taken away, but happily not unprepared for the change, from miseries which may yet await us and from the agonies of a painful disorder. We may be permitted to grieve for the loss of a prince endowed with such various excellencies, so studious of general peace, and so devotedly kind to his people that he may be denominated their *Father* as well as their *Prince*.

" In what dangers and misfortunes the state may hereafter be involved I will not pretend to predict, but most humbly implore the supreme Jehovah, while our departed Elector rests in peace, to look upon the family of his subjects, to bestow his mercies on his son and successor, that he may prove our protector amidst impending dangers ; and give peace to the state for the advancement of his truth and the glory of Jesus

Christ. We acknowledge that God is the only sufficient preserver of the state—to him we fly, from him we implore assistance who has promised to hear the supplications of the afflicted.

" Let me exhort all present earnestly to unite in this prayer to God, to bless the prince under whose protection we are now placed that he may preserve the peace of the church, maintain the doctrines of the gospel and promote every description of useful learning."

Some tributary lines by Melancthon further honour the memory of a name, brighter and more durable than the brass on which it is recorded.

> Tu quoque, Saxonice, Joannes, inclyte Princeps
> Non virtute minor cognite fratre tuo ;
> Eximiâ Christum pietate fideque colebas
> Vita piæ mentis testis eratque tuæ.
> Vindelicis coram tua Cæsare nuper in oris
> Asseruit Christi lingua professa fidem.
> Notior ut fieret divini gloria verbi
> Temporibus fulsit quæ rediviva tuis.
> Utque Evangelii studium deponere velles
> Flectere non ullæ te potuere minæ.
> Ista tui incendit constantia pectoris hostes
> Attulit et passim multa pericla tibi
> Sed te difficili protexit tempore Christus
> Et gratam pacem pro pietate dedit.
> Ac tua sæpe tamen moderatio profuit ingens
> Impia ne quisquam sumeret arma manu ;
> Hâc longè superas aliorum laude triumphos
> Hæc virtus magno Principe digna fuit.
> Ergo tuum a nullo nomen delebitur ævo
> Nec meriti laus est interitura tui.

Hic tua dum Christus meliori corpora sorte
   Restituet justis, molliter ossa cubent.
Spiritus at vivat, cælique fruatur honore
   Interea Christi conditus in gremio.

* * * * * * * * *

Virtuous as FREDERIC, thou, illustrious JOHN !
   Our weeping hearts reluctantly resign'd ;
Whose faith and love to Christ conspicuous shone,
   Whose every action mark'd a pious mind.

Thou didst the faith of Christ with zeal maintain
   Nor dread imperial dictates and decrees ;
Through all our coasts the truth of heaven proclaim,
   Whose glory brightens even times like these.

No threats could move thee and no fears alarm,
   Though foes and dangers closely round thee press'd ;
Christ for thy zeal protected thee from harm,
   And with tranquillity thy country bless'd.

Thy moderation check'd enkindling strife,
   A triumph---and the noblest man can gain !
A praise, surpassing far the hero's life,
   And worthy such a prince, so born to reign !

In Time's vast record a distinguish'd page,
   Thou shalt illustrious JOHN ! for ever grace ;
Thy name shall live through every future age,
   Nor change nor death th' eternal lines erase.

Here in soft slumbers shall thy *ashes* lie,
   Till Christ returns his matchless power to prove ;
While thy immortal *spirit* mounts the sky
   T' enjoy the heaven of her Redeemer's love.

It may be regarded as a favourable circumstance in the history of the Reformation that the

venerable Elector now deceased was succeeded by his son JOHN FREDERIC, who was zealously attached to the Protestant cause, and exerted all the energy of his mind and the vigour of his youth to promote it.

After the retreat of the Turkish army, to which it had been compelled by the menacing appearance of the Imperial forces, Charles hastened to Italy, for the purpose of procuring a personal interview with the Pope to press the appointment of a general Council. Urged by an importunity which he could not resist, he adopted the plausible measure of deputing his Nuncio, Hugo Rangonus Bishop of Reggio, to accompany the Emperor's Ambassador to the new Elector of Saxony, as head of the Protestants, to confer on the subject of a Council which he proposed should be convened at Mantua, Bologna or Placentia. The Elector immediately summoned his principal divines. Melancthon delivered it as his decided conviction " that the Roman Pontiff was practising a piece of dissimulation to cajole them into conditions to which they must not submit—that he made extraordinary concessions to induce them to agree to the decisions of a general convention of his arrangement, to which for his part he could not agree, because it ought to be a free assembly in which opinions on both sides might be discussed fairly and without restraint

—that a deceptive purpose was obvious, and it would be preposterous to consent to a Council before they knew what forms of proceeding were to be adopted, or who were to be implicated in its decrees—that the Emperor *could* not, and the Pope *would* not actually convene it." In this they all concurred, intimating to the Nuncio, that as the controversy had arisen and was principally conducted in Germany, there the Council ought to be assembled. Nothing was effected by this negociation, excepting the Roman Pontiff's purpose of creating delay. *(y)*

Although Zuinglius and Œcolampadius were now dead, the Sacramental controversy did not expire: unquestionably the conciliating spirit of Melancthon, so happily attempering his conscientious integrity, would have reconciled contending parties, had not Luther persisted in the most unwarrantable violence, which is the more to be deplored as he was obviously mistaken. In the latter end of the year 1534, Melancthon was commissioned to go and confer upon the subject with Bucer at Cassel, in the presence of the Landgrave. Bucer, who acted in the name of the Ministers of Upper Germany, and who exerted himself with

(y) PAUL Hist. 61. SECK. Hist. Luth. Lib. 3. CAM. Vit. Mel.

indefatigable zeal to effect an union between the Lutherans and Zuinglians, proposed as the basis of an agreement, that " we received truly and substantially the body and blood of Jesus Christ when we receive the Sacrament—that the bread and wine are exhibiting signs, and by receiving them the body and blood of Jesus Christ are given to us and received by us— that the bread and body of Jesus Christ are united, not by a mixture of substance, but as being given with the sacrament." On the report of this statement to Luther, his hostility was somewhat abated though not eradicated, which was the only ascertainable advantage that resulted from the interview.

An attempt was made during the same year by Ferdinand, Duke George and the Elector of Saxony, to allay religious animosities, and to promote concord. The meeting of persons appointed on each side to confer took place at Leipsic. Vehus, and Christopher Turcus his Chancellor, were the deputies of Ferdinand; Julius Phlug and George Carlovitch appeared on the part of Duke George; the disinterested piety, indefatigable perseverance and excellent spirit of Melancthon naturally induced the Elector to associate him with Pontanus in this new and lovely labour. An account of the conference is still extant in the German lan-

guage, written by Melancthon, which is distinguished by the total absence of all asperity, and
the clear undisguised statement of every transaction. It appears that the attempt to unite
was in vain—the papists adhered to their opinions, and the Saxon deputies would not relinquish truth. Vehus presented a form of concord,
but it distinctly mentioned the errors which
were most objectionable to the Protestants, especially the doctrine of the meritorious power of the
Mass to obtain the remission of sins. *(z)* Nothing is more illustrative of the true character of
Melancthon than these transactions. He was
willing to approximate as far as possible, by con-
ceding every point of difference which did not
regard what he deemed essential truth; but then
he became inflexible. Possessed of the most
benignant temper he was formed to pacify the
world, and inherited the blessedness of the
peace-maker. *(a)* Presenting to our view a
rare combination of excellences, a singular and
pleasing union of the *Christian* and the *Hero*,
we behold him firm but not violent, modest but
not servile, conscientious but not punctilious.

Wherever Lutheranism was known, or
literature admired, the name of Philip Melanc-

<hr/>

(z) Seckend. Hist. Luth. Lib. III. p. 90.
(a) Math. v. 9.

thon was familiar. Francis I. earnestly entreated him to repair to France. Maimbourg relates that Margaret Queen of Navarre and sister to the king, united with other illustrious females attached to the court who cherished sentiments favourable to the Reformation, in requesting that he might be sent for to be consulted on the existing religious contentions. The Queen frequently spoke of him to her brother as a man of exalted piety, profound learning and singular eloquence. Francis, whose active zeal for the revival of literature in France, had acquired him the title of the Father of Letters, listened with pleasure to these representations, and immediately adopted measures to procure a visit. Voræus Fossa was dispatched with a letter from the king, and a command to urge him in his name to repair to his court. The letter is preserved.

" FRANCIS, *by the Grace of God King of France*, *to our Beloved Philip Melancthon, greeting:*

" By means of William Bellaius Langey, our Chamberlain and Counsellor, to whom the management of Ecclesiastical affairs is principally confided, I have for some time known it to be your peculiar study to appease the present disputes in religion; and now I find both from

your letters to him, and from the report of Bar-
nabas Voræus Fossa, who is just returned, that
this is a very gratifying labour to you. I wish
you to come the very first opportunity, and fully
confer with some of our most eminent Doctors
on the reconciliation of opinions, and of other
things susceptible of improvement in the government of the church, for which I feel the
greatest solicitude and anxiety. However, I
will send Voræus Fossa to you immediately with these letters for a safe conduct,
imploring you not to be dissuaded by any
one from this pious and holy undertaking.
Your visit will be most grateful to me, and you
are at perfect liberty to come either in a private
or public character, and be assured you will find
me, as indeed I always have been, most desirous
of promoting your glory, reputation and comfort
both at home and abroad.

" *From the town of* GUISE, *the twenty-eighth
day of June, one thousand five hundred and
thirty five.*"

MELANCTHON'S REPLY.

" *Most Christian and most Potent King!*

" ALTHOUGH the far-famed kingdom of
France greatly surpasses every other in the
known world in many other honourable distinctions, this may be noticed with peculiar ap-

probation that it has always excelled the rest of
the nations in purity of doctrine and perpetual
zeal in defence of the Christian religion.   It has
therefore deservedly obtained the appellation of
most happy and most *Christian*, a title the most
glorious, the most magnificent that can be conferred.   I congratulate your Majesty that at
this juncture you have undertaken the care of
preserving the church, not by the application of
violent remedies, but by rational means, worthy
the name of the *Most Christian King;* and that
in the midst of the present dissensions you have
so studied to moderate the violence of opposing
parties, that the genuine unadulterated doctrines
of Christianity, the glory of Christ, the true
dignity of the ecclesiastical constitution, and
the tranquillity of the state may be promoted.
Nothing can be imagined more becoming a
king than this disposition of mind and these
proceedings.   I beseech your Majesty to persevere in this care and concern for your kingdom : for although public dissension has in
some instances furnished occasion of mischief
to violent and evil-minded Ecclesiastics, yet
good men have brought forward in the church
many things which are essentially conducive
to its welfare.   Although therefore a mis-
chievous disposition of mind ought to be restrained, yet I entreat your Majesty not to be

influenced by the bitter sentiments or writings
of the calumnious, to suffer good and useful regulations to be abandoned in the churches.　For
my own part I have never been pleased with
those intemperate counsels which have degraded
the best and most holy order of the church, and
which ought ever to be held in peculiar veneration: and I am well persuaded that all good
men in your nation, who value the truth as I do,
cherish this feeling.　When I received your
royal invitation, God is my witness how much
I have laboured immediately to comply with
it; for nothing would gratify me so much
as to be of some service to the church according to my feeble capacity, and I indulge the
most pleasing anticipations from my knowledge
of the piety, the moderation, and the constant
aim to promote the glory of Christ displayed by
your Majesty.　But Voræus can detail the numerous difficulties which have delayed my
visit, and which, though they should prevent
this journey, cannot detach my mind from a
steady purpose of checking by my advice and
exertions the existing controversies.　Voræus
however will fully state my views.

" Finally, I commit myself to your royal
favour, promising constantly to contribute my
judgment with that of the pious and learned
men of the church for the general good.　May

Christ preserve your Majesty in prosperity and
safety, that your government may promote the
general happiness of the world and the glory of
God.

Your Majesty's

Most devoted Servant,

PHILIP MELANCTHON.

" *From Saxony, the fifth day of September,
    one thousand five hundred and thirty
    five.*"

In addition to these very curious documents, a further illustration of the dispositions
prevalent at this period in the French Court, at
least amongst some of its most enlightened ornaments, is afforded by a letter addressed to
Melancthon by Cardinal Bellaius, dated the
twenty-seventh of June. *(c)* After applauding
the benevolent wishes which he knew from
Voræus that he entertained for the general
cause of Christianity, the Cardinal proceeds,
" I desire nothing more ardently than that the
dissensions which have so long agitated the
Christian church may be appeased. Apply the
utmost of your power, my dear Melancthon, by
the help of God, to promote this general paci-
fication, and you will have the concurrent ap-

(c) SECKEND. Hist. Luth. Lib. III. p. 109.

probation of all good men, especially of Francis, who, while possessing the supreme authority, is not only the *Most Christian King* in *name* and *title*, but in *truth*, as I have long had occasion to witness. I hope every thing from your meeting, and the matured advice you will give." The warm attachment of the Cardinal may be imagined from his subscribing himself, " Yours, *from my very heart*, Bellaius."

In another letter written by William Langey, and dated the sixteenth of July, Melancthon is urged by a variety of arguments to visit France. " I have explained," says he, " to my friends who are interested in the common cause all circumstances, and have given them your letters, and those of Bucer, to peruse. I feel myself somewhat implicated in this affair, and should be sorry for any thing to occur dishonourable to you, or injurious to the cause of truth and the glory of Christ. The Cardinal Langey was shewn the letters you have received from me previous to their being sent, lest any thing should have been written which he might disapprove or deem contrary to the views of the king." He afterwards alludes to the controversy respecting the place of holding the proposed Council, represents the good inclinations of the king, and alludes to a private consultation with Melancthon upon the best and safest means of reforming the state of ecclesiastical affairs.

Langey apologizes for the severities which had been inflicted upon some persons for their religious opinions, alleging what however is not very admissible, that they were only a set of enthusiasts of notorious character, whom Melancthon himself would have been inclined to punish. After urging various other considerations to induce his compliance with the King's request, who he says was not only prepossessed in his favour, but naturally acute, prudent and willing to listen to sound argument; he concludes thus, " I exhort you, I conjure you for Christ's sake not to neglect the present occasion of accomplishing a business of all others the most glorious in which mortals can be engaged."

The *Sorbonne divines* probably would not have very readily united in these pressing solicitations, for how could they forget or forgive the satirical pen of Melancthon ; and there is reason to suspect that a temporizing policy more than a spirit of sincere inquiry after truth dictated their prince's invitation. Francis had seized the opportunity afforded him by the full employment of the emperor's confederate forces against the Turks to renew his claims in Italy, and used every effort to excite in the different princes of Europe a jealousy of his rival's power. But his measures mere disconcerted, and from the operation of different causes he was generally unsuccessful. The invitation he received from the associated Protestant princes at Smalcald was therefore at this crisis peculiarly welcome, and he was naturally led to use every endeavour to promote his own views by securing their confidence.   For this purpose he negociated and flattered, accommodating himself to their religious prejudices, affecting a wonderful moderation and even a spirit of pious inquiry in matters of controversy.   A very curious affair had been transacted at Paris, to which the preceding letter of Langey refers.   With an indiscretion which no one can defend, some of the Parisians who had imbibed the principles of Protestantism *(d)* posted up hand bills in several of the public places and on the gates of the Louvre, containing reflections on the doctrines, rites and clergy of the church of Rome.   The king being highly incensed at these proceedings, issued a general order against heretics and appointed a solemn procession.   The holy host was carried through the city, the king walked with his feet bare and his head uncovered, attended by the queen, the princes of the blood and all his courtiers.   Six Lutherans were publicly condemned by the parliament to be burnt, a decree which was executed with the most shocking barbarity be-

(d) Mezeray in relating this transaction, says they were Sacramentarians.   *Abregé Chronol. de l'Hist. de France.* Tom. II. p. 898.

fore the procession was finished; and others were sought after with the most eager diligence. *(e)*

For the purpose of explaining these circumstances and securing the Protestant alliance, Bellay was sent to the German princes. He was instructed to assure them " that the persons proscribed and punished were guilty of seditious practices, that the king wished for an accommodation on the subject of religion by a meeting of the Parisian and German divines, and that he was particularly desirous of a visit from Philip Melancthon." Cardinal Tournon however, remonstrated violently against this invitation given to a *heretic, (f)* and the princes of Germany soon saw reason to question the sincerity of Francis. In fact, it is difficult to reconcile his inconsistencies. He protected or persecuted the Reformation as interest or policy dictated. He allowed the Duke of Orleans his second son, to offer the free exercise of their religion to the Protestants in the dukedom of Luxemburg, and his sister the queen of Navarre to promote the reformed cause in her country of Bearn. He courted the Reformers yet opposed the Reformation—panegyrized them at Smal-

(e) SLEID. Hist. 175. DUPIN 181. BELCAR. Com. Rer. Gal. 646.

(f) MAIMBOURG. DUPIN.

cald, yet persecuted them at Paris—almost a Lutheran in Germany, and quite a Catholic in France. (g)

Some of Melancthon's friends urged him to accept the King of France's invitation, believing that it might prove a most favourable occasion for promoting the reformed religion in that country, and for checking the progress of the Catholic persecutions : but others were apprehensive that his visit would be attended with considerable personal danger and advised him to remain in Saxony. Melancthon himself was by no means indisposed to comply with the king's request, supposing that his presence in France was not unlikely to be attended with some advantage to the Reformation. Luther was very urgent with the Elector to allow his friend to go for similar reasons, and alleged that the very expectation of seeing Melancthon had already put a stop to the persecutions in France. (h)

The Elector could not however be prevailed upon to give his consent. He felt apprehensive of offending the Emperor and conceived no hopes

---

(g) Francis even permitted Bellay to explain his sentiments to the German princes, on some of the most important subjects of difference, in terms not very different from those used by the Protestants. SLEID. Hist. 178---180. SECKEND. Hist. Lib. III. 103.

(h) LUTH. Op. Tom. VI. 491.   SECKEND. Hist. Luth. Lib. III. p. 107.

of promoting any real good to the Reformation by such a permission.   Policy of course dictated a different excuse to Francis, to whom he wrote in a courteous manner, assuring him of his inclination to gratify his wishes, but pleading "·the peculiar and distressing aspect of the times and the unpleasant reflections he should be likely to incur.   The Wittemberg Academy he said being dispersed by a pestilential disorder and obliged to retire to Jena, he could not possibly at present part with Melancthon.   If however his services should hereafter be deemed necessary, and the pressure of present difficulties be somewhat alleviated, he would send a more decisive answer to his Majesty's letters and give him permission to visit France.   In the mean time he offered his most ready services in promoting the gospel of Christ, together with the temporal and eternal welfare of the king, his government, and the churches of France."

Melancthon was extremely chagrined at the Elector's interdiction and it may be justly regretted ; for who can doubt that his amiable deportment, elegant taste, nice discrimination and exemplary candour might have produced a very favourable impression upon a prince, who if he were after all a religious bigot, was much addicted to literature and might have been moderated, if not changed by mildness.   The Langean family would have been gratified and con-

firmed in their good inclinations—the queen of
Navarre would have hailed his visit, and a thousand secret machines might have been set in
motion by his influence.   But he was obliged
to content himself with sending a small treatise
into France, containing his opinion and advice
on the best means of_settling religious controversies, and which though never published is
inserted in the collections of Pezelius.

Early in the spring of this year, Doctor
Robert Barnes was sent by Henry VIII. King
of England, to consult with the Saxon Theologians on the subject of the intended divorce of
his queen.   Upon his arrival most of the professors and scholars were removed in consequence
of the plague which raged in Wittemberg, to
Jena in Thuringia.   Luther, Jonas, Cruciger
and Melancthon gave him recommendatory letters to the Elector.   He brought letters of invitation to Melancthon, who was urged by the
King to pay a visit to England.   Henry
offered him ample security from all molestation,
and even hostages if he required it. *(i)*   Luther
was extremely anxious that he should be allowed to go, for " who knows," says he, " what
God may intend to accomplish, his wisdom is
greater than ours and his will superior."   He
wished Melancthon's feelings to be consulted
who was deeply disappointed at the Elector's

(i) " Egregiam Cautionem imo et obsides."

previous refusal of his invitation into France. In his first letter to the King written in March, he compliments Henry in a very elegant style upon his literary inclinations, and after deploring the wretched state of letters in Germany through the intemperate violence of religious controversy, *(k)* he implores him to use every effort to promote them and to take the persecuted Muses under his protection. *(l)*

By means of Alexander Aless, a Scotchman who went into England, Melancthon took the opportunity of presenting a copy of his *Commentary on the Romans* to the King, who with a munificence worthy of a distinguished Sovereign, immediately presented him with two hundred crowns and wrote him a letter in which he expresses his high approbation of his extraordinary zeal in defending the Christian religion, and his disposition to assist and promote his good intentions by every means in his power. To this communication Melancthon returned an answer in the following month of December. He compliments the King upon his professed attachment to religious truth, and assures him that these sentiments had afforded himself and others to whom he had read his letters the greatest satisfaction. *(m)*   In addition to Dr. Barnes's

(k) VALENT. BAVAR. Compil. Vol. I. p. 252.
(l) MELANCTH. Ep. Lib. I. 26. *ad Henric. oct. Reg. Ang.*
(m) MELANCTH. Ep. Lib. I. 27.

commission, Haynes and Mount had been dispatched secretly to Sir John Wallop, ambassador in Paris, for the purpose of dissuading Melancthon from continuing in France if he had undertaken the journey, and to allure him to England. Sir John Wallop was soon able to appease the anxiety of the King of England, by assuring him in a dispatch dated the seventeenth of August, that there was reason to believe Melancthon would not visit France. Henry however hastened Mount to him into Germany, with the view of superseding the French ambassador's application. So solicitous were two of the most distinguished Monarchs of Europe to cultivate the friendship and to obtain the advice of Philip Melancthon. *(n)*

The original documents are not a little curious, and shall be quoted for the amusement of the reader. *(o)*

" *Master Secretary,* *(p)* after our most hearty commendations, ye shal understand that having received the letters sent unto you from Sir John Wallop and shewed the same unto the King's Majesty, his plesure thereupon was, that we should dispatch these our letters incontinentely

---

(n) STRYPE's Eccles. Memorials, Vol. I. HERBERT's Life of Henry VIII.

(o) BRITISH MUSEUM. *Cott. MSS.* Cleop. E. 6.

(p) T. Cromwell.

unto you concerning the accomplishment and doing of these things ensueing.

" First, his Grace's plesure is, that you shal immediately upon the receit hereof dispatch *Barnes* in post with *Deryk* in his company into Germany: commanding him to use such diligence in his journey, that he may and it be possible, meet with *Melancthon* before his arrival in France. And in case he shal so meet with him, not only dissuade his going thither; declaring how extremely the French King doth persecute those that wil not grant unto the Bishop of Romes usurped power and jurisdiction; using in this part al persuasions, reasons and means that he can devise to impeach and let his said journey thither; laying unto him how much it should be to his shame and reproch to vary and go now from that true opinion wherein he hath so long continued: But also on the other side to persuade him also that he may (be willing) to convert his said journey hither; shewing him as wel the conformity of his opinion and doctrine here, as the nobility and vertues of the King's Majesty, with the good entertainment which undoubtedly he shal have here at his Grace's hands.

" And if percase the said Barnes shal not meet with him before his arrival in France, then the said Barnes, proceeding himself further in his journey toward the princes of Germany shal with al diligence return in post to the K. H. the said Diryk, of the certainty of the said Melancthon's coming into France and such other occurrents as he shal then know.   And if the said Diryk be not now ready to go with him, the King's plesure is ye shal in his sted appoint and send such one other with the said Barnes as ye shal think meet for that purpose.

*   *   *   *   *   *

" Furthermore, the King's plesure is yee shal upon the receit hereof immediatly cause Mr. Haines and Christopher Mount, in post to repair into France, to Sir John Wallop in as secret a manner as they can, and coming like his friends to visit him and not as sent by the King. And in case they shal by him or otherwise learn and know, that Melancthon is there arrived, then his Grace wol, that the said Haines and Mount, shal, in such sort, as they be not much noted, resort unto him and for the dissuading of his continuance there, or the alteration of his opinion and the alluring of him hither ; to use such reasons and persuasions as be before written, with such other as they can further devise for that purpose.   To the which Haines and Mount, the King's plesure is, ye shal deliver like copies of the same Dean's Book *(q)* and the Bishops Sermons to be shewed unto the said

(q) Richard Sampson Dean of the Chapel.

Melancthon, or otherwise used, as may be most expedient for thachyevement of the King's purpose in that behalf.

*   *   *   *   *   *

" And to make an end, his Grace wol in no wise that Barnes and Haynes shal tary for any further instruction of the Bishop of Canterbury or any other.   Having his Grace determined to send the same after by Mr. Almoner and Hethe; but that he Mr. Haynes and Mount shal with al possible diligence depart immediatly in post without any lenger tarying than for this their depeche shal be necessary.   So as their abode impeach not the King's purpose, touching the said Melancthon.   And thus fare you most heartily wel, from Langley, in much hast, this Monday at 4 of the clock at afternoon.

" Your loving friends,

" T. NORFOLK,

" GEO. ROCHFORD."

The next letter is from the Secretary Cromwell to Sir John Wallop the King's ambassador in France, from which such parts only are extracted as illustrate the present subject. (r)

" To my right loving frynd Sir John Wallop, Knyght, the Kinges ambassadour resident in the Corte of Fraunce.

(r) Ex. MSS. D. G. H. Esq.

2 c 2

" After my most harty recommendacions ;
these shal be to advertise you that the xviith day
of this monthe I receyvid from you a packet of
letters; which indelayedly I delyvered unto the
Kinges Highnes and conferred with his Grace
theffects both of your letters and al others
within the sayd packet beying directed as wel
to his H. as to me.   And after his H. had with
me perused the hoole contents thoroughly of
your sayd letters ; perceyvyng not only the likli-
hod of the not repayr into Fraunce of Philip
Melancthon, but also your communications had
with the Frenche Kinges Highnes upon your
demaunde made of the Kynges Majesties pen-
sions, with also your discrete answers and repli-
cations made in that behalfe, for the which his
Majestie givethe unto you condigne thanks——

*   *   *   *   *   *

" And touchyng Melancthon—consideryng
there is no lykelihod of his repaire into Fraunce
as I have wel perceyved by your letters, the K.
H. therefore hath appoynted Christofer Mount
indelayedly to take his journey where Melancthon is, and if he can to prevent Mounsr. de Lan-
gye in such wise as the sayd Melancthon his
repaire into Fraunce may be stayed and diverted
into England.   Not doubting but the same shal
take effect accordyngly.   And as to Maister
Haynes, the Kyng's plesure is that he shal go to
Paris there to lerne and dissiphre the opynyons

of the lerned men and their inclynations and affections, as wel towards the K. H. procedyngs as to the Busshop of Rome his usurped power and aucthorite, after such sort as the Kyng's sayd Highnes hath now writen unto hym by his Grace's letters addressed both unto hym and the sayd Christofer Mount: directyng theym what they shal do yn al thynges commyttyd to theyr charge at this tyme ; as I doubt not but they wil put thereto theyr devoires for the accomplishement of the Kynges plesure as apperteynethe......................

.............At *Thornebery* the xxiiith day of August.

" Your assuryd freend,

" THOMAS CRUMWELL."

A larger commission was afterwards sent by Henry VIII. to the Protestant princes of Germany, now assembled at Smalcald, consisting of Edward Fox, Bishop of Hereford, Nicholas Hethe Archdeacon, and Dr. Barnes.   The opinion which Melancthon formed of them is thus expressed in a confidential letter to his friend Camerarius.   " One only of our present guests Nicholas Hethe, the Archdeacon, excels in amiableness of disposition and sound learning ; as for the others they have no relish for our philosophy and mode of discourse, (γλυκυτητος) so that I shun their society as much as possible." (s)

(n) MELANCTH. Ep. Lib. IV. 183.

In the course of these conferences, Fox represented that the King had abrogated the Popish abuses and had abolished indulgences. He
designated the Papal domination by the term
Babylonian Tyranny, and the Pope he called
Antichrist. A variety of articles were drawn
up by Melancthon, and some dissertations which
the ambassadors brought on their return to England on the Marriage of Priests, on Monastic Vows,
and on the Mass. It is intimated in the conclusion that the Protestants feel surprized at the
English decree against abuses, when no amend-
ment was proposed and especially as there was a
total omission of the more flagrant abuses of
which they complained. In a copy of this decree of Henry VIII. still extant in the German
Archives, Melancthon has written in several
places in the margin οὐδὲν ὑγιες, *not at all sound*.

The great purpose however which Henry
really had in view by these negociations, was to
obtain ultimately the sanction of the Wittemberg divines to his divorce; but their opinion
was unfavourable to his proceedings. They
drew up a paper disapproving of the divorce
which was transmitted by the ambassadors, *(t)*
and Melancthon fully concurred with Luther
upon the subject.

(t) A German copy of this document in the hand writing
of Caspar Cruciger, sent from Wittemberg to the Elector, is
preserved in the Archives of Smalcald.

In this same year (1535) Melancthon's acquaintance with the celebrated Archbishop Cranmer commenced. It seems to have originated in the visit which Alexander Aless, who had been long and intimately acquainted with Melancthon in Germany, paid to England in the month of August. Knowing the Archbishop's generous disposition, Melancthon took the liberty of giving him a recommendatory letter as a learned foreigner, and availed himself of the opportunity of conveying a present to the Archbishop of one of his own books. This was probably his Commentary on the Romans. *(u)* Another copy was presented as we have related to the King. This Alexander Aless was the same person whom Cromwell took with him to the Convocation in the year 1536, for the purpose of delivering his opinion about the Sacraments, of which he insisted only two, baptism and the Lord's Supper, were of Christ's original appointment. He wrote also a useful treatise on the subject of *Schism*, with which the dissenters from the Catholic church were charged ;

(u) Strype says, " he should have supposed it to have been his ' Common Places,' but that they came out a year after." This is an evident mistake, for though a new edition might have been published in the following year, we have already seen that this chef d'œuvre of Melancthon first appeared in the year 1521.

but he was furnished with both matter and argument by Melancthon.

Aless originally fled with other learned men from Scotland, in consequence of the persecutions of 1534 and was received into Cromwell's family. Henry VIII. is said to have been considerably attached to him, and to have bestowed upon him the distinguishing epithet of *his sholar*. He was afterwards made a professor in the University of Leipsic.

The recommendatory letters of Melancthon insured his Scotch protegèe a most hospitable reception at the palace of Lambeth, and the Archbishop could not but feel honoured by the sincere praises of his learned and pious correspondent who sought his friendship, and who in his letter said " if the church had but some more such bishops, it would be no difficult matter to to have it healed and the world restored to peace." *(v)*

Several circumstances concurred at this period, to excite that hypochondriacal depression of mind which so much embittered some of the years of Melancthon's life. He had a narrow escape from lightening which produced considerable damage in his immediate neighbourhood, and he suffered severely in his back from a fall,

(v) STRYPE's Mem. of Archbp. Cranmer, B. III. Ch. 23, 24.

but happily it occasioned no permanent injury. *(w)* The removal of the Academy to
Jena, in consequence of a raging infectious disorder alluded to in the Elector's letter cited
above, exceedingly discomposed and incon-
venienced him—but the students and professors
returned in the beginning of the year 1536 to
Wittemberg.

Health required an excursion amongst his
friends. He was accompanied by Jacob Mi-
lichius, a physician, to whom he was particularly
attached on account of his professional skill,
devoted friendship, and literary taste. He was
a native of Friburg, and for a series of years led
a useful and eminent course of public life at
Wittemberg. At the age of fifty nine he died,
much and generally lamented. *(x)* Camerarius
alludes with evident pleasure to the few days
passed in the companionable society of Melancthon at Tubingen, and notices the useful
advice he gave respecting the management of the
University, and the general regulation both of
religious and literary concerns. A violent contention had arisen on the subject of giving letters
of recommendation and conferring honorary
titles upon the students. Many learned men
were applied to for their opinion, amongst the

(w) ADAM. Vit Germ. Theol.   CAM. Vit. Mel.
(x) CAM. Vit. Mel.

rest Melancthon, who sent in a written statement of his views, and the reasons which influenced his decision.   He conceived that they
had been attended with advantages, especially
as such testimonies, publicly and solemnly
bestowed upon meritorious students, tended to
secure the avenues to clerical office against the
intrusion of ignorance and incapacity.

He addressed a long letter to Brentius on
the subject of the Academy at Tubingen, which
is dated from the palace of the Duke of Wirtem-
burg.   It is not to be wondered at that he felt a
peculiar interest in this early scene of his studies
and labours.   He mentions his satisfaction in
some of the professors, but intimates the *great
deficiency* that existed in reference to the Theological departments, and urges his correspondent, by desire of the Duke, to spend one year at
Tubingen, till some *suitable person* could be procured to occupy that important situation.   He
deplores the general state of literature throughout the whole of Upper Germany, and expresses
great anxiety to ameliorate the state of the
Academy. *(x)*

He was doomed to incur in consequence of
this journey what he so often experienced, the
attacks of malevolence.   A variety of vexatious
reports were put in circulation, and instantly

(x) MELANCTH. Ep. IX. *ad Joan. Brentium.*

credited by the weak and the wicked propagators
of mischief. Some asserted that he had separated from the Reformers, and quarrelled with
Luther, to whom his philosophical notions were
disagreeable—that he would not return to Wittemberg, or if he did no further cordiality was
likely to subsist between them. The sowers of
dissension however were disappointed of the
produce they anxiously expected. His methods
of conveying instruction, and especially his uniform and zealous efforts to purify the logic of
the schools, and terminate the endless disputations of former times by introducing juster principles of reasoning, were exceedingly grateful,
instead of being, as his adversaries calumniously
misrepresented, disgusting to Martin Luther.
That eminent Reformer always sought his advice, and with his characteristic ingenuousness
acknowledged his superiority.

An anecdote which is related of them is
confirmatory of this statement. Luther was
writing the following words, " Res et verba
Philippus; verba sine rebus Erasmus; res sine
verbis Lutherus; nec res, nec verba Carolostadius." " *Philip Melancthon is both substance and
words—Erasmus words without substance—Luther
substance without words—Carlostadt neither substance nor words*"—when Melancthon came in
unexpectedly, and overlooking him said with a
smile, " As to Erasmus and Carlostadt it is well

judged and censured, but too much is attributed
to me, and good words as well as matter ought
to be ascribed to Luther, for he speaks exceeding well." *(y)*

Amongst a variety of other important labours, Melancthon was very much occupied at
this time with the furious zealots who had created so much disturbance in Germany under the
name of Anabaptists. During the temporary
removal of the Academy to Jena, he and Cruciger were indefatigable in their efforts to reclaim
them, and it must be owned were in some degree successful. Melancthon wrote an excellent treatise against them in the German language. *(z)*

Soon after his return from Jena, he was
also engaged in a conference with Bucer and
Capito on the sacramental controversy. Pursuing with unabated ardour the great purpose of
forming a general re-union among the Reformers, Bucer and Capito had repaired, in the
month of January, to an assembly of the ministers and magistrates of the Reformed Cantons of
Switzerland, at Basil. They urged a union
with the Lutherans, which they deemed more
than ever probable from their decreased animosity. A meeting was afterwards convened in
May at Eisenach, to which the Swiss divines

(y) COLLOQ. MENSAL. p. 510.
(z) SECKEND. Hist. Luth. Lib. III. p. 115.

sent their confession of faith; but as Luther could not personally attend, Bucer and Capito proceeded to Wittemberg, where, after several conferences with him and his associates, Melancthon was appointed to draw up a formula on the sacrament, which, it is remarkable, the inflexible Lutherans, the moderate Reformers, and the whole Synod composed of the ministers of Upper Germany, concurred in signing. Thus the purpose of unanimity was obtained to a very considerable extent, and was celebrated on the occasion with great mutual congratulations; *(a)* though it may be questioned, from a perusal of this document, whether Bucer and his moderating associate did not manifest too much of a servile and temporizing flexibility.

(a) Myconius says, " Proruperunt lacrymæ Capitoni et Bucero et utrinque cancellatis manibus et gestibus piis Deo gratias egimus."

CHAP. X.

A. D. 1537 to A. D. 1545.

A General Council proposed—Meeting at Smalcald—Melancthon writes on the Pope's Supremacy, and against the manner of appointing the Council—Communications with Francis I.—Passage from the Recess of Smalcald—Melancthon is solicited to visit Augsburg respecting the institution of a Public Library—Letter of Cardinal Sadolet—A second Commission from Henry VIII.—Persons sent into England—Melancthon's letter to the king—Second Letter against the Anabaptists—Another Deputation from Frankfort—Melancthon's third and fourth Letters to the king—Death of George of Saxony—Progress of the Reformation—Diet held at Haguenaw—Melancthon's dangerous illness on the way—Interesting account of Luther's visit to him—Another Diet at Worms—Referred to Ratisbon—Melancthon meets with an Accident on the Road—Conference between Select Persons—Augsburg Decree confirmed—Several Anecdotes of Melancthon—Contentions about the Election of a Bishop at Naumburg—Account of Melancthon and Bucer's co-operation with the Archbishop of Cologne, to introduce the Reformation into his Diocese—Acrimonious Publication of some of the Clergy—Melancthon's satirical Reply—Private Afflictions—Draws up a Plan of Reform for the Elector Palatine—Engages in the Ordination of George Prince of Anhalt—Sketch of his life—Epigram by Melancthon.

PAUL III. who had succeeded to the Popedom in the year 1534, appeared more disposed than his predecessor to convene a general Council, and sent circular letters throughout the states under his jurisdiction, appointing a time and place, namely, the *twenty-seventh of May*, 1537, at *Mantua*. The confederate Protestant Princes re-assembled together at Smalcald, and in the February preceding the proposed Council, Vorstius, the Papal Nuncio, and Heldus, Vice-Chancellor to the Emperor, came to announce it, and exhort them to attend. This occasioned long and close deliberations.

The Wittemberg Theologians were summoned to the meeting at Smalcald, and as Luther was incapable of attending in consequence of a severe illness, the chief trouble, accompanied as usual with no inconsiderable odium, devolved upon Melancthon. They were required to make an accurate comparison of the different sentiments which prevailed among themselves, in order to terminate the existing disputes, and devise some common form of doctrine for the Protestant churches; then to determine upon those articles of faith which from their radical importance were to be retained and avowed at all hazards, in order finally to ascertain what might be conceded to the Catholics for the sake of restoring peace and harmony. *(a)*

(a) MELANCTH. Ep. Lib. IV. ep. 196 *ad Camerarium*. PEZEL. L. I. p. 269.

Whether from the flattering caresses of others, or from the deliberate judgment and affectionate disposition of his own mind, Melancthon could not be induced to renounce the hope of promoting concord, not only between those who were perpetually contending on the subject of the Sacramental controversy, but between the Reformers and Catholics. With respect to the first question, relative to an examination of the points of difference which divided the Reformers themselves, he complains that a calm and impartial investigation could not be obtained, owing to the rigidity of some, and the apprehension of others lest instead of promoting harmony, the discussion of these differences should inflame resentment. With respect to the second, he was deputed to compose a piece on the power and primacy of the Roman Pontiff, and on the jurisdiction of bishops. This performance proved of signal use, and was noticed with marked approbation in the Recess or Decree of the Convention. *(b)* It exceedingly confirmed the minds of all, and removed the suspicions which

(b) " Postquam Theologos nostros primarius et Sacræ Scripturæ peritos hic congregavimus, illi de omnibus articulis confessionis & apologiæ quam Augustæ exhibuimus, Christianum habuerunt colloquium et per Dei gratiam unanimiter in omnibus inter se consenserunt; articulum vero de primatu Pontificis Romani LATIUS & MELIUS CONCEPERUNT, ut scriptum ostendit."

his calumniators had excited even in the Elector
himself, who did not sufficiently distinguish between a bias to Popery and that strong desire for
peace Melancthon laboured to effect, and which
he cherished the hope of obtaining without the sacrifice of principle. He thought it proper to contend only about essentials; here he was firm—
in other respects he aimed with incessant, but
useless toil, to produce reconciliation. In fact
the standard of his piety was superior to the
age in which he lived, and unlikely to be
duly appreciated or sufficiently influential in
the boisterous hour of religious innovation.
The performance referred to was written
with no less zeal against the excessive domination of Rome and her ecclesiastics than
Luther himself would have displayed, though
with milder words; and it affirmed that little or
no hope could be entertained of the results of a
Council so constituted as that to which the
Pope had summoned the Princes of Christendom. Similar sentiments are expressed in the
correspondence which was carried on between
the confederate Princes and the king of France.
In the preceding year Francis had written letters
to the assembly which intimated some offence.
He perceived, he said, from the report of his
ambassador, that they did not cherish exactly
the sentiments he had expected, but he was
disposed to overlook any contempt they had

2 D

manifested from his ardent desire to promote a
general union in Christendom, especially between Germany and France. He was desirous
they should send a deputation to him. They
replied in letters written in their name by Melancthon, who may perhaps not inaptly be termed
the pen of the Reformation. " That they certainly
had intended no contempt, and fully concurred
in his views respecting mutual union. They
excused themselves from sending deputies as
he desired, not feeling themselves warranted to
do so; and with respect to a Council, if it were
not free, but ordered by the Pope merely for the
purpose of condemning them, it would confirm
instead of remove abuses, and inflame greater
discord. They allege the Bull itself, in
which their sentiments are condemned already,
as a proof that the Council would not be a free
one." The King replied in a courteous manner,
declaring that on this subject they were completely agreed.

It is due to the Princes assembled at Smalcald to introduce the following passage from
their Recess. *(c)* " As it has hitherto been the
case, and still is, that some who pretend to holy
orders adhere to the Popish doctrines and ceremonies, and cannot agree with our faith nor
conform to our worship, whence monasteries

(c) SECKEND. Hist. Luth. Lib. III. p. 157.

and other ecclesiastical property have or will
hereafter come into our hands, the Reverend
and Spiritual Christian Teachers, Preachers and
Pastors have advised and requested us that some
of this property should be devoted to the honour
of God and the advantage of the Christian
cause, as our pious will may direct; we therefore unanimously agree, that the parochial
churches in our several districts and jurisdic-
tions, shall be provided with learned, pious and
honourable Teachers, Preachers and Pastors;
and that in their different situations they may
be maintained in a decent and respectable way
with their wives and families. Also we appoint
Superintendants to watch over the said Pastors
and Ministers, that they keep sound doctrine
and live and walk as becometh Christians.
And we order the provision of suitable Funds
for *Schools of Education*, adapted to the local
circumstances of each district, that youth may
be trained up therein in good morals and sound
learning, so that our churches may not in future
be unsupplied with suitable Pastors and Ministers. *We further order proper Funds to be appropriated to the use of those who shall devote
themselves principally to the study of the sacred
Scriptures.* Moreover we order the erection and
endowment of *Hospitals* for the reception of the
poor of both sexes ; and in fine, that every one
in every place shall exert himself to cause such

institutions to be erected, provided and supported, wherever the necessity exists, and whatever else the duty of Christian Princes and Magistrates may require."

Melancthon was solicited by the Senate of
the city of Augsburg to pay them a visit, but
many and weighty reasons induced him to decline their invitation. They were about establishing a public library, and even applied to the
Elector to permit this visit ; but he replied that
he could not possibly spare him, both on account of the discussions upon the subject of a
general Council, and of the great resort of students to Wittemberg. *(d)*

In fact Melancthon could not command a
moment's leisure, and in addition to his exertions in the public cause, he was incessantly
pestered with the reproaches of the malevolent,
who misinterpreted all his actions, and with
the unjust censures of many with whom he
was connected who disliked his conciliating
spirit. It was reported that in consequence of
considerable differences of opinion which occasioned some discussion at Smalcald, he was
alienated from his own party, and several Princes
studiously endeavoured to induce him to relinquish his existing engagements, and become a
professor in their Universities; but he never

(d) Gassar. Annal. MSS.

sought private emolument or honour to the
neglect of public duty, and therefore he could
not be gained.   But as his friend and biographer
Camerarius remarks, no integrity or innocence
of character can escape suspicion and slander.
He could not even receive a letter from the
learned Sadolet, because it came from *Italy*,
without being exposed to suspicion and charged
with the crime of being connected with Catholics.   This letter is produced by Camerarius as
a specimen of that elegant latinity for which the
writer was distinguished ; we may be allowed to
translate it as being no less honourable to the
spirit and character of him who wrote than of him
who received it.

" James Sadolet, Cardinal of Carpentras,
sends his most affectionate salutations to
Philip Melancthon.

" During my residence at Carpentras,
where I had imagined myself fixed for life, but
whence I am suddenly recalled to Rome by the
mandate of the Pope, I was perpetually conversant with your writings, which I read both
on account of the ability they discovered and
the general elegance of the composition.   Often
in the midst of this pleasurable employment,
I became gradually enflamed with affection,
and cherished a great anxiety to commence
a friendship with you.   For although some

difference of opinion exist between us, **this**
need not cause dissension amongst well educated men.

   " At the moment I was deliberating about
writing to you to open, so to speak, the doors of
friendship, suddenly I was sent for to Rome, on
account of an approaching Council, and a consultation respecting various affairs, on which it
would become necessary soon to deliberate.   I
had superintended my spiritual charge for the
period of ten years, when thus summoned by
the secret appointment of the best and wisest of
Pontiffs, to be invested, ignorant and unskilled
as I was, with the dignified office of Cardinal.
This occasioned delay in transmitting as I
wished a letter to you : for it is impossible to
express how many anxieties, cares and troubles
this translation from my former peaceful and
happy life into this tumultuous and bustling
one, has occasioned me.   This indeed was sure
to happen, for my judgment avoided this and
followed my former course of life.   Both, however, fell out contrary to my original inclinations,
so that I cannot rejoice in what I was unwilling
to possess, and not be unaffected with grief in
losing what I wished to enjoy.   But thus appointed by the providence of God, I shall endeavour by his aid properly and fully to discharge this honourable office.

   " As my mind begins to emerge from the

crowd of difficulties which beset me, I have
resolved no longer to defer writing, and thus
give you a pledge, my dear Philip, of my
affection and of your attraction.   My esteem
arises from your exemplary virtues, and may I
not hope that you will equally reciprocate it
from your native kindness?   You will, I doubt
not, accede to my request and eager desire of
friendly intercourse.   I am not one of those who
instantly cherish a violent hatred because another differs in opinion, an arrogance and a
vanity to which my nature is totally repugnant.
I honour intellect, virtue and literature, which,
as you possess them in no common degree,
excite a proportionate regard for you.   I doubt
not your sentiments are similar to my own : for
a person so accomplished in elegant literature
cannot be otherwise than kind and courteous,
and I indulge the greatest confidence that my
letters will not be unacceptable, because however disjoined by distance of place, we may be
united in spirit and affection.   The object of my
greatest anxiety and desire therefore is, to persuade you to admit me into a principal share of
that regard you feel for those, and I know they
must be very numerous, who have been induced
from the celebrity of your name to solicit your
friendship.   Nothing would afford me greater
pleasure than to have an opportunity of expressing and proving my attachment to you, and

if you will furnish me with any such occasion,
I shall esteem it as a high obligation. I am
ready with the greatest zeal to do whatever I
know may be gratifying to you; no one shall
exceed me.   Attachment to you and the nature
of my office, require a constant concern for
literary men.   Farewell, most learned Melancthon, and let me share your best affections.
    ROME, *July* 15, 1537."

The justice of Luther's remark upon the
preceding letter may be left to the reader's own
determination.   " Sadolet," says he, " who
had been the Pope's Secretary fifteen years, a
very witty and learned man, wrote in a most
courteous manner to Philip Melancthon, but
exceeding craftily, according to the Italian custom, in order that, through a *Cardinalate*, they
might have bought him on their side, which
was done by the Pope's directions ; for the good
gentleman, Mr. Pope, is much perplexed, not
knowing how to fall upon us." *(e)*
    Application was again made from the Court
of Great Britain for a deputation of the Saxon
divines and Reformers to take a journey, for the
purpose of conferring with learned men of that
kingdom about ecclesiastical and other important affairs.   William Paget and Christopher

(e) COLLOQ. MENSAL. p. 409.

Mount were employed on this mission. They were instructed to go through France and act in concurrence with the King, and Gardiner the English ambassador at the French Court: but the main purpose of Henry VIII. was to induce the German princes to disregard both the Emperor and the Pope, and to refer all the points of difference to himself and the King of France. (f) A visit from Melancthon in particular was exceedingly urged, but year after year slipt away and other concerns occupying his attention the journey was never accomplished.

A legation however was sent consisting of Francis Burkhard or Burgart, Vice-Chancellor of the Elector of Saxony, George a Boneyburg, a Nobleman, a Doctor of Laws, and Frederic Myconius superintendant of Saxe-Gotha. The former was charged with a letter from Melancthon to the King, in which he expresses his affectionate friendship for the Vice-Chancellor, who would be able to explain his high regard for his Majesty and his disposition to devote himself to the public good by the illustration of Christian truth. " Private men," says he, " very much need the aid of distinguished princes and states, and your Majesty has excited the greatest hopes in every country that you would promote the wishes of the pious

(f) HERBERT's Life of Henry VIII. p. 425.

for the Reformation of the churches.   What else does the Papal faction aim at than the total extinction of divine truth and the infliction of the most barbarous cruelties upon Kings, Princes and nations, and the support of the Catholic abuses by a system of boundless tyranny in the church?   Such being the dangerous situation of her affairs, I will not cease to exhort and implore your Majesty to pay attention to the circumstances of the Christian church now a suppliant at your feet, to promote some firm and durable union, and to dissuade other princes from connecting themselves with Popish counsels. This is an affair of the greatest importance, and therefore worthy the attention of a King so superior to others in learning and wisdom." *(g)*

The ambassadors were received in the most courteous manner, and the King of England frequently expressed his anxious desire to see Melancthon. *(h)*   But nothing of any consequence was effected by this journey, and the commissioners were at length dismissed with strong protestations of royal friendship and an invitation to return during the ensuing year.   The King sent letters to the Elector of Saxony full of the strongest professions of kindness to himself and

(g) The original letter is preserved in the BRITISH MUSEUM, *Cott. MSS.* Cleop. E. 6.

(h) SECKEND. Hist. Lib. III. p. 180.

the Reformed cause, and expressive of the greatest anxiety to enjoy a visit from Melancthon, " from whose distinguished erudition and sound judgment all good men," says he, " form the highest expectations."

The princes having discovered by means of some intercepted letters a secret correspondence between the German and English Anabaptists, wrote a long and elegant epistle to Henry VIII. containing a statement of the pernicious doctrines these persons so eagerly disseminated, and warning him of the danger likely to result from their fanatical proceedings unless prevented by a bold and timely interference. This epistle was composed by Melancthon. (i)

A Protestant conference was held at Frankfort in the beginning of the year 1539, to which place Melancthon accompanied his prince. Violent proceedings being apprehended he was deputed to write a piece on the subject of lawful defence, which he executed with great care and success. From this assembly a deputation was sent into England, which carried another of his letters to Henry VIII. for, being affected by the testimony of his friends respecting the royal benignity, and desirous of promoting in the king every good inclination, he thought it proper to cherish this correspondence. His

(i) SECKEND. Hist Lib. III. p. 180.

letter dated Frankfort, March 26, 1539, was
calculated to produce a good effect.   After ex
pressing his grateful sense of his Majesty's regard for him, which was manifested afresh in his
discourses with the commissioners, he proceeds,
" I commend the cause of the Christian religion
to your Majesty's attention, for your Majesty
knows that the most important duty of great
princes is to regard and promote heavenly truth, on
which account God associates them with himself
in the office of ruling.   I am desirous as I have
written before, that a union upon the basis of
doctrinal agreement should be effected amongst
those churches which reject the domination of
Rome.   This would tend to promote the glory
of God and conduce to general tranquillity.
Your Majesty has happily begun the removal of
some superstitious practices, I entreat you to
proceed to others.   The intention of our adversaries is apparent, but they can never suppress
our doctrine ; God himself will be the keeper of
our states and princes.   They are always most
anxious for public peace and tranquillity, but
if our enemies resort to arms the princes will not
be deficient in their duty.   I frequently call to
mind the inscription upon one of King Edward's
coins, " *Jesus autem transiebat per medium
eorum ;*" *Jesus passed through the midst of
them,* by which that wise monarch doubtless
intended to intimate that the governors of king-

doms are divinely protected whilst they defend
righteous causes; and, indeed, that it is truly
heroic to bear arms in defence of the church
against tyrants.   It is said that Ajax asked
Achilles what were the greatest and most difficult of all labours ? To which he replied, " those
which are undertaken for friends."   Ajax inquired again, " What then were the most pleasant and easy ?"   He answered, " the same."
The hero intimated by this reply, that nothing
could be more delightful than to perform even
the severest duties for the public good, and that
he could cheerfully sustain the heaviest cares for
this purpose.   Such was their greatness of mind
who were ignorant of the true God ; how much
more does it become Christian princes to endure
labour and danger for the church of Christ, when
they know that they are divinely appointed to this
office and are promised celestial rewards for their
services.   I will not cease therefore to exhort
your Majesty to persevere in promoting the cause
of the Christian church, and in resisting the tyranny and violence of its adversaries." (k)

Melancthon addressed letters also to Cromwell and Cranmer, and afterwards being denied
a journey to England by the Elector, who acted
with the concurrent advice of Luther, from an

(k) The original letter is in the BRITISH MUSEUM,
Cott. MSS. Cleop. E. 5.

opinion that nothing could be done with the infatuated monarch; he again, at the instigation
of the Landgrave of Hesse, wrote him a long
epistle in a most magnanimous spirit, many parts
of which merit quotation. *(l)* " Many pious and
learned men in Germany have indulged the hope
that your Majesty's authority would have produced a considerable alteration in the conduct
of other Kings, and that the German princes in
particular might have been influenced to relinquish the unworthy cruelty of their proceedings
and deliberate on the correction of abuses.   You
were hailed as the promoter and leader of this
most holy and illustrious design.   Now, alas!
your prejudices have wounded our minds most
deeply: the animosity of other princes is confirmed, the vexatious obstinacy of the impious
is increased and the ancient errors are strengthened.   The bishops no doubt contend that they
do not maintain errors, but true doctrines and
a divine right;   and though by no means
ignorant that they are in fact opposed to the
divine authority and the apostolical constitution
of the church, yet men will find out very fine
interpretations, σοφα φάρμακα *artful poisons* as
Euripides calls them when policy requires it,

(l) MELANCTH. Ep. Lib. I. 28. It is dated 1529 by
mistake, instead of 1539. Comp. PEZEL. Consil. Theol. P. I.
p. 343. MELANCTH. Op. Tom. IV.

in order to furnish a specious pretext for their
errors. Sophisms of this description may not be
so much admired in England for their wisdom,
but they are very much in repute at Rome,
where the Cardinals Contaranus, Sadolet and
Pole are applying a new paint and varnish to old
abuses. In Germany these sophisms have depraved the minds of many persons of distinction,
and I am not surprized that multitudes are deluded by these fallacies; and though you are neither deficient in erudition nor in judgment, yet
even wise men are sometimes diverted from the
truth by specious arguments.

" It cannot be denied that the church of
Christ was for a long period veiled in tremend-
ous darkness. Human traditions, the torment
of pious minds, were most shamefully introduced
to the utter corruption of divine worship. Vows,
gifts, vestments, meats and drinks, a vain repetition of prayers, indulgencies, and the worship of
images with every species of manifest idolatry
being substituted for the true service of God, exhibited a striking resemblance between the religion of heathens and of Rome. The real doctrines of repentance and forgiveness of sin through
faith in Jesus Christ, justification by faith, the
distinction of Law and Gospel and the use of
the Sacraments were unknown. The keys of
authority were given into the hands of the Pope
to support his tyranny both in civil and eccle-

siastical affairs.   The law of celibacy produced licentiousness of manners, but God has in some measure dispersed the darkness by the reformed doctrine, for this light of truth which now shines in the churches must be attributed to him, because no human skill could have removed the prevailing errors.   The Spirit of God has predicted that in the last times a violent contention would arise between the Saints and Antichrist, and that Antichrist supported by bishops, deceivers and princes, would oppose the truth and slay the pious.   These very things are at this moment transacted.   The tyranny of the Romish hierarchy has partly introduced and partly confirmed the existing abuses, and as Daniel predicted, ' his look is more stout than his fellows.' *(m)* We rejoiced in the separation of your Majesty and hoped that the English church would flourish again, but alas your bishops still adhere to Antichrist in all his idolatries and errors.   The articles they have published are most craftily selected and support every human tradition, especially vows, celibacy and confession.   In retaining the doctrine of private masses they not only confirm priestly domination, but every dangerous error of Popery, artfully avoiding improvement that their dignity and wealth may be secure.   That this is the work

(m) DAN. vii. 20.

of the bishops is obvious ; it speaks for it-self.

"I implore you by our Lord Jesus Christ to mitigate and amend this episcopal decree, by doing which you will both consult the glory of Christ and the welfare of all your churches. May you regard the ardent desires of the pious throughout the world that Kings would use their influence to effect a Reformation of the church, to remove unauthorized services and to propagate evangelical truth. May you consider those holy persons who are in bonds for the gospel and are the true members of Christ, for if this decree be not cancelled the bishops will practise their severities to an incalculable ex-tent. Satan himself can alone inspire this op-position to Christ ; they minister to his rage ; he impels them to these cruel massacres. All good men entreat and implore you not to listen to the impious, the cruel sentiments, and so-phistical cavils in circulation against us, but to regard our just and well-founded petition. In doing this, you will secure no doubt a great and a divine reward, as well as the highest degree of celebrity amongst all Christians. Jesus Christ himself will judge of the conduct of men to his church, and while human language exists these transactions will be transmitted to all future ages. If our churches be indeed the churches of Christ and we seek his glory, the cause will never want patrons and protectors, who will bestow due praises on the deserving, and merited contempt on the persecutor.   Hungry, thirsty, naked, bound, Christ himself complains of the fury of the Roman hierarchy and the iniquitous severities practised by many Kings and Princes: he entreats for the wounded members of his body, that his true church may be defended and the gospel honoured ;—to acknowledge, to entertain, to minister to HIM, is the duty of a pious King and a most grateful service to God."

New cares and labours awaited Melancthon upon his return from Frankfort, but they were pleasureable ones.   George, Duke of Saxony, Sovereign of Misnia and Thuringia, the inveterate enemy of the Reformation was dead, and his brother Henry who succeeded to his dominions espoused it with the utmost zeal.   Melancthon and Luther were immediately employed to regulate the affairs of the University at Leipsic and to investigate the state of the churches. *(n)* The Reformed cause now rapidly spread in every direction, and other princes especially Joachim II. the Elector of Brandenburg and son-in-law to Sigismund the King of Poland embraced it. Raynald quotes some letters written by Cochlæus in which he imputes the *blame*, as he calls it, of this change to Melancthon and Vicelius,

(n) CAM. Vit. Mel.

and Seckendorf has preserved a pleasing letter on the subject composed by the former, addressed in the name of the Elector of Brandenburg to the Polish Sovereign. *(o)*

The Protestants having solicited the Emperor to appoint a general conference between them and the Catholics, in conformity with the resolutions which had been adopted for this purpose at Frankfort, he directed them previously to deliberate on the concessions they were prepared to make to their adversaries. They met at Smalcald in the year 1540, and replied by the pen of Melancthon, that they should adhere to their Confession at Augsburg and the subsequent Apology. *(p)* Amidst a multiplicity of other public engagements he found time also to write a long and admirable vindication of the Reformers, addressed in the name of the Elector of Saxony and the confederate princes to Charles V.; and another piece against Sebastian Frank, Caspar Schwenckfeld and others, who maintained fanatical opinions and pretended to extraordinary revelations.

(o) SECKEND. Hist. Luth. Lib. III. p. 234 and 241.

(p) Melancthon in a letter to Camerarius says, " all the Theologians agreed that the bishops should enjoy their jurisdiction, if they would embrace evangelical truth and remove abuses out of the church." Nothing of this kind however is inserted in the decree of the convention. MEL. Ep. Lib. IV. ep. 222. SECKEND. Hist. Lib. III. p. 258.

The Diet which the Emperor had appointed to be held at Spires, was in consequence of the plague removed to Haguenaw. On his way thither Melancthon became dangerously ill, arising chiefly from the morbid melancholy incident to his constitution. The immediate cause of his present extreme dejection of mind is to be traced to the misconduct of the Landgrave of Hesse, who was forming an illicit connexion which Melancthon foresaw would prove detrimental to the Reformation, by furnishing an occasion of reproach to its virulent adversaries. Varillas and Bossuet are by no means backward to avail themselves of the circumstance. *(q)* Being in consequence of this indisposition detained at Vinaria, he experienced the kindest attentions from the Elector and his friends, who immediately sent for George Sturciad, a physician of Erfurt, to whom he was peculiarly attached. Luther also hastened to his friend whose cheering presence contributed not a little to aid the powers of medicine in producing his convalescence. As he had previously felt a deep persuasion that he should die, he had written his will and deposited it with Cruciger ; *(r)* and on

---

(q) MELANCTH. ep. ad *Bucard. Mythob.* ap. PEZEL. Cons. p. 394. SECKEND. Hist. Lib. III. p. 277. BOSSUET Hist. des Variations.

(r) Vid. Appendix VI.

his way while crossing the Elbe, he suddenly uttered what happily proved an unfounded prediction,

" Viximus in Synodis et jam moriemur in illis."

In councils we have lived, in councils now shall die. *(s)*

The interesting account written by Solomon Glass and preserved amongst the original manuscripts of the German princes, shall be presented to the English reader. " When Luther arrived he found Melancthon apparently dying. His eyes were dim, his understanding almost gone, his tongue faultering, his hearing imperfect, his countenance fallen, incapable of distinguishing any one and indisposed to all nourishment. At such a sight Luther was in the most terrible consternation, and turning to those who had accompanied him in his journey, exclaimed, ' Alas, that the devil should have thus unstrung so fine an instrument!'—Then in a supplicating posture he devoutly prayed, ' We implore thee O Lord our God, we cast all our burdens on thee and WILL CRY TILL THOU HEAREST US, pleading all the promises which can be found in the Holy Scriptures respecting thy hearing prayer, so that THOU MUST INDEED HEAR US to preserve at all future periods our entire confidence in thine

(s) ADAM. Vit. Germ. Theologorum. CAM. Vit. Mel.

own promises.' *(t)*   After this he seized hold of
Melancthon's hand, and well knowing the extreme anxiety of his mind and the troubled
state of his conscience, said, ' Be of good courage, Philip, YOU SHALL NOT DIE: although God has always a sufficient reason for
removing us hence, he willeth not the death of
a sinner but rather that he should be converted
and live,'—' it is his delight to impart life, not
to inflict death.   God has received into his favour the greatest sinners that ever existed in the
world, namely Adam and Eve, much more will
he not cast thee off my dear Philip, or permit thee
to perish in grief and guilt.   Do not therefore
give way to this miserable dejection and destroy
thyself, but trust in the Lord who can remove

(t) This petition is translated immediately from the original German.   " *Allda muste mir unser Herr Gott herhalten
denn ich warff ihm denn sack für die thür und riebe ihm die
ohren mit allen* PROMISSIONIBUS EXAUDIENDARUM PRECUM
*die ich aus der heiligen schrift zu erzehlen wuste dass er mich
müste erhören, wo ich anderst seinen verheissungen trauen
solte.*"   Seckendorf remarks this language is so peculiar and forcible as scarcely to admit of being properly
rendered into Latin, and the same may be said of English. His
words and version are as follow : " Parrhesia hæc vix exprimi
Latinè potest, sensus est, *Se cum Deo magnâ cum confidentiâ
egisse, omnesque ei objecisse et veluti inculcasse, quæ ex Scrip-
turis allegari poterant, promissiones de audiendis precibus,
itaque cogebatur* (ait) *me exaudire, si fiduciam meam in promissiones suas conservare vellet.*"   SECKEND. Hist. Lib. III. p.
314.

it and impart new life.' While he thus spake, Melancthon began visibly to revive as though his spirit came again and was shortly restored to his usual health."

After his illness Melancthon wrote thus to Camerarius, " I cannot express the pain I have suffered during my illness, some returns of which I often feel. I witnessed at that period the deep sympathy of Luther, but he restrained his anxieties that he might not increase mine, endeavouring to raise me from my desponding state of mind, not only by administering kind consolation but salutary reproof. If he had not come to me I should certainly have died." To Burcardus Mythobius he wrote, " In the summer I received two letters from you, the one at Smalcald, the other in Thuringia, at a time when I was confined by extreme illness occasioned only by overwhelmning anxiety of mind on account of some affairs relative to others, of which you also complain. I must have died if Luther had not recalled me from the gates of death."

The Elector of Saxony and the Landgrave of Hesse not being present at Haguenaw, no conclusive measures were adopted, but another Diet was appointed to meet at Worms in October. Thither the Emperor dispatched his Commissioner, Nicholas Granville, and the Pope his Nuncio, Campegius, Bishop of Filtri.

Vergerius also appeared in the name of the king of France. It was long before the preliminary arrangements could be adjusted. On the twenty-eighth of November Melancthon thus addresses his friend Jerome Baumgartner. " The church of God does not often engage the serious attention of Kings, Pontiffs and Princes, for their minds are devoted to ambitious projects, and other occupations. Truth is more generally esteemed and the church upheld by private persons and families; it was not one of the kings of Phœnicia or Syria that cherished Elijah; but a poor widow, in whose house the true religion was maintained. Jonah is said to have been the son of a widow. Abraham, Isaac and Jacob were not only private individuals, but exiles; and therefore I trust that God will still preserve his church amidst the present troubles. I exhort you to pursue your pious labours and cares with increased alacrity and renewed hope. The history of our convention may soon be told: nothing is done except deliberating about the plan of conducting the disputations. You remember the saying of Aristotle, 'It would be a happy thing for the world if *artists* were to be made the sole judges of the *arts*'—but we are *favoured* with canonists and nobility as arbitrators, who are quite unacquainted with our concerns, and these again have certain *managers*, as they are termed on the stage, or, as

Æschines calls them, περιτριμμαῖα τῆς ἀγορᾶς petti-foggers of the forum who cajole the public." *(t)*

In a letter to Granville he intimates his opinion, " that good humoured discussion might tend to remove sophisms and obscurities out of the way, and diminish the number of existing differences; at the same time he nobly avows his dislike of all inexplicitness and dissi-mulation, which rather perplex than disentangle controversies; resolving for his part, whether in private or public conferences, TO SPEAK WHAT HE THINKS FIRMLY BUT MODESTLY, AND TO CONCEDE WHAT HE DEEMS MAY BE CON-CEDED, WITH UNAMBIGUOUS INGENUOUS-NESS." *(u)*

The conference being at length opened in January, 1541, a debate between Eckius and Melancthon ensued. The latter characterizes his antagonist as an apt disputant, but " more solicitous of contending for the prize of ingenuity than for truth." *(v)* At the close of the third day Granville received an order from the Empe-ror to suspend the proceedings, and meet him in person at a Diet which he appointed at Ratisbon. It was opened early in the spring, and all the Princes of the Empire were either personally present or sent deputies. Unfor-tunately in going Melancthon was overturned in

(t) MELANCTH. Ep. 51. ad *Hieronym. Baumgartnerum.*
(u) MELANCTH. Ep. Lib. II. 2.
(v) MELANCTH. Acta Wormat. ap. Pref.

the vehicle in which he travelled, which accident, though it was not a fatal one, so essentially injured his right hand, that he never afterterwards' recovered the proper use of it. His wrist was dislocated by the fall. *(v)*

The Catholics and Protestants having agreed to a proposal by the Emperor that the controversies about religion should be settled by a conference between select persons from both parties, his Imperial Majesty claiming the right of nomination, chose Julius Pflug, John Eckius, and John Gropper on the one side, and Philip Melancthon, Martin Bucer, and John Pistorius on the other. They were commanded to lay aside all passion, and respect only the glory of God in the conference. Granville, the Emperor's prime minister and commissioner at the conference, delivered a book to this Committee, which he said the Emperor desired them to peruse, but they were at liberty to approve or amend it as they pleased. It contained twenty-two articles, and was supposed to be written by Gropper. This paper was artfully constructed, but only led to long and fruitless discussions. Both parties appear to have raised objections

" *(v)* In aditu Bavariæ dextra mihi, cum everteretur currus quo vehebar, adeò duriter quassata est, ut ossa εν κάρπω, ut Medici vocant, luxata sint. Ideo nunc sine cruciatu literas pingere non possum." MELANCTH. Ep. Lib. I. 41. ad *Dom. Georg. Princip. Anhalt.* Comp. CAM. Vit. Mel. MEL. ADAM. Vit. Germ. Theologorum.

against it; and Melancthon remarks in writing
to one of his friends, that Eckius declared in a
letter to the assembly of Princes, that he never
had and never would approve this book, because
it *Melancthonized* too much, for he suspected it
to be either his dictation, or written with his
advice and concurrence. But he totally disclaims it, and says that Eckius injured Gropper
by this imputation. *(w)* The legate however
resented the Protestant objections, and the Diet
was concluded by his Imperial Majesty's commanding that the Augsburg decree should continue in force, and all prosecutions in the Imperial chamber be suspended. *(x)*

In the course of the late discussions Melancthon remarked, that " the Sacrament had
no significance beyond its divinely appointed use, and that Christ was not present for the
sake of the bread, but of the recipient;" a sentiment which so delighted Luther when it was
repeated to him, that he exclaimed, " *Macte
Philippe, tu eripuisti Pontificiis quod ego non
ausus fuissem;* i. e. " Admirable Philip, thou hast
seized from the Popedom what I should not
have dared to attempt!" Eckius himself was
so confounded that he could say nothing, and

(w) MELANCTH. Ep. 16. *ad Brentium.*

(x) At Ratisbon every effort was made to discredit Melancthon with the Emperor; but he addressed a letter to him
refuting every charge in the most satisfactory manner. ME-
LANCTH. Ep. Lib. II. i.

therefore, as persons commonly do in similar circumstances, he uttered a violent speech in default of argument, and went home in a fit of indignation, which, together with an unusual quantity of wine at supper the same evening, operated so powerfully as to produce a fever. He never again returned to the conference. Granville appears to have been considerably affected by his opponent's statements, for a few days afterwards he said, " I have been thinking, Philip, for these several days past, very closely upon your arguments, and I really perceive this controversy to be a most difficult one, and well worthy of itself to occupy the attention of a Council."

Melancthon had declared at the commencement of these discussions, " *Se mori malle, quam conscientiam & veritatem lædere & certissimè ex mærore moriturum, si id faceret;* that he would rather die than injure truth and violate his conscience, and certainly if he could possibly act so he should die with grief;" a noble declaration, and finely illustrated by the following incident. Eckius, during the heat of disputation, made use of some puzzling sophism, at which Melancthon paused, to revolve the statement in his mind, and at length replied, " I will give you an answer to-morrow." " Oh," said his antagonist, " there is no merit or honour in that, if you cannot answer me immediately." To which he replied in these memorable words,

" *Mi Doctor, non quæro meam gloriam hoc in negocio, sed veritatem: cras, volente Deo, me audies.* My good Doctor, I AM NOT SEEKING MY OWN GLORY IN THIS BUSINESS BUT TRUTH: I say then, God willing, you shall have an answer to-morrow." *(y)*

The same remarkable superiority of mind to all the incentives of ambition, was apparent in every part of his conduct. As he did not pursue fame, but truth, in his numerous conferences with the Catholics, so he did not aspire after rewards, but the promotion of the public good in his Academical labours. Indeed he was almost scrupulous to an extreme. Luther, in a letter addressed to the Elector of Saxony on the third of July, mentions Melancthon's hesitating to accept an increase of his salary to the amount of a hundred florins, and his wish to continue his Greek Lectures without any remuneration, that the ordinary stipend might be devoted to augment the revenues of the University. " But," says Luther, " he has sustained the greatest share of Academical labour for upwards of twenty years past, and surely he has the greatest right to enjoy in quiet some of the profits. The junior masters, who are his scholars, are capable of teaching the Greek language. He has been a kind of general ser-

(y) ADAM, Vit. Germ. Theologorum.

vant to the whole institution, and well merits the bounty of your Highness. *The whole Christian world is his debtor, and blessed be God, the Popish fraternity are more afraid of* HIM *and his* SCHOLARS *than all the learned besides put together.*" (z)

A long and violent altercation between the Elector and the Popish party at Naumburg respecting the election of a bishop, occupied a considerable part of the year 1542. The state of the district rendered it a question of great importance. The majority of the ecclesiastical orders adhered to the degrading superstitions of Popery; but the inhabitants both of the towns and villages in the vicinity of the Electorate were panting to enjoy the doctrines of the Reformation. The Catholic influence was exerted to introduce Julius Pflug, one of the persons appointed in the select Committee at the recent conferences of Ratisbon, a man estimable in himself, but a decided Papist; the Elector on the other hand, tenacious of his right of nomination, and anxious to introduce a Reformer, after long and mature deliberations fixed upon Nicholas Amsdorff, who was eventually installed. On this occasion Luther, Melancthon, with many persons of eminence and rank attended. The account of the popish writer Maimbourg is suf-

(z) SECKEND. Hist. Lib. III. p. 356 and 381.

ficiently amusing.   After intimating his displeasure at the *pride* and *insolence* of the abettors
of Lutheranism subsequently to the Council of
Ratisbon, and mentioning the choice of Julius
Pflug, he says, " The Duke of Saxony openly
declared the election invalid, because he did not
conform to the Augsburg confession, and nominated Nicholas Amsdorff in his stead, one of
the principal and most zealous of the Lutherans,
upon whom his master Luther, who played the
Pope at Wittemburg, laid his hands and made
him a bishop!"   The Emperor felt also ex-
cessively exasperated at these proceedings ;
but desired Pflug to exercise patience, " for,"
says he, " your cause shall be mine ;" and accordingly a few years afterwards he employed
the strong arm of imperial power to eject Amsdorff, who fled to Magdeburg, instating Pflug in
the diocese of Saxe-Naumburg. *(a)*

It was a mortifying circumstance to the
Papists that the wide-spreading light of the
Reformation extended at length into COLOGNE ;
and that the Archbishop and Elector Hermannus, or Herman, Count de Wied, whom Maimbourg and other writers highly panegyrize, both
for his personal accomplishments and ardent
zeal for the Catholic religion, became anxious at

(a) ADAM. Vit. Germ. Theol. p. 69, 70. SECKEND.
Hist. Lib. III. p. 382 and 392.

this period to reform his diocese. It was not indeed a sudden or momentary feeling. At the time of the Protestant convention at Frankfort, in the year 1539, the Archbishop sent Peter Medmannus to confer with Melancthon, and to request a visit from him ; but he could at that time only return a congratulatory letter, in which he says, that " though his Lordship's personal regard to him was most grateful to his feelings, yet he was still more rejoiced on account of the public cause, as the Archbishop appeared desirous of applying proper remedies to heal the wounds of the church, instead of adopting measures calculated only to inflame and exasperate them."*(b)* Towards the close of 1541, Hermannus sent for Martin Bucer, and had several conferences with him in the following year at Bonne; the result of which was a resolution to confer with proper persons, and pursue effectual means for the reformation of his diocese. On the fifteenth of January, 1543, he dispatched letters to the Elector of Saxony, requesting him to allow Melancthon to come ; who replied, after a considerable lapse of time, that he had given him permission to be absent from the University six or seven weeks. The letters of Melancthon sufficiently explain the transactions at Bonne. To Luther he writes

(b) MELANCTH. Ep. Lib. III. ep. 38.

thus on the nineteenth of May. " The Bishop wishes a formulary of doctrines and ceremonies to be drawn up, similar to that of the Nuremberg church, and to be given to him for his inspection. I have been engaged in this the last three days. He is desirous of introducing pure doctrinal truth, and of exterminating whatever rites are now publicly practised in opposition to it; but the Canons in general resist this innovation, though there are some amongst them who aim to restrain the violence ef their brethren. The Bishop has been fiercely threatened to be driven from his dignity; on which account the Landgrave has written to the College, and openly avowed his own determination, and that of the confederate Princes, to unite, if it be requisite, in his defence. All the cities excepting Cologne, including the major part of the nobility, are desirous of a better ecclesiastical constitution, which they see plainly enough to be necessary. I do believe that scarcely any part of Germany was in so barbarous and heathenish a state as this, which the prevailing idolatrous practices sufficiently evince; but I perceive the discourses of Bucer and Pistorius are much regarded, and I think they preach the truth. There are others also who teach the people sound doctrine, and administer the Sacraments as they ought, in some of the neighbouring towns and villages." In another letter, addressed to

2 F

Camerarius, he says, " You could not witness without tears the wretched state of these churches, in which the people are daily crowding to the images, and this with the ignorant multitude is the sum and substance of religion. *(c)* The aged Prince rightly judges, that reform is necessary, and seeks to introduce it. I have only at present begun the formulary of doctrine and ceremonies which is to be proposed to the churches. A few assist the Prince; at Cologne he is opposed, but in various places are to be found men of piety and correct sentiments." Again upon his return in August he writes, " After Bucer and myself had finished our work for the regulation of the churches, the aged Bishop, sending for his Dean and assistant Stolbergius, a man of sense, and some other leading persons, desired me to read through the whole book in their presence, to which he paid the greatest attention, remarking upon many parts of it, sometimes suggesting very proper alterations, sometimes after discussing a point submitting to our opinion in preference to his own. This labour occupied four hours every morning in six

---

(c) He makes similar complaints in letters addressed from Bonne to his friends *Pomeranus* and *Caspar Cruciger.* He speaks of the Pastors, where any were to be found, as of the most illiterate class. " Pastores aut nulli sunt, aut indoctissimi. Tota religio populi est in adorandis statnis." ME-LANCTH. Ep. Lib. I. 83, 84.

successive days. I wondered at the assiduity and diligence of the old man." *(d)*

When the Archbishop presented the Articles, which the deputation of Reformers had drawn up, to the Chapter at Cologne; they requested time to examine it, while the Protestant doctors were expelled the city. With the former request he readily complied, but alleged in reference to the latter, he could not consent unless they were convicted of false doctrines and immoral conduct. An acrimonious publication under the following title soon appeared; "*Judicium Deputatorum Universitatis et Secundarii Cleri Coloniensis de Doctrinâ et Vocatione Martini Buceri;*" upon which Melancthon remarks ; " The publication of the Colognians is issued. It is not so much against Bucer as against the doctrine of our churches in general, and against our princes. It is the worthy effort of a well-fed Carmelite, and priest of Bacchus and Venus. They had entitled it, " *The Judgment of the Clergy and the University;*" but when some of the more sane members of the College saw it, and perceived it was much more worthy of buffoons than of Clergymen, they

(d) MELANCTH. Ep. Lib. I. ep. 74. Lib. IV. ep. 298, and ep. 304. In a letter to one of his other friends, dated *Bonne,* he mentions that the Archbishop turned to Luther's German Version of the Scriptures to verify every quotation. MEL. Ep. *ad Joan. Cæsar.* BOSSUET exhibits the good Archbishop in a very different light. *Hist. des Variations* Tom. I. p. 456.

insisted upon a change of the title, and protested they did not approve such a production ; upon which, instead of *The Clergy*, it was agreed to use the term *Inferior Clergy*, by which some understand the *baser* description.   Lutheranism is prodigiously railed at; and upon the subject of marriage the vilest and most obscene language is used, such as would almost disgrace a prostitute.   The jests are culled from the comedies of Plautus, whose writings I dare say are more charming to this Carmelite than the Psalms of David." *(e)*

Bucer and Melancthon both published a reply to this *unclerical* publication; that of the latter is one of his very best writings.   He first singles out the dissentient individuals, for whom he cherishes a sincere regard ; and then with a cogency of argument and a pungency of satire, attacks the remaining part of the fraternity. He tells them that neither Eckius nor Pighius, madly as they wrote, ever equalled the atrocious language of these Colognians.   He jokes upon the word *secundarius* in the title-page, and supposes they mean the *low* and *degenerate* part of the community.   On the subject of the mass he remarks, that there is no more reason for adoring the bread in the Sacrament of the

(e) Pezel. Cons. Tom. 1. p. 536.   Melancth. Ep. Lib. III. ep. 75.

supper, than the water in the ordinance of baptism. " If Ambrose and Augustine were to
rise from the dead, to say nothing of the apostles, and witness the superstitious mockeries
now practised, the long processions of wooden,
silver and marble images, the superintendants
and expositors of sacred mysteries carrying about
the bread, and the surrounding multitude pro-
strating themselves in adoration of it, they
would be absolutely alarmed, and ready to
ask into what heathen land they had got, and
what new ceremonies were invented since their
day, for they could not imagine themselves in
Christian churches. But when they came to
be informed that this was the manner in which
the Lord's Supper was observed, they would
burn with grief and indignation, and begin to
exhort the people to return to the genuine use
of the Sacrament, and to the proper services of
religion. There was formerly a custom of a similar nature prevalent in Persia, in which the
sacred fire was carried about to be worshipped
by the populace, and three hundred and sixty-
five priests, answering in number to the days of
the year, led the way, carrying particular en-
signs." To this statement he adds a solemn exhortation, and relates a circumstance, which he
declares he received from the best authority,
respecting a priest who went to Tubingen,
where he carried about some relics consisting of

bones, promising to every one that kissed them a security from the plague, during the period of a whole year. When Prince Eberhard, who was possessed both of wisdom and influence, had him taken up for his ridiculous impudence, the priest alleged that he had certainly stated what was most true, because the people did not in fact kiss *the relics,* but only *the glass case in which they were put!* " Such," says Melancthon, " are the miserable shifts to which you resort to excuse your ecclesiastical abuses, and think to escape the censures of the pious : the people in the mean time being confirmed in error and superstition." He ridicules their pretended attempts at reform, representing them as " willing to wipe the dust off the images in their temples, to new colour the old worn out pictures upon the walls, and passing an oracular decree to double the size of the square altars, that they may have a more magnificent appearance. They enact laws against letting the beards grow, and concerning the vain repetition of unintelligible prayers. These are the mighty things which they require to be restored, and which they complain of the Prince for hindering." *(f)*

(f) The Pope thinking it necessary to shew the Protestants that he was not averse to every kind of reformation, had appointed four Cardinals and five other eminent persons to draw up a plan for the reformation of the church; but it was ex-

Unhappily, in consequence of the firm resistance of the chancellor, canons and divines of Cologne, to the reforming plans of the good Archbishop, the Popish religion was still maintained in that Electorate. They did not hesitate to avow " that they would rather live under a Turkish government than under a magistrate who approved and defended such a reformation." But the city of Hildesheim abolished the Catholic superstitions, and embraced the Protestant faith. *(g)*

The University of Wittemberg received their illustrious Professor with the most marked respect, after he had finished the transactions at Cologne. Sensible of the lustre his still increasing celebrity shed upon their whole body, impressed with a deep sense of his public efforts in the cause of the Reformation, his academical labours and his numerous private virtues, he was welcomed home by a sort of public entrance. The students and most of the professors in the different branches of literature, went out to meet him on the road, and to hail his return. *(h)*

tremely superficial and partial. It was published about the year 1539 at Antwerp, with the answer of Cochlæus to the objections of Sturmius, who, as well as Luther and Melancthon had turned it into ridicule. In this plan the most intolerable grievances of which the Protestants complained are left totally unredressed.

(g) DUPIN.
(h) CAM. Vit. Mel.

But the cup of human life is never replenished with unmingled good; the sweet and the bitter are mixed in their due proportions by an all-wise providence. It seems upon a close inspection as if human happiness were more equally distributed by the unsparing hand of divine liberality than the envious and the petulant too frequently imagine. Great talents, or external splendours are sometimes connected with inward heartburnings and domestic anxieties; while poverty and rags are often the only patrimony of noble and wisely-contented spirits. Sorrow, like death, visits alike the palace and the cottage. *(i)* Melancthon became at this period involved in the utmost perplexity and grief by the improper behaviour of one of his sons-in-law, and the removal of his daughter into Prussia, circumstances which have been mentioned in an early part of this work, in connexion with a view of his domestic character. *(k)* His mind, always tending to despondency, was much agitated also by the loss of several of his friends, particularly Valerius Cordus, a person of elegant taste and extensive erudition. His death occurred at Rome, and was supposed to have originated in excessive

(i) Æquo pulsat pede pauperum tabernas
Regumque turres. ——— ——   Hor.
     (k) Vid. Ch. 4.

fatigue, incurred by a laborious search, amongst the cold mountains and vallies of Italy, after herbs, roots and plants for medical purposes, to which he was devoted. The Sacramental controversy was renewed with increased asperity, and so violent was Luther, and so conciliating was Melancthon, that, availing themselves of the favourable moment, their mutual enemies attempted to foment their dissension, but in vain; for though at one period a cloud seemed to be gathering over the brightness of their friendship, it soon entirely disappeared. In fact Luther seems to have been kindled with unusual rage against the Sacramentarians, and to have used a provoking intemperance of language, which, though his conscientious convictions and the barbarous usages of the age, may be admitted as some extenuation, could not by any means be approved by his amiable friend. At the same time the Protestants in France were in a deplorable situation, and Francis and Charles V. were engaged in a furious war, which however terminated in September, 1544, by a treaty of peace at Crespy.

The Elector Palatine Frederic, successor to Lewis, being animated with zeal to reform the churches under his jurisdiction, obtained in the beginning of the year 1545 a plan for this purpose, drawn up by the ready pen of Melancthon, and presented with his signature, in conjunction with those of Luther, Bugenhagen or Pomeranus, Cruciger and Major. It is a judicious compendium, in six divisions, stated in these words: *(l)*

" The true and salutary administration of the Christian Church chiefly consists in these six particulars:

" I. In pure doctrinal truth, which God has revealed, transmitted, and commanded to be taught in his church.

" II. In the legitimate use of the Sacraments.

" III. In the maintenance of a gospel ministry, and the due obedience to Pastors, according to the will of God, who has promised to afford his presence and protection to such a ministry.

" IV. In the preservation of strict and holy discipline, by the proper exercise of ecclesiastical authority and jurisdiction.

" V. In a proper regard for the establishment of schools, and the direction of necessary studies.

" VI. To these it is proper to add, the support of officers who may be wanted for necessary services in the church."

Another very important duty in which Melancthon was engaged, was the episcopal

(l) PEZEL. Cons. ADAM. Vit. Germ. Theol.

ordination of the Prince of Anhalt, which shed
such a pleasing lustre on the present year. The
reader will not deem it an uninteresting digression to introduce this circumstance in a connected but necessarily brief sketch of his life.

GEORGE, Prince of Anhalt, and Count of
Ascania, was descended from the Dukes of
Saxony, and was born on the fourteenth of
August, 1507. His father, Prince Ernest
of Anhalt, gave him a liberal education
at the University of Leipsic, under George
Forchem, who was no less celebrated for correctness of conduct than for capacity as a
preceptor. Camerarius, Cruciger and others
studied under this eminent tutor, who had the
pleasure of finding in the Prince of Anhalt an
apt and diligent scholar. He devoted a considerable degree of attention to the civil law,
which his rank in life seemed particularly to
require. At the age of twenty-two his proficiency in every branch of knowledge, and his
reputation for eloquence was such, that Albert
Elector of Mentz chose him to be one of his
Council, and he became, in consequence, very
much engaged in state affairs. At the rise of
the Reformation his ardent mind soon interested
itself in the pursuit of truth; he perfected himself in the Greek and Hebrew languages, searched the Holy Scriptures with diligent investigation, read the best commentators amongst

the Fathers, and cultivated an intercourse with some of the most learned men. Often with tears he was known to pray, " Deal with thy servant according to thy mercy, and teach, O teach me thy righteousness!"

At length he openly embraced the Reformation, planted seminaries of learning, and strenuously opposed the Popish superstitions. Multitudes saw and rejoiced in the wide-spreading light, and he constantly co-operated with his brothers in establishing the reformed religion in their respective territories. For the purpose of more extensive usefulness, he was induced, in the year 1545, to accept the bishopric of Mersburg, in Saxony, an office upon which he entered with fervent prayer, and afterwards discharged with extraordinary assiduity. His letter of episcopal ordination, written by Melancthon, is thus expressed:

" We give thanks to God the eternal Father of our Lord Jesus Christ, who of his infinite goodness has instituted a gospel ministry for the recovery of the fallen race of mankind, and will maintain it through the successive ages of time till the resurrection of the dead; and who raises up learned and suitable persons, giving command to his church that such should be called to the office; and promises through their ministry to dispense the doctrine of the remission of sins, the gift of the Holy Spirit and eternal life. We beseech him not to permit the light of his gospel to be extinguished, but that he would raise up faithful men to advocate and uphold the pure and salutary doctrines of Christ, and now in this territory gather to himself a people to celebrate his praises to eternity. As the most reverend and illustrious GEORGE, PRINCE OF ANHALT, COUNT OF ASCANIA, LORD OF BERNBURG, &c. appointed to this gospel ministry over the church at Magdeburg, has been called in a regular and pious manner to the discharge of ecclesiastical functions in the bishopric of Mersburg, certain serious and learned persons who superintend the neighbouring churches, and whose names are under-written, have been sent for to be present conformably to the custom of the ancient primitive churches, that they might here give their public testimony of ordination in addition to the general call to the office. We are therefore assembled for this purpose because we well know that the illustrious prince GEORGE understands and firmly embraces the pure doctrines of the gospel, which all the churches of God in these parts unite with one voice and one soul with the church universal in professing, and the glory of which is to promote holiness and virtue. We have attended to his ordination in the apostolic manner of laying on of hands ; for Paul admonished Titus that Presbyters should be every where ordained to teach and govern the churches.

Be it known that this ordination to an ecclesiastical function derives its authority from apostolic practice, and as priests are appointed to teach and rule churches, to watch over doctrinal sentiments and moral conduct, let the words of the Son of God be in constant recollection, ' When thou art converted strengthen thy brethren.' And as Christ sitteth at the right hand of the Father to give efficacy to the public ministry, we pray that he would rule over this whole district and bless this ordination. ' Whoso loveth me and keepeth my words, him will my Father love; and we will come to him and make our abode with him.' Such is his promise and we exhort the prince to be encouraged by the declaration; for though the government of a church is attended with many and great dangers, nor can human wisdom avail for such an undertaking, yet let him know that God is truly present and will constantly dwell wherever his gospel is preached; that he will defend and support it. With this conviction the labours of such a ministry may be undertaken and sustained. MERSBURG, Aug. 3, 1545."

This eminent character discharged the duties of his sacred office with exemplary diligence. His whole time was devoted to preaching, reading, writing, devotional exercises and the affairs of the church. He never intentionally injured any one, but benefitted many both publicly and

privately. He was a promoter of peace amongst
the princes, settling many of their disputes, re-
straining turbulence and faction, being himself
superior to all motives of mean ambition. He
sustained many and great injuries with the utmost magnanimity, lived a life of devotion with
God and resignation to his will, often admo-
nishing others to cultivate similar feelings. After
lingering under a painful disease, during which
he settled the affairs of his church, engaged in
the most ardent devotions, frequently conversed
on the most interesting religious topics and
daily read the Sacred Scriptures, particularly the
prophetic and apostolic writings, " on the seventeenth of October, 1553, his spirit was called
away from this mortal state to the assembly of
the heavenly church." *(m)*

The most celebrated German poets wrote
elegies upon his death. Two epigrams by Melancthon are preserved, one of which shall be
inserted.

Ascaniæ stirpis virtus est clara triumphis:
  Ordine quos numerant secula longa patrum.
Cæsar in Adriaco quum gessit littore bellum,
  Et fregit venetas Maximilianus opes :
Duxerat Ascaniâ natus de stirpe Rodolphus:
  Fixit et in Veneto multa trophæa solo.

(m) ADAM. Vit. Germ. Theologorum. *Vit. Georg. Prin. Anhaltini.*

Nunc ad majora decora, hæc laus magna, Georgi,
    Accedit, verè principe digna viro:
Quod sic doctrinam reliquis virtutibus addis,
    Ut verum celebres pectore et ore Deum :
Et Christi illustres ingentia munera scriptis;
    Justificâ supplex quæ capis ipse fide:
Exemploque Esdræ populum dum jure gubernas :
    Doctrinæ spargis semina pura simul.
Summe Deus, solus qui das felicia regna,
    Ascanios fratres, te precor, ipse regas !

For ages past behold Ascania's line,
In martial virtues and achievements shine !
When through the coasts of Italy afar,
Imperial prowess poured the tide of war;
Then Maximilian.---then Rodolphus gains
Trophies of valour on Venetian plains ;---
Still to sustain the glory of his race
A GEORGE is giv'n, the high descent to grace ;
Though for each manly virtue far renown'd,
With brighter honour, brighter glory crown'd,
He lov'd the truth---the God of truth he serv'd,
The faith of Christ he honour'd and preserv'd ;
Like Esdra ruling well, but on each hand,
Spreading the seeds of truth throughout the land.
'Tis thine, Great God ! 'tis thine alone to cause
Nations to triumph in their kings and laws,
To rule o'er rulers, and assign their place ;
Oh, condescend to bless the Ascanian race !

CHAP. XI.

,,,,,,,,,

,,,,,,,,,

Persecuting measures--Death of LUTHER*--Melancthon's*
  FUNERAL ORATION *for him—Tributary lines—Re-*
  marks on the friendship of Luther and Melancthon—
  Position of public affairs—The Emperor and the Pro-
  testants at open war—Perfidy of Maurice—Captivity
  of John Frederic and imprisonment of the Landgrave—
  Diet at Augsburg—The INTERIM*—Meetings of the*
  Wittemberg and Leipsic Divines—Melancthon's pub-
  lication on indifferent things—Extracts from his reply
  to the Interim—Curious preface to an English trans-
  lation of it—The virulent opposition of Flaccus Illy-
  ricus to Melancthon—Reply of the latter.

PERSISTING in his resolution notwithstanding the objections of the Protestants, the
Roman Pontiff summoned a general council to
be held at Trent, while the Emperor at the Diet
of Worms in the year 1545 used every effort to
persuade all parties to acquiesce in that appointment. It was in vain ; and the pen of Melancthon was again employed to prepare a publication in the name of the Reformers, containing

2 G

the chief reasons which induced them to dissent
from the Papal decree.   It is entitled, " *Causæ,
quare et amplexæ sint, et retinendam ducant doctrinam, quam profitentur Ecclesiæ, quæ Confessionem, Augustæ exhibitam Imperatori sequuntur
et quare iniquis judicibus collectis in Synodo Tri-
dentina ut vocant, non sit assentiendum;*" and
" on account of the excellence of its matter, the
weight of argument and a certain original beauty
of style cannot fail of profiting every reader." *(a)*
It is inserted in the fourth volume of his works.

The Emperor being exasperated at the continual objections raised against the council, departed at last from his usual course of conduct
and determined to settle all religious disputes by
force of arms.   The Elector of Saxony and the
Landgrave of Hesse immediately adopted proper
measures for their own defence.   At Worms the
clergy of Cologne had presented a petition to the
Emperor, against the proceedings of their Archbishop in establishing the reformed religion, and
he instantly took them into his protection,
not only interdicting by his imperial letters any
molestation of the Catholics in the electorate,
but summoning the Elector to appear before
him within thirty days.   The Pope issued a
similar summons for sixty days to the Archbishop, Dean and five Canons of Cologne, who

(a) SECKEND. Hist. Lib. III. p. 602.

had espoused his cause. In the succeeding January, 1546, the Protestant princes assembled at Frankfort, made common cause with the persecuted Archbishop, and united to defend themselves against the violent designs of the Emperor. *(b)*

If ever the presiding genius of Martin Luther were requisite to direct the intricate concerns of the Reformation, the present crisis seemed particularly to demand his talents. The gathering tempest frowned with a portentous aspect upon all Germany; the new launched vessel in which many of their princes had embarked with a noble and adventurous spirit, and which had hitherto been driven about by so many raging winds, became at this time exposed to a storm of unusual violence, and every voice was lifted up to demand the pilotage of the first and in many respects the greatest of the Reformers. It is not easy therefore to express or imagine the consternation with which the princes and Reformers in general, and his most intimate friend Melancthon in particular saw him expire at this alarming period. In consequence of repeated attacks of the stone his constitution had been declining for many months, and in the early morning of the eighteenth of February 1546, he

(b) SLEID. Hist. p. 310, 340, 351, 355. SECKEND. Hist. Lib. III. p. 566, 570, 613.

died at Eisleben his native place, whither he had gone a second time to settle some existing differences between the Counts of Mansfeld. A few hours afterwards Jonas communicated the melancholy tidings to the Elector of Saxony, and requested his Highness to inform his wife, Melancthon, Pomeranus and Cruciger. In the first journey to Eisleben a short time before, Melancthon had accompanied him and must have deeply regretted his absence on the last painful occasion. When he first received the intelligence of his death, he exclaimed, " My Father ! my Father ! the chariot of Israel and the horsemen thereof !" *(o)* He was interred at Wittemberg. Pomeranus preached a funeral sermon, and Melancthon pronounced the following

ORATION.

" Although amidst this general mourning my voice is so obstructed by deep affliction and tears, yet something I would attempt to say; not to eulogize the dead as the heathen do, but to admonish the living in this vast assembly, and especially to impress just sentiments upon the junior part of the auditory respecting the government of the church and its dangers, that they may learn what to desire and by what examples to regulate their lives. Wicked and infidel men represent every thing in the present apparent

(c) 2 KINGS ii. 12.

confusion of human affairs as the result of mere
chance, but confiding in the numerous and explicit declarations of God himself, we distinguish
the church from the promiscuous multitude of
mankind, and affirm it is under divine superintendence and protection.   To this we constantly
look, obeying our lawful governors and cherishing a pious reverence for those guides and instructors whom we choose.

    " It will be necessary to advert to these
considerations as often as the name of the Reverend Doctor MARTIN LUTHER, our most beloved father and teacher is introduced, whom
we love and honour, detestable as he appears in
the eyes of many wicked men, and whom we
know to have been raised up by heaven as a minister of the true gospel, by evidences which
notwithstanding the charges of our opponents,
prove that his doctrines were neither seditious
nor dispersed abroad with a blind and impetuous
zeal.

    " In this place and on these occasions,
many things are usually said in a panegyrical
strain respecting the personal endowments of
the deceased; I propose however, to omit these
and advert chiefly to his ecclesiastical function.
Intelligent and pious persons will admit, if he
were the means of promoting useful and necessary truth in the church, we ought to be grateful
to the Providence of God for raising up such a

light, while his labours, faith, perseverance and other virtues ought to be duly acknowledged and his memory tenderly cherished by all worthy men.

" The Apostle Paul represents Christ as ' having ascended on high to give gifts unto men,' that is, the preaching of the gospel and the Holy Spirit; for the purpose of communicating which, ' he gave some apostles, and some prophets, and some evangelists, and some pastors and teachers ;' *(d)* selecting them from amongst those who read, study and delight in the sacred writings. Nor are they only called into the Christian service who occupy the more ordinary stations, but others are frequently introduced under the direction of learned men into this holy warfare, and it is both pleasing and profitable to witness the care of God to his church throughout all ages, in sending a continued succession of useful men, that as some fall in the glorious field, others may instantly rush forward to take their places. The first of our race who nobly occupied the foremost ranks were Adam, Seth, Enoch, Methuselah, Noah and Shem. The latter being yet alive and dwelling in the neighbourhood of Sodom, when the inhabitants of the earth forgetting the instructions of Noah and Shem, became addicted to idolatry ; God raised

(d) EPH. iv. 8. 11.

up a coadjutor of Shem in the person of Abraham, to co-operate in the great work of propagating divine truth.   To him succeeded Isaac,
Jacob and Joseph, who kindled the light of true
religion in Egypt, at that period the most flou-
rishing empire in the world ; and to them Moses,
Joshua, Samuel, David, Elijah and Elisha,
Isaiah, Jeremiah, Daniel and Zachariah.   After
them arose Esdras, Onias and the Maccabees ;
then Simeon, Zacharias, John the Baptist,
CHRIST and his Apostles.   I am delighted to
contemplate this unbroken succession, which
affords conspicuous evidence of the presence of
God in his church.   The apostles were succeeded by a troop, so to speak, of inferior warriors,
but nevertheless distinguished of heaven, Poly-
carp, Irenæus, Gregory of Neocæsarea, Basil,
Augustin, Prosper, Maximus, Hugo, Bernard,
Taulerus and others.   And although the latter
ages present a more barren prospect, God has
always preserved a proportion of his servants
upon the earth, and now through Martin Luther
a more splendid period of light and truth has
appeared.

     " To this enumeration of the most eminent
amongst the sons of men who gathered and reformed the church of God, may be added others
who may be regarded as the flower of mankind.
Solon, Themistocles, Scipio, Augustus and
others, who either established or ruled over

mighty empires were indeed truly great men, but far, far inferior to our illustrious leaders Isaiah, John the Baptist, Paul, Augustin and Luther, and it becomes us to study this distinction. What then are those great and important things which Luther has disclosed to our view, and which render his life so remarkable; for many are exclaiming against him as a disturber of the church and a promoter of inexplicable controversies? I answer, that when the Holy Spirit in his regulation of the church reproves the world for sin, dissensions arise out of the pertinacity of wicked men, and they alone are culpable who refuse to listen to the proclamation of the eternal Father concerning his Son, ' This is my beloved Son, HEAR HIM.' Luther explained the true and important doctrine of penitence which was involved in the profoundest darkness. He shewed in what it consists and where refuge and consolation could be obtained under a sense of divine displeasure. He illustrated the statements of Paul respecting justification by faith and shewed the distinction between the law and the gospel, civil and spiritual justification. He pointed out the true principle of prayer and exterminated that heathenish absurdity from the church, that God was not to be invoked if the mind entertained the least doubt upon an academic question. He admonished men to pray in the exercise of faith and

a good conscience to the only Mediator and Son
of God, who is seated at the right hand of the
Father making intercession for us, and not to
images or deceased saints according to the shocking practice of the ignorant multitude. He also
pointed out other services acceptable to God,
was singularly exemplary himself in all the duties
of life, and separated the puerilities of human
rites and ceremonies which prevent instead of
promoting genuine worship, from those services
which are essential to obedience. In order that
heavenly truth might be transmitted to posterity, he translated the prophetic and apostolic
writings into the German language with so much
accuracy, that his version of itself places Scripture in a more perspicuous light than most commentaries. But he published also various expositions upon the sacred writings which in the
judgment of Erasmus by far excelled all others ;
and as it is recorded respecting those who rebuilt
Jerusalem, ' with one hand they laid the stones
and with the other they held the sword,' so while
he composed annotations on Scripture replete
with heavenly instruction and consoled afflicted
consciences by his pious counsels, he was necessitated at the same time to wage incessant war
with the adversaries of evangelical truth. When
it is recollected that this truth, especially the
doctrine of faith and the remission of sins, is
not discoverable by the merely human eye, it

must be acknowledged he was taught of God, and many of us have witnessed his anxious solicitude to impress the great principle of acceptance by faith. Multitudes of the saints will therefore praise God to all eternity, for the benefits which have accrued to the church by the labours of Luther. To God their gratitude is primarily due, and then they will own themselves much indebted to his labours, although infidels who ridicule the church in general will consider these noble performances as no better than empty trifling or absolute insanity. The true church does not as some falsely affirm promote intricate disputations, throw out the apple of contention and propose the enigmas of the fabled Sphinx; for to those who judge seriously and without prejudice it is easy from a comparison of opposite opinions to perceive what are consonant to the statements of heavenly truth and what are otherwise. Christians are no longer in a state of hesitation on the subject of existing controversies, for when God determined to reveal his will and display his character in the sacred writings, it is not to be imagined that such a communication would be ambiguous like the leaves of the ancient Sibyl.

" Some, by no means evil-minded persons however, express a suspicion that Luther manifested too much asperity. I will not affirm the reverse, but only quote the language of Erasmus, ' God has sent in this latter age a violent

physician on account of the magnitude of the
existing disorders,' fulfilling by such a dispensation the divine message to Jeremiah, ' Behold I have put my words in thy mouth.   See
I have this day set thee over the nations, and
over the kingdoms, to root out and pull down,
and to destroy and to throw down, to build and
to plant.' (e)   Nor does God govern his church
according to the counsels of men, nor choose to
employ instruments like theirs to promote his
purposes.   But it is usual for inferior minds to
dislike those of a more ardent character.   When
Aristides observed the mighty affairs which
Themistocles by the impulse of a superior genius
undertook and happily accomplished, although
he congratulated the state on the advantage it
possessed in such a man, he studied every means
to divert his zealous mind from its pursuits.   I
do not deny that ardent spirits are sometimes
betrayed into undue impetuosity, for no one is
totally exempt from the weaknesses incident to
human nature, but they often merit the praise
assigned by the ancient proverb to Hercules,
Cimon and other illustrious characters, ἀκομψος
μὲν, ἀλλὰ τὰ μέγιςα ἀγαθὸς ' rough indeed, but distinguished by the best principles.'   So in the
Christian church the Apostle Paul mentions
such as ' war a good warfare, holding faith and

(e) JEREM. i. 9, 10.

a good conscience,' *(f)* and who are both pleasing to God and estimable amongst pious men.
Such an one was Luther, who while he constantly defended the pure doctrines of Christianity maintained a conscientious integrity of
character. No vain licentiousness was ever
detected in him, no seditious counsels, but on
the contrary, he often urged the most pacific
measures ; and never, never did he blend political artifices for the augmentation of power with
ecclesiastical affairs. Such wisdom and such
virtue I am persuaded do not result from mere
human skill or diligence, but the mind must be
divinely influenced, especially when it is of the
more rough, elevated and ardent cast like that
of Luther.

" What shall I say of his other virtues?
Often have I myself gone to him unawares and
found him dissolved in tears and prayers for the
church of Christ. He devoted a certain portion
of almost every day to the solemn reading of
some of the Psalms of David with which he
mingled his own supplications amidst sighs and
tears ; and he has frequently declared how in-
dignant he felt against those who hastened over
devotional exercises through sloth or the pretence of other occupations. On this account,
said he, divine wisdom has prescribed some for-

(f) 1 Tim. i. 18, 19.

mularies of prayer, that our minds may be inflamed with devotion by reading them, to which
in his opinion reading aloud very much conduced. When a variety of great and important
deliberations respecting public dangers have
been pending, we have witnessed his prodigious
vigour of mind, his fearless and unshaken courage. Faith was his sheet anchor and by the
help of God he was resolved never to be driven
from it. Such was his penetration, that he perceived at once what was to be done in the most
perplexing conjunctures ; nor was he as some
supposed negligent of the public good or disre-
gardful of the wishes of others, but he was well
acquainted with the interests of the state, and
pre-eminently sagacious in discovering the
capacity and dispositions of all about him. And
although he possessed such extraordinary acuteness of intellect, he read both ancient and modern ecclesiastical writings with the utmost
avidity and histories of every kind, applying the
examples they furnished to existing circumstances with remarkable dexterity. The unde-
caying monuments of his eloquence remain, and
in my opinion he equalled any of those who
have been most celebrated for their resplendent
oratorical powers.

" The removal of such a character from
amongst us, of one who was endowed with the
greatest intellectual capacity, well instructed and

long experienced in the knowledge of Christian
truth, adorned with numerous excellencies and
with virtues of the most heroic cast, chosen by
divine Providence to reform the church of God,
and cherishing for all of us a truly paternal
affection—the removal, I say, of such a man
demands and justifies our tears. We resemble
orphans bereft of an excellent and faithful father; but while it is necessary to submit to the
will of heaven, let us not permit the memory of
his virtues and his good offices to perish. He
was an important instrument in the hands of God
of public utility; let us diligently study the
truth he taught, imitating in our humble situations his fear of God, his faith, the intensity of
his devotions, the integrity of his ministerial
character, his purity, his careful avoidance of
seditious counsel, his ardent thirst of knowledge. And as we frequently meditate upon the
pious examples of those illustrious guides of the
church, Jeremiah, John the Baptist and Paul,
whose histories are transmitted to us, so let us
frequently reflect upon the doctrine and course
of life which distinguished our departed friend.
Let the present vast assembly now unite with
me in grateful thanks and fervent supplications,
saying in the spirit of ardent devotion—' We give
thanks to thee Almighty God, the eternal Father
of our Lord Jesus Christ, the author and founder
of thy church, together with thy co-eternal Son
and the Holy Spirit, wise, good, merciful, just,

true, powerful, and sovereign, because thou
dost gather a heritage for thy Son from amongst
the human race, and dost maintain the ministry
of the gospel, and hast now reformed thy church
by means of Luther; we present our ardent sup-
lications that thou wouldst henceforth preserve,
fix and impress upon our hearts the doctrines of
truth, as Isaiah prayed for his disciples; and
that by thy Holy Spirit thou wouldst enflame
our minds with a pure devotion, and direct our
feet into the paths of holy obedience !'

" As the removal of illustrious men from
the church is frequently a means of punishing
their survivors, such of us as are entrusted with
the office of tuition, myself personally, and all
of us collectively, entreat you to reflect upon the
present calamities that threaten the whole earth.
Yonder the Turks are advancing, here civil
discord threatens, and there other adversaries
released at last from the apprehension of Luther's censures, will proceed with a perverse ingenuity, and with increased boldness to corrupt
the genuine truth. That God may avert these
evils let us be more diligent in the regulation of
our lives and studies, always retaining a deep
impression of this sentiment in our minds, that
as long as we maintain, hear, obey and love the
pure doctrines of the gospel, God will always
have a church and a dwelling place among us.
' If,' said Jesus Christ, ' a man love me, he will

keep my words; and my Father will love him,
and we will come unto him and make our abode
with him.' *(g)*   Encouraged by this ample promise, let us be stimulated to inculcate the truth
of heaven, knowing that the church will be the
preservation of the human race, and the security
of established governments; and let us constantly elevate our minds to that future and eternal
state of being, to which God himself calls our
attention, who has not given so many witnesses,
nor sent his Son into the world in vain, but
delights in the communication of these magnificent blessings.   Amen."

Of all the tributary lines to the memory of
Luther, those of Theodore Beza have been particularly celebrated; the following were composed by Melancthon:

> Occidit omnigena venerandus laude Lutherus
> Qui Christum docuit non dubitante fide
> Ereptum deflet vero hunc ecclesia luctu
> Cujus erat doctor, verius, imo pater.
> Occidit Israel præstans auriga Lutherus
> Quem mecum sanus lugeat omnis homo
> Nunc luctumque suum lacrymoso carmine prodat
> Hoc etenim orbatos flere, dolore decet.

> LUTHER, illustrious name! is now no more;---
> Let the true church with streaming eyes deplore

(g) JOHN xv. 23.

A TEACHER firm in faith---nay, rather say
A FATHER, from his children snatch'd away.
Luther is gone---the Pilot of our course:
O let the tearful Muse his name rehearse---
Let all the pious join with me to mourn,
Orphans should thus bedew a Father's urn.

The sympathizing heart will naturally lin-
ger upon the affecting consideration of Luther's
decease.   It was the earthly termination of
an uninterrupted and unusual intimacy of nearly
TWENTY-EIGHT YEARS with Philip Melancthon.   To judge of the survivor's feelings requires either a mind of remarkable sensibility,
or the experience of a similar loss.   This depri-
vation of Luther's valuable counsels, and friendly reproofs, of his consoling sympathy amidst
the trials of life, and of his directing wisdom amidst the peculiar difficulties incident
to the circumstances of the age in which
they lived must have inflicted a deep and
lasting pang.   Their attachment was founded
on principle, and so completely mutual that they
were become almost necessary to each other.
The agony of separation therefore must have
been exquisite ;—

" O the soft commerce ! O the tender ties,
Close-twisted with the fibres of the heart !
Which, broken, break them ; and drain off the soul
Of human joy ; and make it pain to live---

2 H

And is it then to live? When *such* friends part,
'Tis the *survivor* dies——" *(h)*

I said it was the *earthly* termination of their
intimacy, for religious friendship can never,
never end. If the soul of man be immortal,
and if, as seems more than probable, it will
carry with it into another world those principles
of action, those modes of thinking, those characteristic qualities, which constituted each
one's individuality and very being upon earth,
then the connexions of time will be perpetuated
amidst the raptures of eternity. For though
distances and separations are incident to the
condition of the present life, it neither comports
with our ideas of the benevolence of the Deity,
nor with the representations of Scripture, nor
indeed with our most ennobling desires and
hopes, to suppose these imperfections of our
temporal destiny will attach to our future existence. And not only will the recollection of
past friendship endear our future intercourse,
but the superiority of our celestial character,
acquired by a nearer and more constant approach
to the source of light and holiness, will infinitely purify it. Friendship founded on
just principles arises from the perception of

(h) YOUNG's Night Thoughts, 5.

moral excellence, associated with an y other striking or attractive qualities, besides a consciousness of some natural similarity of taste or character ; it must be allowed therefore that the increase of what constitutes the principle of mutual attraction, will necessarily produce a proportionate increase of attachment.   If moral excellence be now esteemed in its present imperfect degree and degraded state, associated as it is with glaring defects, dwarfish in its growth, irregular in its shape and full of infirmity, unquestionably it will prove hereafter in its maturity and glory, a stronger bond of union.   And because every principle and faculty is capable of continual improvement, and will hereafter, under happier circumstances, admit of more rapid increase, and more extensive augmentation than at present, the friendship of another world may be considered as everlastingly progressive, and, from the constitution of celestial spirits, indissoluble.

The conduct of Melancthon and Luther to each other, affords an admirable illustration of the true *basis* of religious friendship.   They were not perfectly *agreed*, but they were perfectly *united*.   Mutual forbearance admitted the free exercise of an independent mind, and secured the rights of conscience and the purity of principle.   Societies have been distracted, families divided, and even empires convulsed, from

the existence of differences in religious sentiment or practice, far less considerable than those
which subsisted between these eminent friends.
They knew each other, and did not allow the
whirlwinds of a temporary passion to dissipate
feelings founded on the best principles, and cherished by an unreserved intercourse. There
were many who at different times endeavoured
to divide them by fomenting discord, in order to
gain their respective influence and authority to
some other party or interest: but they were too
confident in each other, and too well persuaded
of the magnitude of the cause which claimed
their mutual co-operation and incessant efforts,
to be cajoled into disagreement. If, therefore,
our friendships were formed upon more solid
principles of union than they frequently are, it
is obvious they would prove more satisfactory,
more beneficial and more permanent. In all
our religious intercourse, it would be wise to
aim rather at securing the essentials of Christianity, than to be solicitous of accomplishing
what is notoriously impossible, a perfect agreement in points of inferior consideration. The
pious Baxter has admirably remarked, " Were
we all bound together by a confession or sub-
scription of the true fundamentals, and those
other points that are next to fundamentals only,
and there took up our Christanity and unity,
yielding to each other a freedom of differing in

smaller or more difficult points, or in expressing
ourselves in different terms, and so did live
peaceably and lovingly together, notwithstanding such differences, as men that all knew the
mysteriousness of divinity and the imperfection
of their own understandings, and that here we
know but in part, and therefore shall most cer.
tainly err and differ in part, what a world of
mischief might this course prevent? I oft
think on the examples of Luther and Melancthon. It was not a few things that they differed
in, nor such as would now be accounted small,
besides the imperious harshness of Luther's disposition (as Carolostadius could witness) and
yet how sweetly and peaceably and lovingly did
they live together, without any breach or disagreement considerable. As Mel. Adamus says
of them, ' Etsi tempora fuerunt ad distractiones
proclivia hominumque levitas dissidiorum cu-
pida tamen cum alter alterius vitia nôsset, nun-
quam inter eos simultas extitit ex quâ animorum
alienatio subsecuta sit ;'—so that their agreement arose not hence, that either was free from
faults or error, but knowing each other's faults,
they did more easily bear them. Certainly if
every difference in judgment in matters of religion should seem intolerable or make a breach
in affection, then no two men on earth must live
together, or tolerate each other, but every man
must resolve to live by himself, for no two on

earth but differ in one thing or other, except
such as take all their faith upon trust, and explicitly believe nothing at all. God hath not
made our judgments all of a complexion no
more than our faces, nor our knowledge all of a
size any more than our bodies; and methinks they
that be not resolved to be any thing in religion,
should be afraid of making the articles of their
faith so numerous, lest they should shortly
become heretics themselves, by disagreeing from
themselves; and they should be afraid of making
too strict laws for those that differ in judgment
in controvertible points, lest they should shortly
change their judgments, and so make a rod for
their own backs; for how know they, in difficult disputable cases, but within this twelve-
months themselves may be of another mind,
except they are resolved never to change for
fear of incurring the reproach of novelty and
mutability; and then they were best resolve to
study no more, nor ever to be wiser. I would
we knew at what age a man must receive this
principle against changing his judgment. I am
afraid lest at last they should teach it their children, and lest many divines did learn it too
young: and if any besides Christ and his apostles
must be standard and foundation of our faith, I
would we could certainly tell who they are, for I
have heard yet of none but the Pope or his general Council expressly lay claim to the preroga-

tive of infallibility, and I think there is few that have appeared more fallible." *(i)*

The principal points of difference between Melancthon and Luther were three: 1. Melancthon thought that the ancient form of ecclesiastical government might be retained, on condition of not annulling the authority of Scriptural truth ; to which Luther could not assent. 2. Melancthon conceived that Luther carried his doctrine respecting justification by faith only to such an extent as to nullify the importance and obligation of good works, so that his statements required explanation. 3. Melancthon appears to have differed from Luther in his opinion respecting the sacrament, particularly in the latter period of his life. He did not believe that the opinions of the Zuinglians ought to occasion a disunion among the Reformers ; but Luther was decided upon this point to his dying day. Dr. Maclaine very unnecessarily corrects Dr. Mosheim in his statement of this subject. *(k)*   It is obvious that *at first*, as Dr. Mosheim represents, " Melancthon adopted the sentiments of Luther in relation to the Eucharist," but in consequence of serious examination, his mind became enlightened, so that he

(i) BAXTER's Saints' Everlasting Rest, p. 559. 4to. 2 Ed.

(k) MOSHEIM Eccles. Hist. Vol. IV. p. 325.   *Note* (r) 8vo. Ed.

admitted the scriptural idea by degrees, and towards the close of his life, in his letters to Calvin, intimates his persuasion of the erroneous and idolatrous nature of the doctrine of consubstantiation. The character of Melancthon has been misunderstood on this as on other occasions. It has been intimated that an unwarrantable timidity prevented his avowing explicitly his opinions respecting the Sacrament. It is true it did arise from his apprehension lest such an avowal should enflame discord, and injure the great and general cause of the Reformation. But whether this apprehension were well-founded or not, or whether such a policy were justifiable or not (and we are not prepared by any means to defend it) such was Melancthon's real *principle* of action, and not any mean timidity or fear of personal danger or suffering. If this concealment for the sake of peace had really involved him in personal suffering instead of shielding him from it, it is due to the greatness of his character and the conscientious scrupulousness of his mind, to believe he would nevertheless have adhered to it.

It was not from personal considerations only that Melancthon felt the bitterness of his bereavement in the death of Luther; he was sensible of the public loss, and of the great and daily increasing difficulties of his own situation. Political affairs had never yet assumed so alarm-

ing an appearance, and they became almost
identified with ecclesiastical ones, owing to the
conspicuous part which was acted by the most
distinguished of the German princes. Though
during the past ten years he had been called
to take the lead in most of the public transactions relative to religion, having been employed to write every thing that was to be written, and to do almost every thing that was to be
done, yet he had constantly profited by his unreserved familiarity with Luther, with whom he
consulted and corresponded on every occasion.
Now he was required to act in a great measure
alone, and in consequence of his rare merit as a
divine and a scholar, which had acquired him a
high reputation in every country of Europe, he
became at once elevated to an undisputed preeminence amongst the leading Reformers of
the age.

The zealous efforts of Bucer to unite the
Swiss and German churches by an agreement on
the subject of the Sacrament having been defeated by Luther's determined hostility, his death
seemed to furnish a favourable opportunity for
the accomplishment of this long-projected reconciliation. Melancthon and his followers
were known to be extremely solicitous of this
union, and were disposed to go to the utmost
length which their consciences would permit to

extinguish the flame of discord. The high mutual
esteem subsisting between Bucer and John Calvin, the celebrated Pastor and Professor of Divinity at Geneva, appeared to facilitate this design.
Anxious to promote Bucer and Melancthon's
views, Calvin proposed a mode of explaining the
subject, which, while it denied the corporeal
presence, allowed a divine virtue and efficacy
communicated by Christ with the bread and
wine of the Sacrament to those who partook of
it with a lively faith and integrity of heart: but
he has been generally censured by Protestants
for making unwarrantable concessions for the
sake of peace. The fair prospect however soon
became obscured, in consequence of the occu-
pation of Melancthon in other violent controversies to be mentioned hereafter, which left
him no leisure for that co-operation with Calvin
which probably might have produced the happiest results; and still more on account of the
intemperate zeal of Joachim Westphal, pastor
of the church at Hamburg, who both adopted
the sentiments and manifested the too-unchari-
table spirit of Luther. *(l)*

The Pope and the Emperor were now resolved to accomplish the ruin of the Protestants.

*(l)*Losch. Hist. Motuum P. 2. Lib. III. cap. 8. Grevii
Mem. Joach. Westph.

The Council of Trent decreed, that the Apocryphal writings should be received as of equal authority with the books which the Jews and primitive Christians admitted into the sacred canon, that the traditions of the church should be equally regarded with the doctrines and precepts of the inspired apostles, that the Vulgate translation should be read in the churches, and deemed authentic and canonical: and that all who disputed these truths were anathematized in the name of the Holy Ghost. (m) By this means they aimed a deadly blow at the very root and principle of Protestantism; and the Pope soon afterwards exhibited a striking proof of his disposition to exterminate it root and branch. Availing himself of the appeal of the canons of Cologne against their Archbishop, he convicted him of heresy, and issued a bull by which he was deprived of his ecclesiastical dignity, and his subjects absolved from their oath of allegiance to him as their prince. There was no reason to doubt the concurrence of the Emperor in this sentence, who was maturing the most deep-laid schemes for the subversion of the Protestant faith, under an impenetrable veil of the profoundest dissimulation. In the month of March he contrived to have an interview with the

(m) F. PAUL, 141. PALLAV, 206.

Landgrave of Hesse, who was more suspicious of his design than any of the other confederates, and made such professions of attachment to the interests of Germany, and of his dislike to violent measures, stoutly denying that he was engaged in any military preparations, that the Landgrave, cajoled by his plausibility, dismissed his own apprehensions, and quieted the fears of the Smalcaldian confederacy.

At length public affairs were brought to such a crisis, that the Emperor and the Protestants were at open war. No decisive superiority was acquired on either side during the autumn of 1546; but Maurice Duke of Saxony, and uncle to John Frederic, by an act of perfidy as strange and unnatural as almost any transaction recorded in the annals of history, for the purpose of gratifying a mean and most detestable ambition, invaded the Electoral dominions under the Imperial promises that he should possess them, in consequence of which the Elector was necessitated to retreat homewards. He was eagerly pursued by the Emperor, and eventually defeated and taken prisoner, on the twenty-fourth of April, 1547, at Muhlberg on the Elbe. The Landgrave of Hesse was induced by the infamous Maurice to throw himself upon the clemency of the Emperor, under an express stipulation for his liberty, which availed nothing when self-

interest and policy dictated another act of imperial treachery. *(n)*

During the progress of this war the University of Wittemberg suffered a temporary dissolution. In the month of November 1546, the
students were dismissed, and Melancthon with
his wife and family retired to Zerbst, in the
principality of Anhalt and the residence of the
princes of Anhalt-Zerbst. He was afterwards
invited to the offices of Theological and Philosophical professor at Jena, whither some of the
princes attempted to collect again the scattered
members of the University; but nothing could
detach his mind from the beloved scene of his
early labours and most endeared associations,
and he returned to Wittemberg. His name was
a sufficient attraction and recalled the greater
part of the fugitives. The lectures recommenced
in October, and he successively directed the
attention of his students to the Epistle of Paul
to the Colossians and to the Proverbs of Solomon. *(o)* The new-made Elector who had so
unworthily usurped his present dignities and
possessions, requested him to repair to Leipsic in

(n) See a full and interesting detail of all these transactions, in ROBERTSON's Hist. of Charles V.   Vol. III. B. 8,
and 9. 8vo, ed.

(o) CHYTRÆI Saxonia, p. 422.

1547, to deliberate upon the constitution of an Academy and the regulation of ecclesiastical affairs, but on many accounts he chose to decline the honour of this invitation. Maurice as a matter of course, fully concurred in the Emperor's proposal at a Diet held at Augsburg, soon after the captivity of John Frederic and the imprisonment of the Landgrave of Hesse, to refer the decision of all religious disputes to the long projected council of Trent. It was also easy for his Imperial Majesty with a formidable army at hand to overawe the majority of the assembly into a similar concurrence. Swords are very powerful arguments, and a man may legislate as he pleases when they are drawn in his defence. The purpose however was not answered. The plague was said to infest the city, the consequence of which was the removal of the Council to Bologna, and which proved in effect its dissolution. Anxious to devise some method to preserve a religious tranquillity, the politic Charles commanded Julius Pflug, bishop of Naumburg, Michael Sidonius and John Agricola, of Eisleben, to draw up a temporary rule of faith and worship for the use of both parties. This was called the INTERIM, because it was professedly appointed only for the period of time which might elapse previous to the assembling of a general council. It contained all the essential doctrines of the church of Rome, though veiled under artful and ambiguous modes of expression. *(p)* It was promulgated at Augsburg with the greatest solemnity, and afterwards enforced by the Imperial sword.

The deplorable consequences resulting from this attempt of Charles to legislate for the faith of those whose consciences were proof against the attacks of imperial power, and who resolved like some of the earliest heroes in the same field to obey God rather than men, are thus represented by Melancthon : " Upwards of four hundred pastors in Suevia and the circles of the Rhine are driven from their stations. There is but a single officiating minister at this moment at Tubingen who conforms to the book published at Augsburg ; it has had the effect of driving away all the preachers and pastors. It is truly astonishing therefore that Agricola should

(p) Among a variety of other articles, the Interim affirms " that works of supererogation are to be commanded ; that the church hath the power of interpreting Scripture; that the Pope is head of the church by virtue of the prerogative granted to Peter ; that by confirmation and chrism the Holy Ghost is received ; that extreme unction is to be administered ; that the Sacrament is a sacrifice, and that in it we are to celebrate the memory of saints that they may intercede with God the Father with us and help us by their merits ; that we must pray to God for the dead ; that in every town and every church two masses a day at least be said, but in country parishes and villages one, especially on holidays ; that on Easter Eve and Whitsunday Eve the water in the font be consecrated." SLEID. Hist.

persist in promising in consequence of this publication another golden age, when it evidently
ruins such a multitude of churches, and so many
pious and learned men with their families are
gone into voluntary exile." (q)

Agricola was liberally rewarded by the Emperor and by Ferdinand ; and Sidonius obtained
the bishopric of Mersburg in Saxony. This
furnished occasion for a common joke being
passed upon them, " that they only defended
the Popish Chrism and Oil as being necessary
to Salvation, that they might come off the better greased themselves." (r)

The new and perfidious Elector, notwithstanding his obligations to his equally perfidious
patron, hesitated in dubious neutrality respecting the adoption of the Interim until the year
1548, when he assembled the Saxon nobility and
clergy at Leipsic to assist him in forming a proper
determination. Melancthon attended no fewer
than SEVEN conferences upon this subject, and
wrote all the pieces that were presented as well
as the censure which was passed distinctly upon
the different divisions of that imperial creed. (s)

This was a very critical period in his life.
It will be necessary to examine it with attention,
and to dwell upon it with some minuteness of

.(q) PEZEL. Consil. Theol. p. 87.
(r) SLEIDAN.   (s) ADAM. Vit. Germ. Theol.

detail, in order to afford the reader ample materials for the due appreciation of his character. Not only was Melancthon perpetually exposed to the vilest calumny, but all his conduct and words were misrepresented to the Emperor and plots were laid against his life. The fury of party was raging to cut him off at a stroke, but he was preserved amidst the danger and survived the tempest. The Emperor even sent to summon him into his immediate presence, but Maurice himself became his advocate and protector. (t)

The divines of Wittemberg and Leipsic assembled upon the subject of the Interim successively at Begy, Zell and Juterbock, whither Agricola was sent by the Elector of Brandenburg to meet them. The result of these deliberations was the publication of a book written by Melancthon, and of a decree founded upon it respecting the observance of things of an indifferent nature. The Emperor being anxious to enforce his own creed, and Maurice though a Protestant, not to displease him to whom he had been so highly indebted, consulted the Protestant leaders especially Melancthon, respecting the extent to which concessions might be made with a safe conscience, in order to avoid the extremes of servility and violent opposition. In reviewing

(t) CAM. Vit. Mel.   ADAM. Vit. Germ. Theologorum.

the Interim it was thought this conciliating medium might be discovered in the omission of some practices and opinions while the essentials of Christianity were retained. The volume referred to, contained a particular statement of such articles.

As this publication and the *Adiaphoristic Controversy (u)* resulting from it became a fruitful sourse of the most envenomed disputes, in which Melancthon was represented as having abandoned the truth through excessive timidity or servile compliance, and as ecclesiastical writers have by their statements perpetuated this unfavourable impression to the present hour, it is incumbent on a faithful biographer either candidly to avow the fatal blemish, or by an impartial examination of authentic documents to remove these false impressions, if the aspersed character be indeed capable of vindication. The reader will admit that the first and most direct means of ascertaining the fact, is an appeal to Melancthon's own reply to the Interim, which shall be done by extracting its statements on those topics in particular which occasioned the remomstrances and clamours of his most violent adversaries.

(u) From the Greek word ἀδιαφορος, which signifies *indifferent*. Hence Melancthon and his followers were called *Adiaphorists*.

" If we deny and persecute acknowledged truth we blaspheme God, an unpardonable sin, from which we pray that he would graciously defend us. And although threatened with war and destruction, we must still adhere to the word of God and not deny acknowledged truth. As to the *danger* incurred by the defence of what is preached in our churches and we know to be truth, *we will entrust the affair to God.*

" As the articles in the Interim are various, some right and some wrong, some in which all pious persons concur and some otherwise, *we will plainly avow our convictions, not rejecting what is true out of caprice or violence, nor allowing what is obviously erroneous.*

" The first three articles respecting the Creation and fall of man, original sin and the redemption of the world through Jesus Christ we fully admit; but to the fourth on justification we object: because it states that a man is justified or made righteous by the exercise of love as a work, a sentiment which is afterwards repeated, for a man is righteous before God and pleases him for the sake of Christ and through faith in his name. And though the Emperor's publication states in some places that a man becomes righteous through faith; the meaning evidently is, that faith is a preparation of the heart beforehand, and that afterwards a man is rendered righteous by the work of love. It asserts also

the obnoxious principle that there may be true
faith although a man live with an evil conscience and have no love, and that love constitutes
a meritorious title to eternal life.   So that according to these representations a man is justified and pleases God by his own works, a doctrine long ago taught by monks and friars.   The
truth is, although we must possess love and a
good conscience, yet we are justified before God
or please him through our Saviour and Redeemer
Jesus Christ, FOR HIS SAKE ALONE and through
faith in him, but by no means on account of our
own merit or virtue.

   " At the same time we diligently teach the
necessity of deep repentance, sincere love and a
good conscience, because ' he that loveth not
abideth in death.'   But we must cleave to Jesus
the Mediator and seek the communication of
every grace through him, for ' in thy sight,' to
adopt the language of the Psalmist, ' can no man
living be justified ;' and again, ' for thy *name's
sake* O Lord pardon mine iniquities.'   When in
our necessities we supplicate the Throne of
Grace, it becomes us to be humbled under a
sense of our misery and our guilt, and to implore
consolation through him who is our Great Peace-
maker.   ' Being justified by faith we have peace
with God through our Lord Jesus Christ.'

   " To prove that this is the original and
immutable principle in the church of God in all

ages St. Paul refers to the example of Abraham,
declaring that ' Abraham believed God and it
was counted unto him for righteousness;' that is,
although Abraham was distinguished for his
great and eminent virtues, yet his righteousness
before God whom he pleased, consisted in his
faith in the promises which were graciously
vouchsafed to him.

" There are many points relative to the
order and power of the bishops which we cannot
but oppose—but as these remarks are general
and the language is often ambiguous, we advise
our most gracious prince not to animadvert much
upon this article. The church is a congregation
or assembly of persons who possess real faith in
Christ, and no man ought to separate himself from
the *true* church: but the question is who compose it ?—Separation from the church is charged
upon us as a crime of the greatest magnitude;
but if the adversaries of truth continue obstinate and thus occasion discord and debate, surely
they are guilty before God and not the poor
and pious souls who receive or preach it.
' If,' says Paul, ' an angel from heaven preach
any other gospel let him be accursed,'—but there
exist at the present moment many grievous errors
and abuses under the authority of the Roman
Pontiff, which even the book of the Interim itself
has denounced, but which the councils of Trent

and Bonony have advocated. If the bishops would induce us to obey them it must be upon this condition, that they do not persecute the truth nor re-establish impious ceremonies. God has graciously explained his mind and will in his Scriptures: THESE WE MUST HEAR AND RECEIVE and not as in worldly kingdoms be made to submit to the expositions of some one man who is empowered to give them at his own pleasure.

" Our churches practise those ceremonies which conduce to good order, and if any person imagine there is any thing in such indifferent things which with the good advice of those who regulate the church appears calculated to promote uniformity or order we will readily assist, for on this subject we will not contend. We are indifferent whether men eat flesh or fish. As to prayers and hymns addressed to departed saints, I have before said they are inadmissible ; the same may be said of processions of the Sacrament. It is also well known to our adversaries that private masses, invocation of saints and the procession with other practices, if they might admit of some excuse or extenuation, are however both needless and dangerous, and the re-establishment of them in our churches will strengthen the monstrous errors and abuses of our adversaries ; and they know also that that offence will deeply grieve many pious men and occa-

sion much persecution, proscription, imprisonment and perhaps the murder of priests and
others.

" Let the potentates and rulers consider
amidst the alarms of war now prevalent, what
they will and what they ought to do in this
affair for the defence of the church. As FOR
MYSELF, I AM READY BY THE GRACE OF GOD
TO DEPART HENCE, AND IF NEED BE, TO
SUFFER.

" We have been lately written to and admonished not to preach, teach or write against this
Interim, but necessity compels us to say thus
much with all humility of mind, that we will
not alter in what we have hitherto taught in our
churches; for NO CREATURE POSSESSES POWER
OR AUTHORITY TO CHANGE THE WORD OF
GOD, and it is at every one's peril to deny or
forsake the known truth. As therefore this Interim is opposed in many of its articles to the
truth we have advocated, we feel it necessary to
publish in a Christian spirit an explicit answer ;
*the danger incurred by this measure we cheerfully
face, committing all to the eternal God the Father
of our Lord Jesus Christ.* And as of his infinite
goodness he has gathered to himself a church in
these realms, by means which surpass the wisdom
and thoughts of all men, we earnestly pray that
he will always uphold, preserve and place it
under a good and righteous superintendency."

This performance was translated into English as soon as it issued from the German press by one *John Rogers,* and as it is a curious piece of antiquity we insert the translator's preface entire. It is not only amusing, but elucidatory of the present subject.

" To the Reader, *(v)*

" Because I with great griefe have nowe often heard (most dere Reader) that the highly learned and no lesse godly, jentle and loving man Phillip Melancthon is highlye belyed, in that a great sorte openlye saye that he hath denyed the trueth or (that I maye use their owne wordes) recanted ; (whiche thyng they saye onelye to hyndre the furtheraunce of God's trueth), I coulde do no lesse but turne into our Englyshe speache and also put out this litle treatise of his : not so muche for the defence of his moste named and knowen fames sake, (which he hath yet hitherto kepte undefiled, so that even the greatest enemyes of the gospell neither coulde nor have saied other-

(v) The original edition of this book is in the BRITISH MUSEUM. It is entitled, " *A waying and considering of the* INTERIM, *by the honour-worthy and highly learned Philip Melancthon---translated into Englyshe by John Rogers,* 1548.'' This worthy advocate of Melancthon is considered by Mr. Lewis, in his History of the Translations of the Bible into English, as probably the translator as well as publisher of that edition of the Bible which was issued under the name of Thomas Matthews in 1537 with the King's licence. Rogers was afterwards burnt for printing that Bible in the reign of Queen Mary.

wise of hym) as for the confortyng of many godly
and Christen hertes, whiche have bene not alytell
dismayed and discouraged thorow suche lyes.
And verely not without a cause, for his denying
would do more harme to the trueth in these last
and most perelouse tymes than any tongue or
penne can expresse. And God of his goodnesse,
bountefull mercye and great power, graunt that
that never chaunce. At this tyme also thankes
be to God therfore, he hath not onely not denyed
the trueth but also after his olde accustomed
Christen manier, plainelye confessed and acknowledged it: whiche thyng this his answere
to the Interim, ynough witnesseth.

" And although this his writing be shorte
and answere not to al the poyntes of the Interim, (for that would aske great labour and long
tyme) yet it playnely answereth to the greetest
misuses, and to the very senowes of the Rome-
bushops moste tyrannouse kyngdome contayned
in that boke.

" He also sheweth tokens ynoughe in the
booke that he will at leasure and largelier write
upon manye poyntes thereof. I received also a
letter with this treatise from a nother godly and
learned man, wherein is writen that other and
divers learned men in Dutchlande be in hand to
shewe their meaning in writing as touchyng the
same, so that we may be of muche better com-
forte then our Papistes would gladly se, yea then

manye of the good and faithfull be, that that
Interim will be wstanded and not so sone and
easely receaved as the Papistes hope and many
Christen feare.   This I saie chiefelye caused me
to putte out this litle boke at this time.

   " But for that there be haply many that
know not what that Interim meaneth, for some
have not seen and some have not harde of it, ye
and the moste understande not the worde, as
they that understand no Latine, or not very well,
neede dryveth me to shewe bothe what it is and
also the meanyng of the worde.   Interim is a
booke whiche was at the Emperowres Maiesties
commandement prynted and put forth about the
begynnyng of June, in this yere of our Saviours
birthe 1548, wherein is commanded that al the
cities in Dutchlande that have received the
worde of God, and made a chaunge of cere-
monys accordyng to the word shal reforme their
churches agayne, and turne to the olde Popishe
ordinaunces as a dog dothe to that he hathe
spued out, or a washen swyne to the myre.

   " Thus have ye harde what it is.   Now
heare what the word signifyeth or betokeneth.

   " Interim is as muche to saye, as in the
meane season or in the meane while.   And therfore have they christened the childe and geven
him this name because they wyll that we kepe all
the thynges commanded and contayned in that
booke, in the meane while from this highedutche

parlament holden at Augsburg till there be a generall councell holden.   There they thynke (but
God sitteth above in heaven and thynketh haply
otherwyse) to make that matter worsse.   For
because it had been an hastye worcke to have
chaunged all thynges at once, they of their great
(I had almost sayed) grevouse and mercilesse
mercy have borne with us in two thynges, that
is to saye, in the Maryage of Priestes and receiving of the communion in both the kindes.   But
how long forsoth ?—*Interim*, that is in the meane
while till the generall councell come.   And
thynke then to beare no longer with us, no nor
with Christe himselfe, for then they thynke to
be so strong, that neyther Christe himselfe nor
all that wyll abyde by hym shall be able to with-
stande them.   This is the meanyng of the worde
in Englyshe.

   " Unto this Interim and meaning thereof
hathe thabove named Phil. Melancthon answered and written this present treatise, and
sheweth to what thinges a Christen man maye
agre and which thynges may be chaunged and
whiche not ; in whiche treatise the reader shal
well perceave that he nether hath denied the
trueth that he hath thus longe taught and acknowledged, nor yet thinketh to do : whiche
vertu and high gyfte of God, the Almighti Father
of our Lord Jesus Christ increase in him and all
the Christen to the honour and glory of his holy

name, increase of his knowledge and saving of many soules.—Amen. *At London, in Edward Whitchurch House, by John Rogers,* 1. *Augusti,* 1548."

The affair of the Interim occupied the attention of several conventions in the year 1549, and Melancthon devoted a considerable share of his time, not only in these attendances, but in writing letters of advice respecting indifferent things to the pastors of the different churches in Hamburg, Frankfort, Mansfield, and the various districts of Upper and Lower Saxony. These interesting documents uniformly breathe the same pious and pacific spirit, mingled with their author's characteristic prudence. To the former of these churches he very distinctly states his sentiments respecting what are denominated indifferent things. " We do not call magical consecrations, worshipping of images, the procession of the host and other similar services openly condemned both in our discourses and writings, nor other absurdities, as nocturnal visits to the tombs of saints, *indifferent things:* but they are shockingly multiplied either for the purpose of provoking us, or with a crafty design to impose heavier burdens upon the pastors, and they do us an injury while they humour their own passions. There are many things appointed by the most ancient of churches, and conducive to the beauty of orderly worship and the instruction of the lower classes, as the order of festivals and of lessons, public assemblings, examination and absolution previous to the reception of the sacrament, certain rites in public penitence, examination in confirming, public ordination to the ministry of the gospel, public betrothing to marriage, the form of prayers used in nuptial ceremonies, and funeral orations over the dead." *(w)*

One of the first and most virulent of all the opponents of Melancthon at this period was Matthias Flacius, or Flaccus Illyricus. He was a native of Albona in Istria, and in the year 1541 he went to Wittemberg, where he became a disciple of Luther and Melancthon, and afterwards taught Greek and Hebrew for a subsistence. He was treated with the utmost kindness and liberality by Melancthon, and in 1544, through his and Luther's influence, he obtained a public employment in the University. During the period of dispersion which the scholars suffered in consequence of the war, he resided at Brunswick, and delivered lectures which acquired him considerable reputation, but afterwards returned to Wittemberg in 1547. When the controver-

---

(w) MELANCTH. Ep. Lib. I. 79. Comp. ep. 80, 81, 82. ad Past. Eccles. *in Marchiâ, in Comitatu Mansfeldensi, in urb. Francof. ad ripas Meni.*

sies arose respecting the Interim, he retired to Magdeburg, which was at that time put under the ban of the Empire. He is represented as a man of excellent talents, great wit and extensive learning, but turbulent, furious, and of a most contentious disposition. *(x)*

Flacius at first ventured only upon the private circulation of some sarcastic misrepresentations of the meetings of the divines of Wittemburg; but afterwards he openly slandered them, although he had no certain information of the subjects of their conferences. Melancthon was blamably negligent of his private papers, and would often confess it to his friends, particularly Camerarius, who remonstrated with him upon the subject. Flacius by this means surreptitiously obtained possession of copies of several of his letters and other writings, and considering himself sufficiently armed for a more public attack, he first united himself with some of Melancthon's bitterest enemies, Gallus, Amsdorff, Wigand, Judex, Faber and others: then published at Magdeburg a variety of slanders against him and all his party, advising every one to avoid them as the very pests of the church. He had the audacity to proclaim him-

(x) BAYLE Dict. Hist.   CAM. Vit. Mel.   ADAM. Vit. Germ. Theologorum.

self as " the only true prophet, teacher and defender of the religious interests of the Christian
community, and admonished every one to observe
the evil consequences resulting from their secret
assemblies and conferences—that now there was
an end to all pure religion—that gospel liberty
was betrayed—that they were returned to the
once rejected yoke of Papal domination—and
that the poor flock of Christ were recommended
again to the mitred bishops." To prove these
charges he published a copy of the decree of
Leipsic, and other minor writings which had
been proposed to the states, and compared these
with the book of the Interim. He distorted
every sentence, and by artful misrepresentations
endeavoured to persuade every one that the
different articles of the decree contained the most
deadly poison. In addition to this he declared,
" that the forms of the church ought to be constantly maintained inviolate, without allowing
the smallest alteration according to the appointments of the Interim, and that if the Emperor or
the Papists should molest any one, it would be
proper to resort to arms for defence."

After some time Melancthon, having patiently borne every reproach, wrote a reply to
these statements, which merits insertion, not
only on account of the excellent spirit which
pervades it, but because it effectually refutes
the misrepresentations of Mosheim and his learn-

ed commentator. It is dignified, pious, and solid.

" As it ought to be every one's principal concern to know and worship God aright, and as he has revealed himself in his church, inviting all to hear his voice and to fly to the standard of our Lord Jesus Christ, who is represented by Isaiah as " set up for a standard to the people," *(y)*—it is of the utmost importance amidst this general confusion of mankind, wisely to consider and to inquire what constitutes the true church, and where it is to be found ; that wherever we are we may form a part of it by adopting the principles of the true faith, and connecting ourselves with the people of God. This church is dispersed throughout the world, but is distinguishable from the impious part of mankind by infallible signs ; for such as maintain the truth of the gospel, and the proper use of the sacraments, to the rejection of idolatrous services, constitute, *wherever situated*, the true church of God, and may be satisfactorily distinguished from others by their reception of THE SCRIPTURES.

" Amidst the wreck of empires and the dispersion of their subjects, good men possess this consolation, that wherever they hear the incorruptible word of truth, and witness the legitimate use of sacraments, the rejection of idolatry, and

(y) Is. xlix. 22.

of those errors which oppose the commands of Jesus Christ, there they feel confident of having discovered the true church, there is the family of God, there he is present by the ministry of the gospel, there the supplications of faith are heard, there the genuine worship of God is conducted, and there the Son of God gathers an eternal inheritance. ' Where two or three,' said he, ' are gathered together in my name, there am I in the midst of them.' (z)

" In periods of public dissension we have need of these consoling sentiments, and I have introduced them here, because our churches, which know the importance of these considerations, are at this moment exceedingly disturbed by numerous clamours. The same doctrine is taught in them as is proclaimed in our writings: the Sacraments continue unaltered: errors in faith and images in worship, as our books sufficiently testify, are discarded.

" But Flacius Illyricus exclaims that our doctrine is changed, and that we have restored certain ceremonies which had been abolished. Let us examine these charges; and *first*, concerning *Doctrine*. The instructions of all the public teachers in our churches and seminaries at once refute this claumny, and to avoid any prolix statement let me refer to what I have

(z) MAT. xviii. 20.

2 K

written in the volume entitled, ' Loci Communes Theologici,' which is in many hands, and
in which I did not aim to establish a new faith,
but accurately to represent that which was common to all our churches, as exhibited in the
Confession of Augsburg, presented in 1530 to
the Emperor, which I consider the invariable
sentiments of the true universal church of
Christ; a statement I wish to be understood as
having written without sophism, and without
any calumnious intention.   I am conscious of
having compiled that epitome of doctrine, not
for the purpose of seeking to differ from others,
not from the mere love of novelty, not from a
desire of controversy, nor from any other base
or unworthy motive: but circumstances required it.   When in the first inspection of the
churches we had to encounter a variety of reproaches from ignorant persons, I published in a
compressed form a summary of Doctrine which
Luther had delivered in volumes of discourses
and expositions, and studied a mode of expression which might conduce to accuracy of views in
those who were taught, and to general unanimity; always submitting what was written to
the judgment of our churches, and of Luther
himself, whose opinions on many points I particularly inquired, and copies of whose writings
are in the possession of many.   I now call God
to witness my profession of this doctrine, which,

as I have already stated, I am satisfied perfectly coincides with that of the universal church of our Lord Jesus Christ, and by his assistance I resolve to bring this confession into general use in the church. This I mention lest any one should reproach me for hindering the faith of others by my own doubts.

" In the next place it is requisite to offer a few words of reply to the charge respecting *Ceremonies.* I certainly could have wished, especially in the present afflictive circumstances, that the churches should not have been disturbed by any change, but if such be the case it does not originate with me. But I confess that I have persuaded the people of Franconia and others not to abandon their churches on account of any service with which they could comply without impiety. For although Flacius cries out vehe_ mently that the churches had better be deserted, and the Princes alarmed by the fear of sedition, I should not choose to be the author of such wretched advice. It is plain that we must endure much greater burdens in the cause of literature and religion than mere dress—as the hatred of the great, the insolent contempt of the populace, the malevolence of hypocritical friends, the dissensions of the priesthood, poverty, persecution, and other evils which accompany even a quiet government: but these turbulent times produce many greater miseries.

" But as we must not desert our posts on this account, we may sustain lighter servitude if it can be done with a good conscience. The distressing situation of the present times, in which there are such divisions in sentiment and affection, seem to me to require that these oppressed churches should be comforted and strengthened by all the aids that piety can afford, and that we should take care that the most important doctrines should be faithfully explained and transmitted to posterity, and that the Universities be supported as the depositories of general literature.

" The representation of Flacius respecting somebody (who I know not) having reported, that I have declared we ought not to withdraw from the churches although the ancient abuses should be re-instated, is absolutely false.

" Now mark this crafty man; in order to excite suspicion and inflame hatred, he produces many sentences dropped in familiar discourse, which he calumniously misinterprets, and also attributes sayings to others of his own invention, that he might appear not only to have witnesses, but agents at his command. Nor have I ever thought or said what he falsely imputes to me, that we ought to remain in those churches in which old errors are restored, mass services, invocation of saints, and other impious services which we have condemned in our publications.

I do openly declare that such idolatrous rites should neither be practised nor endured: and that students may be the better instructed in every particular, I have explained the occasions and origin of controversy with great care and labour.

" Here if I were inclined to indulge my grief I might justly complain of Flacius, who circulates such falsehoods to my detriment, and might detail the origin of those distresses which overwhelm the whole church, explaining those circumstances which tend to strengthen the boldness and confirm the power of our adversaries against the truth. But I am unwilling to open these wounds, and I beseech these advocates of liberty to allow me and others at least to endure our afflictions in peace, and not excite more cruel dissensions.

" He boasts that he will be the advocate of the pristine state of things. If by this expression he refers to particular empires and governments, and confines the church only to its own walls, his idea is very incorrect ; for the church is scattered abroad in various kingdoms, publishing the incorruptible word of the gospel, and serving God by the tears and groans of genuine worship. But as he states he was once so familiarly acquainted with me, he could testify my pains and sorrows and zealous care. We lament the disturbed state of public affairs and of kingdoms, nor do we ask for garrisons and ramparts of defence, but in our churches we publish the gospel of truth, serving God in the knowledge and faith of his Son, and aiming to the best of our feeble efforts to promote the literary pursuits of our youth and the preservation of discipline.   If this advocate of the primitive state of things can restore this golden age to our churches, let him triumph as much as he will.

"Why he should particularly attack me who have never offended him as Marius did Antonius, I know not, for he is aware that I have been always opposed to the corruptions of religion and have censured the prevailing errors.   Now he says I have encouraged them, because it has been my advice not to quit the churches on account of a surplice or any thing of that kind. If dissension arises on these subjects, the commandments respecting charity should not be forgotten, especially as he knows our great afflictions, and that we neither seek dominion nor wealth.   We should not imitate the example of worldly disputants whose impetuosity is often such as to exemplify the proverb, ' One serpent eats another lest it should become a dragon.'   He now not only threatens to write against me, but to do something worse.   I could wish that we rather co-operated to illustrate essential truth, for there are sourses enow of contention ; so that we should renounce our hostility and

labour, a mode of proceeding more conducive to
our personal advantage and that of the whole
church : lest it should happen as Paul says,
' take heed that ye do not devour one another.'
I shall frame my answers with a view to utility,
and hope, that both by my writings and by the
opinion of the pious I am sufficiently defended
against calumny. Many good and learned men
in different places are greatly grieved that the
churches are so unjustly censured. But I recommend Flacius and others to consider, what
will be the consequence if mutual animosities
revive the quarrels of thirty years. How deplorable would this be !

" Whenever he reports his idle stories and
things professedly spoken in familiar conversa-
tions, he shews what kind of regard he has for
the confidence of friendship and the rights of
social intercourse. We naturally unbosom ourselves with more freedom amongst our friends, and
often I have myself in maintaining a discussion
strongly opposed an opinion which I really embraced, not in joke, but for the purpose of obtaining information from the views of others.

" Many are acquainted with my natural
turn of mind, and that I am prone rather to indulge in jocoseness even in the midst of afflictions than to any thing like sternness. To catch
and circulate my words on these occasions as he
has done is mean and unkind, to say no worse.

But if, as in some parts of his letter he threatens me with the sword, any evil should occur, and destruction should befall this miserable head, I will commend myself to Jesus Christ the Son of God, our Lord, who was crucified for us and raised again, who is the searcher of hearts and knows that I have inquired after truth with a careful simplicity of mind, not wishing either to gain factions and influence, or to indulge an unbridled curiosity. Nor has it been without great and diligent attention to the whole of Christian antiquity, that I have endeavoured to unravel a variety of intricate questions and to direct the studies of youth to important learning.

" But I will not speak of myself. In all civil dissensions I am aware that calamities are to be expected, the minds of men become inflamed, and I perceive Flacius prepared with his firebrands ; but to God I commit my life and his own true church here and in other places, respecting which I feel far more solicitous than of my own life. This however is my consolation, that God has promised his perpetual presence in the church, and his Son declares, ' Lo! I am with you always even to the end of the world.' He will preserve the people that maintain the doctrines of the gospel and that truly call upon his name ; and I pray with the utmost fervour and importunity of soul that he would preserve his church in these regions.

" This brief reply to the clamours of Flacius, I have written, not so much on my own account as for the sake of our churches in general, among whom many pious minds are deeply wounded by his writings. Let them be consoled by this assurance, that fundamental principles are faithfully retained in our churches, namely, the incorruptible ministry of the gospel, all the articles of faith and the use of Christian Sacraments without alteration. The Son of God it is most certain is present with such a ministry, and as I have already said, hears the supplications of such an assembly. Adieu, candid reader. *October*, 1549."

It will be proper to subjoin to this defence the emphatic language he uses in an epistle to his friend Matthesius—" I trust you will not be influenced by the sycophantic writings of Flacius Illyricus, who invents absolute falsehoods. I have never *said*, I have never *written*, I have never *thought* what he declares I *have* said, respecting the phrase ' *we are justified by faith only*;' namely, that it is absurd and a kind of subtle trifling about words—I have indeed spoken and written many things respecting the manner in which the exclusive term is to be understood as well as many others ; and have been at great pains to correct the misinterpretations of many put upon the word *only* ; but I

purpose replying to these virulent criminations." *(a)*

If, in corresponding with his friends Melancthon spoke of Flacius in very decided terms
as a calumniator, we cannot feel much surprized ; but that the flagrant misrepresentations of this adversary, should have so deeply tinctured as it has done, the accounts of
distinguished historians, is truly deplorable.
Even Mosheim and his learned commentator
have obviously leaned to the unfavourable side
of the subject, and rather perpetuated dishonourable impressions than carefully guarded his
fame.   The language of this great Reformer
which has been copiously quoted in the present
work, is in itself sufficient to evince the nature
of those principles by which he was actuated,
and the extreme absurdity of charging him with
tergiversation.

The Adiaphoristic Controversy occasioned
many other disputes, but we shall neither perplex our readers nor mispend our time by wan-
dering into the briery wilderness of polemical
divinity.   To some of these debates, however,
it will be proper briefly to allude in relating the
events of the time in which they were particularly agitated.

(a) MELANCTH. Ep. Lib. II. 42. *ad Johan. Matth.*

CHAP. XII.

,,,,,,,,,,

A. D. 1550, TO A. D. 1557.

,,,,,,,,,,

*Articles prepared for the Council of Trent—Melancthon
commences his journey thither—but returns in consequence of Maurice changing his conduct, and declaring war against the Emperor—Peace of Passau
—Plague—Withdrawment of the University of Wittemberg to Torgau—Osiander—Stancarus—Private
afflictions—Meeting at Naumburg respecting the renewal of the ancient Friendship subsisting between the
Houses of Saxony, Brandenburg and Hesse—Transactions relative to Servetus—John Frederic's Release
and Death—Death of Maurice — Controversies —
Persecutions of Flacius and his Adherents—Melancthon's letters on the subject—Death of Jonas.*

In the year 1550, in consequence of the
importunate entreaties of the Emperor, Pope
Julius III. who had succeeded the departed
Paul III. appointed a Council to be held at
Trent; and in the Diet of Augsburg all the
German Princes, overawed by the military atti-
tude and resolute spirit of his Imperial Majesty,

consented to this convention. The Elector
Maurice was the least servile of any in this compliance, insisting upon these conditions, which
however the Archbishop of Mentz refused to
enter into the registers, that doctrinal points
should be re-examined and discussed—that this
examination should be conducted in presence of
the Protestant divines—that they should have
the liberty of *voting* as well as *deliberating*—and
that the Pope should not preside in the proposed
council either in person or by his legates.
Deeming it requisite to be fully prepared for
the great occasion, Maurice commanded Melancthon to draw up an explicit statement of the
principal articles of the Protestant faith, to be
presented if required to the proposed council.
A similar paper was written by Brentius in the
name of the Wurtemburghers. When the former document was ready, the prince assembled
all his Theologians at Leipsic on the eighth of
July 1551, to hear it read and to deliberate upon
its contents. It was unanimously approved
and published under the title of " Repetitus
Confessionis Augustanæ."

In the month of January of the succeeding
year Melancthon began his journey to Trent.
" Yesterday,"says he, writing to George, Prince
of Anhalt, " I received letters from the Court
containing the commands of our illustrious
Elector, to George Major and myself to proceed

to Nuremberg, where we are to wait further orders respecting our journey to the general council, the Duke of Wurtemberg and the city of Strasburg having already sent their deputies. But as no particular instructions are given, I purpose proceeding direct to Dresden whence I will write to your Highness. I sincerely wish the Court would not disregard the advice which is approved by so many, that a general commission be sent by common consent to the council from the principal churches in the neighbouring cities and districts. But I commend our cause to God." They were, however, directed to proceed only as far as Augsburg, till they received further instructions from Prince Maurice for their future guidance. With this design they travelled to Nuremberg, where in consequence of the high esteem in which Melancthon was held, they were received with the most marked distinction. They were lodged in a public building of the city and every attention paid them, which the most affectionate and solicitous benevolence could dictate. " The day after our arrival at Nuremberg," says Melancthon, " which was on the twenty-second of January, I received a packet of letters sent by Doctor Padornus, from the city of Trent, in which it was intimated that the answer to the application, for a (Papal) safe conduct was still delayed. I wrote immediately that we were

come to Nuremberg, and requested to be informed whether and when we were to proceed
to Trent. I have also notified our journey to
our own Court. At present I have received no
reply from either. We have been already delayed ten days at Nuremberg, in total uncer-
tainty respecting our future progress, whether or
when we are to go forward. In the mean time
many in this place distinguish us by the most
officious kindness and attention. Sarcerius
preaches publicly to great concourses of people
and I have delivered several lectures."

During this delay public affairs assumed
such a posture as not only to stop the progress
of Melancthon and his associates, but to place
Germany in a new and interesting situation.
The time was at length arrived when the secret
motives which influenced the new-created
Elector of Saxony to a mysteriousness of conduct which had often perplexed and astonished
the Protestants, were at length fully developed.
From the intimacy to which the Emperor had
admitted him, he soon perceived his design of
becoming the absolute dictator of Germany, and
every act convinced Maurice that he was secretly
rivetting on the chains of servitude, which his
ambition had forged for his degraded country.
He had frequently petitioned for the release of
the Landgrave of Hesse from imprisonment; to
petitions he added remonstrances, but nothing

could induce Charles to fulfil his engagements. Maurice was aware at the same time,
that he was elevated to a commanding ascendancy amongst the Protestant princes, and the
fairest prospects presented themselves for the
gratification of his own eagerness for power and
distinction. With the most consummate address
he succeeded in retaining the fatal confidence of
the Emperor while he deceived him, and in not
losing entirely that of the Protestants, while he
was necessitated in public to pursue a course
which they must have often considered dangerous to their religion, if not subversive of their
liberties. He at length prepared to strike the
blow, by soliciting the protection of Henry II.
King of France, who agreed to declare war
against the Emperor, professedly for the sole
purpose of emancipating the Landgrave of Hesse,
as a Catholic prince could not unite with a Protestant association upon a religious account.
Application was also made to the King of England, but the cabals incident to a Court during
a minority (it was the reign of Edward VI.) prevented that attention to foreign and especially to
religious affairs, which might otherwise have
been expected. A last application for the liberty of the captive Landgrave was made in vain,
Maurice still cajoled the Emperor, affected to
be more than ever anxious to remove the difficulties which had arisen respecting a safe conduct

to the Protestant divines, and as we have seen, even commanded Melancthon to proceed on his journey to the council of Trent. He further intimated his intention of meeting his Imperial Majesty in person at Inspruck. Many rumours were beginning to circulate, but the Emperor and his confidential adviser Granvelle, Bishop of Arras, totally disregarded them ; the sagacious minister and his Imperial Master being both lulled into a fatal security.

At length Maurice took up arms and published a manifesto, in which he represented that the defence of the Protestant religion, the liberties of Germany and the release of the Landgrave of Hesse from unjust imprisonment, were the principal motives of his conduct. The council of Trent was instantly prorogued for two years, but circumstances prevented its actually re-assembling for the space of ten. It is impossible not to perceive in the infatuation of Charles V. and his advisers, and the political manœuvres resulting from the ambitious views and private resentments of the Elector Maurice, that superintending Providence, which, though it permitted a sea of troubles to flow in upon the Protestant cause, and almost to inundate the territories of religious Reformation for a time, appointed the happy moment when the tide should ebb and Germany be free.

Melancthon in this extraordinary crisis willingly returned to Wittemberg, to resume his various duties both of a private and public nature. The city which had so welcomed his arrival, rendered him every honour upon his departure. " It would have been a very proper procedure," says he writing to the Prince of Anhalt " to have sent a general deputation from various churches to the council as your Highness thought from the very first, but our advice on this subject, as your Highness knows, was afterwards disregarded. When therefore none of the princes or cities sent deputies, and no commands were given us except by the Elector of Saxony, I felt I confess, the strongest disinclination to the journey ; and when we could not proceed any further, I returned most willingly under the guidance of Providence to Wittemberg, although I was very much persuaded to remain in the country. Aware, indeed, there were many unwise and evil-minded persons at Trent, I would nevertheless have gone had Germany continued in a state of tranquillity. Now distress forces me to return, or rather I judge it a very unseasonable period to be disputing concerning Pontifical authority in a council amidst the alarms of civil war." (b)

The unprepared state of Charles and the vigorous activity of Maurice, combined with a

(b) MELANCTH. Ep. Lib. II. p. 247.

2 L

variety of more private reasons which influenced the different powers of Germany, to produce the peace concluded in the month of August at Passau ; in which, amongst other articles, it was stipulated that a Diet should be held within six months to deliberate concerning the most effectual method of preventing in future all disputes in religion ; that in the mean time neither the Emperor nor any other prince should upon any pretext whatever offer injury or violence to such as adhered to the Confession of Augsburg, but allow them the free and undisturbed exercise of their religion ; that the formulary of faith called the Interim should be considered null and void ; and that if the proposed Diet should not be able to terminate religious disputes, the present stipulations in behalf of the Protestants shall continue in full force and vigour. *(c)*

Amidst the desolations of war, Germany was destined also to suffer the ravages of the plague, in consequence of which the Universities of Wittemberg and Leipsic were dispersed ; but the former re-assembled under the auspices of Melancthon at Torgau, about twenty-two miles distant. He there engaged in delivering lectures on Justin Martyr, prepared a treatise " de unione personali," which does not appear to have been ever committed to the press, and

(c) RECEUIL DES TRAITES, II. 261.

published a refutation of Osiander in the German language. He used to say that " he was not afraid of the plague which had driven them to Torgau, but he was really apprehensive on account of plagues of another kind, which infested the country and seemed to threaten its utter ruin."

Osiander was another of those virulent adversaries of Melancthon, which the conferences and publications on the subject of the Interim had produced. He was pastor of the church at Nuremberg, but retired on that occasion to a divinity professorship at Konigsberg. His character and his opinions were marked by eccentricity. He zealously propagated sentiments respecting repentance and justification, which differed essentially from the Lutheran doctrines, and which consisted in subtle distinctions it is needless to detail. Suffice it to remark, that Stancarus, professor of Hebrew at Konigsberg undertook to refute his statements, but was hurried by his impetuosity into opposite extremes of doctrine. Osiander maintained that the *man* Christ, as a moral agent was obliged to obey for *himself* the divine law, and therefore could not by the imputation of his obedience obtain *righteousness* or justification for *others*. Hence he inferred that the Saviour of the world was empowered by his nature *as God*, to make expiation for our sins and reconcile us to the offended Deity. But Stancarus totally excluded Christ's *divine* nature from all concern in the *satisfaction* he made and in the *redemption* he procured, affirming that the office of Mediator between God and man belonged to Jesus in his human nature alone. Osiander was patronized by persons of considerable rank and influence, but his opinions did not long survive him. *(d)*

These discussions engaged the attention of the most eminent of the Lutheran divines and moved the powerful pen of Melancthon. In the year 1553, he says in a letter to his friend Camerarius, " I have written on the controversy of Stancarus in a manner by far inferior and more concise than the magnitude of the subject requires, but I was not willing to irritate an angry and choleric man." To Matthesius he writes, " About eight days ago the Elector of Brandenburg sent for Pomeranus and myself to examine into the controversy of Stancarus, who contends that Christ is Mediator only in his human nature. But immediately afterwards, information arrived that the Elector's son was dead and his father ill ; and thus at present our journey and the examination is postponed. Nevertheless I have written my solemn declaration, that Jesus Christ is to be viewed as Mediator, as he is our High

---

(d) SCHLUSSELB. Cat. Hæret. Lib. VI. BAYLE Dict. Art. *Osiander, Stancarus.* MOSH. Eccles. Hist. Vol. IV.

Priest in his united natures, divine and human.
St. Ambrose maintains the same sentiment.
The principal arguments for this truth I purpose
sending at a future time. I beg you to notice
for me any evidences on this subject which you
may discover in reading the ancient fathers."

His reply to Stancarus exhibits a mind in
search of truth, and maintaining that dignified
and unruffled tranquillity which a consciousness
of possessing it ought ever to inspire. He begins
in the most pious and conciliatory manner, de-
precating all animosity in religious parties, and
stating that as great contentions frequently originate in small beginnings, it was his anxious
desire to remove rather than to enflame contention. He appeals most convincingly to every
part of the New Testament, in proof of the im-
possibility of separating the two natures of
Christ in the Mediatorial transactions, because
the Son of God in his entire nature became Mediator, Redeemer, Saviour, King and Priest of
the church. He appeals also to the concurrent
opinion of Chrysostom, Irenæus, Ambrose, Jerome and the fathers generally, upon the same
subjects. (e)

Melancthon was at this period occupied
with the care of the churches and academical
establishments in Misnia. To him as the most

(e) MELANCTH. Op. Tom, I.

competent director in every concern of this
description, applications were usually made;
and the very counsellors of princes were
the first to seek his valuable advice : and his
plans were in this and most other cases generally
adopted. *(f)*

His affectionate spirit was deeply grieved
by the loss of several friends during the course
of the year, and by trials in his family. " Domestic afflictions," says he, *(g)* " are superadded
to others. My servant John, remarkable for
his fidelity and virtue, is called from the present
life to the heavenly church; and now my wife is
so extremely ill that nature seems overpowered
by disease. But I pray the Son of God to grant
us his presence and preserve us with his whole
church, as I have often expressed it in the following verse :—

" Te maneat semper servante Ecclesia Christe
　Insertosque ipsi nos tua dextra tegat ;
Tres velut in flamma testes Babylonide servas
　Rex ubi præsentem te videt esse Deum."

O Saviour may thy church unhurt remain,
　And all within thy kind protection share !
Like Israel's sons amidst Chaldean flame---
　The king confessing that a God was there !---

(f) Cam. Vit. Mel.
(g) Melancth. Ep. Lib. II. 77. *ad Joh. Matthes.*

A conference being appointed in the month of March 1554, at Naumburg, in Thuringia, for the purpose of consolidating a union and renewing the ancient friendship that subsisted between the houses of Saxony, Brandenburg and Hesse; the different Theologians with Melancthon at the head of them were summoned to attend. John Foster, a skilful Hebraist, accompanied him from Wittemberg; Alexander Aless, to whom he was peculiarly attached on account of his excellent spirit, polemical knowledge and accurate discernment, was deputed to join them from the University of Leipsic; Adam Craft, from Hesse, and John Sleidan, celebrated for his history of ecclesiastical affairs, from Strasburg. From this convention he writes to Camerarius, "Like the ancient Argonauts who stuck fast upon a quicksand, so I seem to be fixed amongst the numerous perplexities of this troublesome affair. When we arrived at the Court we were directed to give our opinion upon three things, the inspection of the churches and the preparation of a formulary, as they call it, of instruction—the constitution of councils—and finally concerning the affairs of the Academy in Misnia. Afterwards when no one had prepared a copy of such instructions as were required, I received orders to compose it, which though done upon the spur of the occasion, was read in the assembly the next day and approved. The

pastor commented upon some things respecting
your council; of the new Academy I have given
no advice.   The pastor made some observations
in a very free, ingenuous manner.   The third
day was consumed in contention with the Dean
of Friburg, who attacked in the severest terms
the good old pastor respecting the Adiaphoristic
Controversy.   I have written a reply which is
incorporated in the letters of the prince to the
Duke of Prussia, who is aiming to prevent the
circulation of every book that contains any thing
upon the subject of the *Baltic* Controversy."

The purpose of this meeting was at length
accomplished, in the renewal of that ancient
treaty which subsisted between the two Electors
of Saxony and Brandenburg, and the Landgrave
of Hesse; and the insertion of another article
which the peculiar circumstances of the times
suggested, by which the respective parties
agreed to adhere to the Confession of Augsburg,
and to maintain it in their dominions. *(h)*

Impartiality here demands a statement of
the opinion of Melancthon upon those transactions at Geneva respecting the unhappy SER-
VETUS, which have occasioned so many violent
controversies.   Were we to enter into a deliberate and dispassionate investigation of this
affair, it would probably appear that an eager-

(h) CHYTR. Saxon. 480.

ness to criminate on the one hand, and to defend
on the other, has hurried each party into extremes ; the one, whose opinions have coincided
with those of Servetus, have not been sufficiently
disposed to make allowances for the peculiar
circumstances in which the Reformers were
placed, and for the strength of those conscientious
however erroneous—*deplorably* erroneous principles they blended with many valuable discoveries;—the other party cherishing opposite
religious sentiments, have been too anxious to
extenuate a crime committed against the rights
of conscience which no considerations can excuse; absurdly imagining that Calvin and truth
were identical, and that to defend the reputation
the former was essential to the vindication and
glory of the latter.

The case was this. Michael Servetus, a
Spaniard and a native of Villaneuva, in Arragon,
embraced the reformed religion at an early period of his life, in consequence of searching the
Scriptures ; but departed from the general sentiments of the Reformers on the subject of the
Trinity. His zeal was considerable, and going
into Germany to propagate his opinions, he published a book in 1531, entitled " de Trinitatis
Erroribus," which in the ensuing year was followed by two other treatises. These writings
occasioning great dissatisfaction, he removed
from place to place till he settled in Paris,

where he devoted himself to the study of medicine, but at the same time became involved in
disputes of a theological nature with the phy-
sicians, till at length chagrined at the sup-
pression by act of parliament of a book he
had published, he withdrew to Lyons and was
introduced to the Archbishop of Vienna, in
whose house he long resided. During several
years he corresponded with Calvin the Reformer of Geneva, but the contemptuous manner in which he treated his theological antagonist, produced at length an open rupture and a
mortal antipathy. When Servetus was arrested
and committed to prison at Vienna for his publications, together with his printer, Calvin, at
the desire however of the magistrates of that
city, sent his letters and writings—but he was
condemned for his published errors, and not as
it appears in consequence of any interference of
the Genevan Reformer. But having escaped
from prison he fled to Geneva with the design
of retiring to Naples. Here he was arrested;
and as it cannot with probability be denied at the
instigation of Calvin, who had long before intimated " if that heretic came to Geneva, he
would take care that he should be capitally punished."

When tried for heresy the principal accusations against Servetus were, his having asserted
that the land of Canaan was fertile, though it

was unfruitful and barren—his having corrupted
the Latin Bible which he was employed to correct at Lyons, by introducing trifling and impious notes of his own—and having in the person
of Calvin defamed the doctrine that is preached,
uttering all imaginable injurious and blasphem-
ous words against it.   Before sentence was
passed, the ministers of Basle, Zurich, Bern and
Schaffhausen were consulted, who unanimously determined that he ought to be condemned
to death for blasphemy and heresy.   The following verdict was accordingly pronounced—
" You Michael Servetus are condemned to be
bound and led to Champel, and there fastened
to a stake and burned alive with your book written with your hand and printed, until your
body shall be reduced to ashes and your days
thus finished as an example to others who
might commit the same things ; and we command you our lieutenant to put this our sentence into execution."   Thus he perished in
great agonies on the twenty-seventh of October
1553.

     The reader must naturally feel curious to
know the opinion of the amiable Melancthon on
this odious transaction, and it is with the utmost
pain we produce it, as expressed in a letter to
Bullinger.   " I have read your statement respecting the blasphemy of Servetus, and praise

your piety and judgment, and am persuaded that the Council of Geneva has done right in putting to death this obstinate man, who would never have ceased his blasphemies. I am astonished that any one can be found to disapprove of this proceeding ; but I have transmitted you a few papers which will sufficiently explain our sentiments." On more than one occasion he had refuted his statements by an appeal to Scriptural evidence, *(i)* and had he confined his hostility to the *principle*, and not by his concurrence have punished the *man*, we should have enjoyed the delightful opportunity of presenting to the reader, what the whole course of Melancthon's life and the general character of his mind seemed to render probable, a noble exception to the general spirit of the times. But at that period, Christians of every class and party believed that *gross religious errors were punishable by the civil magistrate*, a popish doctrine which they had not yet renounced, and which, it is to be feared, is not even to this day, and in the most enlightened part of the world, totally exterminated from the breasts of all Protestants. Be it remembered however, that by cherishing such a principle in any degree they betray the best of causes—furnish occasion of

(i) MELANCTH. Ep. Lib. I. 3. Lib. IV. 140, &c.

the most injurious representations of Christianity, and instead of learning of their master, who was " meek and lowly of heart," imitate the misguided disciples who were for calling down fire from heaven. Can any thing be more obvious than this, that it is the birthright of every human being to think for himself, that he is amenable alone to conscience and to God for his religious sentiments, and that whatever person or system attempts to legislate for the freeborn soul, and coerce the faith of another, is perpetrating one of the most detestable of crimes, robbing man of his liberty and God of his authority? In such a case *submission to* MAN is *treason against* HEAVEN. Is it not truly astonishing that while the Reformers in their separation from the church of Rome asserted this noble principle, and were daily contending and even bleeding for it, they should so far forget themselves, even the very best of them, as to act in diametrical opposition to their own claims —to impose and to dissent from the same principle at the same time—to discard human authority in matters of religion in contending against the Roman hierarchy, and to vindicate it in establishing their own church?—So inconsistent is human nature!—But let Protestants aim to purify themselves from this deep stain upon their characters, which can only be removed by eternally disclaiming all dominion over another's faith and conscience!

JOHN FREDERIC survived to the present year the release from " durance vile" which the peace of Passau had given him.   He had however only been permitted to take possession of a part of his territories, and although he had laid claim to his electoral dominions upon the death of Maurice, who was shot in battle in the preceding year, that usurper's brother, Augustus, a Prince of considerable talents and great ur- banity of manners, was chosen by the ungrateful states of Saxony to that elevated station.   The death of John Frederic excited the tears of Me- lancthon, who ceased not to admire the virtues which not only flourished in the beams of pros- perity, but which did not appear in the least degree to wither in the most adverse season of his life.   He possessed an inflexible integrity of character that no changes could possibly alter, and a far distant posterity will venerate his name.

The contentions excited by the intemperate zeal of Osiander and Flacius now raged in every direction, and with such excessive violence at Nuremberg in particular, that the whole city was in a state of commotion.   A most urgent application therefore was made to the Elector Augustus, to permit Melancthon, whose advice

had been often sought, to repair immediately
with his principal associates Aless, Camerarius,
and Pomeranus, to afford every requisite assistance on the spot.   The most disgraceful scenes
were transacted, *(k)* but the presence and judgment of these eminent commissioners after some
time restored tranquillity.   Melancthon drew
up a short but comprehensive statement of
truth, in which he displayed the most exquisite
skill, combined with the most Christian spirit.
He maintained truth and refuted error without
indulging in the least asperity of language against
his adversaries.

This affair however, was not adjusted
till the commencement of another year; but
upon his return home he was infested with
crowds of persons inoculated with the wildfire
of Flacius, who absolutely persecuted him for
several months and years.   Unhappily several
persons of distinction espoused his cause, and
encouraged the ignorant hostility of the vulgar.
They cherished a disputative pertinacity of spirit,
made a man an offender for a word, perpetually
stood in the attitude of defiance, filled all the
shops with the most abusive publications, and
denounced with unmerciful scurrility the ami-

(k) " Exarseruntque passim certamina de illis rebus planè
gladiatoria.   Quæ tanta extiterunt Norimbergæ ut ferri in
civitate pacata diutiùs non possent."   CAM. Vit. Mel. p. 341.

able and most insulted Melancthon. Flacius himself was the prime mover of these proceedings, and exerted a never-ceasing activity in the circulation of calumnious misrepresentations. In a letter to Matthesius, Melancthon very justly characterizes him as " a viper whose venom every wise man would avoid;" but the calumniator himself he addressed in the mildest terms. " Homer, in describing the contest between Ajax and Hector, represents the former as being satisfied when the latter yields and confesses that he is vanquished; but there is no end to your criminations. Who ever acts in this manner? Who strikes a foe when he gives up the contest and throws away his weapons? Claim the victory, I yield, I contend no longer about these rites; I am chiefly solicitous that the churches live in concord and peace. I confess indeed that I have committed sin in this affair, and implore forgiveness of God that I did not wholly fly from these subtle disputations: but I feel myself obliged to refute the mistatements of yourself and Gallus." *(l)*

On another occasion he expresses himself in the following manner; " I am not in despair on account of the cruel clamour of my enemies, who threaten not to leave me a foot of ground to stand upon in Germany; but I commit myself

(l) Pezel. Cons. Theol. Tom. II. pp. 255, 257.

to the Son of God. If I am driven away alone, *I have determined to go into Palestine,* and in those lurking places where Jerome retired, by maintaining intercourse with the Son of God, to write clear statements of divine truth, and in death to recommend my soul to God." Again he says, " I am eagerly and with tranquil‑ lity of mind expecting to be banished, as I have told the princes. My adversaries declare they are resolved to accomplish their purpose, and that I shall not have a footing in Germany. I sincerely wish they would *do it quickly,* as the Son of God said to Judas. If I die, there will be a footing for me in heaven; or if I continue in the body, I shall still be associated with pious and learned men either in Germany or else‑ where. I am astonished at the folly of my enemies, who imagine they possess a ruling in‑ fluence in Germany, and can terrify me with their threats."

On Melancthon in a great measure de‑ volved " the care of all the churches;" but will any one credit the representations of his open enemies, or more injurious friends who have carelessly propagated the notion of his abandon‑ ing the truth, after perusing the following pious and affectionate portion of a letter addressed to the pastors of the churches in the provinces of Bohemia and Lusatia?—or, indeed, will it be believed that if he had been guilty of tergiver‑

sation they would have continued to seek his
advice, to value his sympathies, to confide in
his wisdom, and to allow him to maintain the eminence to which public esteem and personal merit had exalted him? " Whether," he observes,
" divine wisdom has appointed still greater troubles than ever existed before in this feeble and
superannuated age of the world, may be doubtful; but amidst the desolation of Empires, the
Son of God will continue to gather an eternal
church, solely by the preaching of his gospel,
till the period when he will recal the dead to
life. These predictions are given to encourage
us to endure the sufferings allotted us, and to
persevere in the labour of extending the truth
in the world, which will not be in vain. It is
with much grief we have heard that pure doctrine is so despised, that the pastors have been
driven from their churches, and that at this
moment many pious and upright men, with their
wives and dear little children, are in a state of
exile. We sympathize most deeply with them,
with you and with your bereaved churches, and
implore the Son of God, who has said, ' I will
not leave you comfortless,' to alleviate these
sufferings, and to afford you all necessary assistance. You so well know the true sources of religious consolation, that we will not enlarge, but
only admonish you under present circumstances
to set your churches an example of stedfastness

in tribulation, lest they should be tempted to unbelief. Nothing will be more efficacious for this purpose than a thorough knowledge of the truth, and an opposition to mere human opinions. The Papists support the most flagrant idolatry, the invocation of departed saints, and numerous absurdities originating from that monstrous sentiment: they turn the Lord's Supper into a gainful traffic, and contrary to the design of this institution, carry about the bread in public procession to be adored. Disparaging the true doctrine of repentance, they invent a multiplicity of foolish rites, to the absolute torment of pious persons, taking away the consolation to be derived from the knowledge of our Lord Jesus Christ, the Son of God, and zealously contending for numerous observances of their own invention. The people then will surely not suppose our determined opposition to these practices unnecessary. Let the principal points of doctrine be frequently inculcated, with these solemn admonitions; 'Keep yourselves from idols.'—' Though we or an angel from heaven preach any other gospel unto you than that which we have preached unto you, let him be accursed.'—' Whosoever blasphemeth against the Holy Ghost, it shall not be forgiven him.'" This letter is dated *February*, 1555. (*m*)

(*m*) MELANCTH. Ep. Lib. I. 78.

2 M 2

The death of Justus Jonas proved an additional source of affliction at this period. He had been particularly intimate both with Luther and Melancthon, and had co-operated with the latter in several important public transactions. He was a native of North..... Thuringia. He was profoundly skilled both in law and theology. For some years he held a pastoral charge at Wittemberg, and was a Professor and Rector of the University. Afterwards removing to Halle, he became extensively useful in promoting the Reformation. For a considerable time after the death of Luther he continued in the Duke of Saxony's court, and was a sympathizing companion to the sons of John Frederic in their afflictions. At last he was placed over the church in Eisfield, where he expired in peace on the ninth of October, 1555, at the age of sixty-two.

Maximilian king of Bohemia exacted a new tax upon the celebrity of Melancthon, by proposing to him a number of questions respecting the principal subjects that occasioned the controversies of the age; to all of which he felt himself obliged to return a circumstantial reply. This was in the year 1556, and the whole memorial was published at Leipsic, by Nicholas Selneccer, about ten years after the author's decease.

It is impossible for those who are not simi-

larly situated fully to realize the perplexity and
toil which Melancthon and his coadjutors sus
tained at this period. As the head of all the
principal literary and ecclesiastical transactions
of the age, consulted by princes, despatched
upon every urgent occasion on different journies,
summoned to private conferences and public
councils, necessitated to maintain a most extensive correspondence, opposed, and even insulted
by a violent faction, and watched as a heretic by
the partizans of the Roman hierarchy ; it is not
surprising that he should represent himself as
tormented upon the rack of incessant engagement, and absolutely distracted with writing disputations, rules and regulations, prefaces and
letters. *(n)*

(n) " Non poëticæ carnificinæ apud inferos pares sunt
meæ carnificinæ, quâ excrucior scribendis disputationibus,
legibus, præfationibus, epistolis. Nunc respondeo optimo in-
veni τῷ ἔχοντι ὄνομα υἰᾶ Θετᾶ Ιᾶ σκιπίωνος, et volumen mitto.
Heri in Pomeraniam Controversiæ Stetinensis disjudicationem
misimus." *ad Joach. Camerarium,* 844.

CHAP. XIII.

············

A. D. 1557 to A. D. 1560.

···········

Last conference of Melancthon with the Papists at
Worms—Visit to Heidelberg—Receives intelligence of
his wife's death—Her epitaph—The Chronicon and
other writings—Loss of friends—Melancthon's in-
firmities—Interesting paper assigning reasons why it
is desirable to leave the world—A variety of particulars
respecting his LAST ILLNESS AND DEATH—*Epitaph*
by Sabinus—Another by Camerarius—Ode.

THE time was now approaching when Providence determined to remove this distinguished
combatant from the field of holy and honourable
warfare in which he had so long " fought a good
fight ;" to share the honours of an eternal triumph. In the year 1557, he met his Popish
adversaries for the last time in a conference at
Worms. The chief subject of dispute was a
most important one, meriting all the zeal and
firmness with which the Reformers maintained
their principles. It respected *the rule of judg.*

ment in religious concerns. This the Papists strenuously affirmed to be *the universal consent or custom of the church ;* and with no less ardour Melancthon and his coadjutors insisted the only legitimate and authorative rule was THE SACRED SCRIPTURE. Let it never be forgotten by a grateful posterity, that however they might differ in some other points *among themselves,* and however widely present or future generations may differ from *them* in topics, either maintained by some of them individually or perhaps all of them collectively, they are to be applauded and venerated for holding with the most tenacious grasp of mind and asserting with the utmost resolution of spirit in defiance of a persecuting world, this noble principle—this *anchora sacra* of the Reformation, that THE ONLY AUTHORITY TO WHICH HUMAN REASON OUGHT IMPLICITLY TO SUBMIT IN RELIGIOUS CONCERNS IS THE INFALLIBLE WORD OF THE LIVING GOD!

From the conference at Worms during a temporary suspension of the business, the Elector Palatine sent for Melancthon to Heidelberg, for the purpose of adjusting some literary arrangements—the Augustine convent having been converted into an academy. In this affair he was assisted by Micyllus and other eminent scholars. The pleasure he felt in meeting his brother George at Heidelberg, and in the affec-

tionate attentions of his celebrated son-in-law
Caspar Peucer, was painfully interrupted by the
intelligence of his wife's death.   His friend
Joachim Camerarius was charged to convey the
melancholy tidings. Knowing the strength of his
affections, he chose to defer the melancholy duty
till the day after his arrival when they walked
together in the prince's garden, but instead of
manifesting any extraordinary emotion, he spoke
like a man who was weaned in a great degree
from the world, uttering a kind of tender farewell to his beloved Catharine, and adding " that
he expected very soon to follow her."   He
pursued a solemn and pious strain of conversation, expressing his prophetic anticipations of
the future troubles that awaited Saxony.   So
firmly convinced was he of the reality of his apprehensions, and so deeply affected at the dark
prospect of future calamitous years, that his
domestic misfortune seemed utterly absorbed in
the greater importance of public affairs. (o)

The last act of conjugal tenderness which
closed the long union of thirty-seven years, was
the composition of the few following lines to
adorn her tombstone :—

Proximus hic tumulus Catharinæ contegit ossa
    Quæ Crappo quondam consule nata fuit

(o) CAM. Vit. Mel.

Conjugio casto fuerat quæ nupta Philippo
Ex scriptis cujus nomina nota manent.
Virtutes habuit donatas numine Christi
Matronæ Paulus quas docet esse decus.
Hic absente viro sepelivit filia corpus
Vivit, conspectu mens fruiturque Dei.

,,,,,,,,,,,

Deposited beneath this hallow'd earth
Lies CATHARINE's dust, of CRAPPIN's house by *birth ;*
To PHILIP join'd by *wedlock's* sacred name---
Philip---whose writings will prolong their fame.
Virtues which Christ bestow'd, adorn'd her life
And such as Paul affirms become a wife !
While, Philip absent, mourn'd the chast'ning rod—
By filial tenderness beneath this clod
Her BODY's plac'd ;---her SOUL is fled to God !

Melancthon only survived his beloved partner
about two years and six months, a period which
he occupied in an unremitting attention to the
duties of his academical station, and in the composition of useful works. His opponents would
not allow him to retire from controversial writing,
and in 1558 he replied to the accusations of
Staphylus and Avius, two of the zealots of
Rome.

In the same year he issued the first part of
his CHRONICON, which is published complete
in the fifth volume of his works by Peucer. It
consists of more than seventy pages in folio, containing the great events of general history from

the creation of the world to the period of the Reformation.   Like all his other compositions it displays a great extent of reading, a remarkable capacity for judicious selection, and a disposition to use up the rich materials with which his mind was stored, in the erection of a structure, adapted both to gratify and to benefit posterity. The Chronicon was written principally as its author states for the youth in the Universities ; " I wish," says he, modestly, " I possessed more time and capacity to finish up these historical narratives, but I hope that others will be stimulated by this example to execute other more copious and better compositions."

Many writers have erroneously attributed to Melancthon a Greek Version of the Augsburg Confession, transmitted in the course of the following year, under the name of Paul Dolscius, to the patriarch of Constantinople. His own words in a letter to Bordingus sufficiently evince the mistake of this statement, while they authenticate and approve the Version.   " I send you a Greek Version of the Augsburg Confession, which was published without my advice. However I approve the style and have sent it to Constantinople by a man of learning, a dean of that city, who has been our guest during the whole summer.   He relates that there were heretofore many churches in Asia, in Thrace and the neighbouring countries, but they have been

gradually diminished by oppression and bondage."
During the same year he composed his reply
to a Decree of the Abbot of Wirtemberg, and to
some papistical scurrilities of which he griev-
ously complains; *(p)* he wrote also his judgment
upon the controversy respecting the Lord's Supper to Frederic III. Elector Palatine, which was
afterwards published, and also finished some
other minor compositions.

During these transactions his earthly ties
were gradually dissolving. Year after year
robbed him of his dearest friends, thus rendering
the world less desirable, and heaven more attractive. On these occasions he usually expressed
himself in a most pious and elevated strain.
For instance, " Let us congratulate Vitus, now
removed to the delightful society of the heavenly
church ; and be stimulated by his example to be
prepared for the same journey." In addition to
his domestic and other bereavements he lost
Micyllus, Justus Menius and John Bugenhagen Pomeranus. The latter was one of the most
remarkable men of the age, and may be justly
ranked with Luther and Melancthon, with whom
he cherished a long and close friendship and to
whom he was in many respects little inferior.
Originally he was a schoolmaster at Treptow, in
Pomerania, and when he first saw the " Babylo-

(p) MELANCTH. Ep. Tom. II. p. 379. *ad Cracovium.*

nish Captivity" by Luther exclaimed, " the author of this book is the most pestilent heretic
that ever infested the church of Christ;" but
after examining it more seriously and with an
inquisitive mind, it wrought so entire a change
of sentiment, that he said " the whole world is
blind and this man alone sees the truth." When
he was chosen to be minister of the great church
at Wittemberg, he not only did not aim at this
elevation, but was almost dragged by force out
of his obscurity to possess it, and assiduously
devoted himself to the duties of this eminent
station during thirty-six years.   He expired in
peace on the twentieth of April 1558, at the advanced age of seventy-three.

It is some satisfaction to find that such a
man as Philip Melancthon was not destined to
spend the latter years of his life in a state of
inanimate decrepitude and half-conscious being.
The flame of his genius and piety burnt with a
bright and steady lustre to the last ; the noon of
fame seemed to shed its undeparted glories upon
the evening of his earthly existence ! How many
have lived only to be pitied or despised, the wreck
of their former selves, alike incapable of receiving or imparting either pleasure or benefit !
Decays of body and infirmities of mind have
worm-eaten a fabric built of the finest materials,
and once presenting to the gratified observer a
happy combination of elegance and utility.   But

in the present instance every thing excites surprize and veneration. A perfect maturity of the
faculties and a singular capability of exertion are
apparent to the very end of his days. *Pulchro-
rum etiam autumnus pulcher est.* It is impossible
to read some of his last letters without emotion.
They breathe an exalted piety, a spirit of sympathy with the sorrows of others, and a state of
preparation for that mighty change he was soon
to experience. Such is his letter to Everard
Roggius. *(q)*

" Dearest Brother,

" I am a father and not insensible or destitute of natural affection, but deeply sympathize
in the calamities which befal sons and daughters.
I cannot therefore but believe that you are painfully affected with yours ; for the strongest mutual affection is implanted in the human breast
between parents and children. I pray that our
Lord Jesus Christ may assuage your griefs, alleviate your adversities, and preserve both you and
your family. Resort to those divine sources of
knowledge which are bestowed upon us, to administer consolation in trouble. God designs
indeed that his church should suffer the cross,
but he would not have us be overwhelmed with
grief, but rather stimulated by afflictions, to call

(q) MELANCTH. Ep. p. 307, 8, *Lugd. Batav.* 1647.

upon his name, to acquiesce, to rejoice in his
dispensations.   You remember the language of
the Prophet Isaiah, whose words are expres-
sively rendered in the Septuagint Ἐν θλίψει μικρᾷ ἡ
παιδεία σου ἡμῖν. It is said to be a *little* or *short* affliction, because all the joys and sorrows of the
present life are hasting to a termination.   Let us
then contemplate and be constantly perparing
for the everlasting society of the blessed God !
......Farewell, the sixteenth of October, the
day on which one thousand eight hundred and
eighty-one years ago Demosthenes died, whom
one cannot but lament for having consumed
such a vigour of genius in such a useless manner
and as being σκεῦος ὀργῆς *a vessel of wrath.*   Let us
be grateful to God who has called us to nobler
pursuits, and implore his Son so to rule and
guide us that we may be σκεύη ἐλέους *vessels of
mercy.*

" From your brother, now an old man and
          not far from his climacteric year 63,
                " PHILIP MELANCTHON."

The last letter, chiefly because it is the
last he wrote, we have thought proper to translate.   It is addressed to John Aurifaber. *(r)*

(r) MELANCTH. Epist. p. 430. *Ludg. Batav.* 1647.

" Reverend Sir and dearest Brother,

" Although I heard that you were in the principality of Breslau, where I indulge the hope of enjoying some intercourse with those learned and pious men Crato, Adam, Peter Vincentius and Mcreburgius, yet I write these few lines though I am in excruciating pain from an intermitting fever, originating in a catarrh which has troubled me for upwards of three years. You will pardon therefore the brevity of my letter. Feeling myself dying, I have commended your doctrine to the illustrious prince, and have written concerning the genuine and holy union of the principal churches. I commend also this doctrine to you and implore you to receive David Voyt with kindness. I trust he will not disagree with you in opinion. Let me entreat you, if I live, to write me soon. Farewell, I return you my thanks for every kind office, and in particular for your assistance in the case of Sickius and Daucis.

" Philip Melancthon will soon be no more!"

About the same time he wrote down in two columns, on a piece of paper, the reasons why he should not be sorry to leave the world. One of these columns contained the blessings which death would procure; namely, *first*, that you will come to the light—*secondly*, that you will see God—*thirdly*, that you will contemplate the Son of God—*fourthly*, that you

will understand those admirable mysteries
which you could not comprehend in the present
life—*fifthly*, that we shall know why we are
created such as we are—*sixthly*, that we shall
comprehend the union of the two natures in
Jesus Christ. The second column assigned two
reasons why we should not regret departure from
the world—*first*, because you will sin no more
—*secondly*, because you will no longer be exposed to the vexations of controversy, and the
rage of Theologians. The following is an exact
copy. *(s)*

A Sinistris.

Discedes à peccatis
Liberaberis ab ærumnis et à
rabie Theologorum.

A Dextris.

Venies in lucem
Videbis Deum
Intueberis filium Dei
Disces illa mira arcana quæ
  in hâc vitâ intelligere non
  potuisti :
Cur sic simus conditi
Qualis sit copulatio duarum
  naturarum in Christo.

It appears from the testimony of the professors at Wittemberg, in their narrative of his

(s) MEL. ADAM. Vit. Philosophorum.

death, *(t)* that Melancthon frequently intimated his conviction that he should not survive his sixty-third year; and a few months previous to his decease he wrote the following distich in anticipation of the approaching event :

> Sic ego quotidiè de lecto surgo precando
> Ut mens ad mortem sit duce læta Deo.

The last journey he performed was to Leipsic, on the *sixth of April*, for the purpose of attending the annual examination of the Students of Divinity, who were supported by the munificence of the Elector; from which service he returned on the *ninth*. Although the season was inclement, he appeared to feel no inconvenience on his way thither, but while there he was suddenly seized during dinner with the windy cholic and diarrhœa, but the symptoms quickly disappeared. Upon his return he complained of the severity of the north wind, and the cold humidity of the atmosphere, which, he said, he had not felt so much during the whole winter;

(t) The interesting little volume referred to was published in the name of all the professors, and is entitled, " BREVIS NARRATIO exponens quo fine vitam in terris suam clauserit Rev. Vir D. Philippus Melancthon, unà cum præcedentium proximè dierum et totius morbi quo confectus est brevi descriptione, conscripta à PROFESSORIBUS ACADEMIÆ WITTEBERGENSIS, qui omnibus quæ exponuntur interfuerunt. *Express. Wit.* *A.* 1560.

and the motion of the carriage had made him painfully sensible of the calculus which had been forming in his kidneys during several years. The night of the *seventh* of April was the first in which his last fatal disorder manifested itself. He was restless from want of sleep, and became afflicted by a considerable and general debility. His cough was extremely troublesome, and the fever which eventually terminated his days began to attack him.

About six o'clock in the morning his son-in-law, Dr. Peucer came to see him, and immediately intimated the great alarm he felt at the situation of his father. It was determined instantly to send the melancholy information of his danger to the friend of his heart Joachim Camerarius, with whom he had lived in the closest friendship for upwards of forty years.

After this he wrote several letters, and used the medical remedies which his son-in-law applied. Having been some time silent he at length exclaimed, " If such be the will of God, I can willingly die, and I beseech him to grant me a joyful dismission;" alluding to the song of Simeon, " Now lettest thou thy servant depart in peace, for mine eyès have seen thy salvation." He dwelt upon the word *peace*, and prayed for such a removal.

At *nine*, the usual hour for the commencement of his public duties in the Academy, he rose from his seat, and began to prepare for going down to deliver a Lecture on Logic, which exercise he thought he could endure for half an hour, if he afterwards used the bath; and he felt unwilling to desist from his public labours. When he was going to set his foot upon a little stool which he was accustomed to make use of when he washed his hands, his weakness was such that he almost fell by the effort upon his knees, which occasioning some bustle—" Ah," said he, " my lamp is almost out." Some of his friends thought it would be expedient to prevent the attendance of the students by issuing private orders to them not to fill up their places, in order that when Melancthon went to lecture, he might be induced to return, and relinquish the idea of perseyering; but he appeared so anxious that it was believed this proceeding would be likely to produce a worse effect, by agitating his mind, than the exertion itself; he was therefore allowed on this and some following days to attend in his place.

The lecture which he delivered was upon a sentence of Gregory Nazianzen, εις τὸ αγιον παχα λυτρον ἰου καἰεσχονἰος; and upon a passage of Isaiah, κατεχει κατεχομεθα μεν γαρ υπο ἰε πονηρε, &c. but his weakness rendered it impossible for him to occupy more than a quarter of an hour. Upon his return home he went into the warm bath, and after taking his dinner he slept very soundly for three hours, and was so revived that a hope was entertained of his recovery. He employed himself before supper in writing, but his debility afterwards returning, annihilated the pleasing hopes that had been cherished.

He did not yet desist from any of his usual employments, and after this period continued to dictate in the second part of his Chronicon.

On the *tenth* of April he appeared to be totally free from his former disease, but was attacked by a semitertian fever or ague. A quantity of bile being soon expelled from his stomach by the use of medicine, he seemed relieved. Though it was of considerable importance he should be kept quiet, yet such was his ardour that, having discovered that the Senate of the University was convened at the hour of twelve, he could not be dissuaded from attending what he believed to be his public duty. As several disputes arose, he spoke with great zeal on the subject for the purpose of promoting peace and reconciliation.

Although extremely debilitated, yet on the morning of the *eleventh* of the month he rose early, and at six, as usual on festival days, delivered a lecture on the last prayer of the Saviour, recorded in the seventeenth chapter of the Gospel of John. He divided the prayer of Christ into three parts, as embracing so many distinct objects: namely, I. That a Church might exist in the world. II. That it might be distinguished by its unity and concord. III. That his people might be heirs of that salvation and eternal life which belongs to the heavenly church. A few days previous to this he had entreated his hearers to remember after his decease some passage or passages to which he particularly directed their attention in this last prayer; and after repeating the above division, he said impressively, " I am a dying man, and these are the three subjects for intercession with God which I leave to my children and their little ones—that they may form a part of his church and worship him aright—that they may be one in him, and live in harmony with each other—and that they may be fellow-heirs of eternal life !"

On the *twelfth* of April, 1560, he delivered his final lecture on the words of the prophet Isaiah, " Who hath believed our report, and to whom is the arm of the Lord revealed?" *(w)* On the same day he wrote the following lines, which are obviously but the commencement of a hymn which his weakness rendered him incapable of finishing.

Æterno genitore nate Christe
Orator patris ex sinu verendi

(w) Isa. liii. 1.

Vocem Evangelii ferens suavem
Qua credentibus exhibes potenter
Vitam justiciamque sempiternam
Et qui sanguine nos tuo redemptos
Exaudis, reputas facisque justos
Ostendisque piis tuum parentem
Nostras Christe semper doceto mentes
Ac in pectora gratiæ arrabonem
Nostra effundito Spiritum moventem
Casta incendia et invocationem :
Fac pars agminis ut tui per omne
Ævum simus, alacriterque semper
Æterni Patris et tuas sonemus
Laudes——

The worthy Professors of Wittemberg relate with great seriousness, that between nine and ten the same night several persons of credibility affirmed, that they saw some remarkable appearances in the air of rods and scourges; upon which Melancthon, who is known to have been addicted to superstitious apprehensions, and to have been deeply impressed with the expectation of approaching calamities to his country, re-marked, " That they were evidently ominous of impending punishments; but as it was *rods*, such as those with which parents correct their children, and not *swords* they saw, they might ex-pect paternal chastisements, and not those destructive ones which were inflicted upon ene-mies." *(x)*

(x) Brevis Narratio à Professor. Acad. Witteb. p. 16.

During the night he enjoyed a comfortable repose, and was heard to chaunt in his sleep in the manner in which the same words were usually repeated in public, " With desire have I desired to eat this passover with you before I suffer." *(y)* He rose at three in the morning, and applied himself to complete his Chronicon. But from this period he rapidly declined: still anxious however to persevere to the last in the assiduous discharge of his Academical duties, two days afterwards, on the fourteenth of the same month, he would have attempted to deliver another public lecture, had he not been prevented by the urgent persuasions of his friend Camerarius, who came from Leipsic to pay him all the attention which affectionate friendship could dictate.

He even put on his Professor's gown, and would have crept to the lecture-room to have delivered a discourse which he meditated on some portion of the Evangelical history, but after being informed by his son-in-law that the students were not assembled, he desisted from his purpose. The fact was, they were dispersed after having crowded to hear him by a proclamation which his friends, unknown to himself, had affixed to the door, stating his incapacity to attend.

(y) LUKE xxii. 15.

His mind was in a very chearful state, and he often betrayed his characteristic humour. *(z)* He spoke of death with composure, and of his friend Pomeranus, who had died about two years before. He said that he dreaded nothing so much as becoming a useless cumberer of the ground, and prayed that if his life were protracted, he might be serviceable to the youth under his care, and to the church of Jesus Christ.

On the *fifteenth* he conversed much with Camerarius on the language of Paul, which he appropriated; " I have a desire to depart, and to be with Christ." He criticised upon the Greek terms, which, he said, ought to be rendered, " Having a desire to remove, pass on, or set about proceeding in the journey:" that is, to go from this life of toil and wretchedness to the blessed rest of heaven.

When Camerarius thought of taking a final leave of him on the *sixteenth*, he said, " My dear Doctor Joachim, we have been joined in

(z) Afferebatur etiam ei vinum rubrum Renanum quod vulgò à similitudine coloris, quam habet cum pede anserino cognominatur et Dominus Philippus duplicato verbo Græco per jocum χηνόπαδα appellare solebat, hoc tum suavius utebatur et sibi sapere dicebat atque laudabat etiam admodum. Etsi autem hilarem se exhibebat et cum amicis præsentibus colloquia habebat suavia, languor tamen magnus erat vel imbecillitas potius non parva, quæ penè in momenta augescebat. *Brevis Narratio.*

the bond of friendship forty years, a friendship mutually sincere and affectionate. We have been helpers of each other with disinterested kindness in our respective stations and employments as teachers of youth, and I trust our labours have been useful; and though it be the will of God that I die, our friendship shall be perpetuated and cultivated in another world."

Camerarius however determined to remain a little longer with his departing friend, and accordingly disregarded, during this interesting interval, the claims both of his public and private affairs. Melancthon continued to manifest great chearfulness, but if it were at any time disturbed, his distress appeared to arise rather from the sympathy he felt with the suffering church, whenever its trials were reported to him, than from even the acute paroxysms of his disease. His friends had conversed with him on this subject during the evening repast, but he afterwards enjoyed a calm night. In his sleep he said he had dreamt of the words of Paul, which were forcibly impressed upon his mind, and afforded him much consolation, " If God be for us who can be against us?"

Early in the morning of the *seventeenth* Camerarius took his final leave. Melancthon had finished some letters to the Duke of Prussia and to several friends, which he had been preparing during the whole of his illness, and expressed his intention of writing more but for the interdiction of his Physician. When Camerarius bid him farewell—with a last and affectionate benediction, he replied, " Jesus Christ, the Son of God, who sitteth at the right hand of the Father, and giveth gifts to men, preserve you and yours and all of us !"

Soon afterwards, having received information that the Roman Pontiff was meditating a general Council, he said he would rather die than attend it, for it was easy to foresee both the dissensions it would occasion, and the inutility of its meeting. Feeling the pressure of increasing pain and infirmity, he said, " O Lord make an end."

On the *eighteenth* his bed was removed, by his own desire, into the library, which he had continually frequented during his illness, upon which occasion he said with great chearfulness, as he was placed upon it, " This may be called, I think, my *travelling couch*—if (alluding to the criticism before mentioned) I should *remove* in it." While several friends were standing about his bed, he said, " By the blessing of God I have now no particular domestic anxieties, for with respect to my grandchildren, whom I tenderly love and who are now before my eyes, I am comforted to think they are in the hands of pious and beloved parents, who will be solicitous for their welfare, as much as I could ever be : but I feel for the state of public affairs, especially for the church of Christ in this cavilling and wicked age. Through the goodness of God however our doctrine is made public." A little afterwards he addressed some present, " God bestows talents on our youth; do you see that they use them aright." In the course of the same day, seeing one of his grandchildren near him, " Dear child," said he, " I have loved you most affectionately : see that you reverence your parents, and always endeavour to please *them*, and fear *God*, who will never forsake you. I pray you may share his constant regard and benediction." He spoke in similar terms of tenderness and piety to all the younger branches of his family, who were deeply sensible of his approaching departure.

On the same day, after discoursing with his son-in-law upon all his private affairs, and having in vain searched for the will he had formerly written, containing an explanation of some of the principal articles of his faith, which he was desirous of transmitting to posterity, he attempted to compose another, which increasing weakness would not allow him to finish. It began thus: " In the year 1560, on the eighteenth day of April, I write this Will briefly, according to the best of those remaining abilities which God vouchsafes me in my present illness. I have twice before written the confession of my faith, and gratitude to God and our Lord Jesus Christ, but these papers are missing; nevertheless I wish my confession to be considered an answer to whatever relates to the Bavarian articles, in opposition to the errors of the Papists, the Anabaptists, the followers of Flacius and others."

After this he conferred with his son-in-law upon a diversity of subjects relative to the interests of the University, and expressed his wish that Peucer might be his successor in that institution.

Letters having been transmitted to him from Frankfort relative to the persecutions which at this period raged in France, he declared " that his bodily disease was not comparable to the grief of his mind, on account of the miseries which the church of Christ suffered."

The *nineteenth of April* was the last day of his mortal existence. After the usual medical inquiries of the morning, he adverted again to the calamitous state of the church of Christ, but intimated his hope that the genuine doctrine of the gospel would ultimately prevail, exclaiming, " If God be for us who can be against us." After this he presented fervent supplications to heaven, mingled with groanings, for the welfare of the church. In the intervals of sleep he conversed principally upon this subject with several of his visiting friends, amongst whom were the Pastor and other officers of the church, and the Professors of the University.

Soon after eight in the morning, awaking from a tranquil sleep, he distinctly, though with a feeble voice, repeated a form of prayer which he had written for his own daily use, and which was as follows:

" Almighty, omnipotent, ever-living and true God, Creator of heaven and earth and men, together with thy co-eternal Son our Lord Jesus Christ, who was crucified for us and rose again, and thy Holy, true, living and pure Spirit; who art wise, good, faithful, merciful, just, the dispenser of life and of truth, independent, holy—and our Redeemer; who hast said thou willest not the death of a sinner, but rather that he should 'return unto thee and live—and hast promised, ' Call upon me in the day of trouble, and I will hear thee.' I confess myself before thy footstool a most miserable sinner and offender against thee in a great variety of respects, on which account I mourn with my very heart, and implore thy mercy for the sake of Jesus Christ our Lord, who was crucified and rose again, seeking the remission of all my sins and justification before thee by and through thy son Jesus Christ, thy eternal word, and image, wonderful and inexpressible in counsel, infinite in wisdom and goodness; and that thou wouldst sanctify me by

thy true, living, pure, and Holy Spirit.   May I
truly acknowledge and firmly believe in thee,
obey thee, give thanks to thee, fear thee, invoke
thee, serve thee, and through grace be admitted
to thy presence in eternity, the almighty and only
true God, Creator of heaven and earth and men,
the everlasting Father of our Lord Jesus Christ,
and to the presence of Jesus Christ thy Son, thy
eternal word and image, and the Holy, true, living and pure Spirit, the Comforter. In thee have
I hoped, O Lord: let me never be confounded:
in thy righteousness deliver me.   Make me righteous, and bring me unto life eternal: thou hast
redeemed me, O Lord God of truth.   Keep and
overrule our churches, our government, and
this Academy, and bestow upon us a salutary
peace and government.   Rule and protect our
princes.   Cherish thy church, gather and preserve it in these provinces, sanctify and unite thy
people by thy Holy Spirit, that we may be one in
thee, in the true knowledge and worship of thy
Son Jesus Christ, by and through him thy eternal Son, our Lord Jesus Christ, who was crucified for us and raised again.   Amen.

" Almighty and eternal Lord Jesus Christ,
the son of God, who art the eternal word and
Image of the eternal Father, our Mediator and
Intercessor, crucified for us and raised again, I
give thee most hearty thanks that thou didst assume humanity, and art become my Redeemer,

and having suffered and risen again in human nature, dost intercede on my behalf. I beseech thee regard and have mercy on me, for I am poor and defenceless. By thy Holy Spirit increase the light of faith in me, and, weak as I am, sustain, rule, protect and save me. In thee, O Lord, have I hoped, let me never be confounded.

" Almighty and Holy Spirit, the Comforter, pure, living, true—illuminate, govern, sanctify me, and confirm my heart and mind in the faith, and in all genuine consolation; preserve and rule over me, that dwelling in the house of the Lord all the days of my life, to behold the beauty of the Lord, I may be and remain for ever in the temple of God, and praise him with a joyful spirit, and in union with all the heavenly church. Amen."

An interval of tranquil repose having elapsed after repeating this prayer, he lifted up his eyes to heaven, and turning to his son-in-law he said, " I have been in the power of death, but the Lord has graciously delivered me." This was supposed to refer to some deep conflicts of mind, as he repeated the expression to others. When some of the bystanders said, " There is now no condemnation to them that are in Christ Jesus," he soon added, " Christ is made to us wisdom, righteousness, sanctification, and redemption." " Let him that glorieth glory in the Lord;" and

often repeated, " Lord have mercy upon me."
After this he took a little refreshment for the
last time, and though he attempted to proceed
with the testamentary paper he had begun the
preceding day, he soon found it impossible to
support such an effort, but signified his ac-
quiescence in the divine disposal.

The coldness of death was now creeping
over him, but his mental faculties continued unimpaired to the very last breath of mortal existence. *(a)*   Having expressed a wish to hear
some passages from the Old and New Testaments, his ministerial attendants read the twenty-
fourth, twenty-fifth and twenty-sixth Psalms,
the fifty-third chapter of Isaiah, the seventh
chapter of John, the fifth of the Romans and
many other passages.   The saying of John respecting the Son of God, he said was perpetually
in his mind, " the world knew him not......
but as many as received him, to them gave
he power to become the sons of God even to
them that believe on his name."

Besides the passages of Scripture already
mentioned, he frequently solaced himself with
the following, " God so loved the world that
he sent his only begotten Son into the world,
that whosoever believeth on him might not pe-

(a) " Mens autem constabat integerrima et sincerissima
usque ed extremum vitæ halitum." *Brevis Narratio.*

rish but have everlasting life ;" " Whoso seeth the Son and believeth on him hath eternal life ;" " Being justified by faith we have peace with God through our Lord Jesus Christ ;" and expressed the great consolation they afforded his mind. He earnestly exhorted his son-in-law to the study of peace, and whenever the prevailing religious contentions were mentioned, he would continually reply in the language of the son of Jesse, " Let them curse, but bless thou," and " my soul hath dwelt with him that hateth peace. I am for peace, but when I speak they are for war."—

In the afternoon a paper was written to the students by the professors, excusing their non-attendance to the usual duties of the day on account of Melancthon's dangerous situation with which they deeply sympathized, and entreating their united prayers during the usual hours of study on his behalf ; for they considered it impossible he should be able long to struggle with his disease unless nature were divinely assisted and supported. *(b)* It may easily be believed that this

(b) " Forma scripti hæc est---Charissimi auditores in quâ solicitudine mærore, et metu versemur propter ægritudinem Reverendi Præceptoris et Patris nostri Domini Philippi non ignoratis et haud dubiè nobiscum seriò adficimini. Patienter etiam feretis, operas lectionum hoc pomeridiano tempore à nobis omitti. Significare autem nobis hoc ideo voluimus ut sciretis morbum ita intendi ut nisi Deus suâ potentiâ naturam

intimation made a powerful impression throughout the University, and that all the passages leading to the house of this beloved tutor became crowded with anxious inquirers.

Upon being asked by his son-in-law if he would have any thing else, he replied in these emphatic words, " ALIUD NIHIL—NISI CŒLUM." i. e. NOTHING ELSE—BUT HEAVEN! and requested that he might not be any further interrupted.   Soon afterwards he made a similar request, begging those around him who were endeavouring with officious kindness to adjust his clothes, " not to disturb his delightful repose."   After some time his friends united with the minister present in solemn prayer, and several passages of Scripture in which he was known always to have expressed peculiar pleasure were read, such as " Let not your heart be troubled, ye believe in God, believe also in me. In my Father's house are many mansions." " My sheep hear my voice and I know them, and they follow me ;" particularly the fifth of

juverit et sustentaverit, dominum Præceptorem vim morbi tolerare diu non valiturum.   Hortamur autem vos ut nobiscum Deum ardenter invocetis ut miseram ecclesiam et in eâ juventutem clementer respiciat et ne ingratitudinem nostram hoc modò puniat, ut hunc fidelem studiorum gubernatorem nobis adhuc quidem eripiat.   His precibus hoc vacuum tempus obsecro tribuite potius quàm aliis studiis et vos, Ecclesiam et valitudinem præceptoris nostri Deo diligenter commendate."

the Romans and the triumphant close of the eighth chapter, commencing " If God be for us who can be against us." Many other parts of Scripture were recited, and the last word he uttered was the German particle of affirmation, *Ia* in reply to Vitus Winshemius, who had inquired if he understood him while reading. The last motion which his friends who surrounded him to the number of at least twenty, *(c)* could discern, was a slight motion of the countenance which was peculiar to him when deeply affected with religious joy!—" Mark the perfect man and behold the upright, for the end of that man is peace!"

At length, " in the midst of solemn vows and supplications," at a quarter of an hour before seven o'clock in the evening, of the *nineteenth of April, one thousand five hundred and sixty,* at the age of *sixty-three years two months and three days,* he gently breathed his last. *(d)* No distractions of mind, no foreboding terrors of conscience agitated this attractive scene. His chamber was " privileged beyond the common walks of virtuous life—quite in the verge of heaven"—and he expired like a wave scarcely

(c) " Item autem hoc *(Ia)* expressè et disertè enunciabat ut exaudiretur à circumstantibus omnibus qui fuerunt numero ad minimum viginti." *Brevis Narratio.*

(d) MEL. ADAM. Vit. Germ. Theologorum. Art. *Melancthon.* BREVIS NARRATIO.

curling to the evening zephyr of an unclouded summer sky, and gently rippling to the shore. It was a " DEPARTURE "—a " SLEEP "—" the earthly house of this tabernacle was DIS- SOLVED !" *(e)*

Surely then, " such a pious and tranquil removal from a toilsome and afflictive life ought to be a subject of joy rather than of lamentation, and each of us should entreat God that in the possession of a similar peace of conscience, firm faith and acknowledgment of the truth and ardent devotion of mind, he would conduct us from our present imprisonment to his eternal pre- sence." *(f)*

Information of this event was immediately transmitted to the Elector, and means were adopted to bury him with suitable circumstances of respect. To gratify the anxious crowds who were desirous of seeing the body of this venera- ble character, the public were permitted for a day and a half after his decease to inspect his mortal remains ; and of the hundreds who availed themselves of the opportunity, none could resist bestowing an abundant tribute of tears upon his beloved memory. Strangers who had never seen

(e) 1 COR. v. 1.

(f) SCRIPTUM publicè propos. in Acad. Wit. quo scho- lastici convocati sunt ad deduc. funus Dom. Phil. Melancthonis, 21 Aprilis: *Geo. Majore Vice Rect.*

him while living pressed to take a view of the yet undeparted symmetry of his amiable countenance, and al lwho came were desirous of obtaining a pen, a piece of paper however small on which he had written, or in short any thing he had used however insignificant in itself, which was scattered on the floor of the library. *(g)*

His remains were placed in a leaden coffin and deposited close to the body of Martin Luther—" lovely and pleasant in their lives, and in their death they were not divided." A long Latin inscription was written on the coffin, containing a chronological notice of the principal circumstances of his life. Some of the professors in the University attended in funereal robes to convey the body to the parochial church, where it was placed before the altar, and after the usual ceremonies and psalms, Doctor Paul Eberus, pastor of the church of Wittemberg delivered a funeral discourse ; after which the body being removed into the centre of the church, Doctor Vitus Winshemius pronounced an oration in Latin. The crowd of students, citizens, strangers and persons of every class attracted together to witness these solemnities, was never exceeded on any occasion within the memory of the spectators. Among the rest were several of the professors from the University of Leipsic, and many

(g) BREVIS NARRATIO.

of the nobility, pastors of churches and others, from a large vicinity. *(h)*

From a considerable collection of Greek and Latin elogies and epitaphs, with which he used to predict that the poets would honour his memory, *(i)* the following by Theodore Beza is selected as a sufficient and very beautiful specimen :—

> Et tu igitur tandem tumuli sub mole repostus
> Die ô Philippe, nunc jaces.
> Et quam invidisti vivus tibi tute quietem,
> Cunctis quietem dum paras,
> Ipsa tibi cura et sancti peperêre labores,
> Carum ô bonis cunctis caput !
> At tu funde rosas, funde isti lilia tellus,
> Ut lilia inter et rosas,
> Quo nil candidius fuit et nil suavius unquam,
> Recubet Melancthon molliter.
> Et gravis huic ut sis, caveas juvenisve senexve,
> Qui nemini vixit gravis.

Here then MELANCTHON lies thy honour'd head
Low in the grave amongst the mould'ring dead !

(h) BREVIS NARRATIO et SCRIP. pub. propos. in Acad. Wit. quo. Schol. convocat. ad deducend. funus Melancthonis.

(i) " Quemadmodum autem ipse vivens sæpe dixerat, *se mortuum laborem relicturum poetis, amicis autem* ἀγῶνα ἐπιτάφιον, ita et factum." MEL. ADAM. Vit. Germ. Theologorum, p. 354.

In life 'twas thine to make all others blest
But to thyself denying peace and rest;
Thine was the holy toil, the anxious tear,
Dear Philip---to the good for ever dear!---
O earth! let lilies here profusely spring,
And roses all around their odours fling!
For rose and lily each their glories blend,
The sweet, the fair, in our departed friend!
Soft let him sleep and none disturb his rest,
None *he* disturb'd while living---none opprest!

Some appropriate lines have been kindly
communicated by a poetical friend.

ODE

On the Death of Philip Melancthon.

Oh! who would envy those who die
   Victims on ambition's shrine!
Though idiot man may rank them high,
And to the slain in victory,
   Pay honours half divine;
To feel this heaving, fluttering breath,
Still'd by the lightest touch of death,
   The happier lot be mine:

I would not, that the murdering brand,
Were the last weapon in my hand.

He, of whom these pages tell,
   He, a soldier too---of truth,
   He, a Hero from his youth;
How delightfully he fell!
   Not in the crash, and din, and flood,
   Of execrations, groans, and blood,
   Rivetting fetters on the good;---
But happily and well.

No song of triumph sounds his fall,
   No march of death salutes his bier,
But tribute sweeter far than all,
   The sainted sigh, the orphan tear !
Yet mourn not, ye who stand around,
   Bid not time less swiftly roll,
What though shade the prospect bound ;
He a brighter world has found,
   Death is the birth-day of the soul.

Witness ! (for ye saw him die)
Heard you complaint, or groan, or sigh ?---
   Or if one sigh breath'd o'er his breast,---
As gentle airs when days of summer close,
Breathe, over wearied nature still repose,
   And lull a lovely evening to rest :
It whisper'd,---" All within is peace,
The storm is o'er, and troubles cease."

His sun went down in cloudless skies,
Assur'd upon the morn to rise,
   In lovelier array,
But not like earth's declining light
To vanish back again to night :
The zenith where he now shall glow
No bound, no sitting beam can know,
Without, or cloud or shade of woe,
   Is that eternal day.

History will not write his name,
Upon the *crimson* roll of fame ;
But Religion, meeker maid,
   Mark him in her tablet fair ;
And, when million names shall fade,
   He will stand recorded there !

Here our labours are nearly closed. The reader it is hoped will accept of this volume as a faithful portrait of Melancthon's character; but before it is parted with, it seems due to the distinguished individual whose likeness we have endeavoured to impress upon these pages, to relate two circumstances as a finish to the picture: the one is illustrative of his fame, the other of his piety.

When Sabinus his son-in-law visited Italy, he carried a letter of introduction from Melancthon to the celebrated Cardinal Bembo; the consequence of which was an invitation to dinner. Among a variety of questions, the three following are particularly mentioned. The Cardinal inquired " what was Melancthon's salary—what the number of his hearers—and what his opinion respecting the resurrection and a future state?"— To the first question Sabinus replied, that " his salary was about three hundred florins," upon which the Cardinal exclaimed, " Ungrateful Germany! to estimate at no higher a price so many and such labours of so great a man!" His reply to the second question was, " that he had usually fifteen hundred hearers." To this the Cardinal answered, " I cannot believe it, because I do not know a University in Europe excepting that of Paris in which one professor has so many scholars." To the third question Sabinus replied, " that Melancthon's works were a sufficient proof of his belief in both those articles."

The Cardinal said, " I should think him a wiser man if he did not believe them." *(h)*.

One is tempted by the other circumstance about to be noticed, to suspect that the judgment which this great man pronounced upon the case of Servetus as before stated, must have been, in *some* measure at least, the result of misinformation. When in consequence of the tyranny of Queen Mary thousands of Puritans fled from England into Germany, Switzerland and France, the Lutherans reproached them as *the Devil's Martyrs.* Melancthon contended strenuously against these calumniators, and expressed his abhorrence at such language being applied to a class of men like Latimer and others with whom he was well acquainted. *(i)*

It is painful to reflect that an event which usually checks the hostile feelings of the most determined enemies, did not however subdue the animosity of those of Melancthon. A persecuting demon seemed to have taken an entire possession of them, for even after his decease they shot the envenomed arrows of malignity at his character and borrowed the vociferous tongue of calumny to blast his fame: but in vain to *him*—he had reached that peaceful asylum so long anticipated, where " the wicked cease from troubling and the weary are at rest !"

(h) MEL. ADAM. Vit. Germ. Theologorum.
(i) MELANCTH. Ep. Lib. IV. p. 959. Lib. II. p. 387.

APPENDIX.

No. I.

(PAGE 3.)

*Biographical Notices of Peter Waldus or Waldo,
John Wickliffe, John Huss and Jerome of
Prague.*

PETER WALDUS or WALDO, of Lyons, was the
founder of the sect of the Waldenses, who inhabited
the valleys of Piedmont. His own convictions of the
truth originated from his having employed a priest,
Stephanus de Evisa, about the year 1160, to translate
the four Gospels from Latin into French, with other
books of Scripture, and the most remarkable sentences
of the ancient Doctors. He soon perceived the essential difference between the religion of the Romish
church and the principles of the gospel. Abandoning
his mercantile profession, and uniting with other pious
men who adopted his sentiments, he became a public
preacher in the year 1180. The Archbishop and other

ecclesiastics vigorously, but unsuccessfully, opposed him in the exercise of his ministry. The purity of his faith, and that of his followers, the unambitious principle that evidently actuated them, and the innocence of their whole character, excited a very general attention, and religious assemblies were at length formed in France, Lombardy, and different parts of Europe; and though pursued by fire and sword, they could never be exterminated.

JOHN WICKLIFFE, the morning star of the Reformation, was born near Richmond in Yorkshire, in the year 1324. He was educated at Oxford, and having been disgusted with the enormities of the see of Rome in general, and its conduct to himself in particular, he at length gave public Lectures, in which he exposed the abuses of the Mendicant orders. He published a defence of Edward III. against the Pope, which introduced him to Court. In 1377 Papal bulls were issued, requiring the Archbishop of Canterbury and the Bishop of London to secure and imprison him as a heretic, and the king and the University of Oxford to deliver him up. Wickliffe however, protected by the government, and by the citizens of London, eluded the persecution. He published a book on the " Truth of the Scriptures," and what he termed " Sixteen Conclusions," directed against the Papacy. But his principal work was a literal translation of the Bible from the Latin Vulgate. This great English Reformer died in December, 1384.

JOHN HUSS, an illustrious martyr to the cause of truth, was born in Bohemia in the year 1376, and was educated at Prague, where he became Professor of Divinity in the University, and ordinary Pastor in the church of that city. He exclaimed with vehemence against the vices of the clergy, and from the year 1408 exerted his utmost endeavours to withdraw the University of Prague from the jurisdiction of Gregory XII. He recommended in the most public manner the writings of Wickliffe, which produced an accusation against him in the year 1410, before the tribunal of John XXIII. by whom he was expelled from the communion of the church. He was burnt alive for his heresy by a decree of the Council of Constance, the 6th of July, 1415, in violation of a safe-conduct which had been granted him by the Emperor Sigismund; "which dreadful punishment," says Mosheim, " he endured with unparalleled magnanimity and resignation, expressing in his last moments the noblest feelings of love to God, and the most triumphant hope of the accomplishment of those transporting promises with which the gospel arms the true Christian at the approach of eternity."

JEROME of PRAGUE was the intimate friend of Huss, and accompanied him to the Council of Constance, with the design of advocating his cause. The fear of a cruel death at first seemed to shake his constancy, but he finally adhered to his principles in the flames, to which he was consigned on the *thirtieth* of May, 1416.

No. II.

,,,,,,,,,,,,

(PAGE 7.)

THIS curious circumstance is related by Camerarius in the following words :—" Harum igitur artium ille peritus et iis virtutibus quas commemoravimus ornatus, in noticiam pervenit maximorum et potentissimorum Principum, iisque carus fuit; in quibus nominasse satis sit et Regem optimum et bellatorem Invictissimum Divum Maximilianum Imperatoris Frederichi filium. Quem Georgius aliquando cum glorioso provocatore Italo, cui nomen Claudio Bataro, certamine singulari congressurum ita instruxit et sic arma ipsius machinando paravit, ut fortissimo Viro Maximiliano victoria certa facilè etiam et celeriter contingeret. Claudius enim non diu repugnans, cum, quantò omnibus rebus esset inferior sentiens ad pedes Maximiliani se adjecisset, ita in potestatem ejus se tradidit." CAM. *Vit. Mel.* p. 3.

No. III.

(PAGE 20.)

PROLOGUS IN ANDRIAM TERENTII.

VESTRÆ periclum fecimus patientiæ
Cum nuper in scenâ exhibuimus militem,
Animosque nobis addidit vester favor
Ut non patiamur scenam consilescere
Sed ne mirere, Quid pompæ Theologicæ
Cum comicis jocis, meræ sunt fabulæ
In pulpitis quas agebant hodie Theologi
Et chirothecæ et annuli sunt fabulæ
Nomen Magistri Nostri planæ fabulæ
Postremo qui condixit operam hujus gregis
Theologus est suoque jussit fabulam

Prolixior ut risus foret præscripto agi
Ut ut placebimus imputari vult sibi
Affertur huc Terentiana fabula
Cui author ipse nomen fecit Andriam
Favete bellus in medium prodit senex.

ALIUS IN EANDEM.

Comica debetur merito tibi palma Terenti
  Tanta etiam parvis gratia rebus inest.

PROLOGUS IN EUNUCHUM.

Salvere jubeo spectatores optimos
Qui scenæ ornandæ confluxere gratia
Favore nostra studia ut excitent suo
Artesque honestas et benigne provehant
Authoritateque ut tueantur hunc gregem
Qui scenicos ludos industria sua
Instruxit hâc in urbe primus, ut jocis
Salibusque personent hæc pulpita atticis
Et barbaros plorare jussit, fabulas
Efferre qui vetabant in proscenium
Quæ cultiores juvenum mores redderent
Terentianum agemus Eunuchum modò
Quæ fabulas latinas vincit cæteras
Sermonis elegantia et facetiis
Vel ipse quas Momus miretur ac probet
Illoque sentiat tinctas sale, quo satam
Amorum et illecebrarum matrem omnium
Venerem ferunt. Sed corrugare tetricos
Quosdam videtis nares, immodestiæ
Hi nos accusant in theatrum quod jocos
Proferre liberiores pauloa usi sumus.
Moresque criminantur viciari bonos

Parum severis dictis atque lusibus;
Sed ô censores asperos et pergraves
Qui quod reprehendunt in theatro ludunt domi
Et curios simulant vivunt bacchanalia
Ludunt poëtæ, at lusus illi seria
Ducunt, simulque morum tradunt optima
Vitæ præcepta, ut nihil melius Solon
Aut sanctius tabulis inscripserit æneis
Sed asperam tamen virtutem condiunt
Jucundioribus illecebris, ut solent
Medici daturi pueris tetra absynthia
Cum melle dulci et saccaro irritant gulam
Facessant ergo iniqui judices hinc procul
Ut æquioribus spectandi dent locum
Nos publici nostrique causa commodi
Terentianam agemus Eunuchum modo
Qua barbaram Thrasonis arrogantiam
Fastumqne inanem irridet, hic est cernere
Perinde ut in speculo ardelionaum imaginem
Qui caudices fungique cum meri sient
Primas tamen sibi rerum ubique vendicant
Proventus hujus generis est uberrimus
Hoc seculo, cum se titulo sapientiæ
Musarum, ubique venditant, hostes feri
Prophana divinaque miscent omnia
Vos ergo favete spectatores optimi
Adfertur utilis et jucunda fabula.

PROLOGUS IN PHORMIONEM

Primum opto vobis spectatores candidi
Salutem, et à vobis vicissim mihi expeto
Ut auribus æquis, cur ego huc processerim
Noscatis, et in humanitate spes mihi

Vestra est benigne facturos quod postulo
Plerique prologi vestrâ abutuntur patientiâ
Qui cum æmulis rixantur in prosceniis
Ubi blanditiis decet emereri gratiam
Non odiose latrare jocosque comicos
Ab amarulentis satyris auspicarier
Si quis caninam meditatur facundiam
Et dicere ac audire vult convicia
Concedat hinc ad Cynicos, si libeat novos
Næ is bene lauteque accipietur arbitror
Ego huc venio indicem ut coronæ, fabulam
Adferri bellulam lepidamque Terentii
A pueris aliquot Phormionem, nunc peto
Ut qui studiis favent, bonisque literis
Faveant et actioni puerorum rudi.

No. IV.

,,,,,,,,,,,,,,

(PAGE 190.)

CONTENTS

OF THE

LOCI COMMUNES THEOLOGICI;

OR,

THEOLOGICAL COMMON PLACES.

2 P

No. V.

(PAGE 229.)

THE title of these volumes is—BIBLIA: das est: die gantze heilige Schrifft: deudsch auffs new zuge_richt.

D. MART: LUTHER.

Begnadet mit Kurfurstlicher zu Sachsen Freipeix gedruekt zu Wittemberg Durch hanslufft, 1541.

Luther has written the following sentences with his own hand.

(In Vol. I.)

Martinus Luther, D.

1542.

Der Herr ist mein Hirte Mir wird nichts mangeln Wer's glanben kunde der ware ein selig fett sicher Schaf dieses trewen Hirten der auch sein Leben hat fur solche Schafe gesetzt wehe dem schandlichen Ver- laumder der solchem. Hirten und lieber will vom Wollfe geffessen sein zum ewigen Tode.

Marthinus Luther, D.

1542.

Translation.

The Lord is my Shepherd, I shall want nothing. Who could believe it! He would rest sound and secure, a sheep of the faithful Shepherd who giveth his life for his flock. Woe to the shameful calumniator who does not follow such a Shepherd, but rather suffers himself to be devoured by the wolf of eternal death.

Martin Luther, D. 1542.

(In Vol. II.)

Und ob ich wandern muste ym fins tern Thal furchte ich mich doch nicht, dem du bist bey mir.

Gottes Wort ist ein Licht; dasym finstern scheinet und lertet Heller denn am Tage denn ym Tode ver- lischt nicht allein das Lichtdieser Sonnen sondern auch der Vernunft: mit aller yhrer Weisheit du liebtest. denn mit aller trero das Wort Gottes ein ewige Sonne welche allein der Glaube sihet und folget bis yns ewige klare Leben.

(In Vol. II.)

Though I **walk thro'** the valley of the shadow of death I will fear no evil, for thou art with me.

The word of God is a light that shines in darkness and is a clearer guide than the day itself, for in death not only the light of this sun but of reason also is extinguished with all her wisdom—still thou lovest with all thine heart the word of God, an eternal sun which is visible alone to faith, and follows it even into the bright and everlasting life.

Martin Luther, D. 1542.

,,,,,,,,,,,,,,,

The hand-writing of Melancthon occupies the fourth page. His words are

Der Spruch des.
Propheten Elias.

Sechs tusent jar bleibet dise welt darnach wirt sie verbrennen.

Zwei Tusent jar oed.

Zwei Tusent jar das gesetz Moisi.

Zwei Tusent jar die tag Messiah ; und von wegen unsre sunden die viel und grosz sind werden die Tar davon abgehen, welche nicht erfullt werden.

Geschrieben Anno 1557 iar nach der giburt der Herrn Christ ausz der Tungfraw Maria.

Anno von Erschaffung der Welt. 5519. Ausz diser Zal ist zu versichern. das dise hochbejahrte Welt : nicht fern vom Ende ist. Der allmachtige Gottes Son Jesus Christus wolle sie velherrlichen nach sein. Armes Kråften gnediglich erhalten regiren bewaren und schutzen..

Script. manu Philippi, 1557. W.

(Literal Translation.)

The words of the Prophet Elias.

Six thousand years this world shall stand and after that be burnt.

Two thousand years void (or without the law).

Two thousand years the law of Moses.

Two thousand years the day of Messiah; but on account of our sins which are many and great, those years which are not yet fulfilled shall be shortened.

Written in the year 1557, after the birth of our Lord Christ, of the Virgin Mary—Year from the Creation of the world 5519; from this number we may be assured that this aged world is not far from its end.— May Jesus Christ the Son of Almighty God, graciously preserve, govern, keep, protect it by the power of his arm.

Written by the hand of Philip, 1557. W.

To what particular passage Melancthon refers in the above quotation I cannot discover, but he appears to have adopted it as the general division of his large historical work the CHRONICON. Thus he states it:—

TRADITIO DOMUS ELIÆ.

Sex millia annorum mundus et deinde confla-gratio.

Duo millia Inane.

Duo millia Lex.

Dno millia dies Messiæ. Et propter peccata nostra, quæ multa et magna sunt, deerunt anni, qui deerunt.

No. VI.

,,,,,,,,,,,,

(PAGE 420.)

TESTAMENTUM

PHIL. MELANCTHONIS.

(Ex PEZEL. *Cons. Theol. P. 1. p.* 389 & 399.*)*

IN Nomine DEI Patris et Filii et Spiritus Sancti.
Apparet, initio præcipue condita esse testamenta propter hanc causam, ut patres relinquerent liberis certum
testimonium suæ sententiæ de religione, quam volebant
gravi autoritate quasi obsignatam propagari ad posteros. Item ut liberos ipsos ad eandem sententiam
retinendam et conservandam obligarent, sicut exempla
ostendunt in testamento Jacob et Davidis. Ideo et
Christus suum quoddam testamentum hoc modo con-
didit. Et quia testamenta continbant explicatas,
certas immutabilesque sententias de doctrinâ cœlesti,
rerum magnitudo auxit testamentorum autoritatem.
Quare et ego meorum liberorum et quorundam amicorum admonendorum caussa, volui initio in Testamento, et meam confessionem recitare, et liberis meis
præcipere pro officio Patris, ut in eâdem sententiâ constanter maneant. *Primum* autem ego gratias Deo
Patri Domini nostri Jesu Christi pro nobis crucifixi,
conditori omnium rerum, quod me vocavit ad pœni-
tentiam, et ad Evangelii agnitionem, ac oro, ut propter

Filium suum, quem pro nobis voluit esse victimam,
mihi condonet omnia peccata, me recipiat, justificet,
exaudiat, et a morte æternâ liberet: sicut credo verè
facturum esse. Nam ita jussit nos credere, et impietas
est, pluris facere peccata nostra, quam mortem filii
Dei. Hanc antefero meis peccatis. Rogo autem, ut
hæc initia fidei in me Deus confirmet Spiritu suo
Sancto, propter Filium Mediatorem. Excrutior equidem et meis peccatis, et scandalis aliorum, sed antefero mortem Filii Dei, ut gratia exuberet supra
peccatum. *Secundo* affirmo me vere amplecti sym-
bola, Apostolicum, et Nicænum, et de totâ doctrinâ
Christianâ sentire, ut scripsi in Locis Communibus et
Romanis (Comment. in Epist. ad Rom.) postremæ
editionis, in quibus explicate de singulis articulis, sine
ambiguitate conatus sum dicere quod sentio. De Cœnâ
Domini amplector Formulam Concordiæ hic factam.
Adjunxi me igitur nostris Ecclesiis, et has judico
profiteri Catholicæ Ecclesiæ Christi doctrinam, et esse
verè Christi Ecclesias ; ac præcipio meis liberis, ut in
nostris ecclesiis maneant, ac fugiant Papistarum Ecclesias et Conjunctionem. Nam Papistæ in multis
articulis profitentur corruptissimam doctrinam: prorsus ignorant doctrinam de justitiâ fidei, et de remis-
sione peccatorum: nihil tradunt de discrimine legis et
Evangelii: de invocatione Dei habent ethnicas aut
Pharisaicas opiniones. Ad hos errores addunt et alios
multos, et manifestam idololatriam, in missis suis
et cultu mortuorum hominum. Peto igitur a meis liberis, ut mihi propter mandatum Dei in hâc re obtem-
perent, nec se adjungant Papistis. Et quoniam video
impendere ad posteros novas conturbationes dogmatum
et Ecclesiæ ac fortassis existent Spiritus fanatici ac
leves, qui labefactabunt articulos de Filio Dei, et de

Spiritu Sancto, volo præmonitos meos, ut constanter
retineant sententiam, quam profiteor in Locis cum
Catholicâ Christi Ecclesiâ, ubi damno Samosatenum,
Servetum et alios, dissentientes a symbolis receptis.
Erant etiam fortassis novæ dogmatum conciliationes
Sophisticæ post hanc ætatem, ubi restituentur ve-
teres errores nonnihil fucati, et hæ conciliationes
corrumpent doctrinæ puritatem, quæ nunc traditur.
De his quoque præmoneo meos, ne Sophisticas conciliationes approbent. Sed hic eruditi hortandi sunt,
ut advigilent, ne specie pacis et publicæ tranquillitatis
recipiant dogmatum confusionem, qualis in Sirmiensi
Synodo facta fuit. Verè hoc possum affirmare me
conatum esse, ut verè et propriè explicarem nostrarum
Ecclesiarum doctrinam, ut juventus rectius intelligere
nostras sententias posset et, ad posteritatem conservare.
Hæc forma si prodest, ut judico, rogo Casparum Cruci-
gerum et alios qui nos audiverunt, ut eam in scholis
conservent. Scio quosdam aliquando suspicatos esse,
me quædam moliri in gratiam adversariorum. Sed
Deum testem facio, me adversariis non patrocinari
voluisse, sed quæsivisse proprietatem in explicando,
ut juventus has res rectius perciperet, sine ambiguita-
tibus, et quam difficile mihi fuerit, hunc ordinem et
methodum in explicando reperire, multi norunt, qui
sciunt, me formam in explicando sæpe mutasse; et
constat Augustinianam formam non satis explicatam
esse. Ideo affirmo, me bono studio hanc methodum
instituisse, quæ extat in Romanis, et quidem cupio
post me relinquere sensentias certas sine ambiguitate;
quia ambiguitas postea parit novas discordias. Nec
meum consilium fuit, ullam novam opinionem serere,
sed perspicuè et propriè exponere doctrinam Catholi-
cam, quæ traditur in nostris Ecclesiis, quam quidem

judico singulari Dei beneficio patefactam esse his postremis temporibus per D. D. Martinum Lutherum, ut Ecclesia repurgaretur et instauràretur, quæ alioqui funditus periisset. Ergo hanc lucem, quam diu possumus, conservemus. Ac precor Deum Patrem servatoris nostri Jesu Christi, conditorem omnium rerum ut piorum studia adjuvet, et conservet aliquam Ecclesiam ac præsertim benedicat nostris Ecclesiis, quæ propter Evangelium sustinuerunt certamina diuturna.

Ago autem gratias Reverendo D. Doctori Martino Luthero, primum, quia ab ipso Evangelium didici ; deinde pro singulari erga me benevolentià, quam quidem plurimis beneficiis declaravit, eumque volo a meis, non secus ac patrem, coli. Ego, quia vidi et comperi, præditum esse excellenti et heroicà vi ingenii et multis magnis virtutibus, pietate ac doctrinâ præcipuâ semper eum magnifeci, dilexi et colendum esse sensi. Ago etiam gratias Illustrissimo Principi, Duci Saxoniæ Electori, Domino Johanni Frederico, cujus erga me fuit singularis clementia et liberalitas. Ac oro Deum, ut servet eum incolumem, defendat ac gubernet, ad suam et communem salutem Ecclesiæ et multarum gentium. Fuit mihi etiam pergrata benevolentia viri clarissimi Domini Cancellarii Pontani, quem et ipsum propter egregiam vim ingenii et virtutem dilexi, eique pro omnibus beneficiis gratias ago. Ago gratias et cæteris bonis viris, qui constantiam in amicitià nostrâ perpetuam præstiterunt, Georgio fratri meo, Joachimo Camerario, Domino Cancellario Francisco *(id est*, Burcardo), D. Jonæ, D. Pomerano, Crucigero, D. Augustino (Schurfio) D. Milichio, Paulo Ebero, Vito. Ac precor Deum, ut eos servet. Nec judico extingui has amicitias mea morte : sed sentio nos paulo post in cœlesti vità conventuros esse, ubi verius frui licebit amicitiâ nostrâ, et erit multo dulcior familiaritas. Precor etiam omnes, ut mihi amanter dent veniam erratorum meorum, si quâ in re quemquam offendi. Certe petulanter non volui offendere. Etiam omnibus in Academiâ Doctoribus, ac collegis meis gratias ago, quod me amanter multis officiis in Republicâ, et privatim adjuverunt.

THE END.

Stower and Smallfield, Printers, Hackney.

Printed in the United States
71581LV00004B/5